THE CRIMINAL ELITE
Understanding White-Collar Crime

Sixth Edition

JAMES WILLIAM COLEMAN

California Polytechnic State University at San Luis Obispo

Worth Publishers

Acquisition Editor: Erik Gilg
Executive Marketing Manager: John A. Britch
Associate Managing Editor: Tracey Kuehn
Project Manager: Richard Rothschild / Print Matters, Inc.
Art Director/Cover Designer: Babs Reingold
Interior Design: Lissi Sigillo
Photo Editor: Patricia Marx
Photo Researcher: Lyndall Culbertson
Production Manager: Paul W. Rohloff
Composition: Compset, Inc.
Printing and Binding: RR Donnelley and Sons

ISBN: 0-7167-8734-2 (EAN: 9780716787341)

First printing 2006

Library of Congress Cataloging-in-Publication Number: 2005927986

Worth Publishers
41 Madison Avenue
New York, New York 10010
www.worthpublishers.com

When the courts are decked in splendor

   weeds choke the fields

      And the granaries are bare

When the gentry wears embroidered robes

   hiding sharpened swords

      gorge themselves on fancy foods

         own more than they can ever use

They are the worst of brigands

They have surely lost the way.

—Lao Tzu

Contents

Preface

To many people, white-collar crime is nothing more than a footnote to the "real" problem of crime in our streets. But I think that a careful reading of the wealth of material presented in *The Criminal Elite* will convince the objective reader otherwise. Whether it is measured in terms of financial losses, deaths and injuries, or damage to our social fabric, white-collar crime is the greatest crime problem of our age. The objective of this book is to ask the reader to look beyond the media's fixation on street crime and to see the full dimensions of the problem of white-collar crime: its common forms, its causes, the legal response, and of course the great damage it causes. Perhaps more important, I have also sought to challenge the reader to think about the problem of white-collar crime, what it tells us about our society, and what we can do to solve it.

The Criminal Elite has enjoyed wonderful success throughout its previous five editions. It has been extremely well received by professional criminologists, students, and the general public alike, and for this I am deeply grateful. The sixth edition of *The Criminal Elite* offers new research and important new case material that attempts to build on this strong foundation.

What's New?

Most of the time the media doesn't pay much attention to the problem of white-collar crime. But every decade or so a huge new scandal seems to erupt that grabs the headlines and provides a wealth of new material and new encouragement for criminologists. Since I finished the last edition of *The Criminal Elite*, the financial scandals involving Enron, WorldCom, and other international corporate giants grabbed headlines around the world. Although careful scholarly analyses of these cases have yet to reach print, and some criminal actions are still pending, the basic facts are now a matter of public record. One of my major tasks in writing this new edition was therefore to analyze this new material and present it in a way that opens up its underlying causes. But these financial scandals were hardly the only important new developments. The rapid growth of the "information economy" led to the addition of two new sections—one on the violation of intellectual property and the other on identity theft. There were also important new legal developments such as the limits on the use of "soft money" in political campaigns and the ratification of the Sarbanes–Oxley Act. New legislation and new attitudes following the terrorist attacks of September 11, 2001, are reflected in the examination of the violation of civil liberties. In addition, I integrated a host of new studies into the text, did a thorough updating of a wide range of material, and deleted old material that seemed too dated. Finally,

I wrote a test bank to help professors who are using this book in class. Please contact Worth Publishers to have a copy of it sent to you on disk.

How to Use the Book

The best understanding of white-collar crime will naturally come from reading the entire book, but because of time limitations, some professors may desire a shorter treatment of the subject to assign to their classes. I have therefore tried to make each chapter as self-contained as possible, so that some parts of the book can be assigned independently of others. The first chapter is a general introduction, which provides enough basic information to enable students to understand any of the subsequent chapters. Rather than giving a summary at the end of each chapter, the concluding chapter contains a restatement of the main points of the entire book, and should help fill in the gaps for students who have not been assigned the whole book. Thus, an instructor who wishes to give beginning students a good introduction to the subject of white-collar crime without dealing with more theoretical issues might assign the introduction, the conclusions, and Chapter 2, which contains many case studies that should maintain students' interest while helping them gain a more realistic understanding of the problem. Students focusing on criminal justice might be assigned the introduction, conclusion, and Chapters 3 and 4, which deal with the origins of the laws against white-collar crime and their enforcement. Instructors wishing to familiarize more advanced students with the theoretical issues involved in the study of white-collar crime without assigning the entire book might omit Chapter 2, since it contains mostly descriptive material. A brief treatment of the basic issues can be gained by reading the introductory and concluding chapters, or even the conclusions alone.

The comments of my academic colleagues and my students have been a great help to me over the years, as were the excellent reviews of the current and previous editions of the manuscript, including those of John Curra, Eastern Kentucky University; Gilbert Geis, University of California, Irvine; Steve Gunkel, University of Nebraska-Omaha; Julia Glover Hall, Drexel University; Emily Noelle Ignacio, Loyola University Chicago; David T. Johnson, University of Hawaii at Manoa; Ron Kramer, Western Michigan University; Paul S. Leighton, Eastern Michigan University; Pat McGeever, Indiana University-Purdue University Indianapolis; Raymond Michalowski, Northern Arizona University; Fred Milano, Appalachian State University; James C. Oleson, Old Dominion University; Brian Payne, Old Dominion University; Nathan Pino, Georgia Southern University; Stephen C. Richards, Northern Kentucky University; Kip Schlegel, Indiana University–Bloomington; Russell Smandych, University of Manitoba; and Kevin Wehr, California State University, Sacramento. Other helpful suggestions came from the editorial staff at Worth Publishers. No work of this kind is the product of only a single person, and I would like to express my thanks to everyone who contributed to this book either with their comments and suggestions or by their work in this vital area.

—*James William Coleman*

About the Author

James William Coleman was born in 1947 and grew up in Los Angeles, California. He received an M.A. and a Ph.D. from the University of California, Santa Barbara. He is currently Professor of Sociology at the California Polytechnic State University at San Luis Obispo, where he teaches courses in criminology, global problems, social psychology, and the sociology of religion, and conducts research in the areas of white-collar crime, religion and society, and international development. He is the author of numerous articles on white-collar crime and other subjects, which have appeared in such journals as *Social Problems* and the *American Journal of Sociology*. In addition to *The Criminal Elite*, he is the author of *Social Problems* (Prentice-Hall, 2005), now in its ninth edition, and *The New Buddhism: The Western Transformation of an Ancient Tradition* (Oxford, 2001).

one

Introduction

*T*o most people, the muggers, murderers, and drug dealers they might encounter on a dark city street are the heart of the crime problem. But the damage such criminals do is dwarfed by the respectable criminals who wear white collars and work for our most powerful organizations. The annual losses from antitrust violations—just one of a long list of major white-collar crimes—are estimated to be ten times greater than all the annual losses from all the crimes reported to the police.[1] The toll of injuries and deaths from white-collar crime is even more shocking. The asbestos industry's cover-up of the dangers of its product has probably cost almost as many lives as all the murders in the United States for an entire decade. Another dangerous product—cigarettes—takes more lives than that every year.[2]

However, until recently the problem of white-collar crime has been nearly invisible. The focus of the media has always been on serial killers, teenage gangsters, and other more visible criminals and more dramatic crimes. The police are ill equipped to deal with all but the simplest white-collar offenses, and even the victims are often unaware of the real source of their difficulties. The criminologists, such as Edward Ross and Edwin Sutherland, who first called attention to the realities of white-collar crime spent their careers as voices in the wilderness calling out to their colleagues, who had little understanding or interest in the problem. Most people in a position to bring it to public attention assumed that the holders of privilege and power were basically honest, or they may simply have been uninterested in biting the hand that fed them.

The first major breach in this wall of silence came from the Watergate scandals of the early 1970s. Since then, year by year, scandal by scandal, public confidence in our political and social institutions seems to have melted away, and the issue of white-collar crime has gained new respectability and importance. But even today those who complain about government corruption or corporate irresponsibility seldom understand the full scope of the problem or the historical, economic, and structural forces that lie at its roots. The goal of this book is to provide that perspective.

The Nature of White-Collar Crime

Ever since Edwin H. Sutherland first used the term in his 1939 presidential address to the American Sociological Society, white-collar crime has been a focus of controversy. Sutherland, who was one of the founding fathers of American criminology, widened the scope of his discipline by helping to bring the "upperworld" crimes of business and government into a field that traditionally focused on crimes of the poor and the underprivileged. Such sweeping changes naturally met with resistance, especially since they challenged both traditional political sensibilities and powerful vested interests. Numerous debates broke out over which offenses could legitimately be called white-collar crime and whether or not they were really crimes.

Part of the problem was of Sutherland's own making. His definition was clear enough: "[A white collar crime is] a crime committed by a person of respectability and high social status in the course of his occupation."[3] Although this definition is broad, encompassing everything from embezzlement and industrial espionage to the bribery of government officials, in his actual research Sutherland focused almost exclusively on the crimes of business and especially on violations of federal economic regulations. Sutherland's failure to devote more attention to violent white-collar crimes probably contributed to the debate that sprang up about whether white-collar crime was really crime. Because price-fixing, false advertising, and most of the other offenses Sutherland studied are usually handled as administrative matters and violators seldom face criminal charges, Sutherland's critics claimed that white-collar crimes weren't crimes at all, or at least that white-collar criminals weren't real criminals.

By today's standards it seems odd to argue that people who have enough political power to prevent the government from prosecuting them are therefore not criminals, but many people were persuaded by such arguments at the time. Because crimes such as price-fixing were prohibited by relatively new legislation and its victims seldom even knew they were being victimized, it was easy to argue that they weren't real crimes, comparable to theft or assault. Had the argument focused on flammable clothing that burned helpless children or on industrial poisons that threatened hundreds of people with slow death, the same argument would hardly have been tenable.

Yet, however he had conceptualized the problem, Sutherland was bound to encounter strong resistance. When he made his famous 1939 address, crime was seen as something that happened primarily among immigrants and poor people who had fallen victim to the social pathology of urban society. The idea that many of the fabled captains of industry should be considered criminals had a very un-American sound to it, even in the midst of the Great Depression of the 1930s. Even more threatening was Sutherland's call for tough action to deal with the problem of white-collar crime. Proposals to treat powerful corporate executives like common criminals were hardly likely to win praise from the upper strata of American society, whose influence on the media and on the distribution of research grants and the other financial rewards that are so important to academic criminologists created some formidable barriers to these new ideas.

Despite these obstacles Sutherland clearly won the first round of the debate, and few criminologists today would claim that white-collar crime is not real crime. But at about the time the original controversy had died down, it appeared that Sutherland had vanquished his critics, a new front opened. This new trend of thought accepted the validity of the concept of white-collar crime but redefined it in a radically different way. The origins of this approach can be dated to a 1970 publication by a former prosecutor with the Department of Justice, Herbert Edelhertz. After recognizing Sutherland's contribution, he went on to argue that the definition of white-collar crime should not be limited to offenses that were occupationally related and that white-collar criminals need not be persons of high social status. Edelhertz defined white-collar crime as "an illegal act or series of illegal acts committed by nonphysical means and by concealment or guile to obtain money or property, to avoid the payment or loss of money or property, or to obtain business or personal advantage."[4] Thus, according to this awkwardly worded definition, any property crime carried out solely through trickery and deception was to be considered a white-collar crime.

The new definition, which no longer required white-collar criminals to have white-collar status, has been particularly influential with the federal bureaucracy. Several research projects relying on official data, most notably the large project on white-collar offenders in the federal courts headed by researchers from Yale University,[5] have also taken this approach. Although Edelhertz explicitly excluded violent offenses, few of the more recent definitions do, because that would eliminate so many environmental and product-safety crimes as to render the term meaningless.

Those who would exclude white-collar status from the definition of white-collar crime generally give two reasons for the change. Some claim that because legal offenses are based solely on the behavior and not on the status of the offender, criminological categories should be as well.[6] Such an argument is hardly convincing, however, because its basic premise is false—the legal definitions of virtually all crimes also include some characteristics of the offenders (that they were sane, had criminal intent at the time of their actions, were more than 18 years of age, and so on). A second argument attacks Sutherland's approach from a more criminological perspective, holding that the inclusion of social status in the definition of white-collar crime is a mistake because it prevents us from also using social status as an explanatory variable. As Gary Green put it, "socio-economic status cannot be an explanatory variable in white collar crime because only higher status persons, by definition, can commit such offenses."[7] But this objection, like its more legalistic cousin, fails to stand up to scrutiny. Although it is true that Sutherland's definition excludes persons of lower status, there is no reason to conceptualize socioeconomic status as a dichotomy. There is still a very wide range of status variation among white-collar offenders under Sutherland's definition. Even if that were not true, socioeconomic status could still be used as an explanatory variable in white-collar crime, just as the sociological and psychological characteristics of adolescents are used as explanatory variables in juvenile delinquency.

The real reason for the popularity of this new definition is more pragmatic. Because it includes a far wider range of offenses as white-collar crimes than the original, it allows government officials to provide a more convincing public account of their effort to stop white-collar crime. The new definition also has an advantage for academic criminologists, because it is far easier to use when analyzing official government statistics. Indeed, many of the studies employing an Edelhertz-style definition would probably have been impossible with Sutherland's approach. For one thing, most official statistics give no information on the class background of the offenders. Moreover, many crimes that were central to Sutherland's definition are so rarely reported in official data as to render statistical analysis virtually impossible.

If the new definition enables us to carry out studies that would otherwise be impossible, why not use it? The answer is simple. What criminologists are studying when they use this definition may be useful and worthwhile, but it is often not white-collar crime. After all, the term *white-collar* or *white-collar worker* directly refers to someone of relatively high status, as opposed to the blue-collar worker or the unemployed. If a skid-row alcoholic conning a friend out of a bottle of wine, a welfare mother hiding her income from a part-time job, and a small-time grifter and con man are included as white-collar criminals (as the Edelhertz-style definition would allow), what meaning does the term have? This approach threatens the whole intellectual thrust of the effort to call attention to the crimes of the rich and powerful and the way they escape punishment, and it could easily lead criminologists back to focusing on nonviolent street crimes, which are far easier and far less threatening to study.

Some of the latest approaches, most notably that of David O. Friedrichs and Susan Shapiro, would make a new element the central factor in the definition of white-collar crime: the violation of trust.[8] As long as the social status of the offender is included in the definition, this approach does far less violence to the original meaning of the term. Indeed, Sutherland himself felt that white-collar crime involved a violation of "delegated or implied trust."[9] However, if the definition doesn't require that white-collar offenders be of high social status, the entire approach breaks down. After all, violation of trust is a rather vague concept, and virtually any crime seems to involve some "delegated or implied trust."

Instead of redefining the concept of white-collar crime, other critics have proposed new terms to take its place. Among the first were Marshall Clinard and Richard Quinney, who suggested two other terms—*corporate crime* and *occupational crime* (which they applied only to crimes committed by individuals acting solely in their own personal interest and not that of their employer).[10]

Although this is a useful dichotomy, those two kinds of offenses are best seen as varieties of white-collar crime, as Clinard himself later recognized.[11] Laura Shill Schrager and James Short proposed the concept of organizational crime as another substitute for white-collar crime,[12] but this term is also more useful when seen as one subtype of white-collar crime, for it does not include many of the offenses covered in Sutherland's original definition.

Green, on the other hand, would use a much broader definition of occupational crime than Clinard and Quinney, and then would substitute it for the entire concept of white-collar crime. Thus, he defines occupational crime as "any act punishable by law which is committed through opportunity created in the course of an occupation that is legal."[13] In one sense, Green's use of the term seems superior to the more narrow conceptualization originally advanced by Clinard and Quinney, since there appears to be no reason that offenses committed in the course of one's job not be included as occupational crimes simply because they are also encouraged by one's employer. However, Clinard and Quinney's definition has been highly influential over the years, and any attempt to make such a radical change in its meaning can only lead to confusion.

As another substitute for white-collar crime, David Simon proposes the term *elite deviance*, which includes not only most white-collar crimes but also deviant activities of elite groups that do not violate the law.[14] The concept of elite deviance and the related concept of corporate deviance[15] are certainly useful ones, but once again, they cannot provide an effective replacement of the concept of white-collar crime. One of the main problems with the deviance approach is the difficulty of determining with any degree of certainty what is and is not deviant. Although criminal law contains ample ambiguities of its own, at least each jurisdiction is covered by a set of explicitly stated legal norms that can be changed only through certain formalized procedures. There are, on the other hand, a huge number of groups with their own sets of norms defining what is deviant. Not only are many of those definitions contradictory, but the operative norms of such groups are subject to rapid and unpredictable change. The use of so evanescent a concept to define this politically charged field of study is a prescription for endless quarreling. Moreover, the concepts of "elite" and "corporate" deviance are weak in another way. Having dropped any explicit link to criminal law, the advocates of the deviance approach cannot effectively address the public's deep-seated concern that rich and powerful criminals are escaping punishment for their behavior.

This is not to imply that students of white-collar crime must don blinders and ignore all unethical behavior that is not against current law. Indeed, such activities are examined in many places in this book. The point is simply that white-collar crime is too useful a conceptual tool to be thrown on the intellectual scrap heap. Because it clearly identifies a specific problem of great concern to people around the world, white-collar crime has become one of the most popular phrases ever to come out of sociological research. Not only is Sutherland's term widely used in criminology, but it has become part of everyday English and has been adopted in several other languages as well. It would be a serious mistake to try to replace it with other, less powerful concepts.

Even if we accept the validity of Sutherland's original approach, however, much work remains to be done to clarify his definition. What, for example, do we mean by a violation of the law? One of the central issues of the early debates about the definition of white-collar crime was whether it included violations of civil as well as criminal law. As the study of white-collar crime has matured, more and more criminologists have accepted Sutherland's contention that it should include both.[16] As Steve Blum-West and Timothy Carter have pointed out, the distinction between torts (civil offenses) and criminal offenses is not in the acts themselves but in the administrative response to them. Most white-collar offenders violate both types of laws, and the decision to pursue a case in civil or criminal court is made largely on extralegal grounds.[17]

A different kind of issue has been created by the increasingly international character of the modern economy. Deviant actions by individuals or organizations may be subject to several different sets of national laws or may manage to stay in the cracks between different jurisdictions. How, then, do we classify such actions? Any behavior that violates the law of the country in which it occurs is obviously illegal, even if it is carried out by foreigners or foreign multinationals. In some cases, the actions of multinationals in foreign countries may also be subject to the "extraterritorial" jurisdiction of their country of origin. But although this standard is a good starting point, it is inadequate to deal with the activities of foreign multinationals in poor Third World countries. As Raymond Michalowski and Ronald Kramer have pointed out, the multinationals are often far wealthier and more powerful than the Third World countries in which they do business and can exercise great influence over the laws those countries do or do not enact.[18] It is therefore necessary to include internationally agreed-upon principles of human rights and national sovereignty in deciding what is and is not criminal behavior. Although these international laws are not as clearly defined or as widely accepted as the statutes in most individual nations, the basic principles governing the conduct of nations and multinational corporations are well established. They have been codified in such United Nations documents as the Universal Declaration of Human Rights, the Guidelines for Consumer Protection, and the Draft Codes of Conduct for Transnational Corporations. Violations of the standards in these documents will therefore be included in our definition of criminal behavior.

In June 1996, the National White Collar Crime Center convened a conference of specialists in the field to examine these perplexing definitional issues. Surprisingly enough, they managed to hammer out a "consensus definition" of white-collar crime: "White collar crimes are illegal or unethical acts that violate fiduciary responsibility of public trust committed by an individual or organization, usually during the course of legitimate occupational activity, by persons of high or respectable social status for personal or organizational gain."[19]

Like all the other definitions of white-collar crime, this one has shortcomings. It lacks the simplicity and directness of Sutherland's original definition, and by including unethical as well as illegal acts it runs the risk of encountering the same problems associated with the deviance approach. However, its flexibility and breadth make it as good a candidate as any to win broad support among criminologists working in this contentious field.

This definition is broader than Sutherland's in two important respects. First, white-collar crime is no longer restricted to persons of high social status. This definition still requires, however, that the criminal hold a respectable position. As we shall see, crimes by those in positions of high status and power still constitute the core of the problem of white-collar crime. Second, although occupationally related crimes are still central, other related offenses, such as income tax evasion, can now be included. Syndicated crime, on the other hand, is clearly beyond the scope of this definition. Although there are many similarities in the operation of a group of syndicated criminals such as the Cosa Nostra and in the criminal activities of a major corporation, respectability is a key difference. Whereas the Cosa Nostra is considered a deviant organization explicitly organized to carry on criminal activities, major corporations, such as Exxon and General Motors, are accepted as legitimate businesses seeking legitimate ends despite any illegal activities in which they may have engaged. So-called career criminals, such as con men or burglars, whose principal occupation is some kind of criminal activity, are likewise excluded by this test of legitimacy.

Measuring White-Collar Crime

By its very nature, crime is a secretive business, and criminologists have been struggling for generations to find accurate ways to measure it. Most of our data about conventional street crimes (non–white-collar crimes) come from three sources: the records of enforcement agencies, reports from the victims, and reports from the criminals themselves. The compilation of data on crimes reported to the police (the Uniform Crime Reports), the comprehensive yearly survey of victimization done by the Department of Justice (the National Crime Victimization Survey), and the occasional studies by criminologists asking a sample of individuals to report the crimes they have committed has allowed us to paint a reasonably accurate picture of most street crimes. Unfortunately, none of these techniques has supplied us with much dependable data on white-collar crime. One of the most basic difficulties in measuring white-collar crime is that the victims often do not realize they have been victimized. For example, almost every reader of this book has probably been victimized by corporate price-fixing when purchasing merchandise, but very few of us know it for sure. The same holds true for the victims of environmental criminals or the voters whose concerns are ignored by politicians who sell their influence to wealthy special interests. People who do not know they have been victimized obviously cannot report the offense to survey takers or to the police. Recognizing this fact, the National Crime Victimization Survey does not even ask about most of the important white-collar crimes. The Justice Department now occasionally publishes data on how many "white-collar crimes" are reported to the police. Unfortunately, most of the crimes included under this heading are nothing more than nonviolent street crimes and would not be counted as white-collar crimes under any of the definitions based on Sutherland's original formulation. The National White Collar Crime Center did a survey that included a series of questions about victimization from "white-collar crimes." But once again the survey only included a narrow range of crimes that excluded almost all government and corporate offenses.[20] Thus, the traditional sources of data on street crime don't give us much useful information about most types of white-collar crime.

The numerous studies that have asked offenders to report on their own criminal behavior have proven much more productive and will be cited in many places in this book. However, most of this research has been based on interviews with convicted offenders and provides little data on the overall incidence or costs of white-collar offenses. To date, there has been no large-scale survey of those in white-collar positions asking them to anonymously report on the offenses in which they have been involved.

Another important source of data about white-collar crime comes from the records of the various government agencies charged with regulating corporate behavior. Numerous studies have been done of these records, and they are a major source of data about corporate crime. Although this data may be the best we have, it still is not very good. Once again, the fact that victims often do not know they have been victimized means that they can't report the offenses to the appropriate agencies. The cases that do show up on the official records are generally uncovered by various kinds of government inspectors and investigators, and it is clear that the funding for such efforts is so small and the investigators themselves are often so compromised that only a small percentage of the offenses ever comes to light (see Chapter 4).

If we have so little hard evidence about the incidence or costs of white-collar crime, how can so many criminologists (including the author of this book) claim that it is our most serious crime problem? The answer is simple. The crimes we do know about are so huge, and their consequences so devastating, that they dwarf any known street crimes. The collapse of the savings and loan industry (caused in large measure but not exclusively by white-collar crime) alone cost the public hundreds of billions of dollars.[21] The yearly toll from antitrust violations is estimated at about $250 billion. Then there is the $150 billion the Internal Revenue Service says is lost to tax fraud every year, the $100 billion believed lost to fraud in the health-care industry, and the fact that employee theft is believed to add 2 percent to the cost of the average retail purchase.[22] In contrast, estimated yearly losses from conventional crimes seems a paltry sum,[23] especially considering the hundreds of other major types of white-collar crimes for which no cost estimates available.

Even though many victims of white-collar offenses never know what happened to them, surveys still report a much higher rate of victimization from white-collar than from street crimes. A 1998 poll conducted by the American Association of Retired Persons found that almost one in five Americans said that they had been the victim of a fraud or major consumer swindle in the last year.[24] The 1999 survey by the National White Collar Crime Center, which, as pointed out earlier, used a very narrow definition of white-collar crime, found that 36 percent of American households reported being victimized by a white-collar crime in the previous year.[25] Even more disturbing was the study of company ethics published in 2000 that found that 76 percent of the employees surveyed had witnessed a violation of the law or company ethical standards in the past six months.[26]

Despite such facts, many people are still more concerned about street crime than about white-collar crime. Much of this attitude can be attributed to simple ignorance. The media focus so much attention on street crime that few people realize how much more costly white-collar crime actually is, and even those who are aware of its enormous financial burden often do not understand the true scope of the problem. The cost of white-collar crimes may be high, the argument often goes, but at least they are nonviolent crimes that pose no direct threat to the public. Even though this argument has been voiced by some reputable criminologists, it too is based on ignorance, for white-collar crime can produce as much violence as any street crime.

According to the National Safety Council, 5,300 people were killed in occupational accidents in 2001 and another 3.4 million people suffered a disabling injury. A different estimate holds that 100,000 people die annually from occupationally caused diseases.[27] The difficulty in accurately determining how many workers are killed and injured each year is compounded by the problem of trying to determine exactly how many of those deaths and injuries result from violations of law and how many are caused by hazardous conditions the law does not prohibit. Although it is impossible to have faith in any exact percentage, some kind of criminal activity is probably involved in the cases. The best evidence we have for this conclusion comes from the work of Steve Tombs on occupational fatalities in Great Britain. After examining a variety of different sources of data, he concluded that some violation of health and safety laws was involved in two of every three fatal injuries that occurred on the job.[28]

Moreover, workers are not the only ones killed by white-collar criminals. The National Product Safety Commission has estimated that 20 million serious injuries and 30,000 deaths a year are caused by unsafe consumer products, and that figure does not include the 400,000 people who die each year from cigarette smoking. Again, it is unclear how many of the products involved violate safety laws or are fraudulently represented by manufacturers or merchants, but it seems likely that illegalities are involved in most of those cases. There is, for example, conclusive evidence that the tobacco companies did their best to conceal the hazards of their product—an effort that included making numerous fraudulent statements.

The toll of deaths and illnesses caused by illegal environmental pollution is even harder to estimate. Not only is it hard to find the exact cause of environmentally related health problems, but the ultimate source of the pollutants can be just as difficult to track down. Because the government still permits many dangerous substances to be released into the environment, most environmental problems probably arise through a combination of legal and illegal contaminants. But whatever the sources, environmental pollution has deadly consequences. The National Cancer Institute estimated that as much as 90 percent of all cancers may be environmentally induced. Cancer is now second only to heart disease as the leading cause of death in North America.[29] It is estimated that 53,000 people die annually from lung problems caused by air pollution. The role of industrial pollution is clearly shown by the variations in the rate of cancer mortality. In New Jersey, the counties with the highest concentrations of petrochemical plants and other heavy industries have cancer rates two and one half times the national average.[30] Moreover, as Stretesky and Lynch have shown, blacks and Hispanics are more likely to suffer from the effects of corporate pollution than those from more privileged groups.[31]

By virtually any criterion, then, white-collar crime is our most serious crime problem. The economic cost of white-collar crime is vastly greater than the economic cost of street crime. And although it may be impossible to determine exactly how many people are killed and injured each year as a result of white-collar crimes, the claim that such crimes are harmless, nonviolent offenses can hardly be taken seriously. Since considerably fewer than 20,000 murders are committed in the United States in an average year, "nonviolent" white-collar criminals undoubtedly kill considerably more people than all the violent street criminals put together.

The Varieties of White-Collar Crime

There are so many kinds of white-collar crime that a book of this length could be devoted merely to describing them. It is all too easy to be overwhelmed by an avalanche of facts, stories, and anecdotal reports, and to lose sight of the fundamental issues. Moreover, there are political and ideological reasons to focus on some types of white-collar crime and to ignore others. When business or civic leaders talk about white-collar crime, they usually discuss crimes against business, such as embezzlement or computer crime. But sociologists, criminologists, and other observers of a more critical persuasion often focus on crimes committed by business—price-fixing, false advertising, and environmental pollution, for example.

A typology is obviously needed that encompasses all the important white-collar crimes. But what sort of typology? From a humanistic perspective, our paramount concern must be the effects white-collar crimes have on the victims. Using such an approach, we can divide white-collar crimes into two large groups: property crimes, which cause only economic damage, and violent crimes, which cause injury, sickness, or death. This distinction is of great importance in the formulation of social policy, but it has serious deficiencies as a device to help us understand the crimes themselves. Even though these two types of white-collar crime have different consequences, their etiologies and internal dynamics often are virtually identical. For example, an executive who claims that a deadly product is "as safe as milk" usually has the same motivation and works under the same organizational pressures as an executive who lies about the durability or effectiveness of a product.

A sociology of white-collar crime can be more effectively organized around the differences between the offenders than around the differences between the victims. Following Clinard and Quinney, many criminologists distinguish between occupational crime that "consists of the offenses committed by individuals for themselves in the course of their occupations and the offenses of employees against their employers," and corporate crime that "consists of the offenses committed by corporate officials for their corporation and the offenses of the corporation itself."[32] This typology has served criminology well over the years, because it emphasizes a distinction that is critical to the actual behavior of the offenders. For example, the motivation of an occupational criminal who embezzles from her employer is likely to be far different from that of a corporate executive who covers up the defects in a product to save her company from taking a huge loss. But the way Clinard and Quinney posed this dichotomy nonetheless has some serious shortcomings. Most obvious, it excludes crimes committed by

---

TABLE **1.1**

Varieties of White-Collar Crime

Occupational Crime: Crimes committed by individuals in the course of their occupation for their own personal gain and without organizational support.

Organizational Crime: Crimes committed with the support of an organization whose goals they are intended to advance.

 –Corporate Crime: Organizational crimes committed by a corporate organization or its agents.

 –State–Corporate Crime: Organizational crimes committed by a private corporation and a state agency working together in a joint endeavor.

 –State Crime: Organizational crimes committed by a government organization or its agents.

the government or other noncorporate organizations. Thus, the term *organizational crime* is more appropriate for this kind of dichotomy. Corporate and state crime then become subtypes under the heading of organizational crime. However, as is often the case with such categories, a simple dichotomy between corporate and government crime fails to capture the full range of this complex phenomenon. Kramer has suggested a third category of state–corporate crime for the numerous offenses that are the "collective product of the interaction between a business corporation and a state agency engaged in a joint endeavor."[33] For example, the 1996 crash of ValuJet Flight 592 that killed 110 people and led to homicide charges against three mechanics was a product of the interaction of both corporate and state actors. At the time, ValuJet was growing rapidly by providing very-low-cost fares. Its intense pressure to cut costs led to the violation of a host of federal regulations both by the parent company and by its subcontractors. But the FAA, concerned that companies like ValuJet succeed in the newly deregulated airline industry, allowed the violations to continue until the crash forced it to clamp down.[34] A similar shortcoming is evident in the dichotomy between occupational and organizational crime. It would certainly make the criminologists' job easier if every white-collar crime could be neatly classified as one or the other. In fact, earlier editions of this book attempted to do just that. But unfortunately, real life is inevitably more complex than the analytic schemes we develop to contain it, and some crimes stubbornly refuse to fit into one category or another. Among the most important examples are the numerous cases from the savings and loan industry in which the top executives of a thrift institution used the organization as a tool to embezzle money from itself. This kind of crime, which Calavita and Pontell dubbed *collective embezzlement,* "thus represents a hybrid (of organizational and occupational crime): 'crime by the corporation against the corporation.'"[35]

The distinction between organizational and occupational crimes is still far too useful to abandon, but rather than conceptualizing it as a simple dichotomy, it is best seen as a continuum. On one end are the individual crimes committed exclusively for personal gain without the support of any formal organization— for example, embezzling by a bank clerk. At the other extreme are those crimes committed with the support and encouragement of an organization whose goals it is intended to advance—for example, corporate price-fixing. In between are several kinds of crimes that combine the characteristics of both individual and organizational offenses. For example, Calavita and Pontell's collective embezzlement is similar to other corporate crimes in most respects except that the victim and the perpetrator are the same organization. On the other hand, police corruption and many forms of professional abuse lie closer to the individual occupational crimes in that they are not supported by a formal organization. But unlike the lone embezzler, such offenses are supported by an occupational subculture that encourages and in some cases even requires illegal behavior by some of its members.

Preview

The next chapter presents a working typology of white-collar crime and illustrates it with numerous case studies and examples. From the huge number of examples that might have been included, I have selected the most important or best-documented cases that fit the various categories. Some cases of unethical behavior in which the participants managed to stay just within the boundaries of the law are also included, both to point out inadequacies in the current legal codes and to clarify the parameters of criminal behavior. The remainder of the book uses this foundation to build a sociology of white-collar crime. Chapter 3 examines the laws that define white-collar crimes and the social forces that led to their enactment. The legislative struggle, however, represents only half the battle. The way the laws are enforced is equally important, and Chapter 4 describes the enforcement effort and appraises its effectiveness. Chapter 5 tackles the most difficult subject of all—the causes of this diverse set of phenomena known as white-collar crime. Finally, Chapter 6 presents a summary of the main themes of the book and allows me to indulge in the arrogance of telling the world how it ought to change.

Review Questions

- What are the different ways white-collar crime is defined? Why are those differences important?
- How have criminologists attempted to measure white-collar crime? How serious is the problem of white-collar crime compared to common street crimes?
- What are the main types of white-collar crime?

Notes

1. The estimate of losses from reported crimes come from Kathleen Maguire and Ann L. Pastore, *Sourcebook of Criminal Justice Statistics—1994* (Washington, D.C.: U.S. Government Printing Office, 1995), p. 329. More recent editions of the Sourcebook no longer contain such an estimate. The estimate for antitrust violations used was $250 billion; see footnote 22.
2. According to the Sourcebook of Criminal Justice Statistics, Table 3.120, October 2004, there were 14,054 murders and nonnegligent manslaughters known to the police in the United States in 2001; asbestos deaths from Joseph A. Page and Mary Win-O'Brien, *Bitter Wages: Ralph Nader's Study Group Report on Disease and Injury on the Job* (New York: Grossman, 1973), p. 22; Richard T. Cooper and Paul E. Steiger, "Occupational Health Hazards: A National Crisis," *Los Angeles Times*, June 27, 1976, pt. I: p. 1 passim; Daniel M. Berman, *Death on the Job: Occupational Health and Safety in the United States* (New York: Monthly Review Press, 1978), p. 85. The yearly death toll from smoking is generally estimated at around 400,000—see Philip J. Hilts, *Smokescreen: The Truth Behind the Tobacco Industry Cover-up* (Reading, Mass.: Addison-Wesley, 1996), p. 105.

3. Edwin H. Sutherland, *White Collar Crime* (New York: Dryden Press, 1949), p. 2.

4. Herbert Edelhertz, *The Nature, Impact, and Prosecution of White Collar Crime* (Washington, D.C.: U.S. Government Printing Office, 1970).

5. For example, Stanton Wheeler, David Weisburd, and Nancy Bode, "Sentencing the White Collar Offender," *American Sociological Review* 47 (October 1982): 641–59.

6. For example, see John Braithwaite, "White Collar Crime," *Annual Review of Sociology* 11 (1985): 1–25.

7. Gary S. Green, *Occupational Crime* (Chicago: Nelson-Hall, 1990), p. 12.

8. David O. Friedrichs, *Trusted Criminals: White Collar Crime in Contemporary Society* (Belmont, Calif.: Wadsworth, 1996); Susan Shapiro, "Collaring the Crime, Not the Criminal: Reconsidering the Concept of White Collar Crime," *American Sociological Review* 55 (June 1990): 407–19.

9. Sutherland, *White Collar Crime*, pp. 152–58.

10. Marshall B. Clinard and Richard Quinney, *Criminal Behavior Systems*, 2d ed. (New York: Holt, Rinehart and Winston, 1973).

11. Marshall B. Clinard and Peter C. Yeager, *Corporate Crime* (New York: Free Press, 1980), pp. 17–19.

12. Laura Shill Schrager and James F. Short Jr., "Toward a Sociology of Organizational Crime," *Social Problems* 25 (April 1978): 407–19.

13. Green, *Occupational Crime*, pp. 12–13.

14. David R. Simon and D. Stanley Eitzen, *Elite Deviance* (Boston: Allyn and Bacon, 1982). See especially pp. 5–6.

15. See M. David Erdmann and Richard J. Lundman, *Corporate Deviance* (New York: Holt, Rinehart and Winston, 1982).

16. Gilbert Geis, "Upperworld Crime," in *Current Perspectives on Criminal Behavior*, Abraham Blumberg, ed (New York: Knopf, 1981), pp. 114–35; Stanton Wheeler, "Trends and Problems in the Sociological Study of Crime," *Social Problems* 23 (1976): 523–34; Schrager and Short, "Toward a Sociology of Organizational Crime"; John Braithwaite, *Inequality, Crime and Public Policy* (London: Routledge and Kegan Paul, 1979); Clinard and Yeager, *Corporate Crime*; John Hagan and Patricia Parker, "White Collar Crime and Punishment," *American Sociological Review* 50 (June 1985): 302–16.

17. Steve Blum-West and Timothy J. Carter, "Bringing White Collar Crimes Back In: An Examination of Crimes and Torts," *Social Problems* 30 (June 1983): 545–54.

18. Raymond J. Michalowski and Ronald Kramer, "The Space Between the Laws: The Problem of Corporate Crime in a Transnational Context," *Social Problems* 34 (February 1987): 34–53.

19. James Helmkamp, Richard Ball, and Kitty Townsend, eds., *Proceedings Definitional Dilemma: Can and Should There Be a Universal Definition of White Collar Crime?* (Morgantown, W.V.: National White Collar Crime Center, 1996), p. 351.

20. Donald J. Rebovich and Djenny Layne, "The National Public Survey on White Collar Crime" (Morgantown, W.V.: National White Collar Crime Center, 2000).

21. See Kitty Calavita and Henry N. Pontell, "'Other People's Money' Revisited: Collective Embezzlement in the Savings and Loan and Insurance Industries," *Social Problems* 38 (February 1991): 94–112; Francis T. Cullen, W. J. Maakestad, and G. Cavender, *Corporate Crime under Attack: The Ford Pinto Case and Beyond* (Cincinnati: Anderson, 1987); Public Citizen Staff Report, *White Collar Crime* (Washington, D.C.: Congress Watch, 1974), pp. 17–18.

22. Stephen M. Rosoff, Henry N. Pontell, and Robert Tillman, *Profit Without Honor: White Collar Crime and the Looting of America* (Upper Saddle River, N.J.: Prentice-Hall,

1998), p. 318; Stuart H. Traub, "Battling Employee Crime," *Crime and Delinquency* 42 (April 1996): 244–56; Robert D. Hershey Jr., "I.R.S. Raises Its Estimate of Tax Cheating," *New York Times,* December 29, 1993, pp. C1, C6; M. Levi, *Regulating Fraud: White Collar Crime and the Criminal Process* (London: Tavistock, 1987); Chamber of Commerce of the United States, *A Handbook on White Collar Crime* (Washington, D.C.: Chamber of Commerce of the United States, 1974), p. 6.

23. See Maguire and Pastore, *Sourcebook of Criminal Justice Statistics—1994,* p. 329, for one such estimate.

24. "Poll: Nearly One in Five Americans Report They've Been Victimized by Fraud," *Corporate Crime Reporter* (March 22, 1999): 3.

25. National White Collar Crime Center, *The National Public Survey on White Collar Crime* (Morgantown, W.V.: National White Collar Crime Center, 2000), p. 15.

26. "Employees Report High Levels of Illegal and Unethical Conduct on the Job," *Corporate Crime Reporter* 14 (June 12, 2000): 1.

27. U.S. Bureau of the Census, *Statistical Abstract of the United States, 2003* (Washington D.C.: U.S. Government Printing Office, 2004), p. 428; J. H. Reiman, *The Rich Get Richer and the Poor Get Prison* (Boston: Allyn and Bacon, 1995), p. 75; Catherine Collins, "Bills Attempt to Give Employees a Voice in Improving On-the-Job Safety," *Los Angeles Times,* August 11, 1991, p. D2.

28. Steve Tombs, "Official Statistics and Hidden Crime: Researching Safety Crimes," in Victor Jupp, Pamela Davies, and Peter Francis, *Doing Criminological Research* (London: Sage, 2000), pp. 68–69.

29. Hilts, *Smokescreen,* p. 105; Friedrichs, *Trusted Criminals,* p. 71; Cooper and Steiger, "Occupational Health Hazards."

30. Yingyi Situ and David Emmons, *Environmental Crime: The Criminal Justice System's Role in Protecting the Environment* (Thousand Oaks, Calif.: Sage Publications, 2000), pp. 7–8.

31. Paul Stretesky and Michael J. Lynch, "Corporate Violence and Racism," *Crime Law & Social Change* 30 (1999): 163–84.

32. Clinard and Quinney, *Criminal Behavior Systems,* p. 188. (The first edition of the book, which originally introduced this distinction, was published in 1967.)

33. Quoted in Ronald C. Kramer, Raymond J. Michalowski, and David Kauzlarich, "The Origins and Development of the Concept and Theory of State-Corporate Crime," *Crime and Delinquency* 48 (April, 2002): 269.

34. David O. Friedrichs, "State-Corporate Crime in a Globalized World: Myth or Major Challenge?" in Gary W. Potter, ed., *Controversies in White-Collar Crime* (Cincinnati: Anderson, 2002), pp. 53–71.

35. Calavita and Pontell, "'Other People's Money' Revisited," p. 99

two

The Crimes

*I*f you were to ask the average person to name a white-collar crime, you would be far more likely to hear about an embezzling bank teller or a high-tech computer scam than the multimillion-dollar crimes committed by an entire corporate organization. For one thing, the media give far more attention to occupational crimes than to the crimes of powerful corporations. Moreover, organizational crimes are often complicated, full of boring legal technicalities. But whatever its popular image, the phenomenon of white-collar crime is far too complex to be easily bound by any simple stereotype. The goal of this chapter is to present examples of the full range of white-collar criminality, from the individual rebel "ripping off" her boss to the intricately coordinated crimes of multinational corporations. The six general categories of white-collar crime used in this chapter are not meant to be anything more than an organizational tool for the material at hand. As new crimes come to light the categories into which they are grouped will undoubtedly have to be changed as well.

Ripping Off the Company

Larceny and Embezzlement

Employee Theft Of all the white-collar crimes, employee theft is probably the one with the lowest-status offenders. It is not so much that top executives don't steal from their employers, but that lower-level employees are excluded from many of the opportunities for other kinds of white-collar crime. In an average year, employee theft is believed to cost more than the losses from all street crimes put together.[1] "Inventory shrinkage" (loss from theft) is estimated to add about 2 percent to the cost of all retail goods, and some put that figure as high as 10 to 15 percent.[2] Since the majority of this loss can be attributed to employee theft, not shoplifting, it is virtually impossible to make any purchase without paying a price for white-collar crime.

Such numerical estimates help define the problem faced by contemporary business, but they can be terribly misleading. Even if the numbers are correct—which is debatable—there is more to this kind of crime than meets the eye. Many managers see certain types of employee theft as a "fringe benefit" that helps make up for low wages or other occupational problems. Some of the alleged cost to the public may therefore be more illusory than real, because an end to employee theft might force employers to pay higher wages or make costly improvements in working conditions. Gerald Mars argues that employee theft actually has positive effects in that it increases job satisfaction, raises production, and makes for a healthier economy.[3] It is doubtful, however, that Mars could get many owners of small businesses to accept his conclusions.

In one of the most comprehensive studies of employee theft, John Clark and Richard Hollinger found that about one-third of the more than 9,000 people they interviewed admitted to stealing from their employers within the past year.[4] They found that the employees most likely to steal were young, male, and unmarried, while another study found higher rates of theft among those who expected to leave their jobs in the near future.[5] Hollinger and Clark also concluded that employee dissatisfaction encouraged higher rates of theft, but the strongest predictor was the perceived likelihood of getting caught. Not surprisingly, those who felt they had the least chance of getting caught were the most likely to steal.

Much of this is petty crime that stems from the conflicting norms held by workers and employers. It has long been recognized that workers develop informal rules on the job that define not only the minimum amount of work expected of each employee but the maximum amount as well. Many eager young employees have been shocked when older workers demand they stop working so hard and making everyone else look bad. Similar rules usually govern stealing and other minor criminal offenses. In his study of a television plant, Donald Horning found that the workers had a clear-cut idea about what kind of property they could and could not legitimately take home.[6] Power tools, heavy machinery, testing equipment, and other large, expensive items were defined as company property, and the theft of such items or of the personal property of other workers was clearly forbidden. But scraps, light tools, nails, screws, electrical tape, and the like were seen as being of uncertain ownership, and the workers viewed the theft of such things as a victimless crime that caused no real harm.

Of course, all work groups do not show such concern about their employers' interests—especially when they feel underpaid or abused by management. Under such circumstances, many employees may go well beyond the kinds of petty crimes just described. It is not unknown for the majority of employees in a plant or office to support, or at least ignore, a ring of criminals operating within the business. Such criminals often make considerably more money from the sale of stolen merchandise to professional "fences" or to their company's legitimate customers than they do from their wages. Of course, some employees are willing to engage in criminal activities that violate their coworkers' code of fair play, but such crimes are more difficult to carry out and the criminals run a substantially greater risk of detection.

Money and property are not the only things taken from unwary businesses. The theft of confidential data or trade secrets has become an increasing problem. In some cases, industrial espionage is carried on by specially hired agents using sophisticated electronic equipment and spy techniques that could be drawn straight from the pages of a pulp novel. Other times, valuable information is purchased directly from a double-dealing employee. Such activities are crimes in most states, but enforcement has been lax. In many states, ambiguities in the law make it difficult to win guilty verdicts, and as is often the case with embezzlers, employers are reluctant to prosecute for fear of the publicity.[7]

Embezzlement

Embezzlers are the aristocrats of chiseling employees. They are, by definition, people who use a position of trust to appropriate someone else's assets for their own personal use. For many people the embezzler is practically the poster child for white-collar crime. Try asking some friends to name a white-collar offense, and there is a good chance the first thing they will mention is embezzlement. Perhaps for this reason, it was one of the first white-collar crimes to fall under intensive scientific scrutiny. Because embezzlers frequently have good jobs and high incomes, the reasons behind their crimes may not be immediately apparent. So a great deal of attention has been focused on the causes of these offenses. Many researchers have concluded that the old saying about being led to ruin by "slow horses and fast women" may contain more than a grain of truth. Research has shown that many embezzlers, both male and female, turn to crime because they are living beyond their financial means.[8] In some cases the problem involves gambling, in others a family emergency, heavy personal debt, or simply extravagant living.

An increasing number of women are now being convicted of embezzlement. In 2002, half (49.8 percent) of those charged with embezzlement were women.[9] The rapid increase in embezzlement by female employees probably reflects two important changes: their growing numbers in bookkeeping and accounting jobs, and the increasing pressure on all women to provide financial support for their families.

The dizzying growth of new technology has transformed white-collar crime every bit as much as it has the rest of society. There is little doubt that computer embezzlement has become one of the growth industries in contemporary crime, and it will be examined in the next section. But despite the large sums taken by some computer embezzlers, they are still not playing for the biggest stakes in the world of occupational crime. That distinction falls to those in top management, who are often the only ones in a position to pull off the multimillion-dollar crimes that may involve the looting of the assets of an entire corporation. In fact, this form of white-collar criminality became so common during the savings and loan scandal that Calavita and Pontell proposed a new name for it—collective embezzlement—which they define as the "siphoning off of company funds for personal use by top management." What sets this type of embezzlement apart is that groups of top executives use the corporation as a tool for committing a crime against itself. It is a "crime by the corporation, against the corporation."[10] Although such crimes are certainly not confined to any one industry, the savings and loan industry does provide numerous definitive examples of collective embezzlement, which are discussed in the case study at the end of this chapter. Whether it was executive compensation out of all proportion to their company's ability to pay, bad loans given in exchange for cash or other favors, or a host of bookkeeping tricks, time and again crooked savings and loan officials got rich while their companies slowly sank into bankruptcy.[11]

Perhaps the most famous case of collective embezzlement outside the American savings and loan industry involved the Bank of Credit and Commerce International (BCCI), which the cover of *Time* magazine labeled as "The World's Sleaziest Bank." Figuring out the full extent of the criminal activities at BCCI is no easy matter, for it operated a complex network of shell companies, branches, and subsidiaries in 70 countries. Even the financial officers and auditors in its Pakistani headquarters had trouble sorting it all out. What is abundantly clear, however, is a classic case of collective embezzlement in which top officials siphoned off so much money that the corporation eventually collapsed from its own weight. Some estimates hold that as much as $15 billion of BCCI's $20 billion in assets were looted by top employees.[12]

As was the case with many American savings and loans, BCCI used millions of dollars to buy friends in influential places. Politicians were used to discourage bank regulators from looking too closely into BCCI's affairs, and numerous Arab sheiks and wealthy businessmen were enlisted to give BCCI an air of respectability and financial integrity. But what set the BCCI affair apart from a run-of-the-mill savings and loan scandal was its involvement in a shadowy world of international intrigue. BCCI is believed to have helped such infamous characters as Panamanian dictator Manuel Noriega and Iraqi president Saddam Hussein stash huge sums of money in secret personal accounts, to have served as a money launderer for South American drug barons, and to have acted as a go-between for secret international arms deals that other institutions refused to handle. In fact, BCCI's ties with drug dealers, international terrorists, and such covert organizations as the Central Intelligence Agency make it as much an example of syndicated crime as white-collar crime.[13]

One of the most interesting things about the BCCI affair was the way such a thoroughly corrupt financial institution was able to avoid official scrutiny by cultivating friends in high places and by hiding in the cracks between the regulatory regimes of the different countries in which it operated. As Nikos Passas notes, "While banking has gone international, its regulation has failed to keep pace and remains largely national or loosely coordinated, which leaves plenty of room for unlawful maneuvers. . . . BCCI demonstrated, once again, that determined law evaders can easily circumvent the fragmented regulatory structures."[14]

Of course, bank and savings and loan executives are not the only ones to loot their own companies. Robert L. Vesco, for example, siphoned off $224 million in cash and securities from a Swiss-based complex of mutual funds known as Investors Overseas Services. Moreover, Vesco was able to flee the country and use his ill-gotten wealth to block the efforts to extradite him to stand trial for his crimes.[15] Even labor unions are the targets of such criminals. The favorite quarry of dishonest union officers is the pension funds on which the financial security of millions of union members depends. The International Brotherhood of Teamsters, the largest single union in the United States, has had a particularly bad reputation in this regard. Investigators have found that at one time organized criminals openly offered to arrange loans from the Teamsters' pension fund in exchange for a finder's fee. There is also substantial evidence that the fund financed numerous underworld projects, and several officials have been convicted of cheating the fund in various ways.[16] Thus, as in the case of so many financial institutions, some unions also seem to be used as tools for their own victimization.

Violating Intellectual Property

Intense pressure from corporate and business interests has helped create a new kind of theft in which the criminal does not take the "stolen" items but merely copies them. The idea behind the legal protection of intellectual property is that just as a person or a business can own physical property, they should also be able to own intangible property such as ideas or artistic creations. The protections for intellectual property include any material that is covered by copyrights or patents, or considered a trade secret or trademark. The laws criminalizing the violation of "intellectual property" are, however, radically different from the traditional crime of theft, since the offender does not deprive the victims of property or its use. Few people would argue against the laws banning the sale of fake copies of consumer products, but there is considerably less consensus about some other aspects of the intellectual property laws, especially the prohibition on copying music or videos that are only put to private use and not resold. A massive campaign sponsored by the music and entertainment industries has, for example, still not convinced many people that downloading a song from the Internet should be a criminal offense.

The Office of the United States Trade Representative, whose job it is to persuade other countries to respect the intellectual property of American corporations, estimates that the theft of intellectual property around the world cost American business $250 billion a year.[17] The Business Software Alliance and the Software Publishers Association estimated that four out of every ten new business software applications were pirated (copied without the permission of the corporation that wrote the program) and that the total loss to the industry was $11.4 billion.[18] Such estimates are probably considerably too high, however, since they assume that everyone who uses copied intellectual property would actually have spent the money to buy it.

What is not in doubt is that the globalization of the economy has helped create flourishing industries producing goods with fake trademarks and logos in many Third World countries. If the copies are of good quality, the consumer may actually benefit from the lower prices of the pirated products, but most often they are not. There is a growing list of consumers who have been injured by shoddily made imitation products, such as the Connecticut teenager whose cell phone exploded in September of 2004 because he unknowingly bought a poorly made counterfeit battery or the New York transplant recipient who suffered serious complications because the antirejection drugs he was taking turned out to be fakes.[19]

The U.S. Department of Justice has been giving increasing attention to the prosecution of those who distribute copied software. In August of 2004, for example, a Virginia Beach man was sentenced to 37 months in prison for selling pirated software, and a Louisiana man was given five months in prison and five months of home confinement for merely helping to distribute copyrighted software without making any personal financial gain.[20] Similar efforts are being made by private corporations. The latest push is coming from the record industry, which has launched a barrage of civil suits to try to prevent Internet sites from distributing copies of copyrighted recorded music.

Computer Crime

The explosive growth of computer technology has led to a similar explosion in the concern about computer crime. Despite all the talk, however, it is not really clear what is and is not a computer crime. The most obvious definition is that a computer crime is simply any crime that involves the use of a computer. But that definition is so broad that many crimes that would have occurred with or without a computer would be included. For example, this definition would consider the electronic filing of a fraudulent tax return but not the filing of an identical return on paper. From a legal standpoint, the offenses commonly considered computer crimes actually violate a host of different statutes. Some so-called computer crimes would be considered embezzlement; others, theft or fraud. Still others run afoul of new laws created to prevent various kinds of computer vandalism.

The differences in opinion about what should be considered a computer crime, and of course the difficulty in measuring any kind of illegal activity, have led to enormous differences in the estimates of its cost. At the low end is the

National Center for Computer Crime Data, which puts the figure at $550 million a year in the United States, whereas the Inter-Pact computer security firm puts it more than twenty-seven times higher, at $15 billion.[21] One thing we do know is that computer crime, however defined, is increasing rapidly. When a 1986 survey asked its respondents if they thought their companies were being victimized by computer crimes, only 7 percent said yes. Another survey seven years later found that 70 percent of the more than 400 companies surveyed felt they had been victimized during the previous year.[22] By 2002, a survey by the Computer Security Institute found that 90 percent of the 503 American corporations and government agencies queried had detected breaches of computer security in the last year, and 80 percent of them had suffered a financial loss as the result of such activities. The average loss reported to the survey takers was lightly more than $2 million. The biggest losses were due to the theft of proprietary information; financial fraud came in a close second. Although many computer security experts believe that the greatest threat comes from within the organization, this survey found that computer attacks were more than twice as likely to originate from the Internet as from an organization's internal systems.[23]

From a legal standpoint most of the computer crime would fall into one of three categories. First, there are the thefts and frauds that involve the use of the Internet and other computer technology to scam the public in much the same way as their low-tech predecessors. But another, increasingly common target of these computer thefts is information—trade secrets, mailing lists, credit card numbers. Closer to the public image of the computer criminal are the hackers who commit computer vandalism, destroying files, disrupting business, crashing computers for nothing other than a sense of power and the thrill of it. Finally, there are a host of other illegal activities that have migrated to the Internet, such as providing child pornography or the sale of other illegal goods, such as weapons or stolen merchandise. Several men have also been arrested for soliciting sex from minors over the Web in recent years. In addition to the outright crimes, the Internet is used for many other highly controversial activities, such as the dissemination of hate literature, lists of the home addresses of physicians who provide abortion services, and step-by-step recipes for making bombs.

Not surprisingly, computer crime does not have much of a history, but what there is is interesting. According to Rosoff, Pontell, and Tillman, the origins of computer crime can be traced to the early 1960s and an innocent-looking blue box—a device that could duplicate the multifrequency dialing system then used by AT&T and allow its owners unlimited free calling. Although an occasional arrest was made, the phone company preferred to downplay the whole problem for fear that publicity might set off an epidemic of phone fraud.

About the same time, the computer was beginning to come into wider use and a new kind of rogue—the hacker—was born. In the 1970s those young computer buffs were soon participating in a variety of minor offenses, most notably changing their grades on their schools' computers. Modems and computerized bulletin boards that came into widespread use by the end of that decade created new possibilities for abuse. But it was the explosion in the use of personal computers in the 1980s and the amazing growth of the Internet in the 1990s that laid the foundations for today's problems. Although the first generation of hackers was mainly out for mischief, the techniques they developed were soon put to use for more criminal purposes, such as fraud and the theft of valuable information.

Today the creators of computer "viruses" are the inheritors of the early hackers' desire for mischievous disruption. Although it is difficult to say who first had the idea to create a program that would mimic living viruses by making copies of itself and sending them off to infect other hosts, it was a brilliant innovation and one that has come to plague the world's computers. Like living organisms, the interconnectedness that makes modern computers so powerful also makes them vulnerable to infection. One of the most famous and destructive computer viruses to date was known as the "love bug." On May 4, 2000, email messages entitled "I Love You" began showing up in computers in Asia. When opened, it infected the host computer, destroyed numerous files, and sent copies of itself to everyone on the hosts' mailing lists. Within hours the virus had spread to Europe and the United States. The virus, which is believed to have been created by a Filipino computer school dropout, is estimated to have caused total losses of around $10 billion and to have paralyzed computers from the Pentagon to the British Parliament.[24]

Although the take from computer crimes is usually far lower than the billions of dollars involved in organizational crimes, the public is fascinated with the popular image of the computer criminal that developed in the early days of computer hackers—young whiz-kids with a bedroom stuffed with exotic equipment and the ability to outsmart huge corporate bureaucracies, with their legions of experts and specialists. The fact the many computer criminals are employees or former employees of the firms they are attacking has done little to change the romantic ideas about computer crime. Even the names given the techniques of computer crime have a humorous, offbeat ring. *Data diddling*, for example, is the term applied to one of the easiest and most common computer crimes. The data diddler simply manipulates the information fed into the computer to his or her advantage. Funds that were intended to be deposited in one account may, for example, be credited to a different account controlled by the criminal. A technique limited to skilled programmers is to place a "Trojan horse" in a program while it is being written. Once the program is installed on a computer, the criminal can activate the Trojan horse and give secret commands, unknown to the legitimate operators. The criminal might, for example, order the computer to make electronic fund transfers, erase personal debts, or reveal confidential information.[25] Another approach to computer embezzlement is known as the "salami technique" because the criminals take "one thin slice at a time." For example, two computer programmers at a large New York garment firm instructed the company computer to increase each employee's income tax withholding by two cents a week and to deposit the money in the programmers' withholding accounts. At the end of the year, the embezzlers planned to receive their profits in the form of refund checks from the Internal Revenue Service. However, those giant-sized refunds touched off an IRS investigation that uncovered the crime. In an operation sometimes known as "superzapping," computer operators can use special programs that override security controls in order to reach confidential data that can be sold to competitors or used in a blackmail scheme. Some security-protected programs have a built-in "trap door" that allows the operator to bypass the safeguards and make changes in a program. Such trap doors are useful when removing bugs from the program, and they may inadvertently be left in the final version, or they may be placed there intentionally for use at a later time. A data thief may also "piggy-back" on a legitimate user, tricking the computer into thinking that the criminal also has clearance to use the machine.[26] Computes are also commonly used to collect the information necessary for the "identity thefts" discussed in the next section.

Financial gain is not the only goal of computer criminals. Many seek revenge or are simply out to work some mischief. Disgruntled employees and former employees often use their knowledge of an organization's computer system to settle a grudge. Typical was the case of Neal Cotton, a network administrator who worked for a Manhattan-based computer consulting firm. After being told he was going to be fired, Cotton went home and hacked into his employer's computer system and destroyed the files of several of its most important clients. Cotton pleaded guilt to charges that carry a maximum sentence of ten years in prison and a $250,000 fine in September of 2004.[27] Another growing problem is the denial of service attack in which hackers direct so many inquiries to an organization's computers that the system overloads and legitimate users can no longer gain access. The Microsoft Corporation, long a target of intense animosity among computer hackers, has been the subject of several recent attacks, but it is certainly not alone. Forty percent of the organizations surveyed by the Computer Security Institute said they had detected a denial of service attack against them in the preceding year.[28]

Computer users and computer criminals are engaged in an increasingly sophisticated game of cat and mouse. Hundreds of millions of dollars a year are now being spent on computer safeguards. Many users are now automatically required to enter a secret password before being given access to files. To prevent unwanted outsiders from tapping into their computer lines and pirating those codes or other confidential information, a growing number of users are employing encryption systems that code computer transactions so that they are virtually impossible to decipher without a special key. But such security systems have an obvious fault—employees who work with those records must be given the password, which may then be used for illicit purposes. It seems doubtful that any new innovation in computer security can do more than buy a little time until a way is found to defeat it, but such a delay may still be well worth the price.

Fraud and Deception

Identity Theft

As the Internet has become a growing marketplace, the security of customers' identities and especially their credit card numbers has become a major issue. It is estimated that fraud in e-commerce transactions cost $1.4 billion in 1999 alone.[29] But identity theft—the use of someone's identity for fraudulent purposes—is certainly not limited to computer users. Criminals can find identity information by everything from dumpster diving to mail theft and purse snatching. It is, moreover, one of the fastest growing of all crimes.[30] The number of identity thefts reported to the Federal Trade Commission increased almost 250 percent between 2001 and 2003.[31] However, some of this huge increase was probably due to better reporting, since data from victimization surveys show that the FTC never hears about the vast majority of identity thefts. A survey released in September of 2003 indicates that identity theft is, in fact, one of the most common crimes in the United States. Almost one in every twenty Americans surveyed (4.7%) reported that they had been victimized by identity theft in the last year, which amounts to about 10 million people. Even though many of the offenses did not involve direct financial costs, the average loss reported was still $4,800, bringing the total cost to almost $50 billion a year.[32]

The most common way these stolen identities were used was to charge something on someone's credit card account. The FTC survey found that 2.4 percent of those surveyed had fallen victim to such a crime in the last year. About 1.5 percent of the respondents said that their identity information had been used to open a new credit card account, take out a bank loan, or commit other types of fraud. The average loss from this type of identity theft was about five times higher than the $2,100 average for the losses from fraudulent charges to existing accounts. About 15 percent of the victims reported that their identity information was misused for something other than financial gain. The most common misuse occurred when the perpetrator gave the victim's name to law enforcement officers when they were stopped by authorities or charged with a crime. Other common uses of fraudulent identity information were in renting an apartment and obtaining medical care. Although the individual victims whose identity information is misused usually do not have to cover the full amount of the losses, the survey found that on the average victims spent about $500 and 30 hours resolving the problems created by the offence.[33]

False Advertising

We spend billions of dollars a year on advertising, and false advertising is certainly one of the best-known forms of fraud and deception. Who has not seen an advertisement that seems patently false or bought a product whose performance fell far short of its promoters' claims? But the legal definition of false advertising is much more generous to the advertisers than most people assume. Although common sense would tell us that false advertising consists of the use of untrue statements in advertising, the law uses a different standard. It is not falsity but deception in advertising that is illegal. According to Section 15 of the Federal Trade Commission Act, deceptive advertisements are those that are "misleading in material respect," and this has been interpreted by the courts to mean that the deceptive advertisement must somehow affect the purchasing decisions of the customer. Although there is usually little doubt about what makes a statement true or false, determining whether or not a statement is deceptive is a much more complex business, because one must not only examine the nature of the statement but also judge its potential effect on the consumer.

This deception standard has a logical rationale. For example, when one petroleum company claimed that its gasoline put a "tiger in your tank," it was making a statement that was literally false yet not deceptive, since no reasonable person would believe that a tiger could actually materialize in a gas tank. The flaw in this approach is that complex legal standards that are difficult to apply tend to be interpreted in favor of those with the money to build the best legal case, and of course it is the advertisers, not the consumers, who command such resources. As a result, a body of case precedent has built up that allows salespeople and advertisers to lie to potential customers, as long as they use only broad, general lies (e.g., "This is the finest soap in the world"), on the grounds that such claims have no effect on purchasing decisions. If this were actually true, and such exaggerated claims ("puffery," as they are called) did not sell products, they would hardly have remained a mainstay of advertising for so many years.

But even with the wide latitude given advertisers to "puff" their products, violations of the law are still common. One of the most famous cases of false advertising that eventually went all the way to the Supreme Court involved an ad for Rise shaving cream. In this commercial, a man was shown shaving first with an "ordinary" lather that dried out quickly after application, and then with Rise, which fulfilled its advertising slogan by staying "moist and creamy." What the television audience was not told was that the "ordinary" lather was not shaving cream at all, but an aerosol especially concocted to come out in a big attractive puff and then quickly disappear.[34] A similar case involved Campbell's "chunky style" soups. The bottom of the soup bowl used in a television commercial was filled with marbles, which pushed the pieces of meat to the top, thus making the soup look a lot chunkier than it really was. Many other cases of false advertising involve claims manufacturers made about the benefits of their product. The manufacturer of Anacin ran into trouble with the Federal Trade Commission for claiming that its product relieved nervous tension, stress, and depression, was stronger than aspirin, brought relief within twenty-two seconds, and was more effective than other nonprescription analgesics.[35] The makers of Listerine mouthwash ran into similar problems with claims about their product's ability to prevent colds. Although such cases can generate a great deal of embarrassing publicity, few sanctions, beyond merely stopping the false advertising, are usually brought against big corporate advertisers.

The huge increases in the advertising budgets for prescription drugs and a new willingness to bypass physicians and appeal directly to the public have led to an increasing number of complaints. In August of 1998, for example, a unit of the BASF Corporation agreed to pay $41.8 million for the false advertising of its synthetic thyroid drug Synthroid. Not only did its advertising falsely claim that Synthroid was unique and superior to competing brands and that no other brand was useful in place of Synthroid, but the company attempted to suppress the publication of research showing that Synthroid and some of the generic products were biologically equivalent.[36]

Deceptive advertising is often tied in to other kinds of deceptive marketing. In 1999, for example, the Pacific Bell telephone company was fined $44 million by the California Public Utilities Commission for misleading advertising and marketing. The judge held that Pacific Bell "sold customers extra services they did not want, used misleading names to sell options like voice mail, and tricked customers into skipping a free option that can block Caller ID for all calls."[37] As is often the case, however, the fines imposed were far smaller than the profits the illegal actions brought. Pacific Bell's own internal documents indicate that it expected to make more than $300 million from the marketing campaign in question.[38]

Deceptive advertising by local retail stores is more likely to be punished, since the victims are more likely to complain and the offenders usually have far less political power than larger corporations. A common form of false advertising used by retail stores is known as "bait and switch." The idea is to bait the customers into the store with advertising that offers merchandise at an extremely low price and then to switch their attention to a more expensive product. When customers ask about the sale merchandise, retailers either claim that "the last one was just sold" or point out some obvious flaw that the advertising failed to mention. Sometimes the customer is not informed of the switch until it is too late to do anything about it. For example, one firm advertised an offer to repair automobile transmissions for only $69.50. But once the mechanics actually dismantled a transmission, they routinely claimed to find new problems that would substantially raise the price.[39]

Consumer Fraud

In contrast to false advertising, more blatant business frauds are usually handled as criminal offenses, but the severity of the punishment varies greatly with the type of offense and the size and influence of the company involved. Consider the case of the Holland Furnace Company, which, as Christopher Stone put it, "seems almost to have been born crooked."[40] Holland's standard sales technique was to send a representative to a private home who would claim to be an inspector from the gas company. Once inside, he would dismantle the heater as part of his "inspection" and then flatly refuse to put it back together, claiming there was grave danger of explosion. In the middle of the family crisis that inevitably ensued, a solution would present itself magically at the door in the form of a Holland furnace salesman, who would make a quick sale. Twenty-two years of legal problems and consumer complaints passed before the company president and two vice presidents were found guilty of criminal contempt, and the president was sentenced to six months in jail.[41] The Holland Furnace Company and other shady home-improvement businesses are part of what Philip Schrag calls the "commercial underworld"—small and medium-sized firms that operate on the fringes of the law.[42]

The Ponzi, or pyramid, scheme is one of the most popular and successful techniques of consumer fraud. Details vary, but the criminal typically offers investors huge returns through one kind of scheme or another, while in fact the money is not invested but goes either into the pockets of the owner or to finance payouts to earlier investors. As long as the number of investors keeps growing, everything appears to be fine and investors continue to receive their interest, but as soon as new investment lags, the whole scheme collapses. In the early part of the twentieth century, Charles Ponzi, after whom the scheme is named, claimed he could make fat profits for investors from the international currency and postal markets. Today these Ponzi schemes involve everything from cosmetic dealerships to stocks and bonds. Other kinds of popular frauds include land sales in which consumers are tricked into believing barren deserts or swamplands are prime home sites, phony contests in which consumers are told they have won a prize that actually ends up costing them far more than it is worth, fee-based employment agencies that deceive the unemployed into thinking a high-paying job will be found for them, and various telemarketing scams in which smooth salespeople talk customers into making an advance payment for some promised merchandise or service that is never delivered.

More sophisticated consumers have long been aware of these kinds of abuses. But fraud and deception have become accepted business practices in many sectors of more legitimate industries as well, and that makes them far more difficult to detect and root out. Consider, for example, American automobile dealers. Common complaints against car dealers include making false claims in the sale of new automobiles, forcing unordered accessories on customers, selling used cars as new cars, and imposing excessive finance charges.

Most people are quick to attribute these problems to the personal character of the dealers, who are depicted as the kind of shady, dishonest characters you would not want living next door. But the real cause of the problem lies in the economic structure of the automobile business. In 1921, there were eighty-eight automobile manufacturers in the United States; now there are only a handful. The small number of potential suppliers makes the loss of a franchise a serious threat and keeps the new-car dealer heavily dependent on the manufacturers. These manufacturers place intense pressures on dealers to sell as many cars as possible, while often providing scant rewards for dealers who excel in the performance of their service and warranty obligations. The system of sales bonuses for the dealers who sell the most cars puts an especially heavy burden on small dealers, who are forced to cut their profit margins to the bone in order to compete with the large dealers who receive those lucrative cash rewards. Since most dealers make so little profit from the sale of new cars, many of them feel compelled to make up the difference through their service departments or used car sales. The manufacturers thus inadvertently promote such illegal practices as charging for more hours of labor than were actually needed for a job, installing new parts when the old ones needed only minor repairs, and charging for work that was never actually done. Part of the failure of some dealers to live up to their warranty obligations can also be attributed to the manufacturers. The factory pays only about two-thirds the amount that dealers would have charged private customers for the same repairs, on top of which dealers are often required to fill out lengthy paperwork and to tag and return parts replaced under warranty.[43]

Manufacturers are sometimes directly involved in such fraudulent schemes as well. In 1987 the Chrysler Corporation admitted that it had reset the odometers on some of the cars it provided to its executives and then sold them to the public as new.[44] Although Chrysler quickly stopped such activities when they came to public light, it is apparently common practice for used car dealers to set back the odometers of high-mileage cars. By comparing the mileage on the odometers of a group of used cars in Queensland, Australia, with the actual mileage reported by their previous owners, John Braithwaite found that more than one-third of the cars' odometers had been set back. An estimate for the state of Georgia puts that figure at a full 50 percent of all used cars.[45]

Nor are automobile dealers and manufacturers the only source of difficulty for motorists. One estimate holds that a third of all the money consumers spend on automobile repairs goes to unnecessary or fraudulent work.[46] Investigators in another study concluded that 53 cents of every car repair dollar were wasted because of faulty repairs, overcharging, and other problems.[47] In an often-cited 1941 study sponsored by *Reader's Digest*, a car in perfect mechanical condition was taken to 347 different repair shops across the country; 63 percent of them invented some kind of work to do. Moreover, when the study was replicated in 1987, the researchers found that the problem was just as bad as it had been four decades earlier.[48] An interesting experiment by Paul Jesilow points to a similar conclusion. In this study, researchers brought dead batteries to 313 firms and asked to have them recharged. Even though the batteries had been checked to make sure they were still good, almost 11 percent of the firms claimed the batteries could not be recharged (which, of course, creates the opportunity for the sale of a new one).[49] The most publicized case of auto repair fraud in recent years occurred in 1992, when the California Department of Consumer Affairs charged the Sears auto repair centers with a host of illegal practices. The bureau's investigators made thirty-eight test visits to twenty-seven Sears auto centers. Unnecessary services and repairs were recommended on thirty-four of those occasions.[50]

Fraud in the Professions

Although the business of automobile sales and repairs has a long-standing rep-utation for corruption and shady dealing, similar abuses are common in even the most respected professions, such as medicine, law, and accounting. For ex-ample, fraud in Medicaid and Medicare—the government-sponsored health-care programs for the poor and the aged—is believed to cost the public billions of dollars a year. The medical insurance industry estimates that about 3 percent of the nation's physicians routinely commit outright fraud and a much larger percentage engage in improper or ambiguous billing.[51] Estimates for 2000 put the total cost of health-care fraud on the part of physicians and other health-care professionals somewhere between $39 and $130 billion.[52]

Some of the most blatant crimes involve fraudulent claims for reimburse-ment. Pharmacies, for instance, commonly bill the government for a larger num-ber of pills than their customers actually receive, and medical laboratories charge for tests that were never performed.[53] In 1992, for example, a large FBI investi-gation known as Operation Goldpill resulted in the arrest of eighty-two phar-macists and a physician for various forms of Medicaid fraud, including billing the government for drug prescriptions that were never filled and secretly sub-stituting cheaper drugs for the ones called for in the prescriptions.[54] In another example of billing for services not performed, a Senate investigator posing as a Medicaid patient was told that her urine sample was normal, when in fact it was a mixture of soap and cleanser that she concocted in the restroom of the clinic she was visiting.[55]

Physicians are also involved in many of the same types of crimes. Although it is extremely difficult to prove fraud in individual cases, there is conclusive evi-dence that physicians make a great deal of money performing unnecessary med-ical procedures (see the next section). Much more clear-cut are the cases in which physicians submit fraudulent medical insurance claims. In some cases, physicians bill for procedures that were never performed. In others they submit several bills for the same services. In a crime known as "upcoding," doctors per-form one medical procedure but bill the insurer for another, more expensive one. Another common crime among anesthesiologists, psychiatrists, and other health-care professionals who charge by the hour is to submit bills claiming that they worked longer than they actually did. Although all but a tiny fraction of such offenses go undetected, many investigative techniques exist to uncover such of-fenders. For example, by comparing billing records submitted to different pri-vate and public payees, investigators have found that some physicians submit claims that total more than 24 hours in a single day. Other investigators have re-sorted to timing the traffic in and out of office waiting rooms to see how long patients actually spend with the physicians.[56]

The fact that such abuses are often directed against anonymous bureaucra-cies may lessen the public's outrage, but patients also pay the price. In one no-torious case, a Los Angeles ophthalmologist was found to have tricked hundreds of poor Hispanic patients into unnecessary eye surgeries to collect the Medicaid fees—subjecting them to many unnecessary risks and leaving at least one woman totally blind. In Texas, a woman was committed to a psychiatric hospital after a psychotic reaction to a pain medication. She believed that she would only be there for a day or two. Instead she was heavily sedated, kept in isolation from friends and family, and warned that she would be held in a mental hospital for the rest of her life if she fought for her release. After her insurance was exhausted, she was finally released and sent home with a bill for $48,000.[57]

Although the public usually blames such problems on the individual professional's lack of personal ethics, once again the economic forces lie at the root of the problem. Because health-care professionals are paid on a fee-for-service basis, a built-in reward is provided for overbilling and overdoctoring. For example, a study of California's Medicaid and Medicare program by Henry Pontell, Paul Jesilow, and Gilbert Geis concluded that "the very organization of the program invites fraud." They found that the "fee-for-service delivery system offers physicians the chance to amass considerable gain with little risk. Diagnostic tests that have not been performed can easily be billed to the state . . . [and] the professional background of the physician affords strong protection against discovery." Even if a physician's crimes are eventually discovered, there is a wide "range of defensive tactics to safeguard against effective sanctions."[58]

Overbilling and other fraudulent practices are also a severe problem among lawyers. Because lawyers generally charge by the hour and much of the time for which they bill involves solitary activities or private meetings that are not readily visible to the client, it is easy for them to overcharge without being detected. One case that did come to public light was that of Webster Hubbell, an associate attorney general in the Clinton administration. Following a public scandal, Hubbell admitted that he had stolen some $394,000 from his former law partners and clients by overbilling and filing false claims for reimbursement.[59] It is doubtful, however, that his crime would ever have come to light had it not been for his close association with President Clinton and the intense personal scrutiny that relationship brought.

Financial Fraud

Although total costs of professional abuses add up to billions of dollars a year, the biggest individual frauds are usually those worked in the glittering world of high finance. One famous example was the Equity Funding case. Estimates of the total losses vary, but this single case may have cost the public as much as $3 billion. From its inception in 1960, Equity was based on a "funding concept" that was designed to appeal to customers' greed. In most cases, customers bought mutual fund shares and an insurance policy from Equity. They were then given a loan with their shares as collateral, which in turn was used to pay the insurance premiums. After ten years the program was to end with the customers making a large cash payment to clear up the loan—presumably from the money they had made from the increasing value of their mutual fund shares. Of course, the whole scheme would work only as long as the stock market never went down, but such an economic decline seemed an unlikely prospect amid the buoyant optimism of the times.

The Equity Funding Corporation itself lost money practically from the beginning. Its directors soon resorted to one of the most common techniques of business fraud to keep the company afloat: They juggled the books to give the company a false veneer of success, thereby increasing the value of its stock and the willingness of bankers to provide loans. Five years after Equity Funding went public, the value of a share of its stock had risen from $6 to an astronomical $80. Equity stock was, however, virtually worthless in another five years. Whether motivated by company loyalty, greed, or fear, more than 130 Equity executives knew of the fraud and said nothing to the authorities. The scandal finally broke when an employee, disgruntled by his layoff, leaked damning information to a securities analyst. The subsequent investigation showed that Equity had written 56,000 bogus insurance policies, created $120 million in phony assets, and even "killed" some of its phony insurees in order to collect on their policies. The entire corporation collapsed soon after the facts came to light. A federal judge later gave Equity's president, Stanley Goldblum, an eight-year sentence for his role in the case, and numerous other conspirators received shorter terms.[60]

The biggest white-collar crimes tend to be anonymous affairs carried on by faceless executives operating behind a wall of corporate secrecy. But much to the satisfaction of the media, the crime wave in the banking and finance industry in the 1980s produced several larger-than-life villains. Foremost among them was Charles Keating, who controlled the now-bankrupt Lincoln Savings and Loan. (The collapse of Lincoln cost around $2.6 billion, making it the single most costly savings and loan failure.[61]) From the time Keating acquired Lincoln Savings in February 1984 until it declared bankruptcy in April 1989, Lincoln was involved in a host of questionable activities. The most famous involved the efforts of five U.S. senators who had received a total of $1.3 million in campaign funds from Keating to intervene with government regulators on his behalf. But it was securities fraud that finally sent Keating to jail. Keating's conviction arose from his program to sell bonds from Lincoln's holding company, American Continental Corporation, directly from Lincoln's branch offices. Because the bonds were purchased from their "bank," many customers apparently did not realize they were not insured. Not only did the salespeople often fail to point out that fact to potential customers, but more important, Lincoln's staff continually lied about American Continental's financial strength. Even when the company was teetering on the brink of bankruptcy, salespeople continued to tout the safety of Continental's bonds. Although many elderly people lost their entire savings when Lincoln went bankrupt, members of the jury that convicted Keating on seventeen counts of fraud in December 1991 said that they were most impressed with the fact that the Lincoln staff never changed their sales pitch even as they watched Lincoln drag American Continental into bankruptcy.[62] In April 1996, however, Keating's lawyers succeeded in overturning his state conviction because of alleged errors in the judge's instruction to the jury. In December they won a reversal of his federal conviction because some jury members had improperly learned about his state court conviction.

Difficult to explain in a short news bite and lacking a bad guy to blame, many of the most complex financial crimes have hardly raised a blip on the media's radar screens. Few, for example, have ever heard of the "yield-burning" cases that resulted in millions of dollars in fines to such top financial firms as Salomon Smith Barney, Goldman Sachs, Paine Weber, Morgan Stanley, and Merrill Lynch in April of 2000. Yield burning is a little-known violation of federal law that occurs when state and local governments seek to refinance their tax-exempt bonds by purchasing U.S. government securities. Federal law forbids them from making any higher interest than the yield earned on the original bonds. So unscrupulous traders inflate the price of the securities beyond their fair market value, thus "burning the yield"; they then pocket the extra money.[63]

The financial fraud at the Enron Corporation might well have met with the same response from the media if it had not led to the bankruptcy of what, at least on paper, was one of the largest corporations in the world. The accounting tricks Enron used to cover up its mounting losses were so complex that it took reporters weeks to figure out what they had actually done. The public attention brought on by Enron's troubles and the complicity of its accounting firm in helping to cover them up spurred the usually lethargic enforcement bureaucracy to step up its efforts. Other major corporations were soon found to have similar problems. Adelphia Communications, once the sixth largest cable television service, filed for bankruptcy after covering up huge losses due to the financial improprieties of its founder and his sons. America's second largest long-distance and data provider, WorldCom, did the same thing after it disclosed that $3.85 billion in expenses were improperly booked and its accounts had another $3.8 billion in "errors." (See the case study at the end of this chapter for more details on these financial frauds.)

Tax Evasion

Every occupation has its own structure of fraudulent opportunities, but even if they wanted to, few people ever have the chance to carry out criminal schemes on the scale that someone like Charles Keating did. Yet almost all workers have a chance to commit one type of fraud—income tax evasion. Most modern-day Americans are probably too suspicious to easily admit their illegal activities to a survey taker, but a survey of 1,698 Americans taken in the 1940s found that 57 percent of the men and 40 percent of the women admitted committing some type of tax evasion.[64] Interestingly, the survey found violations to be the most common among middle- and upper-income people, especially businesspeople and lawyers. Prosecutions by the Internal Revenue Service (IRS) are often concentrated in the higher social strata as well (although part of the reason may be that audits of high-income taxpayers are likely to net more money), and most experts believe that high-income people have the greatest opportunities for tax evasion. The opportunities for tax evasion also vary considerably from one occupation to another. The IRS estimates that auto dealers, restaurateurs, and clothing store operators underreport about 40 percent of their income; traveling salespeople, 30 percent; doctors, lawyers, and accountants, 20 percent; and farmers, 18 percent.[65]

Although the IRS audits less than 1 percent of all tax returns[66] and prosecutes only a few thousand people a year for tax evasion, some criminal cases do occasionally receive a burst of publicity. The most famous case in recent years was probably that of Leona Helmsley, the head of a huge hotel empire who was repeatedly portrayed in the press as the "queen of greed." Helmsley was convicted in 1989 of evading her taxes by charging millions of dollars in personal redecorating expenses to her businesses, and she was fined $7.1 million and given a four-year prison term.[67]

It is tempting to blame income tax evasion on the larceny that is said to be lurking in the hearts of even the most honest women and men. No doubt, there is some truth in this belief—if we were a nation of saints, there would be no tax evasion. But to understand this common crime, we must look to something other than universal human greed. The fact is that U.S. income tax laws could hardly provide more encouragement to would-be violators if they were intentionally designed for that purpose. The laws are so complex that even people who are willing to pay their taxes are often unable to figure out how much they owe, and one person may pay lower taxes than another with the same income simply by being better at the "tax game." The obvious injustice of this situation encourages both contempt for the system of taxation and the attitude that paying taxes is not a responsibility of citizenship so much as a game that one wins or loses. If the percentage of one's income owed in taxes were determined entirely by accounting skills, the system might still claim some shred of respectability. The tax laws, however, are replete with special advantages, loopholes, and benefits for those with the greatest political influence. Because every return cannot be audited, income tax collectors must rely on the honesty of the individual taxpayers; yet the taxation system itself is so riddled with favoritism that it cannot claim the integrity it demands of its clients.

Of course, business organizations have the same motivation to avoid paying their taxes as do individual citizens, but there is one essential difference. Big business has not only the power to obtain specific, industry-by-industry tax breaks and loopholes that make most corporate tax avoidance completely legal, but the talent to create and defend an endless array of new strategies to reduce its taxes. As a result, the tax burden shouldered by big corporations has steadily declined over the last four decades. In 2001, corporate taxes brought in only about half as much of the gross domestic product as they did in 1970, and another round of large corporate tax cuts in 2004 reduced their payments evenmore.[68]

The Internal Revenue Service has often shown surprisingly little concern about tracking down the illegalities of powerful corporate taxpayers. Indeed, the IRS's enforcement efforts are so weak that many of the criminal cases brought against corporations stem from investigations of entirely different activities. For instance, the Wall Street scandals of the late 1980s focused primarily on insider trading, but a number of fraudulent tax schemes were accidentally uncovered. Among the charges to which Michael Milken, the most notorious figure in the scandal, pleaded guilty was a scheme to defraud the IRS by helping one of his clients "park" valuable stocks. Milken agreed to buy blocks of stock below their market value so that the company could record a tax loss, and then sell them back at an agreed-upon price at a later date. (The term *parking* refers to the fact that the control of the stocks really rested in the hands of the original owner; they were merely "parked" with Milken's firm.) It is significant that none of the charges of tax evasion to come out of this scandal originated with the Internal Revenue Service, which is assigned primary responsibility for enforcing the tax laws.[69]

Conflicts of Interest

Most conflicts of interest lie in the vaguely defined gray area between the unethical and the illegal. At their most innocent, such conflicts may result from nothing more sinister than bad judgment, but at the other extreme, they encompass a wide range of clearly illegal behavior usually involving either bribery or fraud. In most cases, there is a tantalizing hint of criminal behavior without quite enough evidence to prove a case. For example, it is completely legal for politicians to accept campaign contributions from a particular interest group as long as they are not buying their vote, but how do we know why a politician votes one way or another? Similarly, it is fraud for a physician to tell a patient that he or she needs an operation when the doctor knows it is unnecessary. But medical judgments are seldom clear-cut. Many times physicians who have a financial stake in performing a particular procedure may simply convince themselves that it is safe and necessary, even when the evidence indicates that it is not.

Conflicts of Interest in Government

The public is probably most familiar with the conflicts of interest among officeholders, since the media pays much closer attention to the world of politics than to that of the professions. There is, moreover, little doubt that the divided loyalties of our elected officials constitute one of the most serious threats to democratic rule we face today. The U.S. Senate's code of ethics, for example, prohibits any member or employee from aiding the progress of legislation for the purpose of advancing his or her own financial interests, yet virtually every day members of Congress vote on bills that directly affect their personal finances.

Of course, the federal government is now so deeply involved in economic regulation that it would be difficult for wealthy legislators to find any high-paying investments that would not be affected by their actions in one way or another. There are, however, two simple steps that even the wealthiest legislators can take to avoid conflicts of interest: abstain from voting on any issue that might affect their financial interests, and place their holdings in a blind trust that is controlled by independent trustees. But very few federal legislators have taken those steps.

A study by the Center for Public Integrity found very similar problems at the state level. Its analysis of financial disclosure reports filed in 1999 found that more than one in five state legislators sat on a committee that regulated their professional or business interests, and that at least 18 percent had financial ties to businesses or organizations that lobby state government. To cite only a single example, the minority leader in the North Carolina House of Representatives, N. Leo Daughtry, owned a fertilizer company and was part-owner of two tobacco warehouses. But such ties did not stop him from supporting a big tax break for the Philip Morris tobacco company or from sitting on the Select Committee on the Tobacco Settlement.[70]

The current system of campaign finance subjects virtually all elected officials, whether wealthy or not, to another fundamental conflict of interest: Do they represent the interests of the public who voted for them or the campaign contributors who gave them the money to run? Unfortunately, the ever-increasing costs of running a serious campaign seem to be tilting the scales more and more heavily in favor of the latter alternative. As recently as 1960, the price tag for an average congressional campaign was only about $25,000. But in the 2000 election, the average race for the House of Representatives cost about $750,000, and the average senatorial campaign, about $4 million. That means that senators need to raise at least $12,000 every week of their six-year term to finance their next campaign.[71]

There are, of course, some legal restrictions on the process of campaign finance aside from the prohibition against directly selling influence. In fact, an elaborate system of regulations has been set up to limit both the sources and amounts of campaign contributions, but it is so full of loopholes that in actuality it does neither. But even without those loopholes, the current legislation governing campaign contributions reveals a curious kind of logic. If campaign contributions are used to buy influence, the logic of democracy would dictate their prohibition and not just limits on their size or the source.

Defenders of the current system argue that the contributions are simply gifts with no strings attached and that they do not influence the way elected officials perform their duties. But even if that highly unlikely contention were true, it ignores the role the big contributors' money plays in putting those with whom they already agree into office. A study by Ralph Nader's Congress Watch found that winners outspent losers by a margin of four to one in congressional races, and that Senate candidates who outspent their opponents won election 85 percent of the time.[72] Although some of this difference is due to the ability of the most popular candidates to attract more campaign contributions, that is only part of the explanation. After a careful statistical analysis of the variables that might affect the relationship between campaign spending and electoral success, Gary Jacobson concluded that "challengers and other non-incumbents do better the more money they spend, because their campaign expenditures purchase the attention of voters."[73] Further, incumbents usually have a lopsided advantage in fund-raising over their opponents.[74]

The general laxity of campaign financing laws might lead one to expect that they would seldom be violated, but that is not the case. Of all the members of Congress who were indicted for criminal offenses between 1941 and 1980, more than 14 percent were charged with violating campaign financing laws.[75] Since then, charges of campaign finance irregularities have become so common that they have been leveled against most of our prominent politicians. Although the existing loopholes allow private individuals to spend as much as they want to help the candidates of their choice as long as they do so independently of his and her campaigns, the ban on direct contributions by corporations and unions has made it more difficult for such organizations to stay within the law. To maintain the appearance of legality, organizational contributors try to persuade their employees, members, or stockholders to give money to political action committees (PACs) that support their organizational interests. And though indictments are rare for such offenses, it is clear that corporations and unions often engage in fund-raising activities that violate not only the spirit of the law but the letter as well. For example, although the law expressly forbids organizations to coerce employees to contribute, many employees still come under intense pressure to chip in to support their companies' political interests. A report in the *Los Angeles Times* indicates that many large corporations actually have automatic deductions taken from the paychecks of "consenting" executives that are sent to company-controlled PACs.[76] Some companies have even given employees special bonuses with the expectation that they will be turned over to the appropriate PAC, or have encouraged employees to pad their expense accounts to reimburse themselves for their contributions. Another common practice, known as "bundling," involves a group of corporate executives with an interest in a particular issue who all send in large "personal" contributions at the same time.[77]

Politicians often play a kind of shell game with their campaign finances. When they first find some new loophole in the law, no one pays much attention. But as more and more candidates jump on the bandwagon, the public starts to take note. As the bad publicity mounts, those same politicians who accepted the money pass some kind of reform bill and turn to the next loophole. One recent example was so-called soft money. Although corporations and labor unions are not allowed to give money directly to individual candidates, they were allowed to give unlimited amounts of "soft" money to the political parties, which could then spend the money to elect those same candidates. According to the Federal Election Commission, the Republicans and Democrats raised almost half a billion dollars in soft money for the 2000 elections.[78] As the huge amounts of money pouring into this loophole became a major political embarrassment, such contributions were banned in 2002.

Well-heeled special interests also hire an army of lobbyists to influence the legislative process. Lavish parties and free entertainment are other devices commonly used to curry favor among elected officials. Although the lobbyists' big entertainment budgets raise few eyebrows in Washington, the process of corruption becomes more apparent when their largess involves free trips and all-expense-paid vacations.

Because most politicians balk at accepting outright bribes, lobbyists often make small personal gifts that allegedly come with no strings attached. The most common inducements are small presents and gratuities—free meals at expensive restaurants, lavishly catered parties, free bottles of perfume, free samples of a company's product, or an all-expenses-paid trip to a corporate-sponsored event at a luxurious resort. A bottle of perfume is obviously not enough to influence a senator's vote on a critical issue, but the hope of the growing army of Washington lobbyists is that the accumulation of small favors will create a sense of obligation that will ultimately be paid back in political favors. Former senator Paul Douglas made this point well: "The enticer does not generally pay money directly to the public representative. He tries instead by a series of favors to put the public official under such a feeling of personal obligation that [he] comes to feel that his first loyalties are to his private benefactors and patrons."[79] Do such tactics work? The answer depends on the individual official involved, but the growing number of Washington lobbyists who spend billions of dollars a year in the effort to win political influence apparently think so.[80]

Conflicts of Interest in the Professions

Conflicts of interest between professionals and their clients are built into the very nature of the relationship. The professional claims, both implicitly and explicitly, to be working in the best interests of the client, yet in many cases the professional's own financial interests and desires clash with those of the client. The ethical practitioner makes an intentional effort to put the clients' interests first and to inform them of any possible conflict of interest he or she may have. But those who are less scrupulous have ample opportunities to manipulate clients for their own gain. Even if those clients are skeptical about the integrity of the professionals who serve them, they seldom have the knowledge necessary to evaluate their performance accurately.

The most common conflict of interest lies in the financial relationship between practitioners, who try to maximize their profits, and clients, who must pay the bill. Most professionals have a direct financial interest in performing the greatest number of the most expensive services possible. On the other hand, the clients' interests are best served if the professional performs only those services that are clearly required and does so as inexpensively as possible. Although such conflicts of interest exist in many types of commercial encounters, they are most serious in the professions because clients are often unable to make an independent judgment about whether or not they actually need the services being recommended.

The greatest problem probably lies in the medical profession, because unnecessary medical procedures not only are costly but may pose a serious threat to the health and even the life of the patient. There is, moreover, ample evidence of large-scale "overdoctoring" of American patients. One study by Dr. Sidney Wolfe of the Health Research Group concluded that the antibiotics prescribed in American hospitals are unnecessary in a full 22 percent of all cases.[81] A study published in the *Journal of the American Medical Association* in 1998 estimated that adverse drug reactions cause more than 100,000 deaths among hospitalized patients every year.[82] But by all accounts, the most serious form of overdoctoring is unnecessary surgery. A Cornell University study found that in nearly one of every five cases in which a patient sought a second opinion, the second physician recommended against the proposed operation. Using such figures, a House subcommittee investigating the medical profession calculated that there were 2.4 million unnecessary surgical procedures a year, which cost the public billions of dollars and resulted in the loss of 11,900 lives. Another estimate put the number of unnecessary operations as high as 4 million a year, with a total cost of over $10 billion.[83] The same problem is reflected in the medical tests physicians order. A U.S. government study concluded that physicians who own an interest in a diagnostic lab order up to 45 percent more tests than those who do not. And to make matters worse, such conflicts are extremely widespread. The U.S. Department of Health and Human Services estimates that one of every four medical labs in the United States is owned by physicians who refer their own patients there.[84]

There is, moreover, a strong element of fraud in the behavior of the physicians who order unnecessary tests or perform unnecessary operations. Although they claim both explicitly and implicitly that their medical decisions are based exclusively on their best judgments about the welfare of patients, the evidence clearly shows that at least some practitioners actually give higher priority to financial considerations. But the desire for a higher income is not the only source of these professional conflicts. Vivienne Walters's study of company doctors in Ontario, Canada, found that they experienced strong pressure from their employers to place the interests of the company ahead of those of their patients—for example, by minimizing the seriousness of on-the-job injuries in their medical reports.[85]

The same kinds of conflicts of interest are found in the other professions as well, but fortunately, misconduct by lawyers and dentists is less likely to have the same life-threatening consequences. Whenever a professional is paid on a fee-for-service basis, the temptation to make extra profits by performing unnecessary procedures is always present. A clinical evaluation of 1,300 Medicaid dental patients in New York State found that 9 percent of the work involved outright fraud and that 25 percent of the amount billed to the state was for unnecessary work.[86] Such abuses are somewhat more difficult for lawyers, since clients are likely to have a clearer idea of the services they actually need. Nevertheless, "overlawyering" is a growing problem. Clients may, for instance, be talked into suits or other legal actions that will provide the lawyer with lucrative fees but stand little chance of success. Lawyers can also try to make it appear that a relatively simple legal procedure, such as an uncontested divorce, requires special legal knowledge, when in fact most people can do it themselves at a fraction of the cost.

Similar problems exist among practitioners of criminal law, although in different forms. Critics of our criminal justice system, such as Abraham Blumberg, have long charged that some defense lawyers run a "confidence game" on their clients. Blumberg has argued that even though a defense lawyer may pretend to be an independent professional who intends to do everything possible for the client, he or she is actually highly dependent on the goodwill of the prosecutor and the court. According to Blumberg, defense lawyers are often more concerned with an expeditious resolution of a case than with its outcome. Unlike civil lawyers, who generally want to perform the longest and most costly procedures possible, the criminal lawyer usually works with low-income clients and hopes "to limit its [the client's case] scope and duration rather than to do battle. Only in this way can cases be profitable."[87] This approach not only maximizes the number of clients the lawyer can handle, but also helps maintain the defense lawyer's relationship with the judge and district attorney, who also want a quick resolution to criminal cases. Defense lawyers often try to appear to be expending every possible effort on their clients' behalf, while actually seeking to convince them to plead guilty and bring their case to a quick conclusion.[88]

Professionals also run into emotional and sexual conflicts of interests with their clients, and even more than in the financial realm, such conflicts revolve around a number of ambiguous issues. Unwanted sexual advances by professionals toward clients or coworkers clearly fall under the heading of sexual harassment and will be examined in the section of this chapter on the violation of civil liberties. But what if the client welcomes or even initiates the relationship? Some writers in this area, such as Peter Rutter, claim that any physical relationship between a professional and a client, or even a former client, is unethical.[89] To this way of thinking, the client invests her or his trust in the professional, and any sexual contact the professional allows is a violation of that trust. But while such relationships may indeed be exploitative, that certainly is not true of them all. There is, for example, no particular reason to believe that a dentist's personal relationship with a patient is likely to be any more or less exploitative than his personal relationship with anyone else. In other cases, however, the clients are in an especially vulnerable position, and any personal relations with the professional unquestionably involve unethical conduct. The two most obvious instances would be when the client is too young to appreciate the full implications of her or his behavior (in many cases the professional in such a relationship would be committing the felony of statutory rape), and when the client is undergoing psychotherapy. Not only is the client in psychotherapy more likely to be in a vulnerable position, but it has long been recognized that a physical and emotional attraction toward the therapist is a normal part of the therapeutic process. When the therapist allows this attraction to develop into a physical relationship, not only is it likely to defeat the goals of therapy but may lead to a catastrophic sense of betrayal on the part of the client. Yet by all indications, therapist–patient relationships are extremely common. One survey of 1,057 psychiatrists found that 7.1 percent of the respondents admitted to having sex with at least one patient, and the actual incidence is undoubtedly far higher. To avoid the problem of asking the respondents to inform on themselves, a different survey asked therapists if they had patients who had had sex with a previous therapist. Seventy percent said they had.[90]

Like the more prestigious fields of law and medicine, accountants face a built-in conflict of interest. But unlike other professionals, accountants usually violate professional standards by being too concerned about the interests of their clients. Federal laws passed after the disastrous stock market crash of 1929 not only made it a crime for a company to file a false financial statement but also required that publicly owned corporations employ an outside auditor to examine those statements. Since a fraudulent statement can easily be used to inflate a firm's credit rating, enhance the value of its stock, or improve its image in the business community, it makes sense to have an outside expert do the review.[91] In actual practice, however, these supposedly independent auditors face a serious conflict of interest, because they are being paid by the same firms they are supposed to be investigating. An accounting firm that gains a reputation for excessive zeal in its audits might find potential clients looking elsewhere for the services it provides.

In the past, it was unusual for an accounting firm to be held responsible for failing to blow the whistle on a financially unsound client. But the crime wave in the financial industry in the 1980s has led to an increasing number of criminal fines and civil judgments against accounting firms. For example, Arthur Andersen & Co., one of the auditors of the notorious Lincoln Savings and Loan, agreed to pay a $30 million fine for helping Lincoln to cover up its bad loans. Ernst & Young, which picked up Lincoln Savings and many other clients after Arthur Andersen began dropping questionable thrifts as clients, ran into more serious problems. After an intensive investigation by federal authorities, Ernst & Young agreed to pay a record $400 million to settle the charges that its auditors had failed to report disastrous financial problems that caused some of the nation's biggest thrift failures.[92] Some law firms have been charged with similar offenses. In March 1992, Lincoln's legal firm, Kay, Scholer, Fierman, Hays & Handler, agreed to pay a $41 million fine (although it did not actually admit its guilt). The firm was accused of obstructing the federal investigation of Lincoln and aiding and abetting its regulatory violations.[93]

The next wave of financial crime was even harder on the accounting industry in general and Arthur Andersen in particular. The problem started when several enormous corporations unexpectedly collapsed into bankruptcy in the first part of the twenty-first century. Investigations showed that they had huge losses that had been hidden by fraudulent bookkeeping that went undetected by their auditors. As it turned out, many of those auditors had been making huge profits as "consultants" for the same firms they were examining. The hardest hit was taken by the firm of Arthur Andersen, which was Enron's auditor. Not only did Andersen make millions providing consulting services to Enron, but several of its executives ended up taking high-paying jobs with them. In June of 2002, Andersen was found guilty of obstructing justice because its employees destroyed more than a ton of Enron-related documents and deleted something like 30,000 emails in an effort to impede the Securities and Exchange Commission's investigation into its activities. Since the law forbids firms convicted of a felony from acting as outside auditors, Andersen's business quickly collapsed. What had for years been called the "big five" accounting firms, became the big four.[94]

Bribery and Corruption

In West Africa it is known as dash; in Latin America, *la mordida* ("the bite"); in Italy, *la bustarella* ("the little envelope"); in France, *le pot de vin* ("the jug of wine"); in the United States, *grease.* Under whatever name, bribery is a universal phenomenon with roots that stretch far back into human history. The Code of Hammurabi, created by the king who founded the first Babylonian empire almost 4,000 years ago, held that if a man was bribed to give false witness against another, he must bear the penalty imposed in the case. An edict by one Egyptian pharaoh proclaimed the death penalty for any official or priest who accepted a bribe for the performance of his judicial duties. References in Greek and Roman laws, as well as in the Christian Bible, show that bribery was condemned with harsh penalties in other ancient societies as well.[95]

Although the record of American history cannot match those others in terms of antiquity, it too is replete with references to the problem of corruption. In 1918, for example, an investigation by the Federal Trade Commission (FTC) found widespread bribery in American business. The FTC reported to Congress that "the commission has found that commercial bribery of employees is a prevalent and common practice in many industries. These bribes take the form of commissions for alleged services, of money and gratuities and entertainments of various sorts, and loans—all intended to influence such employees in the choice of materials."[96] These practices had become so accepted among some workers that one corrupt employee even approached a representative of the commission to ask for his assistance in collection of a "commission" that he said was due him.

Although many people would like to believe that bribery and corruption are confined to past times and poor Third World countries, most studies of the advanced industrialized nations have concluded that it is not only widespread but is accepted as normal business practice in many segments of the economy.[97] Transparency International publishes an annual ranking of the level of corruption in different nations around the world. As we can see from Table 2.1, the industrialized nations are less corrupt than the poor ones, but there are wide variations in the level of overall corruption, and corruption remains a virtually universal problem.

TABLE 2.1

Corruption, 2003
(Lower scores indicate more corruption)

Finland	9.7
Denmark	9.5
New Zealand	9.5
Singapore	9.4
Sweden	9.3
Netherlands	8.9
Norway	8.8
Switzerland	8.8
Australia	8.8
United Kingdom	8.7
Germany	7.7
USA	7.5
Japan	7.0
France	6.9
Italy	5.3
Mexico	3.6
Thailand	3.3
Vietnam	2.4
Indonesia	1.9

*Transparency International, Corruption Perceptions Index, 2003, http://www.transparencyinternational.org.

Although some bribe takers are isolated deviants secretly betraying the interests of their employer, it is clear that many offenders are part of a subculture of corruption that supports their behavior. These subcultures often develop within a single organization, but the structure of opportunity makes it far more likely for the members of some occupations—purchasing agents, police officers, and elected officials, for example—to participate in a subculture of corruption than others. Not only do the holders of such jobs have something of great value to offer, but they are virtually required to be in continual contact with the people who are most likely to be potential corrupters.

This section will examine three general types of bribery. The first is commercial bribery, which is intended to promote sales or obtain confidential business information (thus, both government and private employees may be the recipients of commercial bribery); the second is corruption among the police and other law enforcement personnel; the third is political bribery, which is aimed at influencing government policy.

Commercial Bribery

The bribery of judges and other government officials is an ancient crime, but the concept of commercial bribery is a much more recent development (see Chapter 3). Although it is clearly illegal, many people are willing to brush off commercial bribery as a normal business practice that does not really cause much harm. Supporters of this position argue that the total amount of money paid out in bribes is relatively small and has little effect on the average consumer. One analysis of 34 U.S. corporations that admitted paying overseas bribery concluded that whereas the bribes involved totaled $93.7 million, the total sales revenues of the companies amounted to $679 billion. Thus, the bribe money was only 0.014 percent of the sales of those companies.[98] The question of how much more bribery went undetected, however, remains unanswered. And even if the total amount of money involved in commercial bribery is small, the practice creates a climate of corruption and disrespect for the law and gives major corporations with vast financial resources an unfair advantage over their smaller competitors. A study by the American government found that bribery had been involved in 239 international contract competitions between 1994 and 1998 and that the bribes accounted for $108 billion.[99]

When firms attempt to buy sales for their products, their first targets are often the purchasing agents who are paid to make those decisions. The bribes are usually paid in cash because it is the most difficult to trace, but electronic fund transfers, stocks, bonds, and even such things as drugs and sex are also commonly involved. Although bribe takers are more likely to be fired than criminally prosecuted, they are often vulnerable to tax evasion as well as bribery.

While most recipients of corrupt payments simply try to cover up that income, corporate bribe givers face the difficult problem of how to account for the bribe money on their books. One common way is to make the payoffs through dummy firms set up to act as conduits for illegal transactions. Under this arrangement, the parent corporation can write off bribe money as a legitimate business expense and can claim it knew nothing about the payoffs. One such dummy firm was the Economic and Development Corporation (EDC), which the Northrop Corporation established in Switzerland ostensibly as a sales corporation. In reality, the EDC was a conduit for funds kept in Swiss bank accounts that were used to make various sorts of bribes and "questionable payments." The recipients included numerous political and governmental agents in the Netherlands, Iran, France, Germany, Saudi Arabia, Brazil, Malaysia, and Taiwan.[100]

But rather than go through the elaborate preparations necessary to set up a dummy corporation, which in themselves can be seen as proof that the company was intentionally giving bribe money, most businesses distribute payoff money through sales agents. Because many multinational corporations find it difficult and expensive to set up an office in every country in which they do business, they often employ local agents who know the people involved in making major purchases. Such sales agents also provide an excellent conduit for bribe money, since they know who is likely to accept bribes and what kind of inducements they prefer. More important, the use of local sales agents allows foreign multinationals to avoid direct involvement in the illicit payments and to deny that they have any knowledge of illegal activities. The sales agents do not volunteer information about their corrupt activities, and the multinationals do not ask.

Some of the most persistent questions about domestic corruption concern the Department of Defense's huge yearly purchases of equipment and supplies for the U.S. military. Although the Department of Defense has long been notorious for its inefficiency, it has become increasingly clear that much of the problem can be traced to bribery and corruption. In 1986 the U.S. attorney for a region in southern California with a heavy concentration of defense contractors testified that, "Kickbacks on defense subcontracts are a pervasive, long-standing practice which has corrupted the subcontracting process at most, if not all, defense contractors and . . . defense procurement programs."[101] Publicity about some of the more outrageous amounts the Department of Defense had paid for supplies, such as a $1,118.26 plastic cap for the leg of a stool, led to a coordinated attack on corruption in defense procurement involving the Department of Defense, the FBI, and the Internal Revenue Service that was known as "Operation DEFCON." Although it was criticized for focusing too heavily on small contractors, it did lead to legal action against dozens of individuals and corporations.[102] Aside from taking bribes and kickbacks, other charges concerned the submission of false claims for payment and the sale of substandard merchandise that often had false quality certifications. The list of such merchandise contains everything from aircraft ejection seats to clothing and tools. Several price-fixing conspiracies were also uncovered, involving such widely diverse areas as steel springs and pipeline dredging.[103] Bribery of the legions of government inspectors who supervise one industry or another is also a persistent problem, since there are such powerful incentives for the firms being regulated to win corrupt influence over their government watchdogs. In November of 1999, for example, federal officials arrested eight USDA produce inspectors as part of Operation Forbidden Fruit. USDA inspectors had apparently been accepting bribes from wholesale produce firms for two decades to give fruits and vegetables higher quality ratings than they deserved, thus allowing the producers to overcharge their customers.[104]

In some cases, the bribe givers reach out to locate and corrupt public and private officials whose services they desire. But it is also common for government officials to demand payoffs to do business. Thus, the bribery is actually more like extortion. A 2002 survey by Transparency International found that government officials most often demand bribes for contracts in public works and defense, followed by real estate, telecoms, and power generation.[105]

Corruption in Criminal Justice

Like government inspectors, law enforcement officials have a highly valued commodity to offer potential corrupters: immunity from the law. Numerous investigative committees have, for example, described deep-rooted corruption in urban police departments. Since the turn of the century, New York City's police force has been the subject of four major investigations: by the Lexow Committee in the 1890s, by the Seabury Committee a generation later, by the Knapp Commission in the early 1970s, and by the Mollen Commission in the 1990s.[106] There have been countless official investigations of other departments as well.[107] Virtually all the major investigations reached the same conclusion: police corruption was a widespread and serious problem. Indeed, the pattern of corruption appears to be so pervasive that one highly regarded criminologist commented that "Federal and state investigating committees revealed graft and corruption almost every time they have looked for them."[108] Most victimization surveys, such as the one done by the U.S. Department of Justice, do not ask about victimization by the police. However, the International Crime Victim Survey (ICVS) does ask its respondents both if they have had to pay a bribe and to whom it was paid, so it is possible to make an estimate about police corruption. The percentage of respondents who say they have paid a bribe to the police in the last year ranged widely from country to country. None of the respondents in many of the European nations reported any police bribery, 20 percent of the Argentineans did. The United States had the highest rate of police corruption of any industrialized nation, at 1.5 percent—an extremely high rate considering the fact that the vast majority of Americans have little or no contact with the police in any given year and that the survey did not include such practices as restaurants giving police officers free meals.[109]

The causes of this corruption are not difficult to find. For one thing, police officers simply have a lot of opportunities to receive bribes and payoffs. Not only can police officers offer valuable services merely by being a little less vigilant, but they also are in constant contact with people who desire those services and have no compunctions about breaking the law to purchase them. Moreover, police work is carried out in a unique social environment that may easily come to encourage corruption. Sensing the uneasiness so many of the rest of us feel in the presence of even an off-duty officer, those in police work tend to avoid social contacts with the general public and to retreat into the company of other officers. As one criminologist put it, the police "separate themselves from the public, develop strong in-group attitudes, and control one another's conduct, making it conform to the interests of the group."[110] This sense of occupational solidarity is further reinforced by the dangers inherent in police work and by the need to depend on one's fellow officers for help in difficult situations.[111] The occupational subculture that develops in such circumstances is an ideal vehicle for the transmission of a tradition of corruption. Even the most honest cops hesitate to report minor violations by their colleagues, and once such a custom becomes part of an occupational subculture, it can easily expand to include much more serious offenses.

Another factor underlying the problem of police corruption is the inadequacy of the laws the police are called on to enforce. Criminologists have long recognized that the prohibition of such things as prostitution, gambling, and drug use creates a highly profitable black market that is soon exploited by organized criminals. Although it is vastly stronger and more wealthy than individual criminals, organized crime is also more visible and thus requires some measure of official protection. Considering the billions of dollars in annual earnings that such businesses generate, it would be surprising indeed if the racketeers were unable to find anyone willing to sell them protection. Police corruption is further encouraged by the fact that the victimless crimes, such as gambling and prostitution, that are controlled by organized crime are not usually considered serious offenses by the public. The idea that no one is being harmed by these crimes provides individual officers with an easy rationalization that allows them to continue to see themselves as "good cops" and still receive the financial rewards of corruption. As one officer put it when discussing this attitude toward gambling payoffs: "Hell, everybody likes to place a bet once in a while. It's all part of the system. . . . Sure there are honest cops on the force, and more power to them. You take Captain _____ . Why, you can't buy him a cup of coffee. . . . But most of us are realistic."[112]

Perhaps the most highly publicized investigation of police corruption came as a result of charges made by two whistle-blowing New York City policemen, Frank Serpico and David Durk, in the 1970s. When the two officers first began talking about the abuses they had seen, their colleagues told them to shut up and mind their own business. Serpico and Durk then took their complaints to higher and higher levels in the police administration and city government. Time and again they were told that their charges were being fully investigated, but nothing was ever done. It was not until they began talking to the *New York Times* and the paper ran a series of articles on police corruption that the Knapp Commission was appointed to investigate the problem. It is doubtful the reforms that resulted from the commission's findings rooted out the long-standing tradition of corruption in the New York Police Department (NYPD), but the commission did provide criminologists with one of the clearest and most comprehensive pictures of contemporary police corruption ever assembled.

Although the Knapp Commission found pervasive corruption in the NYPD, minor offenses were much more widespread than serious ones. The acceptance of small gratuities, special discounts, and similar favors was almost universal, but most officers apparently drew the line at petty graft and did not become involved in the big-time payoffs. However, it is also true that opportunities for big-time corruption were not available to all officers. Among those who actively pursued corrupt income, the biggest sources of payoffs were the organized criminals who provided the public with various kinds of illegal goods and services. As a result, the officers who worked in such fields as gambling or drug enforcement raked in the largest profits.

The detectives assigned to gambling enforcement devised the most sophisticated system to divide the spoils. Plainclothesmen in every precinct in New York City were involved in the "pad," a system in which regular payments were collected from gambling interests and then divided up among the officers. The Knapp Commission noted that this system for collecting payoffs from gamblers "has persisted virtually unchanged for years despite periodic scandals, department reorganizations, massive transfers in and out of the units involved, and the folding of some gambling operations and the establishment of new ones."[113]

The commission found that the subculture of corruption was so firmly established in the NYPD that loyalty to one's fellow officers actually became an important motivation to accept petty graft. Officers who refused were looked on with suspicion by their colleagues, both because of the implied criticism of those who had taken bribes and because of the potential threat honest cops posed to the system of corruption. As the Knapp Commission put it: "Accepting payoff money is one way for an officer to prove that he is one of the boys and that can be trusted . . . these numerous but relatively small payoffs were a fact of life and those officers who made a point of refusing them were not accepted closely into the fellowship of policemen."[114] Moreover, generations of administrators adopted a posture of passive indifference toward this corruption, and eventually the occupational subculture of the department became so debased that it was the honest cops, not the crooked ones, who were the deviants.

The Pennsylvania Crime Commission Report painted a remarkably similar picture of police corruption in Philadelphia. The system of payoffs, for instance, was almost identical to that found in New York. In both departments, "bagmen" made periodic rounds of illegal gambling operations to collect payoff money and then distributed it to participating officers. Like officers of the NYPD, the Philadelphia police considered narcotics money to be the dirtiest type of graft. But once again, those attitudes did not deter individual police officers from "scoring" suspected drug dealers for large payoffs. The crime commission heard reports that in 65 to 70 percent of narcotics arrests, a portion of the drugs seized were not turned in. These purloined drugs were used by the officers as "plants" to frame suspected narcotics dealers, sold on the black market, or diverted to personal use. The report indicated that some female addicts were forced to have sex with officers in order to avoid arrest, and that similar sexual harassment was directed at prostitutes as well. The commission concluded that "police corruption in Philadelphia is ongoing, widespread, systematic and occurring at all levels of the Police Department. Corrupt practices were uncovered during the investigation in every police district and involved police officers ranging in rank from policeman to inspector."[115]

The revelations of widespread police corruption in both New York and Philadelphia touched off major scandals, public demands for reform, and a concerted effort to root out corruption. But however effective those campaigns were in the short run, the police departments in both cities (along with those in Miami, Boston, San Francisco, Los Angeles, and numerous other communities) were involved in new corruption scandals as the vigilance of the watchdogs faded away. In 1994, for example, the Mollen Commission found a "willful blindness" to corruption throughout the NYPD that permitted networks of highly organized rogue officers to deal drugs and prey on citizens in Latino and African-American neighborhoods.[116]

The latest police scandal to win nationwide media attention centered on the Ramparts Division of the Los Angeles Police Department. The scandal began unfolding in August of 1998 when a Los Angeles police officer, Rafael Perez, was arrested on cocaine charges. Threatened with a long jail sentence, Perez implicated dozens of officers for drug dealing, making false arrests, giving perjured testimony, and framing innocent people. Most of the officers named by Perez were part of the elite antigang unit of the Ramparts Divisions known as CRASH (Community Resources Against Street Hoodlums). Perez charged that the officers in that unit were acting very much like the street gangs they were supposed to combat—dealing drugs, shaking down members of other gangs, and even wearing a distinctive skull tattoo. Perhaps the most shocking part of Perez's testimony was his admission that he and his partner had shot an unarmed gang member numerous times, planted a gun on him, and then gave perjured testimony claiming that he had attacked the officers. Their victim was ultimately given a 23-year prison sentence. (Once the scandal came to light, the victim was released and pursued a lawsuit against the City of Los Angeles.) As a result of this scandal, more than 100 criminal convictions were overturned because of suspected police perjury, and the CRASH unit was disbanded in March of 2000. As in New York and Philadelphia, the LAPD's initial response had been to deny the charges and cover up its deep-rooted problems. In September of 2000, the responsibility for making reforms was taken away from the department and put in the hands of a federal judge.[117]

Although most of the scandals and investigations have focused on law enforcement's involvement in bribery and extortion, the problem of police perjury is an equally serious one. When officers give false testimony against an accused person, they may end up destroying an innocent person's life. But even more serious is the threat their abuse of power poses to the foundations of a free society. It is impossible to make a precise estimate of how common this practice is. It is, however, generally agreed that many officers who would never get involved in bribery or other forms of corruption do perjure themselves in order to defeat what they think of as "legal technicalities" or to put someone they believe is a criminal behind bars when the evidence is not strong enough to win a fair conviction. One survey of defense attorneys, prosecutors, and judges estimated that police perjury occurs in 20 to 50 percent of the hearings seeking to suppress evidence that may have been illegally obtained.[118] Christopher Slobogin concluded that, "Few knowledgeable persons are willing to say that police perjury about investigative matters is sporadic or rare, except perhaps the police, and . . . many of them believe it is common enough to merit a label all its own."[119]

Although it appears that there is a higher degree of corruption in police agencies than in other branches of the criminal justice system, no part of the system is immune. Until the 1980s, charges of corruption in the judiciary were extremely rare, leading some criminologists to wonder if there was not some truth in the old saying about being "honest as a judge." However, a subsequent wave of charges and criminal indictments makes it seem far more likely that it was the power and status of the office that accounts for the clear record the judicial profession had in the past. One of the first of this new wave of charges was directed against Judge Harry E. Claiborne of the federal district court. The government's case began in response to charges that Claiborne pressured a Nevada brothel owner, Joe Conforte, to pay him $130,000 in exchange for help in winning a reversal of his conviction for tax evasion. Investigation into the bribery allegation revealed Claiborne's failure to report more than $100,000 in taxable income to the IRS. Claiborne's first trial ended in a deadlocked jury, and the government subsequently dropped the charges involving Conforte. At a second trial, Claiborne was convicted by a federal jury of filing false income tax returns, and he was ultimately impeached by the U.S. Senate and removed from his post.[120]

A much more widespread network of judicial corruption was subsequently uncovered in Dade County, Florida. The case began when federal agents persuaded a prominent lawyer to pose as the representative of a Central American drug ring with cases pending in Dade County court. Federal and state agents then appeared in court as defendants in fictitious cases, while the lawyer offered bribes to judges in exchange for such things as lowering bail, releasing confidential information, and suppressing evidence. The agents apparently had little trouble finding jurists to accept their bribes, since the case resulted in the felony indictment of five Dade County judges.[121]

A 2003 study by the Center for Public Integrity also found high levels of misconduct among public prosecutors. In a review of 11,450 appellate cases, the study found more than 2,000 instances in which a conviction was reversed, charges dismissed, or a new trial ordered because of prosecutorial misconduct. Since 90 percent of criminal cases are settled through plea bargaining, which leaves few records that can be the basis of an appeal, the true incidence of misconduct is undoubtedly much higher. The study found that the typical forms of prosecutorial misconduct include making inflammatory comments before the jury, tampering with evidence, failing to disclose exculpatory evidence, and threatening a witness.[122]

Political Bribery and Corruption

Although the more subtle forms of influence peddling are far more common than outright bribery, that offense is most likely to lead to the criminal prosecution of elected officials. Almost 42 percent of the criminal indictments lodged against congressional officeholders since 1940 have involved some kind of bribery.[123] The services that influence peddlers attempt to buy run the gamut of political favors. If the charges brought against federal legislators can be taken as representative, the introduction of special bills and the right vote on a particular piece of legislation are the most sought-after services. More than 30 percent of the bribery charges brought against congressional officeholders involved such favors. Help in winning government contracts, the second-most-sought-after favor, was alleged in 27 percent of the charges. The use of congressional influence with the federal bureaucracy was involved in 15 percent of the charges.[124]

One of the most publicized bribery cases was an FBI sting operation known as ABSCAM. Agents working on this case posed as representatives of Kambir Abdul Rahman, a fictitious Arab sheikh in need of some Washington favors. Eight officials were persuaded to sponsor special bills or use their influence with the federal bureaucracy in exchange for cash payments and other rewards. One senator was given stock certificates in a bogus titanium mine in exchange for his help in winning government contracts. A representative was given $20,000 in cash for his services and was videotaped stuffing the money into his pockets and then asking the FBI agents if any of it showed. The officials involved in ABSCAM were convicted of a variety of crimes and given fines and prison terms. A New Jersey state senator received the most severe sentence—six years in jail and a $40,000 fine.[125]

Similar sting operations have also been carried out in many states, and they have revealed similar levels of corruption. In 1992, for example, another FBI sting operation was touched off when agents caught Kentucky lobbyist John Spurrier III offering a $50,000 bribe to a politician. Spurrier agreed to cooperate and play the role of set-up man for the FBI in exchange for leniency on the corruption charges. The FBI loaded up his hotel suite with electronic gear and gave Spurrier a wad of cash to bribe Kentucky state legislators. Ultimately, sixteen legislators, including the speaker of the Kentucky House, were convicted or pleaded guilty to various crimes.[126]

Some observers have claimed that the ease with which the FBI unearthed crooked officials reflects a pervasive corruption among our elected officials. But others hold that the defendants were lured into crimes that they would not otherwise have committed and that the government agents were actually creating crime, not preventing it. The problem with this line of argument is that the FBI is hardly the only organization seeking to lure government officials into crime.

One of the largest corruption scandals in the federal bureaucracy concerned the Department of Housing and Urban Development (HUD) during the Reagan administration. The administration repeatedly voiced strong ideological objections to the kinds of programs HUD carried on, and HUD was soon riddled with corruption and mismanagement that is estimated to have cost the government $4 billion to $8 billion. The crux of the problem was that lucrative department grants and contacts were given out to Republican party benefactors and well-connected political figures. By the early 1990s a series of HUD officials had been convicted for such offenses as defrauding the government, taking bribes, and lying to Congress. In one of the most famous cases, an agent who was hired to resell houses repossessed by the government became known as "Robin HUD" when she was caught embezzling more than $5 million, which she claimed she gave to charity.[127]

At the state and local level, eight governors have been indicted on criminal charges while in office since the 1930s, and several others have faced charges after they stepped down. Most state and local charges involve commercial bribery in the granting of contracts and other forms of government spending. Under the leadership of William "Boss" Tweed, for example, the famous Tammany Hall political machine in New York City is estimated to have defrauded the city of up to $200 million through overcharges, false vouchers, fictitious bills, and other maneuvers. Tweed was eventually convicted of more than 200 criminal charges and died in prison in 1878. More than a century later, numerous officials in New York were again being charged with corruption dealing with city funds and largesse to favored contractors.[128]

Manipulating the Marketplace

The insecurity of competition is an inherent part of any capitalist economy, but so are the efforts of businesses to manipulate the marketplace and escape from such competitive pressures. Although governments around the world have enacted a long list of legislative measures to safeguard the freedom of the marketplace, major corporations and some professional groups continue to seek market control even if it means breaking the law. Although the public is often unaware of the intricate webs of power that restrain free competition, the benefits reaped from these illegal practices are clearly made at its expense. When fair competition disappears, so does the motivation for innovation and improvement. Research and development dims in importance, production stagnates, the public loses confidence in the investment markets, and complacency replaces the competitive spirit. Worst, the public suffers because those who can control the market for their goods or services can charge exorbitant prices, and the consumer has no choice but to pay them or do without.

Unfair Business Practices

The line between "good business" and "dirty business" is a fine one, and the competitive spirit so central to the capitalist system promotes many kinds of shady practices and dirty dealing. So along with the antitrust legislation created to protect open competition in the marketplace, governments also prohibit a variety of unfair business practices. In fact, such unfair practices have often been a key weapon in the corporate giants' efforts to establish their domination of a critical market. One of the earliest and most effective techniques big companies used to destroy their smaller rivals is price discrimination—the sale of the same goods or services at different prices to different customers. Although this sounds like an innocent practice, it has led to the demise of many small firms. John D. Rockefeller's huge Standard Oil monopoly was built on a foundation of price discrimination. When Rockefeller was laying the first stones of his empire, he concluded that the way to dominate the oil industry was not by producing oil but by refining and distributing it. By winning secret rebates from the railroads, he gained a decided price advantage over competing distributors, who had to pay much higher transportation costs.[129] As the Standard Oil empire grew, Rockefeller used other price manipulations to subdue the competition. Whenever a small local competitor sprang up, Standard would slash its price below its own cost. The small firm would soon be facing bankruptcy, whereas Standard could simply make up its losses with its profits in other markets.

Because these abuses occurred decades ago and have long since been outlawed, they may seem to be only of historical interest. But the laws have not been effectively enforced, and the techniques pioneered by Rockefeller and his contemporaries are still in common use, even among the same multinational corporations that were spawned by the breakup of Rockefeller's Standard Oil empire. For example, after World War II a host of independent "private branders" revolutionized gasoline retailing by erecting large, multipump stations along main suburban highways, doing away with much of the service given in "service stations" and creating the first self-service pumps. As a result, they were able to undersell the majors by as much as five to six cents a gallon and challenge their dominance of gasoline retailing. The giants of the oil industry were slow to react to the challenge, but by the mid-1960s their domestic earnings had begun to decline, and it became clear that something had to be done.

Once again, the majors resorted to the time-tested techniques that Rockefeller had pioneered. Their first response was to give special discounts to their dealers in areas of high competition while continuing to sell gasoline at the regular price in other areas. When the private branders responded with price cuts of their own, the conflicts often escalated into a "price war" in which each station tried to match the price cuts of its competitors. But in the middle of 1972, the tactics of the majors abruptly changed, and the independents watched in amazement as their giant competitors stopped responding to their price cuts. The reason for this unexpected action soon became clear, as the independents found it harder and harder to buy gasoline in the following months. Starting in early 1972, the majors made significant reductions in their refinery operations and slashed the sales they had traditionally made to the "lesser majors," who, in turn, cut their sales to independents. Excluded from many of their sources of supply, the independents were forced to cut back on their operations, and their share of the retail market sharply declined.[130] Both phases of the majors' early attacks on the private branders appear to contain obvious illegalities, but the government took no action to enforce the antitrust laws in either case.[131]

The majors used the same techniques again in 1979 to justify a precipitous jump in the price of gasoline. Following the Iranian revolution, which disrupted the production of Iranian crude oil, U.S. refinery output dropped and a serious gasoline shortage developed. Long lines formed around open stations, and frustrated motorists frequently had to wait for hours to fill up. Most important for the oil companies, the shortages could be invoked to justify large increases in the retail price of gasoline. The majors blamed the shortages on cutbacks in Iranian production and panic buying by consumers—an explanation that seemed logical enough at the time. It was not until many months later, when the gasoline lines had been nearly forgotten, that reports suppressed by the Carter administration surfaced that showed that there had not actually been a gasoline shortage. According to the evidence, other sources had made up for the reductions in Iranian production, and crude oil imports to the United States had not dropped at all. But if the oil shortage was pure deception, the enormous increases in profits reported by the oil companies for 1979 were undeniably real. Some petroleum companies reported increases of more than 200 percent in their already substantial profits.[132]

Another set of charges about the same kind of abuses by the major oil companies came from a 1991 report by Citizen Action, a Washington-based consumer group. Pointing out that the eight biggest oil companies had increased their share of the retail petroleum market by 25 percent during the 1980s, Citizen Action charged that they were once again engaging in predatory pricing—sharply dropping prices in areas with heavy competition from independent companies, and then raising them to new heights after the competition was driven out of business.[133]

Although the economics of the stock and bond markets are vastly different from those of the petroleum industry, they too are famous for their unfair business practices. Some firms have attempted to monopolize the various bond offerings, as Salomon Brothers did for U.S. Treasury notes, but efforts to manipulate the stock market appear to be far more common. The number of Wall Street scandals involving the use of secret "inside" information to buy and sell stocks suggests that such use of information is extremely common despite the federal law expressly forbidding it. The goal of these regulations is to protect the integrity of the markets so that small investors will continue to participate. But there is an enormous temptation for corporate executives and traders who learn some secret information to use it to make a quick profit or avoid an impending loss.

The theft of trade secrets and confidential data has also become an increasing problem in an age ever more dependent on information and advanced technology. In 1996, Congress enacted a new Economic Espionage Act. The first corporate conviction came early in 2000. This case involved a former CEO of a Taiwanese adhesives company and his daughter, who were convicted of stealing trade secrets from the Avery Dennison Corporation. His company was given a $5 million fine, and he was sentenced to six months of home confinement and eighteen months of probation and was given a $5 million fine. His daughter got a year's probation and a $5,000 fine.[134]

The most important antitrust case of the last decade was probably the Justice Department's action against the Microsoft Corporation—a dominating figure in a cutting-edge industry. There was never any question that Microsoft held a near monopoly of computing operating systems software—its products are used on 85 to 90 percent of all personal computers. But the mere existence of a monopoly is not illegal, unless its holders use their position of power to take unfair advantage of their competitors, and that is exactly what the government charged in its antitrust case.

The original case centered about the accusation that Microsoft was trying to use its monopoly on operating systems to force users to adopt its Internet browser and not that of its rival, Netscape—first by threatening to refuse to sell its operating system to computer manufacturers that pushed the Netscape browser, and then by making its browser an integral part of the new versions of its operating system so that users would find it much more difficult to use Netscape's product. As the trial progressed, new allegations arose that Microsoft "had bullied friends and competitors alike, halting innovation that threatened its Windows monopoly."[135]

In June 2000, Judge Thomas Penfield Jackson found against Microsoft and ordered not only that the Microsoft Corporation follow a host of "conduct remedies" that would help prevent it from taking unfair advantage of its competitors, but that the whole corporation be broken into two separate firms. One would control the Windows operating system and the other would own the rest of Microsoft's software applications. Robert E. Litan, who served in the Justice Department's Antitrust Division in the Clinton administration, commented that "Judge Jackson found that Microsoft mounted a campaign of dirty tricks, and the dirty tricks are old tricks. John D. Rockefeller used them all: exclusive contracting, throwing your weight around, scaring off the competition."[136]

The next round in this high-stakes legal battle concluded on June 28, 2001, when a federal appellate court upheld Judge Jackson's finding that Microsoft was engaging in monopolistic practices but sent his order that the huge corporation be split up to another court for reconsideration. In September of 2001, the Department of Justice, by then under the control of the strongly pro-business administration of George W. Bush, announced that it no longer sought the breakup of Microsoft. The final result of the federal case was some relatively minor restrictions on Microsoft's business practices. The states that were involved in the case were somewhat more successful—winning more than $1 billion in settlements for customers Microsoft had overcharged.[137] After the American case was filed, Microsoft soon ran into similar trouble in the European Union. The European Court eventually ruled that Microsoft was illegally restricting competition by bundling its MediaPlayer with its Windows operating system in much the same way it had done with its Internet browser. The Court ordered Microsoft to share some technical information with its competitors and to produce a version of Windows without MediaPlayer. As of this writing, the judgment is still on appeal.[138]

One clear result of this case is that Microsoft and its corporate competitors have made huge increases in their campaign contributions and in their lobbying efforts. In the middle 1990s, before the start of the antitrust case, Microsoft and its employees were donating less than $50,000 a year to federal candidates, and Microsoft had only one lobbyist on its payroll. In the two-year election cycle after the case began, the corporation gave $4.66 million in campaign contributions and spent another $12 million on lobbyists.[139]

Mergers and Acquisitions

Despite the seemingly unequal battle they must wage against the major corporations, many smaller firms manage to survive and prosper. As a result, big corporations have often found it easier and more effective to buy out smaller competitors than to drive them under. Most of the big increases in the concentration of assets in the hands of the largest corporations has resulted from mergers and takeovers, not from the competitive advantages enjoyed by the big firms. In the two decades following the end of World War II, for example, the two hundred largest U.S. corporations increased their share of all manufacturing assets from 42.3 percent to 60.9 percent. Yet without the acquisition of smaller companies, their share of total manufacturing assets would have increased to only 43.2 percent—less than a 1 percent gain.[140] Moreover, there is little doubt that many, if not most, of those mergers could have been held to be illegal, for the Celler-Kefauver Act of 1950 expressly forbids mergers that "may lessen competition or tend to create a monopoly."

Illegal mergers are given different legal treatment from that accorded most of the other white-collar offenses examined up until now. Whereas such activities as price-fixing and bribery are criminal offenses, monopolistic mergers are handled entirely as administrative matters. This approach makes sense, because many mergers among smaller firms are harmless or even beneficial to the economy, and business executives who fail to judge the monopolistic impact of their merger plans correctly can hardly be held to be criminals. Moreover, criminal sanctions are not needed to stop monopolistic mergers. Because mergers are highly visible public events, it should be sufficient for enforcement agencies to examine each proposed merger and take action against those that may have significant anticompetitive effects.

Federal enforcement agencies have, however, failed to do much to enforce the restrictions on corporate mergers. From 1914 to 1969 there were more than 30,000 mergers in the United States, yet the Justice Department and the Federal Trade Commission together brought only about 300 antimerger cases to trial.[141] Part of the failure to block anticompetitive mergers can be attributed to flaws in Section 7 of the original Clayton Act (see Chapter 3). But even after those flaws were corrected by the Celler-Kefauver Act, anticompetitive mergers continued unabated. Ironically, three of the biggest waves of mergers in U.S. history came immediately after the passage of legislation designed to prevent such monopolistic combinations (the Sherman Act of 1890, the Clayton Act of 1914, and the Celler-Kefauver Act of 1950).[142] This fact alone says a great deal about the failure of the enforcement effort.

The dizzying increase in merger activity in recent years has practically overwhelmed the already outmatched federal authorities. In 1991 there were 1,539 mergers in the United States. In 1996 there were 3,087, and by 1998 that figure was near 5,000, with a total value exceeding $1.2 trillion. Yet after controlling for inflation the budget of the Antitrust Division of the Justice Department was actually lower than it was in 1977.[143] These days federal officials seldom do more than force potential merger candidates to divest themselves of one or two lines of business that used be in direct competition. Moreover, there has also been a growing trend toward international mergers and acquisitions that are often beyond the reach of any national laws. Between 1980 and 1999, such international mergers grew at an amazing 42 percent per year.[144]

Conspiracies

The success of the giant corporations in buying up or squeezing out their smaller competitors has left many of the largest markets in the United States in the control of oligopolies of three to five firms. Because antitrust laws make it difficult for a single firm to monopolize an entire industry and because the prospects of attacking a large and firmly entrenched competitor are not particularly attractive, most oligopolists are content to achieve market control by cooperating with their supposed competitors.

One essential task for any oligopoly is to erect the strongest possible barriers to prevent new competition from entering the market. The huge outlays of capital usually necessary to begin production of a new product, along with the intimidating political and economic power of the established firms, normally suffice to ward off new challengers. But most oligopolies also use other techniques to strengthen entry barriers—control of the supplies of essential raw materials, costly advertising campaigns to establish name-brand recognition, and governmental protection in the form of tariffs, import quotas, and favoritism by federal regulatory agencies.

Once their market has been secured, the oligopolistic firms can turn their attention to the creation of a system of mutual cooperation that will keep profits up and competition down. All the different devices used to achieve this goal are, strictly speaking, illegal, because the Sherman Act forbids "every contract, combination . . . or conspiracy in restraint of trade." Enforcement agencies, however, have tended to focus on only a few of the most obvious types of offenses, especially conspiracies to divide up markets or fix prices. And there is strong evidence that such illegal conspiracies are common in many different industries. In a survey conducted by the Ralph Nader organization, 58 percent of the presidents of the 1,000 largest U.S. industrial firms felt that such conspiracies were a "way of life" in U.S. industry.[145] Although only a few criminal antitrust cases are prosecuted each year, they have involved all types of enterprises, from the milk, bread, shrimp, and cranberry industries to those that produce sheet steel, plumbing fixtures, feed additives, and uranium. One early attempt to estimate the extent of price-fixing concluded that it was "quite prevalent" in U.S. industry,[146] and a subsequent study of corporate crime reached a virtually identical conclusion.[147]

The petroleum industry once again provides many excellent examples. Although most people think of the international oil cartel as a child of the OPEC sheikhs, the international oil companies began conspiring to fix prices at least as far back as 1928, decades before most of the Middle Eastern oil fields were even discovered. The problem that originally led to the creation of an international oil cartel was a worldwide surplus of oil, which was accompanied by one of the rare outbreaks of vigorous competition between the major oil companies. Alarmed by the rapid decline in prices, the heads of the world's three largest oil companies—now known as Exxon, Shell, and British Petroleum—met at Achnacarry Castle in the Scottish Highlands for what they claimed was some grouse shooting. The real business at hand, however, was the negotiations that laid the foundation for the international oil cartel that helped shape the economic destiny of the modern world. The goal of the Achnacarry agreement was to establish a framework for international cooperation among the major oil companies, based on the principle that each company accept and strive to maintain its existing share of the market "as is." But because a cartel that included only the three biggest companies was obviously inadequate, all the important participants in the international oil trade were soon brought into the deal.

One of the most striking things about these secret cartel agreements was the great sophistication and specificity with which the participants set down the operating procedures for their criminal conspiracy. Three successive agreements laid out both the functions of each of the local cartels that were to be established in consuming countries and the ways in which the "as is" principle was to be maintained. The preferred method of correcting changes in market shares was by transferring customers from the overtrader that exceeded its quotas to the undertrader that fell short. If such an adjustment were impossible, the undertrader was to receive the net profits the overtrader realized from selling more than its allotted share. Aside from dividing up the petroleum market, the conspirators also agreed on a price-fixing arrangement, also forbidden by U.S. law. They set oil prices at the price of American oil—at that time the most expensive in the world—plus the cost of shipment from the Gulf of Mexico to the point of sale. Thus, even oil purchased in the Middle East at half the U.S. price and shipped only a short distance was to be sold at the full American price plus the "phantom freight" charge from the Gulf of Mexico.[148]

There is some dispute about how long this carefully constructed cartel actually lasted. The oil companies claim it came to an end in September 1939 with the outbreak of World War II. But a special investigative committee reporting to the Swedish parliament found evidence of "continued cooperation among the three major companies" after the war.[149] There is other evidence that difficult issues were brought before a high-level, intercorporate committee of oil executives as late as 1971. George Henry Schuler, a representative of a minor oil company with concessions in Libya, reported that when his proposal for dealing with problems in that country proved too big for the "London Policy Group" to handle, he presented his arguments to a "meeting of the chiefs" held in Mobil's New York headquarters and presided over by the president of Exxon.[150] Such damning testimony, combined with clear evidence showing a continued pattern of parallel actions among the major oil companies, indicates that they are still working together to control the world market for oil. This does not necessarily mean, however, that the oil companies still hold regular high-level meetings to fix prices and conduct other illegal activities. As Ralph Nader put it when surveying the general problem of price fixing, "What begins as conspiracy frequently develops into conditioned response, with only occasional explicit coordination required."[151]

America's latest energy crisis involves electric power, not gasoline, but the effects are just the same: huge increases in the price consumers pay for energy. The story begins when the California legislature was persuaded by a heavy lobbying campaign from the privately held utilities to deregulate its power market. The big utilities were to sell off their generating capacity and buy power from the lowest bidder. According to Common Cause, the utilities and power marketers contributed $17 million to California politicians, and their deregulation bill, backed by their promises of sharply lower power prices, passed with hardly any dissent.[152]

Once the deregulated markets for energy got rolling, the results were just the opposite of what California's big utilities expected. Energy production plummeted and prices went through the ceiling, resulting in rolling blackouts and staggering increases in utility bills. The out-of-state corporations that bought up California's power generators claimed that the cutbacks in production were caused by accidents and repairs needed to keep the power plants going, and energy officials in the Bush Administration laid the blame on California's failure to build enough power plants. But it later became clear that it was actually an intentional effort to manipulate the marketplace and drive up prices. In May of 2002, a series of Enron memos was made pubic that showed that that notorious energy-trading company had played a major role in manipulating the California Market. One illegal scam it used was colorfully named the "death star." The idea was that on days of high demand Enron would give the California Independent System Operator—the agency charged with running the power grid under deregulation—exaggerated estimates of how much power Enron's customers would need. The Systems Operator, worried about meeting that demand, would then offer to pay a premium to energy providers that agreed to send extra power. Enron would then comply by agreeing to reduce its usage—reaping rich profits by cutting back on power it never intended to use in the first place. In another scam known as Ricochet, Enron would create a shortage by sending power out of the state, and then resell the same power back to California at inflated prices.[153] Although Enron's other highly publicized troubles made it an easy target for the media, several other less-well-known energy-trading companies were also involved, as was the El Paso Corporation, which operates the pipelines that supply much of California's natural gas. In September of 2002 a Federal judge found that El Paso had illegally idled 21 percent of its pipeline capacity, and California officials estimated that El Paso's manipulation of the natural gas market cost the state as much as $900 million.[154] Estimates of the total cost to consumers for all the manipulation that occurred run between $6 billion and $30 billion.[155]

Like the energy industry, the pharmaceutical corporations have shown an exceptionally high rate of criminal activity. Although many of their offenses involve the fraudulent marketing of unsafe products, antitrust violations are also common. For example, from January 1990 until February 1999 a far-flung group of multinational corporations conspired to fix the price of vitamins on the world market. Led by the Swiss pharmaceutical giant Hoffmann-LaRoche, vitamin manufacturers on three continents met together to jack up the prices for vitamins A, B_2, B_5, C, E, beta-carotene, and vitamin premixes (which are used as additives to other products). Like the oil companies, they agreed to allocate sales volumes and market shares among themselves, and to rig bidding for vitamin premixes.[156] Commenting on this case, Assistant Attorney General Joel I. Klein said, "This conspiracy has affected more than five billion dollars of commerce in products found in every American household. During the life of the conspiracy, virtually every American consumer paid artificially inflated prices for vitamins and vitamin enriched foods in order to feed the greed of these defendants and their co-conspirators, who reaped hundreds of millions of dollars in additional revenues."[157]

In 2000, it was revealed that Mylan Laboratories and three other firms were involved in an illegal scheme to make astronomical increases in the price of two drugs used to treat Alzheimer's disease and other afflictions. According to government allegations, Mylan developed a plan to cut off its competitors' supplies of the active ingredients necessary to produce the drugs by entering into long-term profit-sharing arrangements with industry suppliers and distributors. Once the competition had been driven out of the market, Mylan raised the price of one drug, Lorazepam, 2,679 percent and the other, Clorazepate, 3,218 percent.[158]

Collusion in the Professions

Large corporations are not the only organizations that violate the antitrust laws. Many medical and bar associations encourage the same monopolistic behavior. In the past, it was common practice for local bar associations to publish schedules of minimum fees and to punish attorneys who charged less. Because they hold the power to control licensure, such associations actually have a much greater ability to enforce their price schedules than do business associations. The American Bar Association used to hold that, "The habitual charging of fees less than those established in suggested or recommended minimum fee schedules, or the charging of such a fee without proper justification, may be evidence of unethical conduct."[159] Accordingly, a lawyer could be disciplined or even disbarred for failing to charge customers a high enough price. In defense of this practice, the American Bar Association claimed that its members were not covered by antitrust law, even though the courts had repeatedly held that fee schedules set by business associations were illegal and the Sherman Act contained no exemption for professional associations.

The case that finally forced the application of the antitrust laws to the legal profession was brought by Lewis and Ruth Goldfarb. When the Goldfarbs purchased a home in Fairfax County, Virginia, they began to shop around for title insurance. The first lawyer they approached told them he charged 1 percent of the total selling price of the house. Thinking that too high a price, the Goldfarbs sent letters to thirty-six other lawyers. All nineteen of the replies they received quoted the identical price of 1 percent of the selling value, which the Goldfarbs later discovered to be the minimum price listed in the local bar association's fee schedule. Lewis Goldfarb was himself an attorney, and he brought suit to stop Fairfax County lawyers from fixing their prices. The case ultimately wound up before the Supreme Court, which unanimously held the mandatory fee schedules to be illegal, noting that they represented "a classical illustration of price fixing."[160]

In addition to such fee schedules, both the legal and medical associations have employed numerous other techniques to exploit their professional monopolies. One good example was the American Medical Association's (AMA) effort to restrict the number of medical school graduates and keep the demand for medical services higher than the supply of physicians. Another was the legal profession's prohibition on advertising. Although advertising and the increased competition it brings might be expected to produce substantial benefits for those in need of legal services, lawyers saw it as a threat to their standard of living. Recognizing the monopolistic intent behind such restrictions, the Supreme Court struck down the prohibition on advertising in 1977.

Legal and medical associations have also fought against the advent of group practices that handle large volumes of clients at lower cost. For example, the first comprehensive group medical practice in the United States, organized by Dr. Michael Shadid in Elk City, Oklahoma, in 1929, ran into fierce opposition from the local medical association. After an unsuccessful attempt to expel Shadid on charges of unethical practice in 1931, the Beckham County Medical Association disbanded itself, waited six months, and then re-formed without Shadid. Futile efforts also were made to get the state legislature to revoke the licenses of the physicians working at Shadid's clinic, and the AMA refused to admit them to the organization. Twenty years of conflict finally reached a climax in 1950, when the clinic filed suit against the medical society, charging it with conspiracy to restrain trade. The society eventually settled out of court and admitted the clinic's doctors to its membership. There was, moreover, nothing unique in this case. The other early group practices, such as Ross-Loos and Kaiser Permanente, faced similar problems.[161]

The same determined opposition was encountered by the early group legal practices. One of the first such low-cost practices was the legal clinic of Jacoby & Meyers. The two lawyers opened up their "clinic" in an inexpensively furnished storefront office in a suburban shopping center, offered unusually long hours of service, and made extensive use of paralegal assistants to cut costs. Within six months of its September 1972 opening, the clinic was handling 1 percent of all the divorce work in Los Angeles, and the more traditional, higher-priced lawyers were getting worried. The response was to charge Jacoby & Meyers with violating the state bar's code of ethics. After several years of maneuvering, the Jacoby & Meyers license was suspended for 45 days and they were ordered to change the name of their clinic. However, in May 1977, more than four years after the charges had first been filed, the California Supreme Court exonerated Jacoby & Meyers of all charges.[162]

Violating Civil Liberties

As the legal systems around the world have matured, the protection of individual rights and liberties has taken on an ever-greater importance. Great documents like the Magna Carta in England, the U.S. Bill of Rights, and the United Nations' Universal Declaration of Human Rights have helped to steadily expand both the definition of basic civil liberties and the range of people who are legally entitled to enjoy them. Of course, the laws of some countries still allow their governments to carry out blatant political repression and give their corporations virtually unlimited freedom to spy on and harass their political opponents. But changing standards and a growing international consensus condemning such activities have served to transform violations of civil liberties into white-collar crime, and as such, they are among the most important topics considered in this book.

Discrimination and Sexual Harassment

Of all the violations of civil liberties, sexual harassment was one of the last to be legally recognized. In the past, the relatively low level of female participation in the workforce and the segregation of most female workers in "women's jobs" tended to defuse the concern about sexual harassment on the job. The general attitude seemed to be that women who violated social expectations and worked outside the home would just have to learn to live with the sexual aggression from male coworkers. But as a new wave of women poured into the workplace and the old barriers of gender segregation began to crumble, complaints about sexual harassment were more and more openly voiced. In California, for example, one out of every five complaints to the state's Department of Fair Employment and Housing now involves sexual harassment. A survey of 13,000 federal employees found that 42 percent of the females reported experiencing some kind of sexual harassment on the job, and other estimates hold that about half of all women experience some form of harassment at work.[163] Most of the victims of sexual harassment never report the offence. But the Federal Equal Employment Opportunity Commission still received more than 15,000 complaints for sexual harassment in 1999 and almost 24,000 complaints of sexual discrimination.[164]

What exactly is sexual harassment? Although definitions vary, sexual harassment may include everything from unwanted sexual comments and gestures to direct physical assault. The law generally recognizes two types of sexual harassment. The first, commonly called quid pro quo harassment, includes any unwanted sexual advances aimed at a particular individual. This kind of harassment involves an implicit or explicit threat, such as loss of a job, if the victim fails to cooperate; or a reward, such as a better grade, if the victim goes along. The other type of sexual harassment is known as environmental harassment and involves such things as unwelcome sexual comments, gestures, and explicit photographs that create an offensive or intimidating environment for female (or male) employees. This kind of harassment may be unintentional, or it may be part of an intentional effort by male employees to drive females out of jobs that they consider to be "men's work."

The most famous case of sexual harassment in the United States stems from the charges made by Anita Hill against her former boss, Judge Clarence Thomas, when he was nominated to the U.S. Supreme Court in 1991. The nationally televised Senate hearings in which both Hill and Thomas testified made for an unprecedented media event. Although Hill gave explicit descriptions of a wide range of highly offensive behaviors by Judge Thomas, he denied all the accusations and was eventually confirmed to the Supreme Court. To many American women, those hearings by an all-male Senate committee symbolized the problems they face on the job and the indifference of the male establishment to their plight. The problem of sexual harassment is, moreover, just as serious among private employers. The list of corporations forced to pay compensation for the sexual harassment of their employees in recent years includes such household names as the Ford Motor Company and the Dial Soap Company.[165]

The conflict of interest many professionals create when they become sexually involved with their clients has already been discussed, but sexual harassment and even outright sexual assault are also common. The problem appears to be especially severe in the medical profession. For example, one well-publicized case involved a gynecologist who used physical examinations to masturbate at least sixteen of his patients for an average of twenty to thirty minutes each. Most of the victims reported being humiliated by the incident but not knowing what to do about it.[166] Numerous allegations of similar activities have been made against other male gynecologists, whose profession obviously places them in a unique position to victimize their female clients. Numerous anesthesiologists have also been charged with similar offenses, including fondling and even having intercourse with unconscious patients.

Although the topic is far too vast to adequately explore in these pages, it is important to clearly locate occupational discrimination against women and minorities within the realm of white-collar crime. At the present time, few works on white-collar crime include this issue, but occupational discrimination meets all the criteria that apply to the more standard white-collar offenses. It is clearly a violation of the law that is committed by persons of respectability in the course of their employment. The Equal Pay Act of 1963, for example, requires that women and men doing the same work get the same pay, and title VII of the Civil Rights Act of 1964 prohibits employment discrimination based on race, religion, sex, or national origin. Perhaps the reasons for the failure to see such behavior as a type of white-collar crime are to be found in the disciplinary divisions within the social sciences. Discrimination and prejudice have traditionally been matters for the student of ethnic relations, and few criminologists see such concerns to be within their field of interest. Although it is probably true that in the past traditional criminology had little to contribute to our understanding of this problem, as the study of white-collar crime has developed an increasing intellectual vigor of its own, it seems that the time has now come to expand our field of view to include occupational discrimination. Certainly, few offenses cause greater psychological, social, and economic damage. In 2001, for example, the average African-American family earned only about 65 percent as much as the average white family, and for Latino families it was about 73 percent. That same year the average woman made 76 percent as much as the average man.[167] Much of that difference can be attributed to one form of occupational discrimination or another.

Violations of Privacy

When we think of some big bureaucracy snooping into our private lives, it is the government that first comes to mind. But the ever-growing size and power of today's corporations has led to increasing concern about their attempts to gather private information about individual citizens as well. For one thing, the concentration of economic control has transformed some long-standing business practices into new threats to civil liberties. For example, many nineteenth-century businesses refused to hire individuals because of their political beliefs. But in that era of independent farmers and small businesses, there were always other employers to be found. The present-day centralization of economic control has made the risks of offending one of the major corporations greater by the year. Perhaps more significant, it has also made the demand for conformity so often associated with life in the corporate world that much more powerful. Another major concern stems from the enormous technological strides that have been made in gathering, storing, and retrieving information. For example, computerized credit services now make it possible for a private business to quickly call up detailed personal information on virtually anyone they choose. Although there is certainly nothing sinister about making sure that someone has paid their bills on time before granting them additional credit, this information is also used in less legitimate ways in such things as political campaigns and hiring decisions.

Drug testing is another relatively new technology that is causing enormous concern among civil libertarians. Although few would question a company's right to fire employees whose drug use interfered with their work, dismissing them for something they do in their private time when their job performance is not affected appears to be a very different matter. Yet an increasing number of employees who are not having trouble on the job are being subjected to this kind of chemical surveillance. A study by the American Management Association found that well over 60 percent of the corporations surveyed had some kind of drug-testing program.[168] The corporations peer into their employees' private lives in other ways as well. It is estimated that 70 percent of companies do background checks on new employees, about 50 percent examine their police records, and around 20 percent administer some kind of psychological test.[169] One study found that 22 percent of the firms surveyed admitted carrying on searches of employees' computer files, voice mail, or other electronic records.[170] While the convenience and portability of the cellular phone has made it a worldwide success, cellular calls are also far easier for a nosy outsider to monitor. One expert estimated that 60 percent of cell-phone calls in California's Silicon Valley were being taped.[171]

Private firms have not, however, limited themselves to these new high-tech forms of information gathering. They have also been caught using private investigators and even funding full-time information-gathering networks. One of the most famous cases was an attempt by General Motors (GM) to smear Ralph Nader, whose book attacking the safety of GM's Corvair was gaining national attention. GM hired a private investigator, Vincent Gillen, to get something on Nader and in Gillen's own words, "shut him up." He looked into Nader's sex life and his political affiliations. Nader even received harassing phone calls until 4:00 A.M. the night before he was scheduled to testify before the Senate subcommittee on auto safety.[172]

No criminal charges were brought against GM, Gillen, or anyone else in the case, but GM did not emerge entirely unscathed. For one thing, the congressional reaction to the revelations about GM's behavior in the Nader affair was one of the primary reasons the auto safety laws GM was fighting were finally passed. GM also had to make substantial payments to the victims of Corvair crashes. Perhaps most bitter of all for the company, Nader won a $425,000 court settlement that he used to establish a "continuous legal monitoring of General Motors' activities in the safety, pollution and consumer relations area."[173]

The question of how common such direct personal assaults on corporate "enemies" actually are is difficult to answer, but numerous incidents involving other corporations have also come to light. The International Telephone and Telegraph Company (ITT) had an especially bad reputation in this regard. For instance, ITT was found to have conducted an organized campaign to repress news stories the company considered unfavorable to its efforts to acquire the American Broadcasting Company. The campaign even included investigations of the personal lives of reporters who were writing articles ITT disliked.[174] The popular opposition to the use of nuclear power has led many utility companies either to create their own network of spies and informers or to hire private detectives to do it for them. The list of firms that have admitted carrying on surveillance programs against their political opponents at their rate-payers' expense include such household names as Pacific Gas and Electric, Boston Edison, and the Philadelphia Electric Company. Other utilities have continued to deny their involvement in such activities despite testimony from disgruntled employees to the contrary. A former employee of Georgia Power charged that the firm spent at least $700,000 a year to maintain a surveillance program on "subversives," who were defined as anyone "who for any reason would be against the rate increases or would have some type of critical opposition to the operation of the power company."[175] Some utility companies have also provided dossiers on their political opponents to trade associations, which in turn distributed them to other companies, thus expanding the network of private spies.[176]

Even though uncovering information about corporate violations of civil liberties is no easy matter, the problem is vastly more difficult where the government is concerned. The government agencies involved in domestic spying wrap themselves in a cloak of secrecy and often claim that national security is being threatened whenever attempts are made to strip away their cover. The historical record indicates that until the 1930s, domestic intelligence operations were put together on an ad hoc basis in response to specific problems.[177] The political developments that culminated in the inferno of World War II also spurred an unprecedented expansion in the effort to gather intelligence information. But unlike past conflicts, the intelligence apparatus was not dismantled after the war but was redirected against citizens who for one reason or another were deemed subversives. The "Red Scare" so skillfully manipulated by Senator Joseph McCarthy, the civil rights movement, the war in Vietnam, the decades of cold war against the Soviet Union and its allies, and finally the threat of international terrorism provided ample justification to maintain and expand wartime surveillance and political intervention, even though this involved many activities that were clearly illegal in peacetime. Reports from the FBI, CIA, IRS, Army Intelligence, and other agencies involved in domestic "operations" show a surprising indifference to their duty to obey the law. Illegal activities were considered a problem only if there was a danger they might be detected and cause political problems for the malefactors or their bosses.[178] The objects of illegal government surveillance and harassment have included the Ku Klux Klan and the American Nazi Party on the Right, Democratic and Republican opponents of presidential incumbents in the center, and various communist and socialist groups on the Left.[179]

Wiretapping is one of the most common techniques used to gather information on U.S. citizens. It was originally declared illegal in 1934, but the FBI simply ignored the law and continued listening in on private phone conversations on the flimsy theory that the prohibition on "any person" wiretapping was not meant to apply to FBI agents. In 1937, the Supreme Court rejected this argument and held the law to be applicable to federal agents. In response to this decision and another one in 1939, Attorney General Robert Jackson issued an order prohibiting all FBI wiretaps; but it stood in force for only two months, until President Franklin Roosevelt unilaterally decided the FBI still had the power to wiretap in cases of "national security." Illegal wiretapping remained a common practice until the law was changed in 1968 to allow wiretapping during criminal investigations if a prior court order was obtained. A second law, passed in 1978, allows court-ordered domestic wiretaps to gather foreign intelligence information, and the laws have undergone further liberalization since then. Although government agents still conduct illegal wiretaps (i.e., without a court order), the changes in the laws have legalized many activities that used to be against the law. The privacy of email messages has not, unfortunately, been given the same protection as phone conversations. In 2000, the FBI announced it had a new software program called "carnivore" that would allow government agencies to almost instantly scan millions of email and Web communications for the exact information about any individual or activity they were looking for.

Most techniques of electronic surveillance, such as those involving hidden microphones, are not specifically mentioned in statutory law, but an illegal entry is usually necessary to plant such devices.[180] One good example of such activities comes from a freedom-of-information suit filed by the Socialist Workers Party (SWP). This suit uncovered documents showing that the FBI regularly burglarized the SWP's national offices as part of the notorious COINTELPRO (shorthand for "counterintelligence program"). According to those documents, the FBI burglarized the Socialist Workers' offices at least ninety-four times between 1960 and 1966 in order to photograph, and in some cases steal, documents outlining the organization's membership, contributions, and political strategy. These break-ins occurred on an average of once every three weeks for six and one-half years. The documents also revealed that the FBI paid 316 different informers more than $1.5 million to spy on the SWP's youth affiliate, the Young Socialist Alliance. At least forty-two informers held office in one of the two organizations, and two informers ran for public office as members of the Young Socialist Alliance.[181]

Although many dismiss such activities as an aberration brought on by the social upheavals surrounding the civil rights movement and the war in Vietnam, there is strong evidence that they continued long after the flames of revolutionary fervor were replaced by the apathy of the 1980s. In 1987, a former FBI informant named Frank Varelli testified before the House Judiciary Subcommittee on Civil and Constitutional Rights that he was paid by the FBI to infiltrate the Committee in Solidarity with the People of El Salvador (CISPES). He said that his FBI handler had told him they had broken into the Dallas offices of CISPES. The subcommittee also heard evidence that fifty-eight unexplained burglaries had occurred in the offices of groups opposed to the Reagan administration's Central American policy, and that in most cases nothing more than membership lists were taken.[182]

The FBI has been more heavily involved in domestic surveillance than other government agencies, but it was by no means alone. The Internal Revenue Service compiled political files on 8,000 individuals and 300 groups during the 1960s and 1970s. The National Security Agency scanned millions of private telegrams sent to foreign countries by U.S. citizens. Even the CIA was involved in domestic intelligence, despite specific legislation forbidding it from engaging in such activities.[183] Numerous local police departments also got into the act with political surveillance operations of their own. The Madison, Wisconsin, police force, for instance, infiltrated agents into the Black Panthers, a welfare mothers' organization, and other leftist groups at the University of Wisconsin. Perhaps the most notorious local intelligence operations of the Vietnam era were conducted by the so-called Red Squad of the Chicago Police Department, which carried on a literal shooting war with black militants. More recently, the Los Angeles Police Department (LAPD) was found to be compiling lists of leftists, antinuclear activists, and critics of police activities. In one case the Los Angeles City Council was shocked to discover that the LAPD had sent a photographic team into the press gallery to take pictures of those who testified against nuclear power at a council meeting. As a result of such revelations, together with civil actions taken by the victims of the investigations, the LAPD agreed to destroy the "subversives" files its Public Order Intelligence Division had accumulated. However, the files apparently were not destroyed but were taken to the home of a police sergeant who leaked their contents to a right-wing political organization known as the Western Goals Foundation, which is alleged to have distributed the files through its computer network.[184] Information that came to light in 2002 shows that the Denver Police maintained secret files on more than 200 nonviolent political organizations, including the American Friends Service Committee, a Quaker organization. A lawsuit filed in March of that year accused the Denver police of breaking in to the offices of the Denver Justice and Peace Committee, an organization that works for social justice in Latin America, and seizing membership, phone, and emails lists that were later used for political purposes.[185]

Political Harassment and Repression

The American government's campaign against political dissidents went far beyond mere surveillance to encompass a program of direct political harassment and intimidation. The roots of the most recent government attacks on the Left go back to the early 1940s, when the FBI began systematically leaking defamatory reports about various leftist leaders and their organizations and preparing antileftist speeches, articles, and books at government expense. In 1956, FBI director J. Edgar Hoover began COINTELPRO, which was to be involved in a host of criminal activities over the next two decades. The original target was the U.S. Communist Party, but the program was soon expanded to include virtually all political groups on the Left and even a few groups on the extreme Right.

One prominent FBI target was Dr. Martin Luther King Jr., the civil rights leader who not only championed nonviolence but also won the Nobel Peace Prize. Once King rose to prominence in the civil rights movement, he was kept under constant surveillance and his phone was illegally tapped by FBI agents with the explicit approval of Attorney General Robert Kennedy. The FBI attempted to stop Marquette University from awarding King an honorary degree and tried to prevent Cardinal Spellman, the archbishop of New York, from appearing at a joint speaking engagement with him. When the FBI uncovered evidence about an alleged extramarital affair, it attempted to plant incriminating stories with two journalists. When that ploy failed, the Bureau sent a tape recording, presumably containing incriminating evidence, and an anonymous letter to King and his wife, Coretta, in an apparent attempt to drive him to suicide.[186] The FBI sent hundreds of letters containing similar personal attacks on other political activists. The Bureau sent a letter to the wife of Elijah Muhammad, the leader of the Black Muslims, which accused Muhammad of having an affair with his secretary. It sent a letter to a Black Panther party youth group leader accusing Fred Hampton and another top Panther leader of having "sex orgies" in party headquarters.

The FBI often enlisted other organizations and agencies in its campaigns against the Left. For example, the Bureau persuaded the phone company to cut off the long-distance phone service of the New Mobe (New Mobilization to End the War in Vietnam) before the Democratic National Convention in 1968 and urged other peace groups' creditors to press for delinquent payments. On several occasions the FBI attempted to get the military to draft political activists on the Left, and it even passed word to the Mafia about activist-comedian Dick Gregory's public attacks on their criminal activities, apparently in hopes of inciting a violent reprisal.[187] On several occasions FBI agents incited right-wing groups to attack leftists working for various political causes the Bureau opposed. For example, according to evidence submitted to the Senate Select Committee on Intelligence, the FBI succeeded in resurrecting a previously disbanded right-wing paramilitary organization known as the Minutemen. The Bureau provided the Secret Army Organization (SAO; the group's new name) with firearms, explosives, and other equipment and supplied at least 75 percent of the SAO's operating expenses. An SAO cell directed by an FBI informant engaged in repeated acts of violence and terrorism against the Left, including the destruction of newspaper offices and bookstores, the firebombing of cars, and assaults on political activists, including a shooting that seriously wounded a young woman.[188]

The FBI also used provocateurs to encourage violence by leftist groups. Here, however, the goal was to incite the members of the group to commit a crime, so that they could be arrested. In his study of agents provocateurs in the American Left, Andrew Karmen found a recurring pattern in the actions of the FBI and other police agencies.[189] First, the FBI or the local police agency selects a group, territory, or situation for infiltration. Next, the agency finds an agent whose background is compatible with that of the intended victims. He or she is then sent in to join the appropriate group and begins doing minor jobs to help win acceptance. After this goal is achieved, the agent seeks out militant individuals and begins urging them to commit violence. Often the agent provides guns, bombs, and other materials and even personally participates in the crimes themselves. Finally, the police close in at the most compromising moment. The agent then withdraws, only to return for the trial with a carefully conceived story admitting complicity with the criminal events but denying entrapment. After examining more than 4,000 reports obtained from a freedom-of-information suit, a *Chicago Sun-Times* reporter summarized the FBI's goals in the 1960s and early 1970s as follows: "The Bureau set out to exterminate the so-called New Left and militant or high-profile black civil rights groups, and even sought to provoke injury or death among their leaders."[190]

American agents have frequently been involved in political harassment and repression in other nations as well. Because these activities occur outside the United States, they do not automatically violate American law, but U.S. agents have repeatedly broken international law as well as the laws of the countries in which they carry on their activities. Moreover, the CIA and other government agencies involved in covert operations have shown almost as low a regard for American laws as those of the other countries in which they operate. The CIA has, for example, repeatedly ignored the explicit constitutional provisions granting Congress the exclusive power to declare war. Acting entirely on presidential directives and without congressional authorization, the CIA has waged a number of secret wars around the globe. In the early 1950s, for example, CIA-sponsored guerrilla led raids against China and launched an invasion of Guatemala. In the late 1950s, CIA aircraft carried out bombing missions in support of a revolt against President Sukarno of Indonesia, and the agency was involved in the coup that finally succeeded in ousting Sukarno in 1965.[191] The 1960s also saw the ill-fated attempt by a group of CIA-backed guerrillas to invade Cuba at the Bay of Pigs. But by far the largest of the CIA's secret wars was carried on in Southeast Asia, where its involvement started as far back as 1954 and reached its peak in the late 1960s and early 1970s. Among other activities in the region, the CIA recruited at least two separate armies—one that fought along the South Vietnamese borders with Cambodia, Laos, and North Vietnam, and a second, larger one that operated inside Laos. When casualties and desertions crippled the original force of Laotian tribesmen, the CIA hired 17,000 Thai mercenaries, despite an act of Congress specifically forbidding the use of mercenary troops. By 1971 almost 50,000 Americans were involved in the secret war, yet this huge operation was successfully hidden from the public and even from most members of Congress.[192] The agency had much less success, however, in concealing its military intervention in Nicaragua. The fact that the CIA organized, funded, and directed the antigovernment rebels in that country became public knowledge almost as soon as it started.

The CIA was also involved in plots to murder many foreign politicians. Direct assassination attempts were launched by the agency against Patrice Lumumba, the leftist leader of the Congo, and against Washington's perennial Cuban antagonist, Fidel Castro. The CIA also encouraged plots that resulted in the deaths of Rafael Trujillo in the Dominican Republic; Ngo Dinh Diem and his brother, Nhu, in South Vietnam: and General Rene Schneider of Chile. The most bizarre of these schemes was surely the campaign against Castro. Aside from the eight different assassination attempts uncovered by the Senate Select Committee on Intelligence, the CIA concocted numerous other schemes to discredit Castro, including a plan to dose him with a strong psychedelic drug before a major speech and a ludicrous scheme to dust his shoes with thalium salts, a strong depilatory the CIA hoped would make his beard fall out and thus ruin his revolutionary image. The assassination plots involved equally bizarre techniques, including poisoned cigars, an exploding seashell, and a wet suit dusted with deadly bacteria. The agency even turned to the underworld, persuading important syndicate figures to organize an assassination attempt.[193]

American agents supported and even instigated numerous coups and revolutions against both dictators and democratically elected governments. Of these, the campaign against the Chilean leftist Salvador Allende is certainly the best documented. Although Chile had a long democratic tradition dating back to its independence in 1818, the U.S. government repeatedly intervened in domestic Chilean affairs. When Allende ran for president in 1958 and again in 1964, the CIA launched secret campaigns to ensure his defeat. But the real trouble began in the late 1960s, when it began to look as if Allende might actually win the next election. As the political winds began shifting in Allende's direction, "leaders of American multinational corporations with substantial interests in Chile . . . contacted U.S. government officials in order to make their views known."[194] The U.S. government soon employed what was termed a "two-track" effort to prevent Allende's election and later to force him from office. Track 1 involved a wide variety of covert techniques aimed at manipulating the Chilean political system. To this end, the CIA paid out millions of dollars to the Chilean media to spread anti-Allende propaganda and encourage civil disorder. Once Allende became president, the U.S. government tried to, in the words of President Nixon, "make the economy scream."[195] This governmental–corporate assault on the Chilean economy included (1) a sharp reduction in American economic aid (however, military aid was continued at its previous level); (2) the virtual termination of short-term credits to Chile from U.S. banks; (3) reductions in funds from the World Bank and other international development agencies; (4) the withholding of supplies necessary for Chile's industry; and (5) pressure on other Western countries and corporations not to trade with Chile. Track 2 employed a more direct approach, for its aim was to foment a military coup and end Chilean democracy. According to the Senate Select Committee on Intelligence, the CIA maintained close contacts with key Chilean military and police officials, and "those Chileans who were inclined to stage a coup were given assurance of strong support at the highest levels of the U.S. government, both before and after a coup."[196] The CIA also encouraged several Chilean plots to assassinate General Rene Schneider, who was strongly committed to the Chilean constitution and refused to cooperate in any attempted coup. After three unsuccessful attempts, General Schneider was finally killed in October 1970. The coup that killed Allende and ended Chilean democracy did not come until three years later, when the Chilean economy was reeling from American economic pressure and from strikes and paramilitary terror supported by CIA money.[197]

There was, however, nothing particularly unusual about the U.S. involvement in Chile. The story of the American role in Nicaragua is much the same. For most of the twentieth century, Nicaragua was ruled by the American-supported dictatorship of Anastasio Somoza and his two sons. In fact, Somoza was originally put into power in 1932 by the U.S. Marines, who occupied Nicaragua after an earlier leftist uprising. However, the Somoza regime's international reputation for brutality and repression lost the support of the Carter administration, and it was overthrown by the leftist Sandinista Front for National Liberation in 1979. The response of the Reagan administration, which came to power the next year, was much the same as Nixon's had been in Chile. Promised economic aid was cut back and then eliminated, economic and military support was provided to anti-Sandinista elements within Nicaragua, a network of bases was established in surrounding countries, and American agents trained and financed an army of Nicaraguan exiles (the Contras), who then invaded the country. Once again, acting under presidential orders alone, American agents violated both domestic and international law. The American government had Nicaraguan harbors mined and ignored the World Court decision that such actions were illegal. The CIA distributed a booklet to the Contras recommending the assassination of public officials who supported the Sandinistas, despite an Executive Order forbidding any American involvement in such activities.

When Congress discovered these activities, a specific prohibition was written into the law that "no funds available to the Central Intelligence Agency, the Department of Defense, or any other agency or entity of the United States involved in intelligence activities may be . . . expended for the purpose . . . of supporting, directly or indirectly, military or paramilitary operation in Nicaragua."[198] The

Reagan administration's response was to set up an elaborate illegal scheme to fund the Contras that eventually came to be known in the media as the Iran–Contra Affair. Foremost among the administration's illegal activities were the use of personnel on the military payroll to raise private money for the Contras, the diversion of profits from the secret sale of U.S. military equipment to the fiercely anti-American regime in Iran for that same purpose, and perjury among top administration officials trying to cover up their crimes and deceptions.[199]

The latest threat to civil liberties comes from the September 11th terrorist attacks, and the "war on terrorism" the federal government launched in response. Although a state of war was never officially declared, the government assumed a variety of wartime powers to restrict privacy and detain suspected terrorists. The most extreme abuses have occurred overseas beyond the reach of American courts. More than 600 people, most of whom were captured during the war in Afghanistan, were brought to the American military base in Guantanamo Bay, Cuba, because no American court has jurisdiction there. They were held without charges, without trial, and without access to legal representation for months on end.[200] Despite strict secrecy it is also becoming clear that the American government used psychological torture, including prolonged sleep deprivation, threats, and nonstop interrogations to extract information from suspected terrorists. But the "war on terrorism" did not stop with psychological torture. In 2004, a series of grisly photographs of the torture and sexual humiliation of prisoners held by the American military in Iraq were leaked to the press and a nationwide scandal erupted. The torture used to obtain intelligence information and simply for the sadistic pleasure of the guards apparently led to the deaths of numerous prisoners.

Violent White-Collar Crimes

No matter how skeptical they may be about the motives of big business or government officials, few people envision white-collar executives as violent criminals. Hardworking, competitive, and successful, these men and women typify the aspirations and ideals of the middle class and seem worlds apart from the violence and disorder of the big-city streets. But the differences between the criminals of the upper world and those of the underworld are as much matters of form as of substance. The young robber who accidentally kills a store clerk displays the same disregard for human life as the engineer who falsifies test results to conceal a deadly flaw in an automobile's braking system. The engineers' distance from their victims allows them the luxury of pretending that no one will really be hurt by their crimes, but the damage is just as real.

Political Violence

From the thugs hired to intimidate a political dissident to a massive international war, political violence is a huge problem. In 1980 Melvin Small and David Singer concluded that there had been an average of 7.9 international and 6.4 revolutionary wars every decade for the previous 165 years,[201] and these conflicts have reaped a staggering toll in human lives—more than 150 million people.[202] The battles of World War II alone are believed to have cost about 15 million lives, and when civilian casualties are added in, the total comes to almost 48 million deaths.[203] Although many think that the world has been relatively peaceful in recent times, there have actually been another 40 million war-related deaths since the end of World War II.[204] Although the number of annual war causalities did drop somewhat after the end of the cold war, the number of wars has been increasing again in recent years. The twenty-first century started off with the 9/11 terrorist attacks and the American-led invasions of Afghanistan and Iraq, as well as the continuation of numerous regional conflicts.

The dead are not, of course, the only victims. Every war leaves a human legacy of the maimed and crippled, widows and widowers, grieving parents, and orphans. There is, moreover, no accurate toll of the number of people tortured or killed because of their political views, but the number is undoubtedly vast. This kind of political violence is far less common in the wealthy industrial democracies than in the poor nations of the Third World. As we saw in the last section, however, even the established democracies use violence against their political opponents, especially when they are in less-developed nations.

There is no question that year by year such political violence reaps a staggering toll in deaths and injuries, but is it white-collar crime? In many cases, the answer is certainly yes. After all, those who commit such acts of political violence—or at least those who give the orders—are almost always persons of high status acting as part of a political career, and often they are clearly violating the laws of one or more nations. The CIA's attempts to assassinate Fidel Castro, for example, were white-collar crimes because they violated not only the laws of Cuba but also those of the United States.

But what if the laws of a particular nation permit it to commit various kinds of violence against its citizens or those of other nations? The answer to such questions can only come from international law. There is, for example, a well-established precedent derived from the Nuremberg trials after World War II that genocide—the attempt to exterminate an entire political, racial, or ethnic group— is an international crime. Although the Nazis' systematic extermination of the Jews is certainly the most famous case of twentieth-century genocide, there have been numerous others: Turkey attempted to wipe out its Armenian residents in 1915; Stalin and Mao Tse-tung liquidated millions of people suspected of membership in opposition groups; the Khmer Rouge government headed by Pol Pot killed as many as 2 million Cambodian civilians, and the Tutsis killed up to 200,000 Hutus in Burundi in 1972. The Hutus took an even greater toll of Tutsis in Rwanda in 1994.[205] More recently, there was the attempt by the Serbs of the former Yugoslavia at "ethnic cleansing"—a euphemism they coined to describe their efforts to kill or drive out all the ethnic Albanians and Croatians from the lands they claimed. Such attempts at genocide are now clearly recognized as an international crime, and offenders are increasingly likely to be tried and punished by international courts, as happened to several Serbian war criminals.

The issue is less clear, however, when it involves military conflicts between two military forces. Many people around the world, for example, condemned the American intervention in Afghanistan and Iraq as a criminal act, but others saw it as justifiable self-defense. The resolution of such issues will have to wait until the World Court or some other international tribunal establishes a clearer set of legal precedents. Similarly, any attempt to move beyond the haphazard retribution wreaked by the victor on the vanquished and to establish more-even-handed punishment for international aggression will have to await the willingness of the world community to grant the agencies of international law stronger enforcement powers. The recent trials of top leaders of the Serbian genocide campaign by an international tribunal show that real progress is being made, but such a forceful response remains very much the exception, not the rule.

Unsafe Production: Dangerous Working Conditions and Environmental Crimes

The explosive economic growth that has made the affluence of the industrialized nations possible has been purchased at an enormous environmental cost. Consider, for example, the problem of toxic chemicals. The National Academy of Sciences estimates that there are almost 710,000 chemicals currently in commercial use. Yet only 20 percent have been thoroughly tested to see if they are hazardous to our health.[206] The United States alone has between 700,000 and 1 million facilities that produce hazardous waste, which are estimated to pump out approximately 1.1 trillion pounds of toxic substances every year. Even the substances that have been proven to be the most highly toxic are often disposed of improperly. It is estimated that 22 percent of hazardous wastes generated in the United States are illegally dumped into streams and sewers. And even the wastes that are disposed of in other ways are often improperly handled. It is estimated that there are approximately 295,000 locations in the United States where hazardous wastes are stored in leaky underground storage tanks that may be polluting underground water resources.[207]

One well-known disaster occurred in Hopewell, Virginia, where the Life Science Products Company set up a chemical manufacturing plant in a converted garage. After only a few weeks in the plant, many workers began to suffer dizzy spells, blurred vision, and tremors. One worker reported that his hands were shaking so badly that he had to have a friend hold his glass when he stopped off for a beer after work. Most of the local physicians blamed these problems on nerves and overwork, but one young cardiologist, Yi-Nan Chou, decided to send samples of a patient's blood and urine to the Centers for Disease Control in Atlanta. Researchers there found the specimens to have a high concentration of Kepone, the toxic insecticide manufactured in the converted garage. Subsequent investigations disclosed that Life Science Products was set up by two former employees of the Allied Chemical Corporation to supply it with the dangerous chemical it used to manufacture under its own auspices. Yet neither the workers nor the community were told anything about the dangers of Kepone.[208]

Although Allied denied responsibility for the damages, Life Science Products was shut down, a federal court fined Allied $5 million, and Allied agreed to donate $8 million to a Virginia environmental fund after Kepone all but destroyed the fishing industry on the James River. In addition, Allied paid approximately $15 million more as a result of civil actions involving the Kepone case. Many of the chemical workers employed at the plant suffered far greater losses, including sterility and other serious disabilities,[209] and the ban on commercial fishing in the James lasted more than a decade.[210] Perhaps most disturbing of all is that Allied's actions were part of a long-term pattern of criminal activities, for the corporation was one of the firms originally identified as a corporate recidivist decades earlier, when the original version of Edwin Sutherland's ground-breaking book on white-collar crime was first published. (Sutherland's publisher forced him to delete the sections of his book that analyzed the criminal records of specific corporations before it was actually published. The uncensored version of this classic work was finally published years after Sutherland's death in 1983.)[211] On the other hand, however, Allied is hardly unique. A study by the General Accounting Office randomly sampled 257 major industrial dischargers and found that almost one-sixth were in "significant (ongoing) non-compliance" with water pollution standards.[212]

Another all-too-typical example of the abuses in the chemical industry comes from the Borden Chemicals and Plastics plant near Geismar, Louisiana, which has repeatedly released clouds of toxic wastes into the air. In 1996, it was a witch's brew of ethylene dichloride, vinyl chloride, and hydrogen chloride. The next year it was a cloud of vinyl chloride and ammonia that shut down Route 73, and in 1998 it was hydrochloric acid. Yet before those releases ever occurred, the EPA had had Borden Chemicals in court on other charges, including illegally storing, shipping, and burning toxic wastes, and contaminating the groundwater used by nearby communities. Borden never admitted its guilt, but it eventually agreed to a consent decree that required it to pay a $3.6 million fine and spend another $3 million to clean up contaminated groundwater. Ironically, those costs were only a fraction of the $15 million tax break the state of Louisiana gave Borden to get them to build the chemical plant in the state.[213]

The story of vinyl chloride, the foundation of a multibillion-dollar plastics industry, follows a familiar pattern. Evidence of the dangers of vinyl chloride began accumulating soon after the end of World War II, when studies from the Soviet Union, Rumania, France, and the United States linked vinyl chloride to liver damage. Although employees exposed to the chemical frequently complained of sore, weak fingers, company physicians in the United States repeatedly denied that the problem had anything to do with their work. As the number of workers subject to long-term exposure increased, evidence of a serious new problem began to emerge. An extremely rare form of cancer, angiosarcoma of the liver, began to show up in an alarming number of vinyl chloride workers. Although angiosarcoma is so rare that one study did not find a single case in more than 200,000 liver specimens examined at the Bronx Veterans Administration Hospital, four cases were found in a single American plant employing only 250 people in vinyl chloride and polyvinyl chloride (PVC) work.[214] In 1971, Cesare Maltoni, a researcher working for the Italian chemical industry, found that vinyl chloride produced angiosarcoma in laboratory animals at levels of exposure far lower than those to which American workers were being exposed. The Manufacturing Chemists Association (the trade association of the American chemical industry) quickly joined with the European firm that had done the research in an attempt to keep these findings secret. But the growing incidence of this otherwise rare cancer could not be hidden from public attention.[215]

As is so often the case with industrial hazards, the damage done by vinyl chloride extends far beyond the workforce directly involved in its production. A study by researchers from Bonn University found serious liver disease in workers who turned PVC plastics into floor tile. Moreover, a study by the Environmental Protection Agency concluded that more than 300 million pounds of vinyl chloride escape into the environment each year. Although the long-range effects of this pollution are difficult to gauge, a study of three Ohio towns in which vinyl chloride was manufactured disclosed an abnormally high incidence of birth defects in infants and tumors of the central nervous system among adult men.[216]

The corporate response to the asbestos problem followed much the same pattern. Asbestos is unique only in that its dangers were recognized much earlier than were those of most other industrial hazards. In fact, the Roman naturalist Pliny the Elder mentioned a lung disease suffered by slaves who mined asbestos and described the makeshift respirators they used to protect themselves from injury. The first modern report of a worker's death from exposure to asbestos was made by a British physician in 1906, and in 1918, U.S. and Canadian insurance companies stopped selling individual life insurance policies to asbestos workers. By 1935 asbestos had been linked to lung cancer and to asbestosis, another crippling lung disease, and by 1955 the causal link between asbestos and lung cancer was conclusively established.[217]

Yet all this scientific evidence seemed to have little impact on the asbestos industry, whose members repeatedly denied that any problem existed. Although company physicians at the nation's leading asbestos producer regularly diagnosed lung problems among asbestos workers, company policy prevented doctors from informing their patients about abnormal chest X-rays or recommending outside treatment. After publication of the 1955 study establishing a link between asbestos and lung cancer, the industry took the offensive, hiring numerous researchers to "prove" that asbestos was harmless. By 1960, sixty-three scientific papers had been published on the problems of asbestos exposure. The eleven studies funded by the asbestos industry all rejected the connection between asbestos and lung cancer and minimized the dangers of asbestosis. All fifty-two independent studies, on the other hand, found asbestos to pose a major threat to human health.[218] Such evidence suggests that the asbestos industry knowingly perpetrated a massive fraud on its workers and on the public. (See Chapter 5 for a discussion of what happened to the asbestos industry when these facts finally came to light.) Apologists for such corporate crimes argue that "everything causes cancer" and that the risks of getting the disease from exposure to most carcinogens are very slight. But that line of reasoning will not work here, for it has been shown that even relatively low levels of asbestos exposure can have fatal effects on some people, and that hundreds of thousands of people with higher levels of exposure have died from such diseases as lung cancer, mesothelioma (a rare cancer of the lining of the lungs and stomach), and asbestosis.[219]

A famous case of a different sort came from Love Canal, New York—an old dumping ground that the Hooker Chemical Corporation gave to the Niagara Falls School Board in the early 1950s. In June 1958 three schoolchildren were burned near the dumping site, and internal memos indicated that Hooker officials attributed the problem to the toxic chemicals left there. But this information remained secret for twenty years, until massive leaks from the site contaminated a group of nearby homes with a potent mixture of toxic chemicals.[220] In 1978 the state was forced to evacuate 239 families and demolish their homes, and more than 900 families were eventually forced to move. Hooker Chemical was made to pay $227 million in damages, but the taxpayers were left with $280 million in expenses for the evacuation and cleanup. It took decades before most of the Love Canal area was once again considered safe, but in 2004 the EPA recommended that it be removed from the list of sites on the Superfund list.[221] Like Allied Chemical, Hooker Chemical has had a long record of illegal dumping activities, including such places as Bloody Run Creek, New York (which was used to dump chemicals after Love Canal was closed); Taft, Louisiana; White Lake, Michigan; and Syosset and Bethpage, New York. In fact, Matt Tallmer has described Hooker's illegal dumping "as a corporate way of life."[222]

As regulations controlling the disposal of hazardous wastes have grown progressively more restrictive, manufacturers have turned to private contractors to get rid of the dangerous substances they produce. Although the law requires the licensing of all firms that dispose of hazardous wastes, there has been so little supervision or control that blatantly illegal techniques are commonly used to get rid of the unwanted chemicals. Indeed, many firms that rushed into the hazardous waste control business were actually run by organized crime.[223] No matter who controls those companies, this is a profitable venture for both parties: Disposal firms make fat profits by illegally (and inexpensively) dumping the wastes, and the large corporations get rid of their pollutants cheaply and easily while avoiding any financial responsibility for them. The public is, once again, the principal loser.

Of course, industrial violence is hardly limited to the United States. One of the most notorious cases of industrial contamination was the Chisso Corporation's poisoning of Minamata, Japan, with mercury emissions from its local plant. The first symptoms of mercury contamination at Minamata surfaced in the early 1950s. Birds began to lose their sense of balance and fly into buildings or simply fall out of the trees, and some cats began walking with a strange, stumbling gait and then suddenly going mad, running in circles and foaming at the mouth until they collapsed. Local fishermen and their families were the next victims. Unusual tenderness in the gums and mouth would be followed by trembling that grew progressively worse, until the victim began violently thrashing about and eventually lapsed into unconsciousness. Most frightening of all were the mental effects of "Minamata disease"—confusion, hallucinations, and mania. By 1975, health surveys had uncovered 3,500 victims and more than 120 deaths.[224]

When faced with the violence it had done to the people of Minamata, the Chisso Corporation responded in the same way its American counterparts did in similar situations: It denied responsibility. When that position became untenable, it fought bitter court battles to avoid paying compensation to the victims and their families. Chisso finally was forced to admit its guilt and pay some claims in 1973,[225] but most of the victims still received nothing. It was not until 1996, more than four decades after the first cases of Minamata disease, that the thousands of victims suing Chisso agreed to drop their cases in exchange for a lump sum payment per victim of about $24,000.[226]

As corporations in the rich industrial nations seek to move their most polluting operations overseas to nations with fewer environmental protections, more and more of the most serious environmental disasters are occurring in the Third World. One of the first to gain wide publicity occurred in December 1984. A Union Carbide plant in Bhopal, India, that had apparently cut corners on safety emitted a massive cloud of poisonous gas that is believed to have killed at least 5,000 people and injured 200,000 more.[227] Subsequent investigations found that the plant was storing a dangerous amount of deadly methyl isocyanate, that it lacked proper safety equipment, and that normal training, staffing, and maintenance were neglected because of pressure to cut costs.[228]

The Third World is also becoming a major dumping ground for the toxic waste of the wealthy countries. Poor nations in Latin America, Asia, and especially Africa, desperate for any source of foreign income, are being deluged by an increasing stream of pollutants from the developed nations. Of course, such arrangements are usually kept as secret as possible, for the glare of international publicity can cause even the poorest nations to have second thoughts. One of the most fascinating examples of the international game of hot potato that sometimes develops involved the *Khian Sea,* a cargo ship of Bahamian registry that sailed from Philadelphia with 13,476 tons of toxic ash. The ash turned out to contain frightening amounts of dioxin and the Bahamian government barred the ship from landing. From there the ship began a 14-month journey to find a port in Latin America that would accept its cargo. Finally, impoverished Haiti agreed to let it dock. But after unloading only about 3,000 pounds the Haitians changed their minds and sent the ship packing. Next, it tried a variety of European ports. Finally, after 18 months at sea the crew secretly dumped the remaining ash in Bangladesh Bay.[229]

Another area of growing concern is the damage workplace hazards can cause to reproductive health. The federal government estimates that 15 to 20 percent of all jobs in the United States expose workers to some chemicals that might cause reproductive injury. At least half a million American workers are exposed to glycol ethers that are known to cause testicular atrophy and birth defects in test animals. About 200,000 hospital and industrial employees work with anesthetic gases and ethylene oxide, both of which are linked to miscarriages in humans. Finally, 90 million or so American workers are exposed to radio frequency or microwave radiation that causes embryonic death and impaired fertility in animals.[230]

Radiation is one of the most feared and least understood forms of environmental hazards, and here it has been the government, not the private corporations, that has been the most cavalier with the health and safety of the public. Between 1945 and 1989, the United States government tested more than 1,800 nuclear bombs, often showing scant concern about the effects the radiation they released would have. The U.S. Public Health Service found that American nuclear testing poisoned soil in Virginia, milk in New England, wheat in South Dakota, and fish in the Great Lakes. But the worst victims were often the military's own personnel, who were in some cases actually ordered to observe the test unprotected from nearby trenches to study the possible effects on enemy troops. Numerous "downwinders"—people who lived near nuclear test sites—are also believed to have died from radiation exposure. When the Atomic Energy Commission (AEC) was finally forced to open up its files, an "AEC conspiracy to hide its environmental record was exposed: The agency had lied in Congressional hearings, destroyed documents, given false testimony in court, and denied in the media any harm to the public. The courts eventually ruled in victim lawsuits that a terrible miscarriage of justice had occurred and that the AEC had perpetrated a fraud."[231]

The government's safety record in the manufacture of nuclear weapons has proven no better. The Hanford Nuclear Reservation in Washington state near the Columbia River was America's major source of plutonium for much of its nuclear program. In the first decade of operation alone, the plant is believed to have released 53,000 curies of radioactive iodine into the air—the equivalent of a major nuclear accident—and millions more curies of radioactive material were dumped into the Columbia River. The Hanford Reservation is one of the most polluted places on earth, containing more than 1,300 nuclear waste sites within its perimeter. Trenches, tanks, ponds, sand-covered pits, and underground storage cribs hold more than a billion cubic meters of hazardous materials. More than 13,000 people living near the Hanford Nuclear Reservation are believed to have received significant dosages of radiation that leaked out from the facility.[232] The facility used by Rockwell International to manufacture nuclear weapons in

Rocky Flats, Colorado, is another environmental disaster where more than 166 hazardous waste sites have been discovered.[233]

Of course, all industrial violence does not involve some kind of exotic chemicals, radiation, or toxic waste. Consider the famous case of the Imperial Food Products chicken processing plant in Hamlet, North Carolina. The 100-year-old plant had no fire alarms, no sprinkler system, and no windows to provide an escape route in case of an emergency; so when the owner decided to have most of the exit doors locked to prevent employees from stealing chicken parts, the building became a veritable death trap. When a fire broke out in September 1991, twenty-five of the 90 employees present died and 56 more were injured.[234]

Unsafe Products: Violence against Consumers

It is estimated that more than 20,000 people are killed by defective products every year in the United States and that another 30 million people are injured.[235] The manufacturer that produces and sells a dangerous product may violate some of our most deeply held ethical standards, but it does not automatically violate the law. Most of the cases examined here involve not only the manufacture of dangerous products but also fraudulent or deceptive statements made by corporate officials to avoid a sales disaster or costly civil suits. It is these fraudulent statements that turn corporate irresponsibility into corporate crime.

The potential for harm varies greatly from one type of product to another. The hazards of an improperly made hat and an improperly made airplane are obviously quite different. But of all consumer products, automobiles and other motor vehicles have proven to be one of the most dangerous (only tobacco causes more deaths and injuries to the public). There have been considerably more than 2 million traffic deaths since the first recorded U.S. automobile fatality in 1899, and perhaps ten times that many injuries. However, many of those casualties can be attributed to defects in the vehicles. The fact remains that automobiles are extremely dangerous machines, and one would expect that responsible manufacturers would do everything possible to make them safer. Unfortunately, the conventional wisdom in the automobile industry has been that "safety doesn't sell." Alfred P. Sloan, the former president of General Motors, expressed the position of his industry years ago in replying to the urgings of the DuPont Corporation to use its safety glass in the Chevrolets: "I am trying to protect the interest of the stockholders of General Motors and the corporation's operating position— it is not my responsibility to sell safety glass. . . . You can say perhaps that I am selfish, but business is selfish. We are not a charitable institution—we are trying to make a profit for our stockholders."[236]

It would be interesting to know how many of Mr. Sloan's stockholders died because GM cars did not have safety glass. Whatever the number, it is clear that the automobile industry has not merely been indifferent to proposals to improve vehicle safety but in many cases has actively opposed them. Time after time, the manufacturers bitterly fought legislation to require tougher safety standards and refused to recognize the safety problem with their vehicles or order recalls until forced to do so by the regulatory agencies or the courts.

Probably the most highly publicized of any automotive safety defect was the unsafe gas tank in 1971 to 1976 models of Ford Pintos and Bobcats. According to the National Highway Traffic Safety Administration, "Low to moderate speed rear-end collisions of Pintos produce massive fuel tank leaks due to puncture or tearing of the fuel tank and separation of the filler pipe from the tank."[237] There is evidence that Ford knew about these safety defects before the Pinto was ever put on the market but declined to make the necessary changes for economic reasons. For example, internal company documents uncovered by investigative reporters showed that Ford conducted secret crash tests of the Pinto and that the gas tank ruptured in every crash occurring at more than 25 miles per hour. Nevertheless, Ford later denied that the tests had ever been made, and it repeatedly claimed that the charges against the Pinto were unwarranted.[238]

The original allegations against the Pinto came from Ralph Nader's Center for Automotive Safety and a subsequent article in the muckraking magazine *Mother Jones.* As the publicity increased, the National Highway Traffic Safety Administration finally issued an "initial determination" that the Pinto's gas tank was unsafe. Ford continued to deny the charges against the Pinto vehemently until a week before the public hearings were scheduled to begin and then suddenly agreed to recall the Pintos and Bobcats.[239] Although the entire cost has never been totaled, Ford's decision to cut corners on the gas tank safety of the Pinto and Bobcat and to continue to deny the dangers of the vehicles for years after they became apparent probably cost the company well over $100 million. In addition to the cost of the recall, Ford was subject to dozens of civil suits, some of which brought multimillion-dollar judgments. But, of course, Ford's losses were slight compared to those of the families of the more than fifty people who are believed to have died as a direct result of automobile accidents involving gas tank ruptures.[240]

The safety problems with automotive tires have been just as severe as those with the vehicles that rely on them. The Firestone Corporation has a particularly bad reputation in this regard. In 1972, Firestone began production of a steel-belted radial tire known as the Firestone 500, and the complaints soon began pouring in. Chevrolet threatened to stop using Firestone tires as standard equipment,[241] and the Atlas Tire Company, which sold Firestone tires under its own name, sent a 1973 memo to Firestone stating that "it appears Firestone is coming apart at the seams, and drastic action is necessary."[242] Montgomery Ward complained in 1976 that "we were given a bad product."[243] The problem they were all complaining about was that the tread would unexpectedly separate from the steel-belted inner layer of the tire, causing a blowout that might send the car careening out of control. A Firestone engineer sent out to investigate the complaints found that 32 percent of the tires he examined at one location showed signs of tread separation.[244]

Firestone's management responded to the overwhelming evidence against the 500 with a concerted campaign to keep the truth from the public. When a government survey of tire safety produced damning evidence against Firestone's tire, the company filed a suit to block the survey's release, claiming it was inaccurate and would create the impression that there were widespread defects in radial tires.[245] In July of 1978, a Firestone representative had the temerity to claim that "There is no safety-related reason for the public to be concerned about continuing to use Firestone steel-belted radial 500s or any other properly maintained Firestone-made tire."[246] In light of the evidence in Firestone's possession at the time, this statement and the numerous others like it can only be considered acts of blatant fraud.

By the time Firestone stopped production of the 500 at the end of 1977, 23 million of them had been produced, tens of thousands of which failed on the road, contributing to numerous accidents and at least forty-one deaths. The company's president eventually resigned, Firestone had to pay hundreds of millions of dollars to recall the tires and settle the lawsuits, and of course it suffered a huge loss of public confidence.[247]

After this financial disaster Firestone was acquired by Bridgestone, the Japanese tire manufacturer. One would certainly assume that the new ownership would not soon forget the lessons from the tire that had nearly destroyed the company. Amazingly, however, a few decades later Firestone tires were again in the headlines with a tread separation problem. This time the problem was linked to the tires on a particular vehicle—the Ford Explorer SUV—which came with Firestone tires as standard equipment. By the time Bridgestone/Firestone announced the recall of some 6.4 million tires in August 2000, their failure had been linked to nearly 300 accidents and at least forty-six deaths,[248] and that figure ultimately rose to at least 174 deaths.[249] Once again, more forthright action by management might have prevented most of the problems, since Firestone had clearly known of the problem for some time before the recall was announced. More than a year before the American recall, Ford had been forced to issue a recall of the Firestone tires it sold on its Explorers in the Middle East. (Since driving at high temperatures apparently promotes the tire separation problem, it showed up first in the desert countries.[250])

As bad as the safety record of the automobile industry has been, that of the pharmaceutical industry has been worse. According to the Multinational Monitor, thirty-one of the top 100 corporate crimes of the 1990s were committed by pharmaceutical companies.[251] Time after time, respected pharmaceutical firms have shown a cavalier disregard for the lives and safety of the people who use their products. Industry salespeople are trained to routinely downplay the dangerous and sometimes fatal side effects of their products, and many pharmaceutical manufacturers apparently see nothing wrong with encouraging their representatives to make deceptive statements that stop just short of fraud. The former medical director of E. R. Squibb described his reasons for resigning as follows: "I reached a point where I could no longer live with myself. . . . I had to choose between resigning myself to total capitulation or resigning as medical director." He went on to say that a drug company doctor "must learn to word a warning statement so it will appear to be an inducement to use the drug rather than a warning of the dangers inherent in its use."[252] Of course, such behavior is not illegal, and as defenders of the industry point out, the same kind of sales approach is used for countless other products. But a company that manufactures products on which many lives depend must assume a greater burden of responsibility than other firms, and the pharmaceutical industry has largely ignored this obligation, choosing instead to pursue the maximum possible profit.

Although the major pharmaceutical firms certainly attempt to stay within the law, this exploitative philosophy has led to numerous criminal activities—particularly in the falsification of tests required by the Food and Drug Administration (FDA) before a new drug is certified and in the use of fraudulent and deceptive advertising. One of the best-documented frauds involved a new drug from the Richardson-Merrell Company, MER/29, a cholesterol inhibitor intended for use by heart patients. When the drug was first developed, Richardson-Merrell foresaw a multimillion-dollar sales potential; but while top management was preparing a major marketing campaign, bad news began to come in from the research department. In one laboratory test all the female rats given a high dose of MER/29 died, and all the rats in a later test involving a lower dosage of the drug had to be destroyed before the experiment was completed. Autopsies revealed abnormal blood changes in the rats, and these disturbing results were confirmed from tests with other animals. Monkeys, for instance, suffered blood changes, loss of weight, and serious visual problems. Richardson-Merrell's response to this clear evidence of problems with MER/29 was not to withhold the potentially dangerous drug from the market but to falsify the data. One technician testified that she was ordered by a Richardson-Merrell executive to falsify the lab reports, and when she complained to her supervisor, she was told, "He [the executive] is higher up. You do as he tells you, and be quiet."[253] As a result of such pressures, Richardson-Merrell's application to the FDA was full of major omissions and fraudulent statements.

Clinical data about the dangers of MER/29 began building up as soon as the drug hit the market. But the discovery of Richardson-Merrell's fraud came about quite by accident, when an investigator for the FDA happened to share a ride with the husband of one of the laboratory technicians who was asked to falsify data. Had the husband not felt talkative that day, Richardson-Merrell might never have been caught—indeed, it seems quite likely that most cases of the falsification of data by pharmaceutical manufacturers never come to light. As the FDA inspector who first uncovered the MER/29 fraud put it, "I didn't think the [MER/29 case] was typical, but I was wrong. . . . They were totally geared to the dollar sign. I am sure there are many other firms similar to them—even today. I suspect [Richardson-Merrell] got away with the same thing many times before."[254]

By the time MER/29 was finally taken off the market, more than 400,000 people had used the drug and at least 5,000 users had suffered serious side effects—

usually the "classic triad" of hair loss, severe skin problems, and cataracts.[255] Criminal charges were brought against a Richardson-Merrell vice president and two laboratory supervisors. Each could have received five years in prison and a $10,000 fine, but instead the judge gave them only six months' probation. After pleading no contest to eight of twelve counts against it, the Richardson-Merrell Company was given a fine of $80,000—not much more than a slap on the wrist for a company that made a profit of $17.79 million that year.[256] Indeed, the $80,000 represented only a small fraction of the money Richardson-Merrell made from its crime: In its first year of production, MER/29 brought in more than $7 million in gross revenues.

The MER/29 case is exceptional only because Richardson-Merrell was caught red-handed falsifying data. A more common ploy by pharmaceutical companies is to conceal the data they have about the hazards of their products. This was the case, for example, with Oraflex, a painkiller marketed to arthritis patients by Eli Lilly and Company. The use of Oraflex has been linked to the deaths of at least sixty-two patients, and evidence shows that the company knew about twenty-six of these deaths in foreign countries before it applied to the FDA for permission to sell the drug in the United States. Lilly did not reveal any of this information to the FDA, however, and Oraflex was approved for sale in April 1982. By August, the drug had to be withdrawn from the market when reports of these deaths and of a growing number of new ones began circulating in the media.[257] Three years later, in August 1985, Lilly pleaded guilty to misdemeanor charges arising from its attempts to conceal the hazards of Oraflex. The total punishment handed out for a crime that is believed to have killed forty-nine people and injured 916 more was a $25,000 fine for Lilly and a $15,000 fine for one executive.[258]

The case of the Dalkon Shield was, however, far more devastating to its developer, the A. H. Robbins Company. At one time the Dalkon Shield was an extremely popular intrauterine birth control device, but as it turned out, every woman who used it was risking serious complications. The most dangerous problem was that the wick used to insert and remove the device also served as a pathway for bacteria-laden fluids to travel up into the uterus. It is estimated that at least 17 women died and as many as 200,000 more were injured by complications involving the Dalkon Shield.[259]

A. H. Robbins was involved in a web of unethical dealings right from the beginning, when it relied on safety tests conducted by a physician who had a substantial financial interest in the shield. As evidence of the dangers of the shield mounted, the company, in the words of two court-appointed special masters, "engaged in an ongoing fraud by knowingly misrepresenting the nature, quality, safety, and efficacy of the Dalkon Shield."[260] A quality control supervisor for Robbins reported that when he told his boss that he must speak up about his concerns with the safety of the shield, he was accused of insubordination and was warned that if he valued his job he had better do as he was told.[261] By 1985, Robbins had paid out more than $378 million to settle 9,200 suits from the victims, but those cases were only the tip of the iceberg. In August of that year Robbins declared bankruptcy, indefinitely postponing compensation to the 40,000 to 50,000 more women who legally deserved it.[262] In June 1989 a federal court accepted a plan to reorganize Robbins that included the creation of a $2.5 billion fund to compensate the victims of the Dalkon Shield.[263]

Another pharmaceutical product to victimize hundreds of thousands of unsuspecting women was diethylstilbestrol—popularly known as DES—a synthetic estrogen discovered in 1938. At first, the drug was approved only for use in menopausal disorders and to suppress lactation. In the early 1940s, however, several gynecologists began claiming that DES helped prevent miscarriages and produced babies with higher birth weights, and the pharmaceutical companies soon saw a huge potential market for the drug as the post–World War II baby boom approached. In 1947 several companies applied to the Food and Drug Administration to market DES as a treatment for the "accidents of pregnancy." The lure of huge profits once again seemed to blind the pharmaceutical companies to their ethical and legal responsibilities, for those applications never mentioned the growing body of research reporting the carcinogenic properties of DES or the studies that showed that babies of pregnant rats given DES had an alarming number of deformities in their sexual organs. Soon after DES was approved to prevent miscarriages, a number of studies showed it was not even effective for that purpose. The dosing of hundreds of thousands of American women with a dangerous and ineffective drug nonetheless continued unabated until a study found a high incidence of an otherwise rare form of cancer among women whose mothers had taken DES. Year by year the evidence against DES mounted, and it is now known to cause not only cancer in "DES daughters" but also sterility and deformities in their reproductive organs. The damage of DES is even passed on to a third generation of children, since DES daughters who do manage to become pregnant have an unusually high rate of premature delivery and other problems in pregnancy. Some DES sons also develop fertility problems and testicular abnormalities.[264]

Another unethical practice in the pharmaceutical industry is the "dumping" of unsafe products in poor nations with lax drug-safety regulations. Although U.S. law forbids the export of any drug that has not been approved by the FDA, manufacturers have often found ways to skirt the law. A. H. Robbins, for instance, continued to market the Dalkon Shield overseas long after the publicity about its side effects had made it virtually impossible to sell in the United States, and those sales continued until the shield was officially ruled unsafe by the FDA.[265] The same tactic was used by the manufacturers of birth control pills containing high dosages of estrogens. After the publicity about the dangers of these contraceptives made them unsalable in the United States, at least two manufacturers sold off their stocks of pills at cut-rate prices for distribution to women in Third World countries. A different form of dumping that is apparently quite common is to ship old drugs whose shelf life has expired to unsuspecting Third World countries.[266]

Another reflection of the pharmaceutical companies' priorities can be seen in the fact that they often admit the harmful side effects of their drugs only when forced to do so by the countries in which the drugs are sold. Consider the adverse reactions listed by the Searle Company for its oral contraceptive Ovulen. In the United States, Searle listed "nausea, loss of hair, nervousness, jaundice, high blood pressure, weight change, and headaches" as side effects. The farther south the product is sold, however, the safer it seems to become. In Mexico only two side effects, nausea and weight change, were named; and in Brazil and Argentina, Searle would have physicians believe that Ovulen has no harmful side effects at all.[267] Such deception is, moreover, a much more serious matter in Third World countries. Because Third World physicians often do not have access to current journals or the latest medical information, they must rely more heavily on the information supplied by drug companies and their salespeople.[268]

At least Third World consumers who use drugs manufactured by the major pharmaceutical companies usually get what is listed on the label, but a host of criminal firms now produce counterfeit drugs that look like the drugs sold under the brand name of the major firms. Some of the fake pharmaceuticals actually contain what is listed on the label and only violate the copyrights of the firm that paid the costs for that drug's research and development. But many fake drugs actually contain little or nothing of medical value, and in some cases they have even proved toxic to users. In October 1990, for example, 109 children in Nigeria died after being given an industrial solvent that was sold to hospitals as a pharmaceutical chemical manufactured in the Netherlands.[269]

Despite all the problems in the automobile and pharmaceutical industries, nothing comes close to the tobacco companies in the competition for the title of the world's most deadly corporate killers. Cigarette smoking has been conclusively linked to cancer of the lungs, larynx, mouth, and esophagus as well as to bronchitis, emphysema, ulcers, and heart and circulatory disorders. The most widely accepted estimate is that smoking kills more than 400,000 Americans every year—making it the number 1 cause of preventable deaths.[270] A study published in the *Journal of the American Medical Association* in 1993 went a step further, concluding that tobacco smoking is implicated in almost one in every five deaths in the United States, making it America's number 1 cause of death—period.[271]

As with the other examples examined here, merely selling an unsafe product is not necessarily a crime unless the companies involved make fraudulent statements to cover up its hazards. The tobacco industry, however, has racked up a long history of deception, denials, and outright lies in its attempt to deceive the public about the deadly consequences of cigarette smoking. The tobacco companies funded research to "prove" smoking was safe, concealed the findings of their own researchers about the health dangers and addictive qualities of tobacco, launched one of history's most intensive public relations campaigns to delude the public into thinking their products were safe, and employed a formidable battery of high-priced legal talent to sue numerous people who challenged their campaign of disinformation. Philip J. Hilts's careful study of the history of the tobacco cover-ups shows that there were two distinct phases. In the 1950s, when evidence about the dangers of smoking first started coming out, the tobacco companies and their top executives launched an impressive public relations blitz, but as Hilts put it: "The company executives who had fought for a decade to hide the effect of smoking had begun their work in a different world, one where smoking was more acceptable, it was fashionable and proud. They had wanted to believe that smoking really couldn't be as bad as the doctors were saying." As irrefutable evidence about the dangers of smoking piled up, study by study, year after year, the new generation of tobacco executives could have few illusions about the dangers of their product. They "learned from the beginning . . . that tobacco executives did not say certain things in public and were required to say others, whether those statements were true or not."[272]

Perhaps the classic example of this technique came in 1994 during the congressional hearings on smoking. The heads of America's seven top tobacco companies were called to testify, and every one of them denied what had already been proven by their own researchers and was certainly common knowledge among the American public—that smoking tobacco was addictive. They even went so far as to suggest that cigarette smoking was no more dangerous than eating Twinkies or drinking coffee, and to deny that smoking causes cancer.[273]

In addition to this campaign of disinformation, the tobacco multinationals have battled every significant government effort to reduce smoking and, perhaps worst of all, have made an intentional effort through advertising and promotions to induce young people (many of whom are not even legally allowed to smoke) to take up the deadly habit. The reasons tobacco companies target the young involve simple economics. Of lifetime smokers, 89 percent take up the habit by age nineteen, and three-quarters do so by age seventeen. Among those who start smoking after age twenty-one, more than 90 percent soon drop the habit completely.[274] If the tobacco companies cannot attract young smokers, their business will die. Way back in 1929, an ad for Lucky Strikes showed a young man in short pants reaching for a cigarette and breaking an "ancient prejudice," as the ad put it. At one time Chesterfield printed up high school football programs for free in exchange for including a two-page centerfold advertisement. Cigarette manufacturers have frequently used cartoon characters to attract young smokers, the latest and most controversial being the famous Joe Camel campaign that was begun in 1988 and only recently discontinued under intense public pressure. Three generations earlier, Philip Morris captured the market for adolescent males with its cowboy hero the Marlboro Man, and in 1967 it began targeting young girls with the Virginia Slims brand and its famous "You've come a long way, baby" slogan.[275]

The political clout of the tobacco companies was, at least until recently, only surpassed by its legal prowess. The legal threat to the industry that makes such a deadly product is obvious, and the industry's strategy was to intimidate its opposition with an overwhelming superiority of resources. Not only did tobacco manufacturers use the civil courts to attempt to prevent information about the dangers of their product and the ruthless policies they pursued from reaching the public, but they launched one of the most effective long-term campaigns of legal defense ever mounted. Time and again in generations of lawsuits by the victims of tobacco use and their survivors, the industry was able to convince jurors that smokers knew the risks they were taking and that they must bear the responsibility for their own personal decisions. No court ever ordered the tobacco industry to pay a single penny in damages until 1996. (In 1988, jurors in New Jersey handed down a $400,000 award against the Liggett Group, but it was voided upon appeal.[276])

However, as the evidence mounted about the efforts of the tobacco corporations to cover up the dangers of smoking and to get people to start using their addictive product, the legal tide shifted decisively against them. In 1998, a Florida court ordered the first punitive damages—$1 million—ever awarded against a tobacco company in a product liability suit, and other defeats have followed. In July of 2000, another Florida jury handed the tobacco industry the largest single damage award in American history—$144.8 billion. Although this judgment was later reduced, such a verdict would have been unthinkable only a fewer years earlier.[277] Big tobacco's opponents have also been successful with a different kind of legal strategy that involves suits from the states and other parties that have been forced to foot the bill for the cost of treating sick and dying tobacco users. In such cases, the industry's claim that smoking is just an individual choice has had far less success. As the result of several defeats in cases brought by individual states, in 1998 the tobacco industry agreed to a $206 billion settlement that covered all the states and ended the thirty-eight cases then pending against them in various courts. In addition, the industry also agreed to some minor restrictions on its advertising practices and to fund a new foundation dedicated to help reduce smoking.[278]

Although the tobacco industry had hoped this settlement would be the end of its legal troubles, year by year these difficulties have continued to mount. In the single most important case to date, a massive suit against the industry by the Department of Justice went to trial in September of 2004 after five years of pretrial skirmishes. This time the government used anti-racketeering statutes originally intended to help combat organized crime. The government was seeking to force the industry to disgorge $280 billion of what it claims are illegal profits that resulted from a massive conspiracy to defraud the public. Among other things, the government charged that the tobacco industry lied about the addictive properties of nicotine and made false claims about the health benefits of "light" cigarettes and the dangers of secondhand smoke.[279]

A Case Study: Two Financial Crime Waves

If nothing else, this chapter has certainly shown the great variety of white-collar crime. But this kind of taxonomic approach that groups together large numbers of crimes with similar characteristics can blind us to other important dimensions of the problem, such as the distribution of the offenses within different sectors of the economy. This final section examines a crime spree that appears to have swept through the financial industry in two huge waves—one during the 1980s and early 1990s and a second at the start of the twenty-first century. The convictions of Wall Street's top brokerage houses for various sorts of criminal schemes, the guilty pleas and convictions of dozens of the nation's leading traders on charges of fraud and insider trading, the jailing of the most successful financier of the era (Michael Milken), the highly successful sting operation on the Chicago commodities exchanges, the revelations of the international criminal conspiracies of the Bank of Credit and Commerce International, and most of all, the collapse of the savings and loan industry, rocked the financial industry in the first wave of scandals. The second wave of crime, which came to light at the start of this century, had more to do with plain old fraudulent bookkeeping (albeit utilizing some creative new accounting tricks) than with the manipulations of big financial institutions and investors. The bankruptcy of the huge Enron Corporation, quickly followed by the bankruptcy of other corporate giants such as WorldCom and Parmalat, led investigators to uncover widespread fraud and deception in the way the corporate world was keeping its books. Whether these scandals reflect an actual increase in corporate crime or just an increase in media attention and the arrests and convictions it brings is harder to determine. Clearly, these offenses had been going on for many years before they came to light, but it does appear that there are some cycles in corporate and state–corporate crime. Corporate offenses appear to increase during periods of rapid financial growth and speculation. When times get harder or the fraudulent schemes collapse of their own weight, the higher rollers attract the attention of the media and the enforcement bureaucracy and things start to cool down again; only to reheat in the next wave of speculation.

One of the first major financial crimes to come to light in the 1980s was the "check-kiting" scheme run by the brokerage house of E. F. Hutton. The scheme began as a relatively innocent attempt to recapture some of the "float" (the interest that banks make on funds they hold while waiting for a check to clear) by writing checks for some funds that had not yet been deposited. But Hutton was having severe financial problems, and it soon seized on the idea of writing much larger overdrafts and pocketing the interest it earned. Although the details are often confusing, a check-kiting scheme is much the same whether practiced by a respected business firm or an individual con artist. Hutton would pay its bills with a check that was covered by another check written on a different bank, which was covered by a check written on still another bank, and so on. While the banks were waiting for these checks to clear, Hutton was getting a kind of interest-free loan. In 1980, the first year the scheme got into full swing, Hutton saved about $27 million in interest, which accounted for about one-third of its profits. In early 1982 two small banks blew the whistle on Hutton, and the company finally agreed to plead guilty and to pay several million dollars in fines and restitution in 1985. The penalties were, however, far less than the profits from the scheme, and as part of the deal the government agreed not to prosecute any of the people involved in the scam. The biggest cost to Hutton was probably to its reputation, and after the settlement was completed the company was sold to another firm.[280]

The next major Wall Street firm to confess to its criminal activities, the high-flying Drexel Burnham Lambert, did not get off so lightly. In December 1988, as part of its involvement in the insider trading scandal discussed later, Drexel pleaded guilty to six felony counts and agreed to pay $600 million in criminal fines and civil penalties. As part of the plea-bargaining deal, Drexel was allowed to decide which of the numerous charges it would plead guilty to, and it selected four counts of "stock parking" (violating securities laws by illegally concealing the ownership of stock) and two counts involving illegal stock manipulations. The huge fines and the loss of public confidence constituted a major blow to the firm, and in February 1990 it declared bankruptcy after fifty-five years on Wall Street.[281]

Drexel was followed into the legal dock by Salomon, Inc., the nation's largest trader in government securities. In 1991, it admitted to an illegal scheme to manipulate that $2.2 trillion market. To prevent a single company from cornering the market, government rules expressly forbid any firm from buying more than 35 percent of a treasury bond issue. But Salomon used a variety of subterfuges to exceed that limit and even traded bonds in the name of some customers without informing them of the transactions. In May 1992, Salomon agreed to pay $190 million in fines and to set aside another $100 million to compensate the victims of its crimes.[282]

As pervasive as such corporate crimes seem to have been, most of the offenses to come to light were intended primarily for individual gain. In fact, some of the individuals involved were so highly placed and so powerful that they used entire companies as tools for their personal enrichment. Violations of disclosure laws, stock parking, and insider trading were all common among traders and investors. Of these offenses, insider trading is one of the most difficult to prove, because the guilty parties can always claim that they made their trades on the basis of market research, good judgment, or just plain luck, and not inside information. Yet this era saw a major increase in prosecutions and convictions for this crime, and one such case became the focus of a scandal that rocked Wall Street to its very foundations.

The affair started with Dennis Levine, a highly placed merger and acquisitions specialist with the Wall Street firm of Drexel Burnham Lambert. Levine seemed to be a classic American success story—a middle-class boy made good. At age thirty-three he drove a red Ferrari, lived in a luxurious New York apartment, and had a million-dollar-a-year compensation package from his employer. But his success story took an unexpected turn when he was charged with using inside information to make $12 million in illegal profits and was sentenced to a two-year prison term.[283] The trail soon led investigators from Levine to Ivan F. Boesky, one of the most successful stock traders of the decade. Boesky had been making huge profits from the tips he had received from Levine and others, and was fined a record $100 million for his offenses and given a three-year prison term.[284] After Boesky, Securities and Exchange Commission investigators uncovered one crooked deal after another. By April 1987, more than sixty people had been indicted. An examination of the list of defendants reveals what can only be described as pervasive corruption among the employees of the top Wall Street firms. Although it took another three years, Boesky's evidence eventually helped send the biggest fish of all to prison: Michael Milken, the billionaire "junk bond king" who was until then one of the most successful financiers in American history.[285]

But the financial scandals were by no means confined to Wall Street. Similar revelations of widespread corruption hit the major commodities markets in 1989, when the arrests began from a sting operation in which two FBI agents posed as commodities traders.[286] If anything, the corruption in the savings and loan industry was even worse than in the financial markets. The virtual collapse of the industry in the late 1980s cost the government and the American taxpayers hundreds of billions of dollars.[287]

There is no doubt that the sharp increase in interest rates in the 1980s created serious economic problems for many savings and loans as their inventories of low-interest, fixed-rate loans became increasingly unprofitable. But most of those staggering losses were due to crimes and grossly unethical conduct by top savings and loan executives. A study of twenty-six savings and loan failures by the General Accounting Office found evidence of fraud or abusive insider dealing in every single case. A more general estimate by the House Committee on Government Operations holds that crimes or misconduct played a major part in the insolvencies of 80 percent of the institutions slated for closure, and the Resolution Trust Corporation (the agency created to supervise the bailout of the industry) puts that figure at about 60 percent.[288]

Shady savings and loan operators used a variety of techniques to enrich themselves at their firms' expense. One way they robbed their own banks was by going on a shopping spree with company funds. Unlike the staid bankers of the past, corrupt savings and loan officers lived a lifestyle of ostentatious luxury. They threw lavish parties, traveled around the world in private airplanes, and bought everything from classic art to antiques and yachts—all with company money. Although federal regulations limit permissible compensation to that which is "reasonable and commensurate with their duties and responsibilities," top executives of money-losing thrifts not only paid themselves multimillion-dollar salaries but put a host of friends and relatives on the payroll as well. To circumvent the $100,000 limit on the loans a firm can make to one of its own officers, executives from different firms often made large loans to each other. One of the most common scams was known as the "land-flip." A piece of property would be "sold" back and forth among the conspirators, until its price was far above its real value. The property was then used as collateral for a loan. When the conspirators finally walked away from their debt and let the savings and loan foreclose, the property could be sold for only a fraction of the value of the loan. Thrift executives also padded their income with kickbacks from borrowers who wanted far larger loans than their credit rating and collateral justified. When the government audited the books of these "go-go thrifts," they often cooperated with each other to cover up their crimes. One technique, known in the jargon of the savings and loan industry as swapping "dead horses for dead cows," was for two thrifts to buy each other's bad loans, thus making them appear as good investments on the books. In another subterfuge, known as "cash for trash," savings and loan officials got borrowers to take more money than they originally wanted and to use some of the extra to buy repossessed properties from their savings and loan.[289]

In addition to the waves of fevered financial speculation that periodically sweep through all the capitalist economies, the financial crime wave of the 1980s was stimulated by the Reagan administration's fervent support for the deregulation movement. The goal of this movement was, in a much-repeated phrase, to get the government "off the backs" of business, which meant, among other things, cutting back on government supervision and regulation of the economy. To the ideological free marketers who dominated the Reagan administration, cutbacks in the government's regulatory efforts would inevitably produce big economic benefits for the whole nation. In fact, the cutbacks produced something closer to national bankruptcy. The corporate raiders and takeover artists who fueled the speculative boom of the 1980s were unquestionably violating the spirit and often the letter of the antitrust laws, but there was little interest in the administration to enforce those statutes. The effects of the antiregulatory movement were even more apparent in the collapse of the savings and loan industry. Not only did the government eliminate the cap on the interest thrifts could charge (a move dictated as much by the economic conditions of the times as ideological fervor), but it eliminated most of the regulations that kept the savings and loans from taking on too many high-risk investments. When the savings and loan regulators asked for more staff to keep an eye on these new savings and loan activities, they were turned down flat by the White House budget office. (Paradoxically, the antiregulatory sentiment did not prevent the federal government from more than doubling the size of the deposits that were backed by its insurance.) As a result of these developments, the savings and loan operators came to feel that they could do whatever they wanted with their depositors' money without government interference, and that if things really got bad, the government could be counted on to step in and pay off the losses. When President Reagan signed the Garn–St. Germain Act, which stripped away many of the old restrictions on the savings and loan industry, he is quoted as saying, "All in all, I think we've hit the jackpot."[290] Unfortunately, the jackpot went to crooked savings and loan operators, and the public was left to foot the bill.

After a brief period of intense scrutiny, the issue of corporate crime seemed to fall from public attention. But while the media and the enforcement bureaucracy were looking the other way, many major corporations were apparently taking bigger and bigger risks with their books in order to make their firms look more successful to stockholders and potential investors than they actually were. More than any other event, it was the collapse of Enron—at one time the seventh largest corporation in the United States—that brought corporate crime back into the headlines.

In 1984, when Ken Lay became chairman and chief operating officer of Houston Natural Gas, the firm was nothing more than a rather stodgy pipeline company. But Lay had big plans and even bigger dreams. He quickly acquired other pipeline companies, and in 1986 he changed Houston Natural Gas's name to Enron. With an ideological fervor for deregulation and a knack for winning influential friends, Lay rode the same deregulation bandwagon that carried the savings and loans to disaster. Backed by the deregulation crusaders of the Reagan administration, Lay won changes in the federal energy rules that allowed natural gas to be sold in open markets like wheat or pork bellies. His success helped create a new industry and made Enron a corporate–political powerhouse. In 1990, he hired a bright young Harvard MBA, Jeff Skilling, and together they moved Enron away from the pipeline business to become the nation's largest energy trader. They set up the first "gas bank," purchasing large quantities of gas from producers and reselling it to industrial customers on long-term contracts. Skilling persuaded federal regulators to let Enron use "mark-to-market" accounting that allowed the company to count revenue from long-term contracts as immediate profits, even though the money might not come in for years, if at all. This victory was something of a watershed at Enron, because from then on much of its explosive growth in profits came from creative accounting and not sound business. But that did not stop Enron from becoming a Wall Street darling, or being ranked by *Fortune* magazine as the most innovative company in the nation for six straight years. Between 1998 and 2000 Enron's stock tripled in value. Lay, Skilling, and other Enron insiders got rich in the process, cashing in almost half a billion dollars worth of stock on top of their already enormous salaries. In April of 2001, only two months after Skilling had taken over from Lay as Enron's CEO, *Worth* magazine ranked him number 2 on its list of the fifty top CEOs— second only to Microsoft's Steve Ballmer.

Skilling, along with his favorite subordinate, Chief Financial Officer Andrew Fastow, moved aggressively toward what was called "structured finance"—complex deals in which Enron set up a series of separate partnerships to generate tax deductions and move debts off the company books. Fastow named himself to head some of the most important of these partnerships and earned tens of millions of dollars in personal profits as part of the deal. Whenever Enron needed to fatten its balance sheets, it would turn a deal with one of the partnerships that produced big profits—on paper. Enron was also booking huge profits from a variety of high-risk investments. It set up a complex web of financial exchanges involving financial entities known as raptors to protect it against potential losses. The raptors acted as a hedge that was supposed to cover the losses if the stock in those start-up ventures dropped. The problem was that the Raptors were almost entirely funded by Enron stock, so they provided protection only if the value of Enron's stock stayed high.

By 2001 Enron's house of cards began to collapse. The value of some of those risky investments did plummet, and the ability of the raptors to hedge Enron's losses came increasingly into question. Once Enron's image of invincibility began to fade and outsiders started to look seriously at its finances, the corporation's fate was sealed. On December 2, 2002, Enron, which only a few years earlier had been one of the most powerful corporations in America, filed for bankruptcy protection. As of this writing, fifteen Enron executives have been convicted of various criminal offences, including Andrew Fastow, who pleaded guilty to conspiracy to commit wire and securities fraud in January of 2004. Jeff Skilling is now being tried on a thirty-five-count indictment that includes securities fraud, conspiracy, and insider trading, and prosecutors are continuing with their investigation of Ken Lay—the last of the Enron kingpins. Arthur Andersen, the accounting firm that signed off on Enron's shady financial schemes, was also forced into bankruptcy after it was found guilty of obstructing justice for destroying ten of thousands of documents and emails relating to its Enron audits.[291] Two reporters for the *Washington Post* who carried out a detailed investigation of the fall of Enron summed it up this way:

> Enron was a fundamentally self-destructive institution, a house of cards where human error and a culture of ambition, secrecy and greed made collapse inevitable . . . Enron's arc toward scandal and bankruptcy exposed the failure of watchdogs at every level. Its board defaulted on its oversight duties. Outside accountants ceded their independence and violated their profession's rules. Outside lawyers approved misleading deals and failed to vigorously pursue crucial allegations of accounting misdeeds. Wall Street analysts lead a cheering section while their firms collected enormous banking fees from the company. Regulators were overwhelmed by Enron's complexity. The media were blinded by its image of success. Nobody looked inside the company and saw what wasn't there.[292]

The story of WorldCom, once America's second-largest long-distance and data provider, reads much like that of Enron. In a little more than a decade, a former milkman, bouncer, and gym teacher named Bernie Ebbers started a small long-distance company in Jackson, Mississippi, and built it into an empire by buying up several major telecommunications corporations. Like his cohorts at Enron, Ebbers and his associates made a failing venture look like a huge success by juggling its books. Among other things, the company systematically booked routine business costs as capital expenses so that WorldCom appeared to be making huge profits when it was actually losing money. Overall, WorldCom's accounting fraud amounted to around $15 billion. WorldCom descended into bankruptcy just a few months before Enron did in July of 2002. In 2004, Ebbers was indicted on fraud charges, and WorldCom's Chief Financial Officer, Scott Sullivan, pled guilty and agreed to cooperate with prosecutors.[293] With Sullivan's help, the prosecutors won a conviction in March of 2005.

In addition to Enron and WorldCom, several other major corporations collapsed around this time as their own financial frauds came to light. Parmalat, the Italian dairy conglomerate, was declared insolvent when it missed a bond payment and it was discovered that $4.9 billion in assets it claimed to have in a Bank of America account in the Cayman Islands did not exist. A similar scenario of fraud and deception also played itself out at Adelphia Communications, America's sixth largest cable television service.[294]

Review Questions

- What are the most common ways employees victimize their employers?
- What are the most common computer crimes?
- How are fraud and deception used to victimize the public?
- What are conflicts of interest, and how do they affect those who work in government and the professions?
- Are bribery and corruption serious problems in business, government, and law enforcement?
- How do corporations and the professions manipulate the marketplace, and what impact do such manipulations have?
- In what ways do white-collar crimes pose a threat to our civil liberties?
- What are the most common violent white-collar crimes? How serious are they, compared with violent street crime?
- What was the "financial crime wave" and why did it occur?

Notes

1. Norman Jaspan, *Mind Your Own Business* (Englewood Cliffs, N.J.: Prentice-Hall, 1974), p. 201; U.S. Congress, Joint Economic Committee, *The Cost of Crime in 1976* (Washington, D.C.: U.S. Government Printing Office, 1976), p. 8.
2. David O. Friedrichs, *Trusted Criminals: White Collar Crime in Contemporary Society* (Belmont, Calif.: Wadsworth, 1996), p. 116; David McCintick, "Inside Jobs," in *Crime and Business*, Editors of the *Wall Street Journal* (Princeton, N.J.: Dow Jones Books, 1971), p. 16.
3. Gerald Mars, "Dock Pilferage: A Case Study in Occupational Theft," in Paul Rock and Mary McIntosh, eds., *Deviance and Social Control* (London: Tavistock, 1974).
4. John P. Clark and Richard C. Hollinger, *Theft by Employees in Work Organizations* (Washington, D.C.: National Institute of Justice, September 1983); also see David L.

Altheide, Patricia A. Adler, and Duane Altheide, "The Social Meaning of Employee Theft," in *Crime at the Top: Deviance in Business and the Professions*, John M. Johnson and Jack D. Douglas, eds. (Philadelphia: J. B. Lippincott, 1978), p. 90.

5. M. W. Boyle, Self-reported Employee Theft and Counterproductivity as a Function of Employee Turnover Antecedents, Ph.D. Dissertation, Depaul University, 1991.

6. Donald N. M. Horning, "Blue Collar Theft: Conceptions of Property Attitudes Toward Pilfering and Work Group Norms in a Modern Industrial Plant," in *Crime Against Bureaucracy*, Erwin O. Smigel and H. Lawrence Ross, eds. (New York: Van Nostrand Reinhold, 1970). Tim Metz, "Hot Stocks," in *Crime and Business*,. Editors of the *Wall Street Journal* (Princeton, N.J.: Dow Jones Books, 1971), p. 93.

7. August Bequai, *White Collar Crime: A 20th Century Crisis* (Lexington, Mass.: Lexington Books, 1978), pp. 89–90.

8. For some works on embezzlement, see Donald R. Cressey, *Other People's Money: A Study in the Social Psychology of Embezzlement* (Belmont, Calif.: Wadsworth, 1971, originally published 1953); Virgil W. Peterson, "Why Honest People Steal," *Journal of Criminal Law and Criminology* 38 (July–August 1947): 94–103; Svend H. Riemer, "Embezzlement: Pathological Basis," *Journal of Criminal Law and Criminology* 32 (November–December 1941): 411–23; G. E. Levens, "101 British White Collar Criminals," *New Society* (March 26, 1964): 6–8.

9. Bureau of Justice Statistics, *Sourcebook of Criminal Justice Statistics, 2002* (Washington, D.C.: U.S. Government Printing Office, 2003), Table 4.8.

10. Kitty Calavita and Henry N. Pontell, "'Other People's Money' Revisited: Collective Embezzlement in the Savings and Loan and Insurance Industries," *Social Problems* 38 (February 1991): 94–112.

11. Barry Bearak and Tom Furlong, "Totting Up Blame for S & L Crisis," *Los Angeles Times*, December 16, 1990, pp. A1, A34–36; Associated Press, "White Collar to Blame for S & L Crisis, GAO Tells House Panel," *Los Angeles Times*, March 23, 1989; Scripps Howard News Service, "GAO: Fraud, Not the Economy, Caused Most S & L Failures," *San Luis Obispo Telegram-Tribune*, March 23, 1989, p. A2.

12. Walter Russell Mead, "In International Banking, Don't Forget Regulation," *Los Angeles Times*, July 28, 1991, pp. M1, M6.

13. Victor F. Zonana, "BCCI, 2 Founders Indicted; U.S. Imposes Record Fine," *Los Angeles Times*, July 30, 1991, pp. A1, A14; Jonathan Beaty and S. C. Gwynne, "The Dirtiest Bank of All," *Time*, July 29, 1991, pp. 42–47; John Greenwald, "Taken for a Royal Ride," *Time*, July 22, 1991, pp. 46–48; Associated Press, "Report Says Crooked Bank Tied to CIA," *Honolulu Sunday Star-Bulletin & Advertiser*, July 21, 1991, p. C4.

14. Nikos Passas, "Structural Sources of International Crime: Policy Lessons from the BCCI Affair," *Crime, Law and Social Change*, 20 (1993): 293–309.

15. There are many good descriptions of Vesco's exploits. See, for instance, Lester Sobel, *Corruption in Business* (New York: Facts on File, 1977), pp. 51, 163–67.

16. Walter Sheridan, *The Fall and Rise of Jimmy Hoffa* (New York: Saturday Review Press, 1972), pp. 531–32; Ovid Demaris, *Dirty Business: The Corporate-Political Money-Power Game* (New York: Harper's Magazine Press, 1974), p. 332; Robert W. Peterson, *Crime and the American Response* (New York: Facts on File, 1973), p. 172.

17. U.S. Department of Justice, *Report of the Department of Justice's Task Force on Intellectual Property* (Washington, D.C.: U.S. Government Printing Office, 2004), p. 8.

18. "Four Out of Every Ten Software Applications Are Pirated, Losses Hit $11.4 Billion in 1997," *Corporate Crime Reporter* (June 22, 1998): 1.

19. U.S. Department of Justice, *Task Force on Intellectual Property*, p. iii.

20. U.S. Department of Justice, Press Release, "Former Virginia Beach Man Sentenced to 37 Months in Prison for Selling Illegal Copies of Software," August 25, 2004; U.S. Department of Justice, Press Release, "Internet Distributor of Pirated Software Sentenced for Criminal Copyright Infringement" August 25, 2004.

21. Stephen M. Rosoff, Henry N. Pontell, and Robert Tillman, *Profit Without Honor: White Collar Crime and the Looting of America* (Upper Saddle River, N.J.: Prentice-Hall, 1998), p. 367.

22. Ibid.

23. Computer Security Institute, "Cyber Crime Bleeds U.S. Corporations, Survey Shows," April 7, 2002, http://www.gocsi.com/press/20020407.jhtml?-requestid=44810.

24. Mark Landler, "A Filipino Linked to 'Love Bug' Talks About His License to Hack," *New York Times*, October 21, 2000.

25. Sloan, *Computers and the Law*, pp. 9–10.

26. Ibid.

27. Department of Justice, Southern District of New York, "Ex-Official of Manhattan Computer Consulting Firm Pleads Guilty to Computer Attack Charge, September 9, 2004, http://www.cybercrime.gov

28. Computer Security Institute, "Cyber Crime Bleeds U.S. Corporations."

29. Paul Fichtman, "Identity Fraud: The Threat to the Internet," *The Informant* (National Center for White Collar Crime, September 2000), p. 4.

30. Debra E. Ross, "Identity Theft" in Lawrence M. Salinger, ed., *Encyclopedia of White-Collar and Corporate Crime*, Vol 1 (Thousand Oaks, Calif.: Sage, 2005), pp. 412–13.

31. Federal Trade Commission, *National and State Trends in Fraud and Identity Theft*, January 22, 2004.

32. Synovate Research, *Identity Theft Report*, Federal Trade Commission, September, 2003.

33. Ibid.

34. Daniel Pope, "Advertising as a Consumer Issue: An Historical View," *Journal of Social Issues* 47 (1991): 41–56; Ivan Preston, *The Great American Blow Up: Puffery in Advertising and Selling* (Madison, Wis.: University of Wisconsin Press, 1975), pp. 233–38.

35. David R. Simon and D. Stanley Eitzen, *Elite Deviance* (Boston: Allyn and Bacon, 1982), p. 87.

36. "AGS, SASF Unit Reach $41.8 Million Settlement in Synthetic Thyroid Hormone Case," *Corporate Crime Reporter* (August 9, 1999): 3.

37. *Corporate Crime Reporter* 14 (January 3, 2000): 3.

38. Ibid., p. 4.

39. Bequai, *White Collar Crime*, p. 55.

40. Christopher D. Stone, *Where the Law Ends: The Social Control of Corporate Behavior* (New York: Harper & Row, 1975), p. 175.

41. Ibid., pp. 175–76.

42. Philip G. Schrag, *Counsel for the Deceived: Case Studies in Consumer Fraud* (New York: Pantheon Books, 1972).

43. William N. Leonard and Marvin Glenn Weber, "Automakers and Dealers: A Study of Criminogenic Market Forces," *Law and Society Review* 4 (February 1976): 407–24.

44. See Ronald J. Ostrow, "Chrysler, 2 Executives Face Odometer Fraud Charges," *Los Angeles Times*, June 25, 1987, pt. I, pp. 1, 25.

45. John Braithwaite, "An Exploratory Study of Used Car Fraud," in *Two Faces of Deviance*, Paul R. Wilson and John Braithwaite, eds. (Queensland, Australia: University of Queensland Press, 1979); Gary Green, *Occupational Crime* (Chicago: Nelson-Hall, 1990), p. 215.

46. Paul Blumberg, *The Predatory Society: Deception in the American Marketplace* (New York: Oxford University Press, 1989), p. 66.

47. Simon and Eitzen, *Elite Deviance*, p. 89.

48. Blumberg, *The Predatory Society*, p. 64.

49. Paul Jesilow, Deterring Automobile Repair Fraud: A Field Experiment, Ph.D. Dissertation, University of California, Irvine, 1982.

50. Friedrichs, *Trusted Criminals*, p. 99.

51. Ibid., p. 104.

52. National Health Care Anti-Fraud Association, "Health Care Fraud," http://www.nhcaa.org, 2002, p.2.

53. Stephen Rosenberg and James Posner, "Medicaid Surveillance and Utilization Review: A Description of the Medicaid Surveillance, Review and Enforcement Activities of the New York City Department of Health," in Allen Spiegel and Simon Podair, eds. *Medicaid: Lessons for National Health Insurance* (Rockville, Md.: Aspen Systems Corporation, 1975), pp. 93–100.

54. "The Medicaid Grifters," *Time*, July 13, 1992, p. 20.

55. Stuart Auerbach, "Medicaid Examiners Find Fraud Rampant," *Los Angeles Times*, August 30, 1995, p. 1 passim.

56. Gilbert Geis, Paul Jesilow, Henry Pontell, and Mary Jane O'Brien, "Fraud and Abuse of Government Medical Benefit Programs by Psychiatrists," *American Journal of Psychiatry* 142(2) 1985:231–34; Green, *Occupational Crime*, p. 194.

57. Rosoff, Pontell, and Tillman, *Profit Without Honor*, pp. 326–27, 333–34.

58. Henry N. Pontell, Paul D. Jesilow, and Gilbert Geis, "Policing Physicians: Practitioner Fraud and Abuse in a Government Medical Program," *Social Problems* 30 (October 1982): 117–25.

59. Friedrichs, *Trusted Criminals*, p. 106.

60. William E. Blundell, "Equity Funding: I Did It for Jollies," in *Crime at the Top: Deviance in Business and the Professions*, John M. Johnson and Jack D. Douglas, eds. (Philadelphia: J. B. Lippincott, 1978), pp. 153–85; Sobel, *Corruption in Business*, pp. 172–74.

61. Robert A. Rosenblatt, "Lincoln Savings Law Firm Faces $275 Million Penalty," *Los Angeles Times*, March 3, 1992, pp. A1, A10.

62. James S. Granelli and James Bates, "Keating Guilty of Fraud; Faces 10-Year Term," *Los Angeles Times*, December 5, 1991, pp. A1, A18; Tom Furlong, "Holders of Worthless Bonds Cheer, Say Justice Is Served," *Los Angeles Times*, December 5, 1991, p. A18; Associated Press, "Keating Guilty on 17 Counts," *San Luis Obispo Telegram-Tribune*, December 5, 1991, p. A1.

63. "Lazard Settles Yield-Burning Case for $11 Million," Corporate Crime Reporter (April 26, 1999): 3–4; "Alex Brown Inc. to Pay $15.3 Million to Settle Fraud Charges in Municipal Bond 'Yield-Burning' Case," *Corporate Crime Reporter* (November 22, 1999): 1, 3; "Big Securities Firms to Pay $140 Million to Settle Yield-Burning Cases," *Corporate Crime Reporter* (April 10, 2000): 4–5.

64. James S. Wallerstein and Clemett S. Wyle, "Our Law-Abiding Law-Breakers," *National Probation* (March–April 1947): 107–12.

65. Friedrichs, *Trusted Criminals,* p. 206.

66. Robert D. Hershey Jr., "I.R.S. Raises Its Estimate of Tax Cheating," *New York Times,* December 29, 1993, pp. C1, C6.

67. Friedrichs, *Trusted Criminals,* p. 208.

68. "A Taxing Battle," *The Economist,* January 31, 2004, p. 71.

69. See James B. Stewart, *Den of Thieves* (New York: Simon & Schuster, 1991).

70. "State Government Riddled by Conflicts of Interest, Study Finds," *Corporate Crime Reporter* (June 12, 2000): 4–5.

71. Federal Election Commission, http://www.fed.gov, March 2000.

72. Mark J. Green, *Who Runs Congress?* 3rd ed. (New York: Bantam Books, 1979), p. 74.

73. Gary C. Jacobson, *Money in Congressional Elections* (New Haven, Conn.: Yale University Press, 1980), p. 157.

74. Stephen Labaton, "On the Money Trail, Most 'Insiders' Had the Advantage," *New York Times,* November 9, 1994, p. B1.

75. This figure was calculated from data in *Congressional Quarterly, Congressional Ethics,* pp. 172–75; and in Green, *Who Runs Congress?,* pp. 156–57.

76. Robert W. Stewart and Tracy Wood, "Political Giving: Corporate Contributions Buy Access," *Los Angeles Times,* October 26, 1986, pt. I, p. 1 passim.

77. Sara Fritz and Dwight Morris, "Political Money by the Bundle," *Los Angeles Times,* July 30, 1990, pp. A1, A14–15.

78. "Campaign Finance Reform," http://www.opensecrets.org, July 26, 2001.

79. Paul H. Douglas, *Ethics in Government* (Cambridge, Mass.: Harvard University Press, 1952), p. 44.

80. See James William Coleman and Donald P. Cressey, *Social Problems* (New York: HarperCollins, 1996), pp. 62–91.

81. Lawrence K. Altman, "Drug Errors and Adverse Reactions Are Studied," *New York Times,* January 22, 1997, p. A10; Boyce Rensberger, "Thousands a Year Killed by Faulty Prescriptions," *New York Times,* January 28, 1976, p. 1 passim.

82. "Adverse Drug Reactions May Cause Over 100,000 Deaths Among Hospitalized Patients Each Year, Study Finds," *Corporate Crime Reporter* (April 20, 1998): 5.

83. Green, *Occupational Crime,* p. 182.

84. Rosoff, Henry and Tillman, *Profit Without Honor,* p. 328.

85. Vivienne Walters, "Company Doctors' Perceptions of and Response to Conflicting Pressures from Labor and Management," *Social Problems* 30 (October 1982): 1–12.

86. Herbert Denenberg, "A Shopper's Guide to Dentistry," as quoted in *Power, Inc.,* Morton Mintz and Jerry Cohen, (New York: Daily Press, 1971)pp. 495–96.

87. Abraham S. Blumberg, "The Practice of Law as a Confidence Game: Organizational Cooptation of a Profession," *Law and Society Review* 1 (1967): 15–39.

88. Ibid.; and Abraham S. Blumberg, *Criminal Justice* (Chicago: Quadrangle Books, 1970).

89. Peter Rutter, *Sex in the Forbidden Zone* (New York: Fawcett, 1989).

90. Ibid., pp. 39–40.

91. James E. Sorenson, Hugh D. Grove, and Thomas L. Sorenson, "Detecting Management Fraud: The Role of the Independent Auditor," in *White Collar Crime: Theory and Research,* Gilbert Geis and Ezra Stotland, eds. (Beverly Hills, Calif.: Sage, 1980), pp. 221–51.

92. Robert A. Rosenblatt, "Auditor Pays $400 Million for Not Signaling S&L Crisis," *Los Angeles Times*, November 24, 1992, pp. A1, A21; Associated Press, "Accountants to Pay $400 Million Fine in S&L Case," *San Luis Obispo Telegram-Tribune*, November 24, 1992, p. A2.

93. Robert A. Rosenblatt, "Lincoln Savings Law Firm Faces $275 Million Penalty," *Los Angeles Times*, March 3, 1992, pp. A1, A10; Robert A. Rosenblatt, "Lincoln Savings Law Firm to Pay U.S. $41 Million," *Los Angeles Times*, March 9, 1992; Donna K. H. Walters, "New Liability Twist Has Lawyers, Accountants Scurrying," *Los Angeles Times*, March 29, 1992, pp. D1, D7.

94. Kristen Rouse, "Arthur Andersen," in Lawrence M. Salinger, ed., *Encyclopedia of White-Collar and Corporate Crime*, Vol. 1 (Thousand Oaks, Calif.: Sage, 2005), pp. 57–58; *Washington Post*, Corporate Scandal Primer, http://www.washingtonpost.com, April 15, 2004.

95. Yerachmiel Kugel and Gladys W. Gruenberg, *International Payoffs* (Lexington, Mass.: Lexington Books, 1977), p. 12.

96. "Commercial Bribery: Letter from the Federal Trade Commission," May 15, 1918, 66th Cong., 2nd sess., Senate Document No. 258, March 20, 1920, p. 3.

97. See Clinard and Yeager, *Corporate Crime*, p. 186; W. Michael Reisman, *Folded Lies: Bribery, Crusades, and Reforms* (New York: Free Press, 1979), p. 44.

98. Neil H. Jacoby, Peter Nehemkis, and Richard Eells, *Bribery and Corruption* (New York: Macmillan, 1977), p. 119.

99. Jason Davis, "Bribery," in Lawrence M. Salinger, ed., *Encyclopedia of White-Collar and Corporate Crime*, Vol. 1 (Thousand Oaks, Calif.: Sage, 2005), pp. 110–13.

100. Kugel and Gruenberg, *International Payoffs*, pp. 61–63; Clinard and Yeager, *Corporate Crime*, p. 172.

101. Karen Tumulty, "Kickbacks Common in Southland, Panel Told," *Los Angeles Times*, February 28, 1986, pt. IV, p. 2.

102. *Corporate Crime Reporter* 1 (April 27, 1987): 14–18.

103. Ibid., 10–16.

104. "'Operation Forbidden Fruit' Busts USDA Inspectors in Bribery Scheme," *Corporate Crime Reporter* (November 1, 1999): 4.

105. Transparency International, Corruption Perceptions Index, 2003, http://www.transparencyinternational.org.

106. Commission to Investigate Allegations of Police Corruption and the Anti-Corruption Procedures of the Police Department, *Commission Report* (New York: City of New York, 1994); New York Legislature, *Report and Proceedings of the Senate Committee Appointed to Investigate the Police Department of the City of New York* (Lexow Committee) (Albany: State Printing Office, 1895); New York Legislature, *Report of the Joint Committee on the Government of the City of New York* (Seabury Committee) (Albany: State Printing Office, 1932); *The Knapp Commission Report on Police Corruption* (New York: George Braziller), 1972.

107. Special Committee to Investigate Organized Crime in Interstate Commerce, *Final Report*, U.S. Senate Report no. 307, 82nd Cong. (Washington, D.C.: U.S. Government Printing Office, 1951); *Chicago City Council, Report of the Commission on Crime* (Chicago: Author, 1915); Pennsylvania Crime Commission, *Report on Police Corruption and the Quality of Law Enforcement in Philadelphia* (1974).

108. Edwin H. Sutherland and Donald R. Cressey, *Criminology*, 10th ed. (Philadelphia: J. B. Lippincott, 1978), p. 402.

109. Sanja Kutnjak Ivkovic, "To Serve and Collect: Measuring Police Corruption," *The Journal of Criminal Law and Criminology*, 93 (Winter and Spring, 2003): 593–650.

110. William A. Westley, *Violence and the Police* (Cambridge, Mass.: MIT Press, 1970), p. 110.

111. On police subcultures, see Westley, *Violence and the Police*; and Jerome H. Skolnick, *Justice Without Trial: Law Enforcement in Democratic Society* (New York: Wiley, 1966), pp. 42–70.

112. Skolnick, *Justice Without Trial*, p. 208.

113. Knapp Commission Report, p. 71.

114. Ibid., p. 65.

115. Pennsylvania Crime Commission, *Report on Police Corruption*, p. 5.

116. Commission to Investigate Allegations of Police Corruption and the Anti-Corruption Procedures of the Police Department, *Commission Report.*

117. "The Rampart Scandal, http://www.pbs.org/wsbh/pages/frontline/shows/scandal/ July 26, 2001; Miles Corvin, "Judge Orders Perez Released from Prison," *Los Angeles Times*, July 5, 2001.

118. Sean Purdy, "Perjury," pp. 603–607 in Lawrence M. Salinger, ed., *Encyclopedia of White-Collar and Corporate Crime*, Vol. 2 (Thousand Oaks, Calif.: Sage, 2005).

119. Christopher Slobogin, "Testifying: Police Perjury and What to Do About It," *University of Colorado Law Review*, 67 (Fall 1996).

120. Robert Welkos, "Nevada Inquiry Becomes a Clash of Personalities," *Los Angeles Times*, January 13, 1984, pt. I, p. 1 passim; Bob Secter, "House Unanimous in Vote to Impeach Judge Claiborne," *Los Angeles Times*, July 23, 1986, pt. I, p.1 passim; "U.S. Judge in Nevada Convicted of Filing False Income Tax Forms," *New York Times*, August 11, 1984, p. 1; "Senate Impeaches Claiborne," *San Luis Obispo Telegram-Tribune*, October 10, 1986, p. 2A.

121. Associated Press, "Four Florida Judges Indicted in a U.S. Corruption Inquiry," *New York Times*, September 25, 1991, p. A15.

122. Henry Weinstein, "Prosecutor Misconduct Probed in National Study," *Los Angeles Times*, June 26, 2003, p. A24.

123. The figure was calculated from data in *Congressional Quarterly, Congressional Ethics*, 2nd ed. (Washington, D.C.: Congressional Quarterly, 1980) pp. 172–75, and Green, *Who Runs Congress?* pp. 156–57.

124. Ibid.

125. "Congress Feels the Sting," *U.S. News & World Report*, February 18, 1980, pp. 19–21; "Abscam's Toll," *Time*, August 24, 1981, p. 20; "End of a Sleazy Affair," *Newsweek*, March 22, 1982.

126. David R. Simon and Frank E. Hagan, *White Collar Deviance* (Boston: Allyn and Bacon, 1999).

127. Friedrichs, *Trusted Criminals*, p. 147.

128. Ibid., pp. 148–149.

129. See Anthony Sampson, *The Seven Sisters: The Great Oil Companies and the World They Shaped* (New York: Bantam Books, 1975), pp. 27–28.

130. See John M. Blair, *The Control of Oil* (New York: Random House, 1976), pp. 246–51, for an explanation of the reasons for the vulnerability of the independents.

131. Ibid., pp. 235–60.

132. Judith Miller, "U.S. Aides Withheld Data on Oil, House Report Says," *New York Times*, January 4, 1980.

133. Eric Young, "Oil Companies Rig Gas Prices, Watchdog Days," *Los Angeles Times*, September 23, 1991, pp. D1, D6; Patrick Lee, "Overpricing Report Wrong, Arco Charges," *Los Angeles Times*, October 25, 1991, pp. D1, D12.

134. "In First Corporate Sentence Under Economic Espionage Act, Four Will Pay $5 Million," *Corporate Crime Reporter* 14(2): 1. 2000.

135. Joel Brinkely and Steve Lohr, "Retracing the Missteps in Microsoft's Defense at Its Antitrust Trial," *New York Times*, June 8, 2000.

136. Linda Greenhouse, "If Microsoft Is Sawed in Half What Does Antitrust Mean in a Software Driven World," *New York Times*, June 8, 2000; Joel Brinkley, "Microsoft Breakup Is Ordered for Antitrust Violations," *New York Times*, June 8, 2000, p. 1 passim.

137. Reuters, October 28, 2003; "Memorandum Opinion," United States District Court for the District of Columbia, Civil Action No. 98–1232, September 22, 2003.

138. Eric Bangeman, "EU Court of First Instance hears Microsoft Antitrust Appeal," October 10, 2004, http://arstechnica.com/news.ars.

139. Michael Hiltzik and Jube Shiver, Jr., "Breakup of Microsoft Is Overturned on Appeal" *Los Angeles Times*, June 29, 2001; Stephen Labaton, "Microsoft Case Back in Play, and the Lobbying Heats Up," *New York Times*, June 30, 2001.

140. Samuel Richardson Reid, *The New Industrial Order: Concentration, Regulation and Public Policy* (New York: McGraw-Hill, 1976). The figures are for the years 1947–1968, from Chart 5.1, p. 64.

141. Ibid., pp. 152–53.

142. Ibid.

143. "Public Interest Coalition Calls for Increased Budgets for FTC, Justice Antitrust Enforcement," *Corporate Crime Reporter* (September 20, 1999): 3–4.

144. Eva Cheng, What's driving the wave of corporate mergers? October 2004, http://www.greenleft.org.

145. Mark J. Green, Beverly L. Moore, and Bruce Wasserstein, *The Closed Enterprise System: Ralph Nader's Study Group's Report on Antitrust Enforcement* (New York: Grossman, 1972), pp. 149–50.

146. *Northwestern Law Review* 151 (1962), as quoted in Green, Moore, and Wasserstein, *Closed Enterprise System*, p. 150.

147. Marshall B. Clinard, Peter C. Yeager, Jeanne Brissette, David Petrashek, and Elizabeth Harries, *Illegal Corporate Behavior* (Washington, D.C.: U.S. Government Printing Office, 1979), p. 184.

148. Blair, *Control of Oil*, p. 60.

149. Ibid., p. 71.

150. Ibid., p. 63.

151. Ralph Nader, "Introduction," in Green, Moore, and Wasserstein, *Closed Enterprise System*, p. x.

152. "Big Money and the Energy Crisis," March 2002, Common Cause, http://www.commoncause.org.

153. Richard Simon, Ricardo Alonso-Zaldivar, and Tim Reiterman, "Enron Menos Stir Calls for Wider Investigation," *Los Angeles Times*, May 7, 2002; Ricardo Alonso-Zaldivar, Joseph Menn, and Nancy Rivera, "Ex-Enron Trader Admits Rigging Energy Market" *Los Angeles Times*, October 18, 2002.

154. Ricardo Alonso-Zaldivar and Nancy Vogel, "Energy Dealings Ruled Illegal," *Los Angeles Times*, September 24, 2002.

155. Ibid.; James Sterngold, "5 Power Generators Sued in California," *New York Times,* May 3, 2001.

156. "Hoffmann-LaRoche and BASF to Pay Record Criminal Fines for Participating in International Vitamin Cartel, LaRoche to Pay $500 Million, Highest Criminal Fine Ever," *Corporate Crime Reporter* (May 24, 1999) 1, 3; "Three Japanese Companies Plead Guilty, Pay Fines for Participating in International Vitamin Cartel," *Corporate Crime Reporter* (September 13, 1999): 5; "Four European Executives Plead Guilty to International Vitamin Cartel," *Corporate Crime Reporter* (April 10, 2000): 6.

157. "Hoffmann-LaRoche and BASF to Pay Record Criminal Fines for Participating in International Vitamin Cartel, LaRoche to Pay $500 Million, Highest Criminal Fine Ever," *Corporate Crime Reporter* (May 24, 1999): 3.

158. "Mylan Settles Price-Fixing Charges, to Pay $100 Million," *Corporate Crime Reporter* (July 17, 2000): 1; "FTC Charges Generic Drug Maker Mylan Labs with Restraint of Trade. From $11 to $337 a Bottle," *Corporate Crime Reporter* (January 4, 1999): 4.

159. Quoted in Jethro K. Lieberman, *Crisis at the Bar: Lawyers' Unethical Ethics and What to Do About It* (New York: Norton, 1978), p. 111.

160. Ibid., 110–13.

161. Ed Cray, in *Failing Health: The Medical Crisis and the AMA* (Indianapolis: Bobbs-Merrill, 1970), pp. 182–99.

162. Lieberman, *Crisis at the Bar,* pp. 79–87.

163. Rebecca S. Katz, "Sexual Harassment," in Lawrence M. Salinger, ed., *Encyclopedia of White-Collar and Corporate Crime,* Vol. 1 (Thousand Oaks, Calif.: Sage, 2005), pp. 737–41; Theodore Caplow, *American Social Trends* (San Diego: Harcourt Brace Jovanovich, 1991), pp. 153–54; Carol McGraw, "Employers, Workers Act to Fight Job Harassment," *Los Angeles Times,* October 21, 1990, pp. A1, A30; Lloyd D. Elgart and Lillian Schanfield, "Sexual Harassment of Students," *Thought and Action* (Spring 1991): 21–42.

164. Rebecca S. Katz, "Sexual Harassment," in Salinger, ed., *White-Collar and Corporate Crime,* pp. 737–41.

165. Ibid.

166. Green, *Occupational Crime,* p. 188.

167. U.S. Bureau of the Census, *Money Income in the United States,* 2001, p. 2.

168. Marcia Staimer, "Do Workers Have Private Lives?" *USA Today,* May 13, 1991, pp. A1, A2.

169. Elys A. McLean, "Working to Avoid Violence," *USA Today,* April 27, 1994, p. B1.

170. Thomas B. Rosenstiel, "Someone May Be Watching," *Los Angeles Times,* May 18, 1994, pp. A1, A12.

171. Ibid.

172. S. Prakash Sethi, *Up Against the Corporate Wall,* 2nd ed. (Englewood Cliffs, N.J.: Prentice-Hall, 1974), p. 374.

173. Ibid., p. 398.

174. Ibid., pp. 424–51.

175. Quoted in Norman Solomon, "Nuclear Big Brother," *The Progressive* 44 (January 1980): 9.

176. Ibid., pp. 14–21; Vasil Pappas, "Some Utilities Generate Sparks by Keeping Close Eye on Critics," *Wall Street Journal,* January 11, 1979, pp. 1, 32.

177. See Richard E. Morgan, *Domestic Intelligence: Monitoring Dissent in America* (Austin: University of Texas Press, 1980), pp. 15–36, for a review of the early history of domestic intelligence in the United States.

178. See Athan Theoharis, *Spying on Americans: Political Surveillance from Hoover to the Houston Plan* (Philadelphia: Temple University Press, 1978).

179. Gary T. Marx, "Thoughts on a Neglected Category of Social Movement Participant: The Agent Provocateur and the Informant," *American Journal of Sociology* 80 (September 1974): 402–42.

180. See Theoharis, *Spying on Americans*, pp. 94–132.

181. Nelson Blackstock, *COINTELPRO: The FBI's Secret War on Political Freedom* (New York: Vintage Books, 1975), p. ix; Julian Roebuck and Stanley C. Weeber, *Political Crime in the United States: Analyzing Crime by and Against Government* (New York: Praeger, 1978), p. 111.

182. "FBI Behind Burglaries of Central American Agencies?" *San Luis Obispo Telegram-Tribune*, February 21, 1987, p. 14A; Eric Pianin, "Hill Told of FBI Drive on Foreign Policy Critics," *Washington Post*, February 21, 1987, p. A8.

183. Roebuck and Weeber, *Political Crime*, pp. 107–10, 114–15.

184. Solomon, "Nuclear Big Brother"; Roebuck and Weeber, *Political Crime*, p. 114; Gene Blake, "New ACLU Suit Aims at Right-Wing Group," *Los Angeles Times*, April 19, 1984, pt. III, p. 1.

185. Julie Cart, "Denver Police Spied on Activists, ACLU Says," *Los Angeles Times*, March 22, 2002.

186. See Noam Chomsky, "Introduction," in Blackstock, *COINTELPRO*, pp. 7–8; Roebuck and Weeber, Political Crime, pp. 29–31; David Wise, "The Campaign to Destroy Martin Luther King," *New York Review of Books* 23 (November 11, 1976): 38–42.

187. Charles Nicodemus, "Anti-Dissent Techniques Varied Widely," *Los Angeles Times*, August 22, 1979, pt. I, pp. 4–6.

188. Chomsky, "Introduction," pp. 15–16; Patrick Dillon, "San Diego Police Linked to 1972 Cover Up," *San Diego Union*, June 2, 1976.

189. Andrew Karmen, "Agents Provocateurs in the Contemporary U.S. Leftist Movement," in C. Reasons, ed. *The Criminologist: Crime and the Criminal* (Pacific Palisades, Calif.: Goodyear, 1974).

190. Charles Nicodemus, "Newly Opened Files Shed Added Light on FBI's War," *Los Angeles Times*, August 22, 1979, pt. IA, pp. 3–4.

191. David Wise and Thomas B. Ross, *The Invisible Government* (New York: Random House, 1964), pp. 136–46.

192. Morton H. Halperin, Jerry J. Berman, Robert L. Borosage, and Christine M. Marwick, *The Lawless State: The Crimes of U.S. Intelligence Agencies* (Middlesex, England: Penguin, 1976), pp. 42–44; Fred Branfman, "The Secret Wars of the CIA," in Howard Frazier, ed., *Uncloaking the CIA* (New York: Macmillan, 1978), pp. 90–100.

193. Select Committee to Study Governmental Operations with Respect to Intelligence Activities, *Alleged Assassination Plots Involving Foreign Leaders* (Washington, D.C.: U.S. Government Printing Office, November 18, 1975).

194. Select Committee to Study Governmental Operations with Respect to Intelligence Activities, *United States Senate, Covert Action in Chile: 1963–1973* (Washington, D.C.: U.S. Government Printing Office, 1975), p. 12.

195. Ibid., p. 33.

196. Ibid., p. 225.

197. The best source on the CIA's covert action in Chile is Senate Select Committee, Covert Action in Chile. For information on the plot against General Schneider, see Select Committee, *Alleged Assassination Plots*, pp. 225–54. Other sources include Harold R.

Kerbo, "Foreign Involvement in the Preconditions for Political Violence: The World System and the Case of Chile," *Journal of Conflict Resolution* 22 (September 1978): 363–91; and Halperin et al., *Lawless State*, pp. 15–29.

198. Public Law 98–473, October 12, 1984, p. 1935.

199. See Richard Alan White, *The Morass: United States Intervention in Central America* (New York: Harper & Row, 1984); Steven Strasser, "The CIA's Harbor Warfare," *Newsweek*, April 11, 1984; Margaret Shapiro, "House Committee Rules CIA Manual Was Illegal," *Denver Post*, December 6, 1984, p. 14A.

200. "The Argument about 'Enemy Combatants: A Few Good Men,' *The Economist*, January 17, 2004, p. 26.

201. Melvin Small and J. David Singer, *Resort to Arms: International and Civil Wars, 1816–1980* (Beverly Hills, Calif.: Sage, 1982), pp. 293–94.

202. James F. Dunnigan and William Martel, *How to Stop a War: The Lessons of Two Hundred Years of War and Peace* (New York: Doubleday, 1987), p. 81.

203. Ibid., p. 239; Small and Singer, *Resort to Arms*, p. 91.

204. Mark Hatfield, "US Needs Code of Conduct for Conventional Arms Trade," *Christian Science Monitor*, April 15, 1994, p. 18.

205. Friedrichs, *Trusted Criminals*, p. 129.

206. James William Coleman and Harold R. Kerbo, *Social Problems*, 8th ed. (Upper Saddle River, N.J.: Prentice Hall, 2002).

207. Rebecca S. Katz, "Hazardous Waste," pp387–391 in Salinger, ed., *The Encyclopedia of White-Collar and Corporate Crime*.

208. Richard T. Cooper and Paul E. Steiger, "Occupational Health Hazards—A National Crisis," *Los Angeles Times*, June 27, 1976, p. 1 passim; Daniel M. Berman, *Death on the Job: Occupational Health and Safety in the United States* (New York: Monthly Review Press, 1978), pp. 82–83; Brent Fisse and John Braithwaite, *The Impact of Publicity on Corporate Offenders* (Albany: State University of New York Press, 1983), pp. 63–70.

209. Oliver S. Owen, *Natural Resource Conservation: An Ecological Approach*, 3rd ed. (New York: Macmillan, 1980), p. 522.

210. Associated Press, "10 Years after Kepone, Fishing Ban Remains," *San Luis Obispo Telegram-Tribune*, July 29, 1985.

211. Edwin Sutherland, *White Collar Crime: The Uncut Version* (New Haven: Yale University Press, 1983).

212. Gary E. Reed and Peter C. Yeager, "Organizational Offending and Neoclassical Criminology: Challenging the Reach of a General Theory of Crime," *Criminology* 34 (1996): 357–82.

213. Donald L. Barlett and James B. Steele, "Paying a Price for Polluters," *Time*, November 23, 1998.

214. Paul Brodeur, *Expendable Americans* (New York: Viking, 1974), pp. 253–54.

215. Morton Mintz in the *Washington Post*, as reprinted in Brodeur, pp. 271–72.

216. Cooper and Steiger, "Occupational Health Hazards"; Brodeur, *Expendable Americans*, pp. 270–71.

217. R. Doll, *British Journal of Industrial Medicine* 12 (1955): 81.

218. Berman, *Death on the Job*, p. 85; John Coyners, "Corporate and White Collar Crime: A View by the Chairman of the House Subcommittee on Crime," *American Criminal Law Review* 17 (1980): 287–300; Henry Weinstein, "Did Asbestos Industry Suppress Data?" *Los Angeles Times*, October 23, 1978, p. 1 passim.

219. Cooper and Steiger, "Occupational Health Hazards"; Joseph A. Page and Mary-Win O'Brien, *Bitter Wages: Ralph Nader's Study Group Report on Disease and Injury on the Job* (New York: Grossman, 1973), p. 22.

220. Grayson Mitchell, "Firm Knew of Peril in Love Canal Chemical Waste 20 Years Ago, Investigators Say," *Los Angeles Times,* April 11, 1979; Bill Richards, "Ex-Residents of Love Canal Area Bitter about Contamination Results," *Sacramento Bee,* November 25, 1979, p. A22; Stephen W. Bell, "Love Canal: The Chemicals and the Hard Feelings Linger," *San Luis Obispo Telegram-Tribune,* November 15, 1986, p. 1C.

221. Debra E. Ross, "Love Canal," pp. 501–503 in Salinger, *The Encyclopedia of White-Collar and Corporate Crime.*

222. Matt Tallmer, "Chemical Dumping as a Corporate Way of Life" *in Corporate Violence: Injury and Death for Profit,* Stuart L. Hills, ed. (Totowa, N.J.: Rowman and Littlefield, 1988).

223. Andrew Szasz, "Corporations, Organized Crime, and the Disposal of Hazardous Waste: An Examination of the Making of a Criminogenic Regulatory Structure," *Criminology* 24 (1986): 1–27.

224. Paul R. Ehrlich, Anne H. Ehrlich, and John P. Holdren, *Ecoscience: Population, Resources, Environment* (San Francisco: W. H. Freeman, 1977), p. 574.

225. Ibid.

226. Reuters, "Mercury Poison Case Is Resolved in Japan," *New York Times,* May 23, 1996, p. A7; Marcia Stepanek, "'Minamata Disease': A Japanese Scandal," *San Francisco Examiner,* July 14, 1991, pp. A1, A14.

227. Friedrichs, *Trusted Criminals,* p. 72; Russell Mokhiber, *Corporate Crime and Violence* (San Francisco: Sierra Club Books, 1988).

228. Yingyi Situ and David Emmons, *Environmental Crime: The Criminal Justice System's Role in Protecting the Environment* (Thousand Oaks, Calif.: Sage Publications, 2000), p. 58.

229. Ibid., p. 55.

230. Ibid., p. 54.

231. Ibid., p. 87.

232. Ibid., pp. 91–96.

233. Rebecca S. Katz, "Hazardous Waste," in Salinger, *The Encyclopedia of White-Collar and Corporate Crime,* pp. 387–391.

234. Sally S. Simpson and Lori Elis, "Theoretical Perspectives on the Corporate Victimization of Women," in *Corporate Victimization of Women,* Elizabeth Szockyj and James G. Fox, eds. (Boston: Northeastern University Press, 1996), pp. 33–58; John P. Wright, Francis T. Cullen, and Michael B. Blankenship, "The Social Construction of Corporate Violence: Media Coverage of the Imperial Food Products Fire," *Crime and Delinquency* 41 (January 1995): 20–36.

235. Matthew B Robinson, "Defective Products," in Salinger, *The Encyclopedia of White-Collar and Corporate Crime,* pp. 247–52.

236. Quoted in Mintz and Cohen, *Power, Inc.,* p. 110.

237. Reginald Stuart, "U.S. Agency Suggests Ford Pintos Have a Fuel System Defect," *New York Times,* May 9, 1978.

238. "Ford Pinto Scored in Coast Magazine on Peril from Fires," *New York Times,* August 11, 1977; Jeffrey Mills, "Supplementary Material," *New York Times,* August 31, 1978; Mark Dowie, "Pinto Madness," in *Crisis in American Institutions,* 4th ed., Jerome Skolnick and Elliott Currie, eds. (Boston: Little Brown, 1979), p. 26.

239. Reginald Stuart, "Ford Orders Recall of 1.5 Million Pintos for Safety Changes," *New York Times,* June 10, 1978.

240. Ibid.; Fisse and Braithwaite, *Impact of Publicity*, pp. 41–54.

241. "Internal Memo Reportedly Noted Firestone Tire Failures in 1972," *New York Times*, December 23, 1978.

242. "Forewarnings of Fatal Flaws," *Time*, June 25, 1979, pp. 58–60.

243. Jo Thomas, "Firestone Knew of Tire Defects 5 Years Before Recall, Papers Show," *New York Times*, December 24, 1978.

244. Ibid.

245. *New York Times*, March 28, 1978, p. 63.

246. Steven Rattner, "Tire Tentatively Found Defective," *New York Times*, July 9, 1978.

247. "Fatal Flaws," *Time*, June 25, 1979.

248. John Odell and Edmund Sanders, "Firestone Begins Replacement of 6.4 Million Tires," *Los Angeles Times*, August 10, 2000, pp. A1, A21.

249. Ed Garsten, "Ford to Spend $2.1 Billion Replacing Firestone Tires," *San Luis Obispo County Tribune*, May 23, 2001, pp. A1, A8.

250. Ricardo Alonso-Saldivar, "Firestone Worried about Tire Recall in '99," *Los Angeles Times*, September 6, 2000.

251. Debra E. Ross, "Pharmaceutical Industry," pp. 610–14 in Salinger, *The Encyclopedia of White-Collar and Corporate Crime*.

252. Quoted in Mintz and Cohen, *Power, Inc.*, p. 249.

253. Quoted in Stone, *Where the Law Ends*, p. 54.

254. Stanford J. Unger, "Get Away with What You Can," in Robert L. Heilbroner, *In the Name of Profit* (Garden City, N.Y.: Doubleday, 1977) p. 126.

255. Don C. Gibbons, "Crime and Punishment: A Study in Social Attitudes," *Social Forces* 47 (June 1969): 392.

256. Morton Mintz and Jerry Cohen, *America, Inc.* (New York: Dial Press, 1971), p. 268.

257. Nelson, "Health Safety Cutbacks"; Morton Mintz, "Lilly Official Knew of Deaths before U.S. Approved Drug," *Washington Post*, July 22, 1983; Morton Mintz, "Lilly Chairman Decided to Sell Oraflex Despite Deaths," *Washington Post*, November 13, 1983.

258. Russell Mokhiber, "Greedy Corporations: Criminals by Any Other Name," *Los Angeles Daily Journal*, August 28, 1986, p. 4.

259. Mark Dowie and Tracy Johnston, "A Case of Corporate Malpractice," *Mother Jones*, November 1976. Also, Barbara Ehrenreich, Mark Dowie, and Stephen Minkin, "The Charge: Genocide; The Accused: The U.S. Government," *Mother Jones* 4 (November 1979): 28.

260. Barry Siegel, "One Man's Efforts to Tell Dalkon Story," *Los Angeles Times*, August 22, 1985, p. 1 passim.

261. Mokhiber, "Greedy Corporations."

262. Jonathan Peterson and Jesus Sanchez, "Merger May Clear Way to Settle Dalkon Shield Cases," *Los Angeles Times*, July 4, 1987, p. 1 passim.

263. Green, *Occupational Crime*, p. 128.

264. Lucinda M. Finley, "The Pharmaceutical Industry and Women's Reproductive Health," in Szockyj and Fox, *Corporate Victimization of Women*, pp. 59–110; Friedrichs, *Trusted Criminals*, p. 76; Mokhiber, *Corporate Crime and Violence*.

265. Ehrenreich, Dowie, and Minkin, "The Charge: Genocide," pp. 28–31.

266. John Braithwaite, *Corporate Crime in the Pharmaceutical Industry* (London: Routledge and Kegan Paul, 1984), pp. 260–61.

267. Morton Mintz, "If There Are No Side Effects, This Must Be Honduras," *Mother Jones* 4 (November 1979): 32–33; also see Braithwaite, *Corporate Crime in the Pharmaceutical Industry*, pp. 247–56.

268. Ibid., p. 250.

269. Tom Masland and Ruth Marshall, "'A Really Nasty Business,'" *Newsweek*, November 5, 1990, pp. 36–43.

270. Philip J. Hilts, *Smokescreen: The Truth Behind the Tobacco Industry Cover-up* (Reading, Mass.: Addison-Wesley, 1996), p. 105; Friedrich, *Trusted Criminals*, p. 79; David R. Simon, *Elite Deviance*, 5th ed. (Boston: Allyn and Bacon, 1996), p. 136.

271. Sheryl Stolberg, "Mortality Study Finds Tobacco Is No. 1 Culprit," *Los Angeles Times*, November 10, 1993, pp. A1, A33.

272. Hilts, *Smokescreen*, p. 55.

273. Ibid., pp. 122–23.

274. Ibid., p. 65.

275. Ibid., pp. 65–70; Richard W. Pollay, "Targeting Tactics in Selling Smoke: Youthful Aspects of 20th Century Cigarette Advertising," *Journal of Marketing Theory and Practice* (Special Issue) 3 (Winter 1995).

276. Myron Levin, "Verdict Deals Tobacco Firms a Historic Defeat," *Los Angeles Times*, June 11, 1998, p. A1.

277. Ibid.; Rick Bragg, "Tobacco Lawsuit in Florida Yields Record Damages," *New York Times*, July 15, 2000.

278. Myron Levin, "Last of 46 State Officials Sign Tobacco Accord," *Los Angeles Times*, November 21, 1998, p A1.

279. Marc Kakufman, "U.S. Case Against Tobacco to Begin," *San Luis Obispo County Tribune*, September 20, 2004, pp. A1 and A4.

280. James Sterngold, *Burning Down the House: How Greed, Deceit, and Bitter Revenge Destroyed E. F. Hutton* (New York: Summit Books, 1990), esp. pp. 75–80, 86–87, 126–33.

281. Dan G. Stone, *April Fools: An Insider's Account of the Rise and Collapse of Drexel Burnham* (New York: Donald I. Fine, 1990), esp. pp. 156–57; Scot J. Paltrow, "Drexel Admits Guilt; to Pay $650 Million," *Los Angeles Times*, December 22, 1988, pt. I, pp. 1, 28; Mary Zey, *Banking on Fraud: Drexel, Junk Bonds, and Buyouts* (New York: Aldine de Gruyter, 1993).

282. Scot J. Paltrow, "Salomon Admits More Bond Auctions Violations," *Los Angeles Times*, August 15, 1991, pp. D1, D4; Associated Press, "Salomon Agrees to Pay $290 Million for Scandal," *San Luis Obispo Telegram-Tribune*, May 21, 1992, p. A3.

283. Susan Dentzer, "Greed on Wall Street," *Newsweek*, May 26, 1986; *Corporate Crime Reporter* 1 (April 13, 1987): 13.

284. Michael A. Hiltzik, "Inside Trader to Pay Penalty of $100 Million," *Los Angeles Times*, November 15, 1986, pp. 1, 30; Stewart, *Den of Thieves*, p. 448.

285. See Stewart, *Den of Thieves*; Zey, *Banking on Fraud*.

286. Douglas Frantz and Larry Green, "Sting in Chicago Shows FBI's New Skill at Cracking 'Crime in the Suites,'" *Los Angeles Times*, February 12, 1989, pt. IV, pp. 1, 6.

287. Barry Bearak and Tom Furlong, "Totting Up Blame for S&L Crisis," *Los Angeles Times*, December 16, 1990, pp. A1, A34–36.

288. Robert Rosenblatt, "U.S. Recoups Only a Fraction of the Funds from S&L Frauds," *Los Angeles Times*, February 7, 1992, pp. A1, A23; James S. Granelli, "Probe of Local S&L Hindered by Shortages," *Los Angeles Times*, July 5, 1990, pp. D1, D8; Calavita

and Pontell, " 'Other People's Money' Revisited"; General Accounting Office, "Thrift Failures: Costly Failures Resulted from Regulatory Violations and Unsafe Practices," Report to the Congress, GAO/AFMD-89–62, June 1989; Associated Press, "White Collar to Blame for S&L Crisis, GAO Tells House Panel," *Los Angeles Times,* March 23, 1989.

289. Frank Hagan and Peter Benekos, "What Charles Keating and 'Murph the Surf' Have in Common: A Symbiosis of Professional and Occupational and Corporate Crime," paper presented at the American Society of Criminology, San Francisco, November 1991; Calavita and Pontell, "'Other People's Money' Revisited."

290. Quoted in Steven Waldman and Rich Thomas, "How Did It Happen?" *Newsweek,* May 21, 1990, p. 27.

291. Peter Behr and April Witt, "The Fall of Enron: Visionary's Dream Led to Risky Business," *Washington Post* July 28, 2002, p. A1, passim; Peter Behr and April Witt, "The Fall of Enron: Dream Job Turns into Nightmare," *Washington Post,* July 29, 2002, p. A1, passim; Peter Behr and April Witt, "The Fall of Enron: Concerns Grow Amid Conflicts," *Washington Post,* July 30, 2002, p. A1, passim; Peter Behr and April Witt, "The Fall of Enron: Losses, Conflicts Threaten Survival," *Washington Post,* July 31, 2002, p. A1, passim; Peter Behr and April Witt, "The Fall of Enron: Hidden Debts, Deals Scuttle Last Chance," *Washington Post,* August 1, 2002, p. A1, passim; Michael Siegfried, "Enron," pp. 289–90 in Lawrence M. Salinger, ed., *Encyclopedia of White-Collar and Corporate Crime,* Vol. 1 (Thousand Oaks, Calif.: Sage, 2005).

292. Peter Behr and April Witt, "The Fall of Enron: Visionary's Dream Led to Risky Business," *Washington Post,* July 28, 2002, p. A1, passim.

293. Elizabeth Purdy, "WorldCom," pp. 871–872 in Salinger, ed., *Encyclopedia of White-Collar Crime and Corporate Crime*; *Washington Post,* "WorldCom: Overview," http://www.washingtonpost.com; Terry Frieden, "Ebbers Indicted: Ex-CFO Pleads Guilty," March 2, 2004, http://money.cnn.com

294. Gail Edmondson, "How Parmalat Went Sour," January12,2004,http://www.business week.com; *Washington Post,* "Corporate Scandal Primer," http://www.washington post.com;

three

The Laws

*F*ew people ever ask why murder, assault, or robbery are illegal. The social consensus condemning such acts is so strong that the answer appears obvious. But many of the laws defining criminal behavior in the white-collar occupations arose in a climate of controversy and dissension that has continued long after their enactment. Indeed, the opposition has been so strong that many observers have been puzzled by the very existence of these laws, and others have argued that they represent nothing more than clever ruses intended to placate the public while carefully avoiding any real restrictions on the prerogatives of privileged individuals or powerful corporations.

An understanding of this issue must start with a general analysis of the origins of law. Numerous theories have been proposed over the years, but most of the work in this area can be grouped in one of two broad schools. What might be called the consensus or functional theory sees the law as a reflection of widely held values and of the general consensus of public opinion.[1] According to this view, new laws result from the effort to apply society's "core values" to new situations and events, and those laws reflect the attitudes and needs of society as a whole.

The interest theory of law creation, on the other hand, sees the formation of new legal norms as a struggle between competing groups striving to promote their own interests. Thus, the law is seen to reflect the structure of power in a society, whereas its norms and values have only secondary importance. Advocates of this theory are divided, however, about which interests control the creation of new laws. The pluralists hold that constantly shifting alliances of different interest groups vary with each individual issue and that no single group holds a monopoly on power.[2] Accordingly, the efforts of competing groups tend to cancel each other out, so that the legislative process ultimately reflects the will of the people and the interest of society as a whole. The elite theorists, in contrast, hold that government is controlled by a more or less unified "power elite," or ruling class, composed primarily of those with great wealth and/or key positions in the corporate power structure.[3] This group wields such enormous power that legislative proposals that threaten its domination are never given serious attention. According to many elite theorists, the various laws defining white-collar crimes are nothing more than symbolic gestures intended to allay public discontent without threatening the powers that be. A third camp, known as the structuralists, also sees the legal system as a reflection of the interests of a small elite. But in their analysis, it is the structural necessities of capitalist society that dictate the legal patterns and not necessarily the direct involvement of the members of the elite. Thus, the government may enact environmental or regulatory legislation opposed by the elite in order to head off mass discontent that would threaten the overall stability of the system (and, of course, the long-term interests of the elites themselves).[4]

Obviously, the proponents of these theories cannot all be right. But before we attempt to evaluate the usefulness of these paradigms for the task at hand, we must explore the historical context and development of white-collar-crime legislation. With this foundation laid, we will return to this critical theoretical issue.

Protecting Business: Embezzlement and Pilferage

Of all the laws examined here, the prohibition of theft is the most ancient. Indeed, the roots of this prohibition go too far back into legal history to concern us here. The nature of the early common-law crime of larceny is important, however, because it provides the context in which the crimes of embezzlement, pilferage, and fraud were first defined. The most interesting thing about the crime of larceny was its extremely narrow definition. It originally included only the taking or carrying away of the property of another without the consent of the owner and with the intent to deprive him or her of its use. According to the strict style of legal interpretation followed by the early English courts, this meant that if someone were given a piece of fine clothing with instructions to have it cleaned, and the receiver absconded with it, no crime had been committed. At first glance this distinction may appear arbitrary and unreasonable, but closer examination of its social context reveals an inner logic. The fact that the common law prescribed the death sentence for anyone convicted of stealing any item valued at more than 12 pence makes such judicial nit-picking much more comprehensible. An extremely strict legal construction was one of the principal ways through which judges avoided imposing the harsh punishment demanded by common-law tradition. Moreover, the misappropriation of another's property was still covered under civil law, and a victim could sue the offender for damages.[5]

This anomalous legal system worked well enough in the medieval English economy. Most people lived directly off the land, and the few consumer goods available were manufactured on a small scale and under strict control of the guilds. But as commerce and the lucrative wool and textile trades grew, the increasingly influential mercantile class began pushing for a new legal approach.

The result was the famous Carrier's case of 1473, in which a shipper was charged with breaking open a bale entrusted to him and stealing the contents. In a major breach of tradition, the defendant was found guilty on the grounds that although the bales had been entrusted to him, their contents had not, and the appropriation of the latter therefore constituted larceny. As important as this expansion of the larceny law was, it appears to have made the legal system more rather than less illogical: After the new ruling, it was illegal to steal the contents of a package one had been entrusted with, but perfectly legal to steal the whole thing.[6]

A statute enacted in 1529 continued the legal trend begun in the Carrier's case by making a servant's theft of his or her master's property a felony. However, the courts of the day, deeply conditioned to strict legal interpretation, held that the master did not have technical possession of property entrusted to the servant by a third party, and thus its appropriation did not constitute a crime. This ruling was of only minor importance in governing the relationships between masters and servants, but the courts soon applied the new standards of "larceny by servant" to employees as well—a development of much greater significance. Whereas servants only occasionally received their masters' property from others, the acceptance of money or goods from third parties was an important part of the jobs of many clerks and employees. The courts' response to the problem this ruling posed for the politically powerful merchant class was to steadily expand the definition of what constituted the "possession of the master." One of these interpretations held, for instance, that if the servant placed money or goods received from another in a receptacle owned by the master, it was therefore in the master's possession. But there were limits beyond which these interpretations could not be stretched, and the growing power and importance of banks made the situation increasingly difficult. In 1742, John Waite, a cashier for the Bank of England (which had been established in 1694), stole six East Indian bonds with a value of more than £13,000, yet he could not be convicted of any crime under the common law of that time. This case led to the enactment of the first embezzlement statute later that same year. However, it was very narrowly drawn and applied only to employees of the Bank of England. The first general embezzlement statute was passed in 1799, after a similar case involving another bank. Although that act applied only to servants and clerks, subsequent legislation applied criminal penalties to all persons who misappropriated property or money that had been entrusted to them.[7]

Protecting Competition: Antitrust Legislation

Although some critics have pictured antitrust legislation as a radical form of economic experimentation, the opposition to monopoly is actually deeply rooted in the common law. If the courts have not always ruled in opposition to monopoly, that has been the general tenor of their decisions for more than five centuries. English records dating as far back as the twelfth century recount the efforts of kings and judges to prevent monopolistic practices at local fairs and markets. As commerce became more developed, opposition to the monopolistic practices of the trade guilds also grew. In later years, popular opposition helped to stymie Queen Elizabeth I's efforts to grant national monopolies to court favorites, and even the great trading companies of the colonial era were eventually forced out of operation. There is, therefore, considerable evidence to support Franklin D. Jones's contention that the "history of Anglo-Saxon people discloses an undying hostility toward monopoly."[8]

Because of these inherited traditions, the laws of the American republic were opposed to monopoly from their very inception. Aside from the common law itself, several states wrote specific antimonopoly clauses into their constitutions. But if this legal foundation was more than sufficient to meet the problems of an agrarian economy with only small-scale cottage industry, it proved wholly unequal to the task of meeting the problems of monopoly and the concentration of power that developed out of the industrial revolution. States with their own antitrust statutes found that they had great difficulty controlling the monopolistic practices of corporations that spanned the nation. The common law did cut across state boundaries and was thus more widely applicable, but the laws themselves were inadequate to regulate modern economic relations. The common law held agreements in restraint of trade to be null and void and allowed victims of such practices to sue to recover the losses they suffered, but there were no criminal penalties, and state prosecutors were unable to instigate cases on their own. When the victims of monopolistic practices did bring suit, they were almost always heavily outgunned by the legal firepower of the big corporations they sought to restrain. Thus, the old approach to the control of monopolies and the preservation of fair competition proved increasingly impotent in the face of the growing concentration of corporate power.[9]

The federal government's first important piece of antitrust legislation was the Sherman Act of 1890, which remains the cornerstone of U.S. antitrust policy to this day. The passage of the Sherman Act is generally regarded as a major victory for the nineteenth-century reformers who sought to curtail the growing power of the corporate giants. There are, however, many critics of this view. Often citing the ease with which the Sherman Act passed the Fifty-first Congress—nicknamed the "Billion-Dollar Congress" for its largesse toward big business—these critics have argued that the Sherman Act was intentionally couched in vague, ambiguous terms in order to pacify the voters without materially affecting the interests of the major corporations.[10]

To understand the forces pushing for antitrust legislation, it is necessary to place them in the context of the profound social and economic changes that swept through the nation in the last part of the nineteenth century. The old middle class, composed principally of independent farmers and the owners of small businesses, was in decline. Its traditional political power and its economic base were being eroded by an emerging corporate elite that was riding the wave of industrialization that was fundamentally transforming the national economy.

The vast new plots of land available for cultivation in the West and the growth of railroad transportation were changing farmers into small capitalists growing cash crops for market. But for most of them, the 1880s and 1890s were hard times. As more and more land was put to the plow, farmers found that the prices their crops brought were declining. Yet the cost of the industrial commodities on which they had come to depend was not going down. As economic conditions worsened on the farm, migration to urban centers drained away rural population and agrarian discontent intensified. Although the farmers were often confused about the exact mechanisms involved, they recognized that they were being made to pay the price for the growth of industrial capitalism. High tariff barriers provided a sheltered environment for U.S. industry and kept it free from the international competition that would have meant lower prices for the manufactured goods farmers consumed. Because American goods were not competitive on the world market, the capital needed to purchase foreign technology and equipment was accumulated through the sale of cheap agricultural products.[11] Thus, as in virtually all industrializing countries, the surplus generated by the farmers was being used to finance the economic transformation that ultimately put them in a position of secondary social importance.

The first target of the farmers' discontent was the railroads, which charged exorbitant rates to ship the small farmers' grain to market but offered large rebates and other special favors to big corporations. Grain storage facilities (which were often owned by the railroads), along with grain buyers and middlemen, were also targets of the farmers' wrath. Several "Independent," "Reform," and "Antimonopoly" parties sprang up to press the farmers' cause. The most successful of these pressure groups was the Granger movement, which owed much of its popularity to the fact that it served both the social and the political needs of the farmers. The Grangers eventually forced a variety of regulatory legislation through the state legislatures, but the conservative courts threw most of it out.[12] As the farmers' frustration grew, the focus of their discontent expanded to include the manufacturers of agricultural machinery and, ultimately, monopolies, trusts, and big business in general. These disaffected agrarians eventually came together under the banner of the Populist (or People's) Party. The preamble to the Populist platform of 1892 (two years after the passage of the Sherman Act) shows the depth of feeling against big business and those in Washington who supported its interests:

> We meet in the midst of a nation brought to the verge of moral, political, and material ruin. Corruption dominates the ballot-box, the Legislatures, the Congress, and touches even the ermine of the bench. . . . The newspapers are largely subsidized, homes covered with mortgages, labor impoverished, and the land concentrated in the hands of capitalists. The urban workmen are denied the right to organize for self-protection; imported pauperized labor beats down their

wages, a hireling standing army, unrecognized by our laws, is established to shoot them down, and they are rapidly degenerating into European conditions. The fruits of the toil of millions are boldly stolen to build up colossal fortunes for the few, unprecedented in the history of mankind; and the possessors of these, in turn, despise the Republic and endanger liberty. From the same prolific womb of governmental injustice we breed the two great classes—tramps and millionaires.

The Populists won almost 10 percent of the presidential vote that year and carried five Midwestern and western states. They did not do as well in the South, but the southern wing of the Democratic Party was deeply influenced by the Populist ideas of such men as William Jennings Bryan. The surprising success of this small, newly organized party competing in its first presidential election provides persuasive evidence of the strength of public discontent with the growing economic and political dominance of big business.

Thus, there seems little doubt that the legislators of the Fifty-first Congress recognized the depth of the agrarian feelings about the need to limit the power of the trusts and feared the challenge of more Populist candidates if they openly opposed the final version of the Sherman Act. Not only did farmers still constitute well over half the U.S. population in 1890, but antitrust, unlike the tariff question, was an issue on which urban workers and the petty bourgeoisie supported their rural counterparts. Moreover, the Sherman Act was very much in tune with the dominant ideology and the legal traditions of nineteenth-century America. The deep-seated American principles of individualism, free competition, and equality of opportunity could all be mustered to support the principles of antitrust. As Hans Thorelli pointed out, "Congress believed in competition. Most congressmen, indeed most Americans, would say in 1890 that antitrust legislation was but the projection of the philosophy of competition on the plane of policy."[13]

The evidence is thus persuasive that the passage of the Sherman Act was indeed a defeat for corporate interests at the hands of a popular mass movement.[14] But was that defeat merely symbolic—the passage of a piece of vague and useless legislation—or was it really a substantive change? The Sherman Act is certainly broad and general, but it is not, by most legislative standards, particularly vague. The first sentence of the first section specifically spells out its intention: "Every contract, combination in the form of trust or otherwise, or conspiracy in restraint of trade or commerce among the several states or with foreign nations is hereby declared to be illegal." Violations of this statute are declared to be a misdemeanor punishable by a $5,000 fine and/or up to one year in prison. Victims of antitrust violations are given the right to sue the monopolist for treble damages—that is, damages equal to three times the amount of the losses they actually suffered. It is true that the specific acts that constitute a restraint of trade are not spelled out, but the common law contained many precedents from which to draw, even if such precedents did not always fit the new realities of industrial capitalism.

Despite its promise, the Sherman Act proved ineffective both because of the resistance of the Supreme Court and the failure of the executive branch to enforce it. For more than a decade no federal agency was established to investigate and prosecute antitrust violations. In 1911 the Supreme Court invoked the "Rule of Reason," unmentioned in the original act, which limited federal prosecution to "bad" trusts that abused their dominant position in the market. Nevertheless, Presidents Theodore Roosevelt and William Howard Taft did eventually bring major antitrust actions that forced the breakup of such monopolies as Standard Oil and American Tobacco.

The prodigious growth of holding companies, which bought up large chunks of stock in many competing firms, soon posed the same threat in a new form, however. Continued political pressure from the Progressives—the urban, middle-class successors to the Populists—and the repeated failure of the executive branch to enforce the Sherman Act resulted in the passage of the Clayton Act of 1914. Aimed primarily at the holding companies, the Clayton Act prohibited corporate stock acquisitions that would substantially lessen competition, forbade the directors of one corporation to be directors of a competing corporation (interlocking directorates), and restricted several other anticompetitive practices. But whereas the Sherman Act was broad, flexible, and at least a potentially powerful weapon against economic concentration, the Clayton Act had none of these attributes. It prohibited interlocking directorates but not interlocking management; it prohibited the acquisition of stock for monopolistic purposes but not the acquisition of assets. Thus, the Clayton Act failed to provide effective new weapons against the growth of economic concentration.

The Robinson–Patman Act, an amendment to the Clayton Act passed during the depths of the Great Depression, represented a response to the pressure from owners of small businesses seeking protection from what they saw as unfair corporate competition. The Robinson–Patman Act forbade firms to give their largest customers special discounts that were not justified by the cost reductions from a higher volume of sales and prohibited anticompetitive pricing practices. However, it delineated those offenses with such specificity and in such turgid language that it often served to prevent firms from lowering prices in order to gain a legitimate market advantage—certainly not one of the goals of antitrust legislation. In many ways, the Robinson–Patman Act is more a piece of special-interest legislation than an antitrust bill, because it often served to restrict fair competition in order to protect a special class of businesses.

The last major antitrust act passed by Congress was the Celler–Kefauver Act of 1950, which was enacted in another period of strong public antagonism toward big business—this time touched off by reports of secret corporate dealings with German firms during World War II. This bill corrected several of the problems in the original Clayton Act but did nothing to untangle the snarl created by the Robinson–Patman Act. The Celler–Kefauver Act prohibited the acquisition of stock and the acquisition of assets when "the effect of such acquisition may be substantially to lessen competition or tend to create a monopoly." The inclusion of the prohibition on asset acquisition, as well as the use of the general term *may be* helped create new weapons against corporate concentration—weapons that were reinforced by the Supreme Court under Chief Justice Earl Warren, which held a more favorable attitude toward antitrust enforcement than its predecessors.[15]

The increasing concentration of corporate power associated with the growth of industrial capitalism spurred antitrust legislation in other English-speaking countries as well. Canada passed its Anti-Combines Act in 1889, one year before the Sherman Act. Like the Robinson–Patman Act, this bill was enacted largely as a result of pressure from small business. Large combines such as the Dominion Wholesale Grocer's Guild and the Canadian Packers Association were gaining control of the markets for many retail goods and were threatening to wipe out smaller firms. However, big business interests were so successful in committee actions that the bill that was finally passed was unenforceable. As part of a general watering down of the language of the bill, the law was made to apply only to "unlawful" conspiracies that "unduly" restrained trade. Ten years later, however, the act was rewritten, the word *unlawful* was dropped, and the bill became at least potentially enforceable.[16]

The Australian Industries Act of 1906, which prohibited combines that damaged the public interest, was a product of much the same social pressures as the Canadian act. Andrew Hopkins has argued that several more recent bills designed to strengthen the original act had their origin in another problem caused by oligopolistic market control—inflation. Australian legislators apparently believed that they had to do something to reduce inflation in order to be reelected and that greater industrial competition would help achieve that end.[17] Great Britain remained cool to antitrust legislation for a longer time, at first preferring to depend on the common law and later eliminating antitrust problems by nationalizing many key industries. However, British Parliament did eventually enact an antitrust bill, the Monopolies and Restrictive Practices Act of 1948.[18]

Protecting Democracy: Fair Political Practices

The problem of government corruption is hardly a new one. Current laws against the bribery of public officials have deep roots in common law, but the earliest definitions of this crime were much narrower than they are today. The common law's greatest concern was not with the corruption of elected officials but with that of judges and other agents involved in the administration of justice.[19] Where the law did apply to officeholders, it focused on officials who bribed voters, and not the other way around. Since the list of eligible voters in the eighteenth century was restricted to a small group of landed gentry, it was easy for a politician to bribe his way into office—indeed, the voters in many boroughs expected to be rewarded for their support. In an effort to stop such abuses, Parliament passed an act in 1695–96 prohibiting candidates from giving voters money, food, or entertainment before an election. In 1729, Parliament required voters to take an oath that they had received no such gratuities before they were allowed to enter the voting place, and voters who lied were subject to perjury charges. But by all accounts these measures were of no avail, and the bribery of voters continued unabated.[20] Similar abuses occurred in America both before and after independence. George Washington, for example, was accused of campaign abuses in his 1757 race for the Virginia House of Burgesses for allegedly dispensing 50 gallons of rum, 24 gallons of wine, 46 gallons of beer, and 2 gallons of cider. Because there were only 391 voters in his district, this represented an average outlay of more than 1.5 quarts of spirits per voter.[21]

Over the years, the definition of bribery broadened as the number of voters grew, and the general direction of bribery shifted. Today bribery statutes generally apply only to officials who receive money from the public; those far rarer instances in which candidates attempt to pay off voters are usually considered election fraud. Bribery is now defined as "the offering, giving, receiving, or soliciting of anything of value to influence action as an official or in the discharge of legal or public duty."[22] The trend in judicial rulings has been to expand the definition of bribery to encompass agents of private firms as well as government employees and officials. In 1975, for instance, a federal appellate court held that it could "discern no reason why the Congress, in using the term 'bribery,' intended that it be limited to the corruption of public officials."[23] Many individual states also have enacted specific "commercial bribery" laws to supplement the older statutes dealing with the corruption of public officials. The massive bribery scandal touched off by revelations that the Lockheed Corporation had paid off foreign officials to promote sales of its airplanes gave rise to another important piece of antibribery legislation, the Foreign Corrupt Practices Act of 1977. This act explicitly prohibited the bribery of officials of foreign governments except in cases involving national security.[24] In November of 1997, the Organization of Economic Cooperation and Development adopted the Convention on Combating Bribery of Foreign Public Officials in International Business Transactions which made the bribery of foreign officials a crime in 34 member countries including the United States.[25]

Another perennial source of political corruption has been the need to generate campaign funds to pay for the cost of running for office. In some cases, large campaign contributions have actually become legal substitutes for bribery. In the early days of the Republic, the costs of political campaigns were low and were met largely from the candidate's own pocket or from "contributions" made by government employees subject to veiled (and sometimes not-so-veiled) threats to their jobs. As the cost of running for office grew, the old sources of funding proved inadequate and politicians turned increasingly to the "spoils system"—handing out government jobs in exchange for campaign contributions.[26] Among the numerous legislative efforts in the United States to stop the extortion of money from public employees, the most significant was the Civil Service Reform

Act of 1883. This act protected employees against reprisals for failing to make campaign contributions and made it a crime for federal employees to solicit campaign funds from their coworkers.[27] But the sources of campaign funding had begun to change even before passage of that act, as public employees were replaced by financiers and industrialists seeking government favors.[28]

The ability of corporations to buy offices for the candidates of their choice was never more apparent than in the presidential campaign of 1896. William Jennings Bryan, the Democratic candidate, had a total campaign fund of around $300,000, whereas his Republican opponent, William McKinley, received almost that much from the Standard Oil trust alone. Under the direction of master fundraiser and political manipulator Mark Hanna, McKinley raised a war chest that was estimated at $3.5 to $10 million.

The specter of big business buying election after election inspired a movement to reform campaign financing. The National Publicity Law Association, an organization dedicated to campaign reform, counted many notable figures of the time as members—including Bryan himself, as well as a future Supreme Court justice and the presidents of the American Federation of Labor and Howard University.[29] Pressure from such organizations and the growing influence of the Progressive movement led to the passage of the Tillman Act of 1907, which prohibited corporations or banks from contributing campaign funds to anyone seeking federal office. Then, in 1910, Congress passed a law calling for disclosure of the names and addresses of all contributors who donated more than $100, and in the following year campaign expenditures were limited to $5,000 for candidates for the House and $10,000 for candidates for the Senate.

The Federal Corrupt Practices Act of 1925 codified and revised the earlier legislation without making substantive changes. Although the Federal Corrupt Practices Act remained the principal law governing federal political campaigns for 47 years, it was notorious for its ineffectiveness. Lyndon Johnson called it "more loophole than law," and there were indeed numerous ways to evade it.[30] For one thing, it did not apply to primary campaigns, which in many parts of the country were more important than the final elections. Another problem was that campaign committees were required to report contributions only if they operated in more than one state, and few actually did. But the principal reason the act failed to achieve its ends was that enforcement was left up to the secretary of the Senate and the clerk of the House, who simply did not do the job.[31]

The Hatch Act of 1939, augmented by an amendment passed in 1940, prohibited federal employees from actively participating in national politics and forbade individuals or businesses working under contract to the government to make campaign contributions. The act also placed a $5,000 limit on the amount an individual could give in political contributions in a single year, but this provision was framed with so many glaring loopholes it was virtually meaningless. Later in the 1940s, the prohibition on corporate campaign contributions was extended to include labor unions as well.[32]

Despite repeated complaints from government officials, political scientists, and public interest organizations, nothing was done to plug the loopholes in the Federal Corrupt Practices Act until 1971. In that year Congress passed the Federal Election Campaign Act, which set limits on the amount of money a candidate could spend on advertising or contribute to his or her own campaign from personal funds and required political committees and candidates to file itemized totals of their expenditures and report all contributions in excess of $100. Although this act represented a significant improvement over its predecessor, it too was filled with loopholes that allowed astute politicians to evade the intent of the law. Its most glaring inadequacy probably was the failure to establish an independent election commission to oversee electoral proceedings. Instead, enforcement was once again left up to the secretary of the Senate and the clerk of the House—the same offices that had failed to enforce the Federal Corrupt Practices Act.[33]

When the Watergate affair became a national scandal in the early 1970s, the unprecedented intensity of media coverage created strong new demands for reform. In a series of amendments to the Federal Election Campaign Act, the existing system of campaign financing was completely overhauled. For the first time, spending limits were placed on both primaries and general elections, a system of public financing was created for presidential campaigns, and a Federal Election Commission was established to enforce the law. However, the sweeping new provisions of these amendments soon ran afoul of the Supreme Court. In a milestone 1976 decision, the Court held that the limitations on campaign spending, the limitations on the independent expenditure of personal funds, and the limitations on the use of personal funds for one's own campaign were unconstitutional. The Court also required that the Federal Election Commission be reconstituted so that all its members were appointed by the president, in order to avoid any mixing of the legislative and executive duties. The justices did approve some provisions of the act, including the limits on campaign contributions to candidates and political committees, the requirements for public disclosure of those contributions, and the public financing of presidential campaigns. This weakened version of the amended Federal Election Campaign Act, combined with a few procedural refinements passed in 1976 and 1979, now stands as the principal regulatory legislation for federal election campaigns.

Today even the limits and restrictions that survived the courts have been neutralized through various subterfuges. For example, although there are limits on how much an individual can give to a particular candidate or political action committee (PAC), there is no limit on the number of PACs representing the same interests, so wealthy contributors channel their money into many different PACs that can all contribute to the same candidate.

Although not directly related to campaign finance, the Ethics Bill of 1978 was also of considerable importance. This act gave the force of law to provisions in the new Senate and House codes of ethics that required public financial disclosures by all federal legislators and high-ranking officials in the executive branch. It also placed some restrictions on the so-called revolving door through which federal employees move directly from government positions to jobs in the same industries that they had previously regulated. In an attempt to curtail the use of lucrative job offers as a lure to gain special favors from government regulators, the bill imposed a two-year waiting period on government employees seeking to make such a move. The Ethics Bill also provided for the creation of an Office of Government Ethics to help administer the law, and it set forth civil penalties for violators of the disclosure provisions and criminal penalties for those government employees who ignored the restrictions on their future employment.[34]

Protecting the Public: Consumers, Workers, and the Environment

The earliest consumer protection laws in Great Britain go back to the common-law crime of "cheating"—that is, fraud by use of false weights and measures. But following the tradition of strict legal interpretation, a crime was considered to have occurred only when ordinary prudence would not have been sufficient to safeguard the victim. A statute passed in 1541 expanded the law of criminal fraud somewhat but still required that some device, such as a false letter or seal, be employed in the commission of the crime. Other types of fraud were not explicitly included in the criminal law for more than two centuries. However, dishonest business practices were commonly punished by public shaming and many of the other types of informal sanctions possible in traditional communities.[35]

As in the case of larceny, the early common-law doctrines proved inadequate to meet the needs of the modern era. The problem was that the growth of mass production and nationwide marketing greatly weakened the traditional restraints on commercial behavior that develop when buyers and sellers live and work in the same small communities. Meanwhile, the explosive increase in the volume of trade also multiplied the opportunities for fraudulent gain. The tonnage of shipping leaving English ports, for instance, increased more than 300 percent during the eighteenth century, as commerce began to take center stage in British life.[36] As the problem of commercial fraud grew, it became increasingly obvious that something had to be done.

The modern law of criminal fraud began during the reign of King George II, with the passage of a 1757 statute that declared, "Whereas divers ill-disposed persons, to support their profligate way of life, have by various subtle stratagems, threats and devices, fraudulently obtained divers sums of money . . . all persons who knowingly and designedly, by false pretense or pretenses, shall obtain from any person or persons, money, goods, wares, or merchandises, with intent to

cheat or defraud any person or persons of the same . . . shall be deemed offenders."[37] As its wording makes clear, this statute was intended to restrain the
practices of charlatans and confidence men, not "legitimate" business people.
Subsequent judicial interpretations, however, steadily expanded its scope until
the crime of false pretenses came to fill the gap left between the larceny and the
embezzlement laws—that is, crimes in which the thief acquires the property of
another through fraud and thus receives it voluntarily but without rightful possession in the legal sense. Today, fraud is one of the most universally recognized
crimes against consumers, although, as we shall see in the following chapter,
enforcement agencies have failed to apply the broad legal principles contained
in the fraud statutes to many types of white-collar crime.

Although the problem of fraud is as old as commerce itself, a multitude of
new problems for consumers, workers, and the general public sprang from the
growth of industrial capitalism. Of these, the first to win widespread public interest was the problem of monopoly and the ever-increasing concentration of
economic and political power in the hands of the industrial corporations. But
as the battle for effective antitrust action against the monopolists dragged slowly
on, other abuses of the new economic order came to the fore. Improved technology in printing and paper production made possible the growth of cheap
mass-market magazines, and editors soon discovered that muckraking exposés
sold magazines. A new breed of investigative reporter sprang up and began ex-
ploring the seamy side of urban life and contemporary government. But the primary target of these muckrakers was big business, which many of them saw as
the root cause of a pervasive national corruption.[38]

From a legislative standpoint, the muckrakers were most successful in attacking the abuses of the food-processing industry, which was just putting together
the first nationwide food distribution network. Much of the credit for the passage of the Pure Food and Drug Act and the Meat Inspection Act of 1906 must
go to the efforts of a host of crusading reformers. Harvey W. Wiley, head of the
Department of Agriculture's Bureau of Chemistry, did much to publicize the problem of unsafe food with his famous experiments on a group of volunteer subjects known as the Poison Squad.[39] Even more important was Upton Sinclair's
muckraking classic *The Jungle,* which shocked the nation with its graphic descriptions of the foul conditions found in Chicago's packing houses:

> These rats were nuisances, and the packers would put poisoned bread out for
> them, and they would die; and then rats, bread, and meat would go into the
> hoppers together. . . . Men, who worked in the tank rooms full of steam . . . fell
> into the vats; and when they were fished out, there was never enough of them
> to be worth exhibiting—sometimes they would be overlooked for days, till all
> but the bones of them had gone out to the world as Durham's Pure Beef Lard![40]

Despite the public outcry, the system of federal inspectors established by the
Pure Food Act might never have been put into place if Sinclair's revelations had
not triggered a 50 percent drop in sales and threatened the packers with the loss

of their lucrative European markets.[41] As Gabriel Kolko pointed out in his study of the Progressive Era, these events forced the large meatpacking firms to become supporters of regulatory legislation. Not only did meat inspection offer the best way to restore public confidence in the product, but the costs of maintaining adequate sanitation were a much greater burden on small meatpacking firms, thus helping the large corporations to consolidate their control over the market.[42]

The muckrakers were also concerned about the growing toll of deaths and injuries among industrial workers. But with the coming of World War I and the ensuing economic boom of the 1920s, the muckrakers passed from the American scene without winning any significant victories in the battle for industrial safety. Theoretically, injured workers and their families always had the right to sue employers under the provisions of the common law, but employers were actually provided with such generous legal defenses that the victims had little chance to win a case in court. If the employee had caused the accident in whole or in part, if he or she had voluntarily chosen to work at the hazardous job, or even if another employee was responsible for the accident, the employer could escape liability.[43]

The increasing number of industrial accidents and mounting pressures from workers led many states to pass employer-liability laws that greatly reduced the defenses allowed under common law. Judges, more and more often faced with destitute complainants who had been crippled or maimed in industrial accidents, also began formulating new interpretations that held employers more strictly accountable. As a result, there was a flood of lawsuits from injured workers, and employers began reevaluating their opposition to proposals for a workers' compensation plan. As Lawrence M. Friedman and Jack Ladinsky put it, "The existing tort system crossed an invisible line and thereafter . . . represented on balance a net loss to the industrial establishment. From that point on, the success of a movement for change in the system was certain."[44] The result of those reforms was the state-run workers' compensation system that developed in the first quarter of the twentieth century. The new statutes were a trade-off between workers and employers. The employers agreed to pay for injuries and deaths arising in the course of employment, and the workers agreed to a legal limit on the amount of damages for which the employer would be liable.

Despite serious flaws in this system (occupational disease, for instance, was not covered at all), it represented a major step toward just compensation for injured workers. But except for a prohibition on the production of white phosphorous matches and a few railroad safety acts, little was done at the federal or state level to actually improve worker safety. The Gauley Bridge disaster of 1930 and 1931 brought the problem of worker safety back to public attention. In this tragedy, almost 500 workers were killed by the silica dust churned up during tunneling work for a hydroelectric plant. Most of the fatalities occurred well after the project had been completed, although 169 black workers literally dropped dead during construction and were buried two or three to a grave in a nearby field. Despite the national attention the Gauley Bridge disaster received, no significant legislative action was taken to improve worker safety during the Great Depression.[45]

Although the economic crisis of the 1930s paralyzed the effort to win greater protection for workers, hard times did stimulate a new concern among consumers that their purchases bring the best possible value per dollar. The beginning of the consumer movement is often dated to the 1927 publication of Stuart Chase and F. J. Schlink's *Your Money's Worth*.[46] This pioneering work vehemently attacked deceptive advertising and high-pressure sales techniques and called for the scientific testing of consumer goods to make more accurate information available to the public. The book received such a strong public response that in 1929 Schlink established Consumer's Research, Inc., to carry on scientific consumer research, and he soon began publishing *Consumer's Bulletin* in order to publicize its findings. The legislative achievements of the fledgling consumer protection movement were meager, however. Kallett and Schlink's attack on the pharmaceutical industry, *100,000,000 Guinea Pigs,* won national publicity,[47] but it was not until 1938, in the wake of the Elixir Sulfanilamide tragedy, that a bill tightening governmental regulation of the drug industry was finally passed. (This "elixir" was a sulfa drug mixed in an entirely untested solvent, diethylene glycol. It was not until the drug was put onto the market and more than 100 people had died that the manufacturers discovered that the solvent was toxic.) The consumer movement was also able to win representation on several of the new government agencies set up to stimulate economic recovery during the Great Depression, but these representatives were usually overwhelmed by powerful and well-financed business opposition.[48]

The outbreak of World War II eclipsed public concern about the protection of consumers and workers, and there was little change in this attitude amid the conservative climate that prevailed in the early postwar years. By the mid-1950s, however, there was new interest in social reform that led to the activism of the 1960s and early 1970s. This era of social concern and political involvement produced important breakthroughs in occupational safety and consumer and environmental protection. One major cause of the new activism was the example set by the civil rights movement. Not only were reformers encouraged by the success of the struggle to abolish the segregation system, but many of them also gained firsthand experience with the techniques of grassroots political organization. At the same time, the ever-growing size of industrial and marketing concerns and the beginnings of the computer revolution left the public facing a marketplace that was more complex, more dangerous, and more depersonalized than ever before. The unprecedented affluence of this era also played a role in the growth of these movements by encouraging higher expectations and the belief that social problems could be solved through collective action.

The issue of consumer protection was the first to reemerge during this era. Works such as Vance Packard's *The Hidden Persuaders* began calling attention to consumer problems toward the end of the 1950s,[49] but an equally important factor was the political appeal of the issue. Because everyone is a consumer, consumer protection bills tended to draw broad-based support. Moreover, consumer protection was much cheaper to implement than were the other major social programs of the 1960s. As the war in Vietnam became an increasingly heavy financial burden, the political appeal of consumer protection grew stronger and stronger.[50]

The first important piece of consumer legislation to come out of this era was the Pure Food and Drug Act of 1962. Originally begun as an effort to limit price gouging and other abuses in the drug industry, in its final form the bill dealt exclusively with improvements in drug safety and effectiveness. The major reason for the transformation and eventual passage of this bill was the thalidomide tragedy and the horrible pictures of the deformed babies born to women who had taken the drug.[51]

Automobile safety was another consumer issue that had received sporadic attention for years until a dramatic incident finally brought matters to a head. Congress had been holding periodic hearings on auto safety since 1956, but only a few minor pieces of legislation had resulted. The 1966 Senate hearings on auto safety might well have had the same result if the chairman had not called for testimony from a young lawyer who had just written a book on auto safety. It was not so much what Ralph Nader said at those hearings—although he did provide a damning account of corporate irresponsibility—but what General Motors (GM) did to try to discredit him that spurred congressional action. The scandal that broke when GM's efforts at harassment and intimidation came to light made Ralph Nader's name a household word and ensured the passage of the National Traffic and Motor Vehicle Safety Act of 1966. Among other things, this act authorized the National Traffic Safety Commission to set safety standards for the automobile industry and to require that manufacturers recall defective vehicles.[52]

The political influence of organized consumer groups continued to grow throughout the 1960s and into the 1970s, when they won what some observers consider to be the single most important piece of consumer legislation of the contemporary era—the Consumer Product Safety Act of 1972.[53] This act established a commission that was given broad powers to set safety standards, recall or ban hazardous products, and institute criminal proceedings against companies that disregarded its orders. Several other pieces of consumer protection legislation were also passed during the 1960s and 1970s. Rapid expansion in the use of consumer credit led to the enactment of regulations governing truth in lending, fair reporting of credit information, equal opportunity for credit regardless of gender or ethnic group, and unfair or deceptive banking practices. Other acts set standards for product warranties and established controls on the use of lead paint and other toxic substances.[54]

Like many of the other social movements we have been discussing, the environmental movement can trace its origins to the early twentieth century. But unlike present-day environmentalists, the early "conservationists," such as Theodore Roosevelt, were primarily concerned with managing the natural environment for the maximum economic benefit and paid less attention to environmental protection itself. The conservation movement sprang in large measure from the realization that the frontier, which had played such an important part in American history, was finally gone, and the concomitant fear that the nation was squandering the resources on which its economic survival depended. The modern environmental movement was born in an era of much greater industrial development. It was in large measure a response to the endless miles of new highways, to urban sprawl, to the threat to animal species, to the frightening increase in pollution—in sum, to the nagging fear that our planet might eventually become unfit for human habitation.

Although local problems created serious concern in many parts of the nation, the environment barely existed as a national political issue in 1960. But the increasing severity of environmental problems, combined with greater media attention, created a tremendous upsurge of interest in the last part of that decade. Between 1969 and 1971, environmental issues jumped from tenth to fifth in the ranks of public concerns.[55] One of the major causes of this change was the increasing size and militance of the organized environmental groups. On April 22, 1970, these groups came together to celebrate Earth Day in nationwide observances that attracted millions of people and focused public attention on environmental issues as never before. In an hour-long television special, Walter Cronkite of CBS-TV described the crowds as "predominantly white, predominantly young, and predominantly anti-Nixon,"[56] and more of those young, well-educated, middle-class Americans soon flocked to environmental organizations. Between 1970 and 1971, the membership in the five largest organizations increased by 33 percent. Such groups as the Sierra Club, the National Wildlife Federation, the Friends of Earth, and the Environmental Defense Fund grew increasingly militant during the 1970s, openly supporting and opposing candidates, lobbying legislators, launching numerous lawsuits, and staging marches and mass demonstrations.[57] But as the environmentalists became increasingly organized and assertive, so did their opponents—especially the manufacturers and developers who saw environmentalism as a threat to their profits.

Water pollution was one of the first environmental problems to receive the attention of the government, probably because it was so clearly linked to the transmission of contagious disease. The first water pollution laws were enacted at the state level, but those early statutes were ineffective, both because of lax enforcement and because of the lack of jurisdiction over pollution carried downstream from other states. The history of federal legislation goes back to an 1899 act forbidding the dumping of debris in navigable water, but the first significant federal water pollution legislation wasn't passed until 1948. Over the following two decades, the federal government slowly expanded its involvement in water purity regulation and began providing financial assistance for the construction of local water treatment plants. Publicity surrounding the 1967 sinking of the giant oil tanker *Torrey Canyon* and the massive oil spills from offshore drilling near Santa Barbara, California, led to the passage of a bill to increase private liability for the cost of cleaning up oil spills and repairing the damage they cause. The toughest water pollution bill to date was passed in 1972; it set a five-year deadline for polluting industries to adopt the "best practicable" control technology and another deadline four years after that for the installation of the "best available" pollution control devices. The bill also gave the Environmental Protection Agency (which had been created in 1970 to bring the federal government's environment programs under a single bureaucratic roof) authority to initiate legal action against polluters.[58] The passage of the Safe Drinking Water Act of 1974 required that the EPA set national drinking water standards and impose sanctions where necessary to ensure that public water systems comply.

The government was much slower in responding to the problem of air pollution, which had been growing progressively worse since the end of World War II. The frightening siege of air pollution in Donora, Pennsylvania, in 1948, which killed twenty people and sickened half the town's population of 12,000, failed to stimulate any new legislation. Fierce opposition from the automobile industry delayed the first federal effort to regulate auto emissions until 1965, and a timetable requiring significant reductions in emissions from new cars and the creation of national standards for stationary emissions was not adopted until 1970. Twenty years later the Clean Air Act of 1990 tightened the restrictions on air pollution by phasing in tougher standards for automotive emissions. It also required that smog equipment have longer warranties, that manufacturers use the best available control technology to reduce certain kinds of toxic emissions, and that new industrial polluters create offsetting reductions in pollution from other sources.[59]

Numerous other kinds of environmental legislation were passed in the 1970s. Many were trivial, but others were of considerable long-term importance. Particularly significant was the Toxic Substances Control Act of 1976, which required detailed reporting on chemical manufacturing and processing, and gave the Environmental Protection Agency authority to seek a court order to limit, delay, or ban the sale of any dangerous chemical. Numerous amendments to the Federal Insecticide, Fungicide and Rodenticide Act of 1947 authorized the EPA to regulate the sales of pesticides, and other legislation placed new controls on the environmental damage caused by strip mining.

In addition to the federal government, the states have become increasingly involved in environmental regulation. Although the states often focus on more specialized issues than those addressed in federal law, there has been a virtual explosion of state environmental laws in recent years. In some cases, federal law specifically allows the state environmental standards to exceed federal standards, but federal preemption remains a serious barrier to the states' efforts to combat many kinds of environmental problems.[60]

The new spirit of environmental activism soon spilled over into the effort to protect the health and safety of the American workforce. It was the workers in one of the world's most dangerous occupations—coal mining—who pushed through the first new occupational safety legislation. In the mid-1960s, coal miners began a concerted effort to persuade the states to include black lung disease (an often fatal ailment caused by the inhalation of coal dust) in workers' compensation programs. After encountering considerable opposition from the leadership of the United Mine Workers Union, angry miners formed independent organizations—the Black Lung Association and the Association of Disabled Miners and Widows. The drive for new legislation gained impetus from a Farmington, West Virginia, mine disaster that claimed the lives of seventy-eight miners in November 1968. In February 1969, West Virginia coal miners went out on a three-week wildcat strike and staged a march on the state capital to press their demands for workers' compensation for black lung disease. Later that year, they finally won federal assistance with the passage of the Coal Mine Safety Act.[61]

Faced with the indifference of union leadership to the problem of occupational safety, workers in other industries also took independent action. In June 1965, 12,000 Teamsters walked off the job in Philadelphia to protest the firing of four employees for refusing to work under dangerous conditions. Jimmy Hoffa, the president of the Teamsters, called the strike illegal and ordered the workers back to the job, but they refused. Similar wildcat actions were taken by the members of other unions. In July 1966, 9,000 members of the United Automobile Workers (UAW) walked off the job at three Ford plants, citing a long list of grievances centered around health and safety issues. In February 1967, the members of a UAW local struck a General Motors plant in Ohio because of the firing of two workers for refusing to carry out hazardous work. Rank-and-file discontent over health and safety issues also cropped up in the International Longshoremen's and Warehousemen's Union, the International Association of Machinists, the International Union of Electrical Workers, and the United Steelworkers of America.

This grassroots activism finally forced union leadership to take up the issue of worker safety. President Johnson, faced with deep party division over his conduct of the war in Vietnam and anxious to solidify his union support, submitted a worker safety bill early in 1968. The bill won widespread union support but was defeated in Congress. The same motivation led Johnson's successor, Richard Nixon, to propose another worker protection act. Although weaker than the previous bill, the Occupational Safety and Health Act of 1970 remains the most significant piece of worker safety legislation enacted to date. This act requires employers to provide a workplace "free from recognized physical hazards that are likely to cause death or serious physical harm to employees" and to meet the standards promulgated by the Occupational Safety and Health Administration (OSHA). It also gives OSHA the power to shut down any operation that places workers in "immediate danger" and grants workers the right to make complaints directly to OSHA with a guarantee of anonymity and protection from employer reprisals.[62]

Corporate Criminal Responsibility: Who Can Commit a Crime?

Although an examination of the origins of laws against such traditional crimes as murder, assault, or robbery would take us too far afield, we do need to consider the question of whether or not a corporation can commit such offenses. The primary concern of the law has always been the regulation of relations between persons, but as far back as the twelfth century, other entities began to be recognized as "persons" for legal purposes. The origins of this concept lay in the efforts of the medieval clergy to free itself from the control of local lords. In the early medieval era, churches were considered to be the property of the regional landowner, but as the clergy began to assert its independence, it rejected claims of outside ownership. But if the lord did not own the church, who did? At various times it was said that the church was owned by its "four walls" or its patron saint, but ultimately the collective body known as "the church" was recognized as the legal owner. Later, as the capitalist economic system grew, the corporation also won recognition as a "juristic person." This development proved a great boon to corporations, who as juristic persons enjoyed many of the legal rights and protections of real persons.[63]

There was, however, a price to be paid, for the logic of the law ultimately required that new responsibilities accompany the new privileges. There is some dispute about exactly when these new "persons" were first held civilly liable for their actions, but it certainly occurred soon after the inception of the concept. However, criminal liability was much slower to develop. The first application of criminal law to a corporate entity was based on the ancient common-law doctrine that a master was criminally responsible if a servant threw something out of the master's house onto a street or highway and thereby caused a public nuisance. The organizations involved in the earliest cases were cities that failed to maintain safe roads and waterways; later, the same law was applied to railroads and other private corporations. This precedent was slowly expanded on a case-by-case basis, until corporations came to be held liable for all criminal offenses that did not require criminal intent (mens rea).

But the doctrine that corporations were unable to form criminal intent was no more legally defensible than the earlier restrictions on corporate liability, and it was rejected in a 1908 case involving railroad rebates. In this ruling, the judge cited the language of the specific statute at issue and went on to point out the obvious contradiction involved in holding that a corporation could act through its agents but could not form a criminal intent through them. It is now common for corporations to be charged with criminal violations of the regulatory statutes as well as more serious offenses such as fraud and perjury.

Another legal development in the centuries-long expansion of corporate responsibility came in an Indiana case in which the Ford Motor Company was charged with reckless homicide in connection with the gas tank problems of the Ford Pinto (see Chapter 2). Although the company was ultimately acquitted, the court ruled that the Indiana homicide statute was applicable to corporations as well as to individuals.[64] Prosecutors were more successful in a 1985 case in Illinois, where a far smaller firm, Film Recovery Systems, was found guilty of involuntary manslaughter for causing the death of one of its workers. (This conviction was, however, ultimately overturned—see Chapter 4.[65]). In 1987, a Texas construction company and its president both pleaded nolo contendere (no contest) to charges of negligent homicide in the death of a worker who was crushed when an excavation ditch collapsed.[66] In October 1989, the Supreme Court let stand a lower court ruling that a state could bring criminal charges against employers for exposing their workers to hazardous wastes even if the employer had complied with standards set by the Occupational Safety and Health Administration.[67]

The issue of corporate criminal responsibility is still far from settled, however. Although the criminal sanctions contained in regulatory legislation are no longer an issue of debate, many corporate interests continue to make vehement objections to the application of traditional criminal statutes against such things as murder or manslaughter to corporate offenders. As we have seen, a slowly expanding body of case law has established corporate responsibility for those offenses, but the courts still do not agree on exactly when a corporation is criminally responsible for the actions of its employees and when it is not. The dominant approach and the one used in the federal courts is known as the imputation theory, because the criminal intent of employees is imputed to the corporation. Under this theory, a corporation is responsible when one of its agents (1) has committed a crime, (2) was acting within his or her authority, and (3) was intending to benefit the corporation. Of these three conditions, the second has been by far the most controversial. The corporations have often argued that they should be held criminally responsible only for the actions of their employees that the company has specifically authorized by its charter (a doctrine known as *ultra vires*) or at least those actions carried out or authorized by top management. Following this line of thought, the Model Penal Code drafted by the American Law Institute would require the prosecutor to prove that the illegal action was performed, authorized, or recklessly tolerated by the board of directors or top managers, who themselves must have been acting on behalf of the corporation within the scope of their employment.[68] Although a few states have adopted this kind of standard, most states and the federal courts still hold corporations criminally liable for the actions of lower-level employees even if they have not been specifically sanctioned by those at the top.

Some laws, especially those regulating offenses that cause widespread harm to public welfare, do not require proof of criminal intent to obtain a conviction at all. Conviction on one of these "strict liability" crimes requires only that the defendants committed the prohibited action regardless of their intentions. For example, in an Ohio case against the Budd Company, an employee noticed an oil slick near a storage tank but failed to report it. In its appeal, the company argued that the state had to prove it had intentionally caused the emissions, but the courts ruled that under the strict liability doctrine the defendant's intent is irrelevant.[69]

Origins of the Laws

Having examined the historical development of the laws creating white-collar crimes, we can now return to the theoretical issue posed at the beginning of this chapter: Are those laws a reflection of society's normative consensus, are they a product of a pluralistic struggle among many more or less equal groups, or is their principal aim really to protect the privileges of the ruling elite and the capitalist system that supports them?

The weakness of consensus theory is immediately apparent from the historical evidence. Most of the numerous antitrust, consumer protection, campaign financing, environmental protection, and worker safety laws were controversial issues at the time of their enactment. Many powerful interest groups tried to influence the content of those bills and worked to prevent or promote their ratification. Only a handful of the laws in question can be said to have reflected an uncontested social consensus. Even those laws—for example, the prohibitions on larceny, embezzlement, and pilferage—can be explained as the products of pressure from specific interest groups, albeit with little significant opposition.[70] Equally damaging to consensus theory is the fact that many activities that violate society's "core values" are not prohibited by criminal law. The inadequacies of consensus theory should not, however, lead us to conclude that society's norms and values played no part in the genesis of these laws. On the contrary, there is little doubt that an appeal to the public's sense of justice and fair play is one of the reformers' most powerful weapons in their battle to restrain the abuses of the elite. In the end, however, pressure from special interest groups appears to have been the sine qua non of legislative action.

But if the interest theory provides the best explanation of the creation of these "white-collar laws," which version of it are we to accept—the pluralists who see a democratic balance of power at the roots of legal innovation, or the elite theorists and structuralists who see the system operating in the interest of the privileged few? The immediate temptation is to say that the pluralists have the better case, since the mere existence of laws restricting the activities of the corporate elite indicates that no single group controls all facets of the legislative process. However, the elite theorists argue persuasively that many of these so-called reforms were of little practical import, and the structuralists point out that even the most sweeping reforms may actually work to the advantage of the ruling elites by protecting the long-term viability of the system that is the source of their privilege.

More careful analysis shows all sides to be needlessly polemic. Although the elite theorists can rightfully claim that many legislative reforms appeared to be much more substantive than they actually were, there is no doubt that this network of legislation contains many provisions that were strongly opposed by significant segments of the corporate elite.[71] Although the structuralists are often right that such reforms are actually in the long-term interests of the elite, that is certainly not universally true. By the same token, the pluralists' claim that the legislative process has been controlled by shifting alliances of groups that ultimately balance each other out, so that the "will of the people" has prevailed, comes much closer to ideology than to empirical fact. Although various reformist groups and defenders of the status quo have indeed shifted alliances from time to time and from issue to issue, there can be no doubt that the corporate elite controls a vast concentration of political and economic power that dwarfs its opposition.

To understand the origins of this legislation, we must look beyond the dynamics of interest group politics to the historical forces that lie at the heart of the system of industrial capitalism. The social movements that led to the reforms discussed here arose out of the dislocations and conflicts caused by the historical development of that system. In many cases, traditional segments of society threatened by new economic developments still had considerable political power to muster in their defense. For instance, both the antitrust movement and the more general populist movement of which it was a part represented an attempt by small farmers and business people to strike back at the corporations that were choking off their means of subsistence. The early reforms prohibiting political contributions by corporations also sprang from the same sources.

The demand for legislation to protect workers, consumers, and the environment was stimulated by other facets of the process of industrialization. Traditionally, producers and consumers lived together in the same small towns, and there was little need for formal consumer protection legislation. If a local merchant or craftsman used shady techniques to exploit consumers, complaints spread quickly through the community and various informal controls could easily be brought to bear. With the growth of big cities and mass marketing, the relationship between producers and consumers was fundamentally altered. The consumer movement was part of an effort to find an effective substitute for the informal controls of the small town. The growth of industrial capitalism also brought about fundamental changes in the techniques of production. As new technologies and methods of production sprang up, a frightening array of poisons and pollutants was soon being spewed out into the environment. The environmental movement stemmed from people's desire to protect themselves from the new hazards created by industrial technology and to preserve the quality of their environment.

Thus, conflicts and contradictions in the political economy of industrial capitalism provided the original impetus for the social movements that agitated for many new pieces of legislation. The conflicts between producers and consumers, labor and business, small farmers and corporations are inherent in industrial capitalism, and any changes in the delicate balance between those conflicting groups may spur appeals for legislative intervention. But other problems, such as environmental pollution, stem directly from industrial technology itself, whether a society's system of economic organization is capitalistic or not. Yet although such general problems may ultimately lead to new legislation, the dynamics of the process of law creation soon transform them into a struggle between specific interest groups, some battling to change, and others to defend the status quo.

Few, if any, of the antitrust, fair campaign practice, environmental, or consumer protection laws examined here would have been passed if large-scale, grassroots movements had not pushed for their enactment. In most cases, one version or another of these laws was under consideration for years, slowly shuffling from committee to committee until the popular pressure grew great enough to force reluctant legislators to vote against the desires of the economic elite—to which most of them were tied with both economic and political bonds.

Because reformers are usually outspent and outmaneuvered by their more highly placed opposition, the chances for significant reforms are slim as long as the public remains apathetic. But hardships created by the failures and contradictions of the political economy can arouse the public from its lethargy. The emergence of effective leadership has proven to be a key factor in transforming popular discontent into the kind of social movements necessary to force reforms. These "moral entrepreneurs," as Howard Becker called them, work to bring disaffected people together in political organizations and to spread public awareness of social problems.[72] Media attention focused on a dramatic disaster or scandal has often provided an important rallying point for reform. Deadly pharmaceuticals, mine disasters, oil spills, the revelations of the muckrakers, Watergate, and numerous other political scandals have all served to galvanize the forces of reform and to cut the ground out from under their opposition. Yet it is a reciprocal relationship: Without the efforts of an organized social movement, even such a dramatic incident as the Gauley Bridge disaster failed to stimulate meaningful reform.

The legislative history of successful reforms often follows a similar pattern. The original efforts of reformers are met with strong resistance from elite interests, effectively blocking any legislative action. But if the reformers gain strength and continue pushing for action, the elite may come to accept the idea that some reform is necessary. Elite interests then begin working to reshape the reformers' proposals in order to minimize their negative impact and/or to win some compensatory benefits. The final shape of the reforms often emerges from intense political infighting about issues of which the public has little knowledge or awareness.

The power of elite interests can be seen in the fact that most proposed reforms, including many needed to deal with urgent social problems, are never enacted. Moreover, many of the reform bills that have been passed were gutted of any real content or rewritten to benefit various powerful vested interests. On the other hand, even nations in the advanced stages of industrialization retain some degree of economic decentralization, and successful reform movements often benefit from divisions within the ruling elite. For example, the insurance industry has generally supported automobile safety legislation, even though the automobile industry has been vehemently against it. A similar split between high-sulfur coal producers in the East and low-sulfur producers in the West occurred in the battle over the enactment of emission regulations for coal-fired power plants.[73]

The ratification of a new law, even if it is a strong one, is not the end of a successful reform movement. As we shall see in the next chapter, the enforcement process plays a critical role in determining whether or not the reforms remain symbolic or result in significant social change. This is particularly true because of the tendency of many politicians to avoid tough decisions that are likely to offend either the organized reformers or the entrenched elites. As a result, many of the lawmakers' most difficult problems are, as Neal Shover puts it, "transformed into administrative problems to be worked out between regulators and the industry."[74] It is the result of this administrative struggle that often determines the success or failure of a reform movement.

Review Questions

- What are the major theories about the origins of criminal law? What do they say about the laws defining the white-collar crimes?

- Describe the historical developments that led to the creation of the laws prohibiting the various types of white-collar crime.

- How has the law's view of the criminal responsibility of corporations changed over the years?

- Are the laws defining the white-collar crimes the product of social consensus, a pluralistic struggle among many more or less equal interest groups, or the domination of a powerful elite?

Notes

1. Many social theorists of the first half of the twentieth century accepted this position. For example, see Emile Durkheim, *The Division of Labor in Society,* George Simpson, trans. (Glencoe, Ill.: Free Press, 1947); Pitirim A. Sorokin, *Society, Culture, and Personality* (New York: Harper & Row, 1947). For a more recent version of this theory, see W. Friedmann, *Law in a Changing Society* (London: Ballantine, 1971).

2. Influential pluralist works include David Reisman, *The Lonely Crowd* (New York: Doubleday Anchor, 1953); Arnold M. Rose, *The Power Structure: Political Process in American Society* (London: Oxford University Press, 1967). For a study that focuses more exclusively on the sociology of law, see Lawrence M. Friedman, *Law and Society* (Englewood Cliffs, N.J.: Prentice-Hall, 1977).

3. The elitist position is the dominant one in contemporary sociology. For examples, see William J. Chambliss, "Sociological Analysis of the Law of Vagrancy," *Social Problems* 12 (1964): 67–77; Richard Quinney, *Critique of Legal Order: Crime Control in Capitalist Society* (Boston: Little, Brown, 1974); Austin Turk, "Law as a Weapon in Social Conflict," *Social Problems* 23 (1976): 276–91; and Neil Gunningham, *Pollution, Social Interest, and the Law* (London: Martin Robertson & Co., 1974).

4. For example, see Nicos Poulantzas, "The Problem of the Capitalist State," in *Ideology in the Social Sciences,* Robin Blackburn, ed. (London: Fontana, 1972), pp. 238–53; Theda Skocpol, *States and Revolutions: A Comparative Analysis of France, Russia, and China* (New York: Cambridge University Press, 1979).

5. Allen Z. Gammage and Charles F. Hemphill Jr., *Basic Criminal Law,* 2nd ed. (New York: McGraw-Hill, 1979), pp. 226–27.

6. Jerome Hall, *Theft, Law and Society,* 2nd ed. (Indianapolis: Bobbs-Merrill, 1952), pp. 3–33.

7. Ibid., pp. 35–40, 62–66.

8. Franklin D. Jones, "Historical Development of the Law of Business Competition," *Yale Law Journal* 35 (June 1926): 905.

9. Hans B. Thorelli, *The Federal Antitrust Policy* (Baltimore: Johns Hopkins University Press, 1955), pp. 9–53; also Jones, "Historical Development of the Law of Business Competition."

10. Among the numerous authors who have taken this position are Charles Beard and Mary Beard, *The Rise of American Civilization*, rev. ed. (New York: Macmillan, 1930), p. 327; Samuel E. Morison and Henry Steele Commager, *The Growth of the American Republic*, 4th ed. (New York: Oxford University Press, 1951), p. 144; Carl Solberg, *Oil Power* (New York: Mason/Charter, 1976), pp. 48–49.

11. For a concise analysis of the relationship between agriculture and industrial development in nineteenth-century America, see C. Wright Mills, *White Collar* (London: Oxford University Press, 1951), pp. 13–33.

12. Harold Faulkner, *Politics, Reform and Expansion: 1890–1900* (New York: Harper & Brothers, 1959), p. 67; also Thorelli, *Federal Antitrust Policy*, pp. 58–59.

13. Thorelli, *Federal Antitrust Policy*, pp. 226–27.

14. On this point, see Albert E. McCormick Jr., "Dominant Class Interests and the Emergence of Antitrust Legislation," *Contemporary Crises* 3 (1979): 399–417.

15. See Mark J. Green, Beverly C. Moore Jr., and Bruce Wasserstein, *The Closed Enterprise System* (New York: Grossman, 1972), pp. 47–60, 298–412; A. D. Neale, *The Antitrust Laws of the United States of America* (New York: Cambridge University Press, 1960).

16. Colin H. Goff and Charles E. Reasons, *Corporate Crime in Canada: A Critical Analysis of Anti-Combines Legislation* (Scarborough, Ontario: Prentice-Hall of Canada, 1978), pp. 41–49.

17. Andrew Hopkins, *Crime and Business: The Sociological Sources of Australian Monopoly Law* (Canberra: Australian Institute of Criminology, 1978).

18. Charles E. Reasons and Colin H. Goff, "Corporate Crime: A Cross-National Analysis," in *White Collar Crime: Theory and Research*, Gilbert Geis and Ezra Stotland, eds. (Beverly Hills, Calif.: Sage, 1980), pp. 126–41.

19. Gammage and Hemphill, *Basic Criminal Law*, p. 314.

20. William Holdsworth, *A History of English Law* (London: Sweet and Maxwell, 1938), pp. 573–77.

21. *Congressional Quarterly, Congressional Ethics*, 2nd ed. (Washington, D.C.: Congressional Quarterly Press, 1980), p. 193.

22. *Allen* v. *State*, 72 P.2d 516, 63 Okla. Crim. 16.

23. *U.S.* v. *Pamponio*, 511 R2d 953 (1975).

24. See W. Michael Reisman, *Folded Lies: Bribery, Crusades, and Reforms* (New York: Free Press, 1979), pp. 151–66, 176–77.

25. Jason Davis, "Bribery," in Lawrence M. Salinger, ed. *Encyclopedia of White-Collar and Corporate Crime* (Thousands Oaks, Calif.: Sage, 2005), pp. 110–12.

26. Herbert E. Alexander, *Financing Politics: Money, Elections, and Political Reform*, 2nd ed. (Washington, D.C.: Congressional Quarterly Press, 1980), pp. 45–46.

27. *Congressional Quarterly, Congressional Ethics*, p. 194.

28. Alexander, *Financing Politics*, pp. 46–47.

29. Ibid., p. 26.

30. Mark Green, *Who Runs Congress?*, 3rd ed. (New York: Bantam Books, 1979), p. 17.

31. Ibid., pp. 17–18; *Congressional Quarterly, Congressional Ethics*, pp. 194–95; Alexander, *Financing Politics*, pp. 26–27.

32. *Congressional Quarterly, Congressional Ethics*, pp. 194–95; Alexander, *Financing Politics*, pp. 26–27.

33. *Congressional Quarterly, Congressional Ethics*, pp. 197–98.

34. Larry V. Sabato and Glenn R. Simpson, *Dirty Little Secrets: The Persistence of Corruption in American Politics* (New York: Times Books, 1996), pp. 10–18; *Congressional Quarterly, Congressional Ethics*, pp. 48–56, 182–88.

35. See Gilbert Geis, "From Deuteronomy to Deniability: A Historical Perlustration on White Collar Crime," *Justice Quarterly* 1 (March 1988): 1–32.

36. Hall, *Theft, Law and Society*, p. 77.

37. Quoted in Hall, *Theft, Law and Society*, p. 40.

38. For a comprehensive account of the activities of the muckrakers, see C. C. Reigier, *The Era of Muckrakers* (Chapel Hill: University of North Carolina Press, 1932).

39. James S. Turner, *The Chemical Feast* (New York: Grossman, 1970), pp. 107–37.

40. Upton Sinclair, *The Jungle* (New York: Vanguard Press, 1927).

41. Robert O. Herrmann, "The Consumer Movement in Historical Perspective," in *Consumerism: Search for the Consumer Interest*, David A. Aaker and George S. Day, eds. (New York: Free Press, 1971), pp. 10–22; Mark V. Nadel, *The Politics of Consumer Protection* (Indianapolis: Bobbs-Merrill, 1971), pp. 7–19.

42. Gabriel Kolko, *The Triumph of Conservatism* (New York: Free Press, 1963).

43. Joseph A. Page and Mary-Win O'Brien, *Bitter Wages: Ralph Nader's Study Group Report on Disease and Injury on the Job* (New York: Grossman, 1973), pp. 49–50.

44. See Lawrence M. Friedman and Jack Ladinsky, "Social Change and the Law of Industrial Accidents," *Columbia Law Review* 67 (January 1967): 50–82; Neal Shover, "The Criminalization of Corporate Behavior: Federal Surface Coal Mining," in Geis and Stotland, *White Collar Crime*, pp. 98–125; Elliott Currie, "Sociology of Law: The Unasked Questions," *Yale Law Journal* 81 (November 1971): 134–37.

45. Page and O'Brien, *Bitter Wages*, pp. 59–63; Daniel M. Berman, *Death on the Job: Occupational Health and Safety Struggles in the United States* (New York: Monthly Review Press, 1978), pp. 27–28.

46. Stuart Chase and F. J. Schlink, *Your Money's Worth* (New York: Macmillan, 1927).

47. Arthur Kallett and F. J. Schlink, *100,000,000 Guinea Pigs* (New York: Vanguard, 1933).

48. Lucy Black Creighton, *Pretenders to the Throne: The Consumer Movement in the United States* (Lexington, Mass.: Lexington Books, 1976), pp. 19–29, 113; Nadel, *Politics of Consumer Protection*, pp. 36–43; Herrmann, "The Consumer Movement in Historical Perspective," pp. 12–14.

49. Vance Packard, *The Hidden Persuaders* (New York: McKay, 1957).

50. Nadel, *Politics of Consumer Protection*, pp. 121–39.

51. Ibid., pp. 36–43.

52. S. Prakash Sethi, *Up against the Corporate Wall: Modern Corporations and Social Issues of the Seventies*, 2nd ed. (Englewood Cliffs, N.J.: Prentice-Hall, 1974), pp. 373–98; Nadel, *Politics of Consumer Protection*, pp. 137–43; Creighton, *Pretenders to the Throne*, pp. 52–55.

53. Creighton, *Pretenders to the Throne*, pp. 38–39.

54. Joel R. Evans, *Consumerism in the United States* (New York: Praeger, 1980), pp. 391–439; Creighton, *Pretenders to the Throne*; Nadel, *Politics of Consumer Protection*.

55. John C. Whitaker, *Striking a Balance: Environment and Natural Resources Policy in the Nixon-Ford Years* (Washington, D.C.: American Enterprise Institute for Public Policy Research, 1976), p. 9.

56. Ibid., pp. 2–7.

57. Walter A. Rosenbaum, *The Politics of Environmental Concern* (New York: Praeger, 1973), pp. 53–91.

58. J. Clarence Davies III and Barbara S. Davies, *The Politics of Pollution*, 2nd ed. (Indianapolis: Bobbs-Merrill, 1975), pp. 27–44.

59. Larry B. Stammer, "Federal Rules Take Back Seat," *Los Angeles Times*, November 1, 1990, p. A5; John Laidler, "Northeast States Move to Adopt Strict California Emissions Rules," *Los Angeles Times*, May 12, 1992, p. A5.

60. Yingyi Situ and David Emmons, *Environmental Crime: The Criminal Justice System's Role in Protecting the Environment* (Thousand Oaks, Calif.: Sage, 2000), pp. 39–41.

61. Page and O'Brien, *Bitter Wages*, pp. 143–44; Berman, *Death on the Job*, pp. 31–32.

62. Page and O'Brien, *Bitter Wages*, pp. 167–89; Patrick G. Donnelly, "The Origins of the Occupational Safety and Health Act of 1970," *Social Problems* 30 (October 1980): 13–25.

63. James S. Coleman, *Power and the Structure of Society* (New York: W. W. Norton, 1974), pp. 13–31.

64. Thomas J. Bernard, "The Historical Development of Corporate Criminal Liability," *Criminology* 22 (February 1984): 3–17.

65. Barbara J. Hayler, "Criminal Prosecution of Corporate Crime: The Illinois Corporate Murder Case," paper presented at the Western Political Science Association, March 20–22, 1986, Eugene, Oregon; Larry Green, "3 Officials Guilty of Murder in Cyanide Death at Plant," *Los Angeles Times*, June 15, 1985, pp. 1, 5; Ray Gibson and Charles Mount, "3 Former Executives Guilty in Cyanide Death," *Chicago Tribune*, June 15, 1985, pt. 1, pp. 1, 5.

66. "Texas Construction Company and President Plead Guilty to Negligent Homicide in Connection with Work Related Death," *Corporate Crime Reporter* 1 (April 20, 1987): 4–5; Barry Siegel, "Murder Case a Corporate Landmark," *Los Angeles Times*, September 15, 1985, pt. 1, p. 1 passim.

67. David G. Savage, "Unsafe Work Sites May Result in Criminal Charges" *Los Angeles Times*, October 3, 1989, pt. IV, pp. 1, 7.

68. Barbara A. Belbot, "Corporate Criminal Liability," in *Understanding Corporate Criminality*, ed. Michael B. Blankenship (New York: Garland, 1993), pp. 211–38; S. Walt and W. S. Laufer, "Why Personhood Doesn't Matter: Corporate Criminal Liability and Sanctions," *American Journal of Criminal Law* 18 (1991): 263–87; J. C. Coffee, "Corporate Criminal Responsibility," in S. Kadish, ed., *Encyclopedia of Crime and Justice* (New York: Free Press, 1983), pp. 253–64.

69. See Situ and Emmons, *Environmental Crime*, pp. 154–57.

70. For an excellent discussion of the social and economic forces that reshaped the common-law crime of larceny, see Hall, *Theft, Law and Society*, pp. 13–14, 62–79.

71. Clinard and Yeager comment that "there is little recognition by radical or Marxist thinkers that even the largest corporations are increasingly being subjected to severer restrictions, heavier penalties, and stronger governmental control, largely in response to the activities of the consumer, environmental, and other groups." Marshall B. Clinard and Peter C. Yeager, *Corporate Crime* (New York: Free Press, 1980), p. 75.

72. See Howard S. Becker, *Outsiders: Studies in the Sociology of Deviance* (New York: Free Press, 1963), pp. 147–64.

73. See Bruce A. Ackerman and William T. Hassler, *Clean Coal/Dirty Air* (New Haven: Yale University Press, 1981).

74. Shover, "Criminalization of Corporate Behavior," p. 120.

# *four*

Enforcement

Most people recognize the importance of the struggle for new legislation, but the public is surprisingly naive about the enforcement process. It is commonly assumed that once a new law is enacted, it is more or less automatically enforced. Enforcement agencies are seen to be mere servants of the law, carrying out the dictates of the people as codified by their legislators. But criminologists have long recognized that such agencies do not merely enforce the law—they create it as well. When resources are allocated to one sort of enforcement and not to another, the law as it actually affects the man or woman on the street is changed. If enforcement agencies decide that they will not prosecute a certain kind of offense, they in effect cancel whatever sanctions the law may contain.

This question of discretionary enforcement is critical to all criminal justice, but especially so for white-collar crimes. The power and influence of the offenders often make the decision to prosecute a major corporate crime as political as the legislative process that created the original law. Even when the enforcement process is less overtly political, the huge size and complexity of many white-collar offenses—and the chronic shortage of resources for investigation and prosecution—may require many difficult decisions about which cases to pursue and which to ignore.

Such complexity also necessitates a much more elaborate enforcement bureaucracy than is necessary for common street crimes. Local police and prosecutors handle many small-scale occupational crimes, but they are hopelessly outmatched by big-time white-collar criminals. The FBI is the only traditional law enforcement agency in the United States with the resources to deal with major corporate offenders, but it is still more concerned with individual occupational criminals. The principal responsibility for enforcement of the laws regulating the corporate world rests with specially created regulatory agencies, such as the Securities and Exchange Commission, the Federal Trade Commission, and the Environmental Protection Agency. In addition, many private corporations and the leading professions have set up their own structures of self-regulation designed to uncover illegal activities within their own ranks, and it is to them that we first turn our attention.

Self-regulation

Professionals tend to regard themselves as an independent group of specialists whose unique knowledge makes them the only ones qualified to regulate behavior within their occupational fields. Over the years physicians, lawyers, and other professional groups have struggled to establish and enhance their professional autonomy, and they have succeeded in keeping most of the occupational offenses of their members out of the criminal justice system. By their very nature, the occupational duties of the professional are complex and difficult for the outsider to understand. Thus, even in the best of circumstances, a criminologist or police investigator might have considerable difficulty in determining whether the self-serving actions of a particular practitioner are simply bad judgment or outright fraud. To add to this problem, many professionals have sought to create an aura of mystery about their work and to generate a sense of awe in the public mind. This professional mystification has helped to insulate professionals not only from the outside "meddling" of the criminal justice system but from the complaints of their customers as well.

A related problem is the spirit of camaraderie and mutual support that exists in most professions. Although at first glance such a normal communal spirit hardly seems dangerous, it has contributed to the professionals' reticence to report abuses by their colleagues or give legal testimony against them. As one expert on discipline in the medical profession put it, "There's a great reluctance on the part of doctors to interfere with another doctor's reputation and means of livelihood. The philosophy apparently is that a man's reputation is more important than the welfare of his patients."[1] The same attitudes are present in the legal profession. As Martin Garbus and Joel Seligman noted, "Attorneys and judges generally refuse to report instances of professional misconduct. They will not testify against each other. There is a strong tendency to treat serious misconduct complaints as private disputes between attorney and client."[2] Aside from the obvious harm such attitudes cause clients, they also make it much harder to investigate criminal activity in the professions.

Professionals enjoy such a high degree of occupational autonomy that some sociologists have come to see it as the defining characteristic of a profession. Eliot Freidson holds, for example, that "a profession is distinct from the other occupations in that it has been given the right to control its own work . . . only the profession has the recognized right to declare . . . outside evaluations illegitimate and intolerable."[3] Most recognized professions have won the legal right of self-regulation, including the control of licensing and disciplinary proceedings. Self-regulation has many advantages for the professionals, but few for the general public. The boards and agencies charged with controlling professional misconduct deflect criminal complaints away from the justice system, thereby protecting fellow professionals from prosecution. Although the agencies of self-regulation have strong sanctions at their disposal, their members have generally shown great leniency toward their fellows—perhaps on the assumption that they themselves might someday be on the other side of a consumer complaint.

The principal responsibility for regulation of the medical profession lies with each state's board of medical examiners. The boards are composed of physicians (in some states a few other medical professionals are included), who are usually appointed by the governor on the recommendation of the state medical society. The main power of these boards lies in their control of medical licensure. Most of their time is devoted to granting licenses to new physicians, but they are also charged with taking disciplinary actions against incompetent or unethical practitioners. Medical examiners generally maintain high standards for the granting of a medical license; once a license is issued, however, it is rarely revoked. Once admitted to the fellowship of physicians, incompetent or even criminal practitioners are apt to be given the protection of their colleagues. Of the 770,370 physicians practicing in the United States in 1999, only 2,696 were subject to serious disciplinary action—less than one-half of 1 percent of all physicians. Yet a report by the National Academy of Sciences estimated that 98,000 hospital patients in the United States are killed every year by the medical treatment they receive.[4] A study in the *Journal of the American Medical Association* found that forty of the physicians disciplined for sex-related offenses such as rape, sexual molestation, and trading drugs for sex before 1995 were still licensed to practice in March of 1997.[5] Another study found that two-thirds of the doctors disciplined in 1995 for substandard, incompetent, or negligent care were allowed to continue practicing with little or no restrictions.[6] It is clear that only the most serious kinds of offenses, committed in a blatant and public fashion, result in the loss of a medical license. In one notorious case, an eight-year-old Colorado boy died during minor surgery after his anesthesiologist fell asleep during the operation. It turned out that the doctor had been reported for falling asleep on at least six previous occasions, but he was still allowed to practice.[7]

The legal profession regulates itself in much the same manner. In most jurisdictions, the local bar association is responsible for processing complaints and initiating investigations of misconduct, but the ultimate responsibility usually rests with the courts. Disciplinary proceedings are often prosecuted by a local grievance committee and tried by a court-appointed referee. State bar associations seldom provide adequate funding for disciplinary agencies, and most place complicated procedural obstacles in their way. Consequently, few consumer complaints receive much action, and the few cases that are brought are extremely time-consuming, sometimes taking more than five years from start to finish.[8] Most of the complaints that are brought against American lawyers are dismissed without any investigation at all, and only a tiny fraction of the cases that are investigated result in any actual sanctions.[9] One survey found that state bar associations investigated approximately 84,000 complaints in 1997, but only 859 attorneys were disbarred and 2,327 lesser sanctions handed out. There were more than a million lawyers practicing that year, which means that less than 0.08 percent of the active lawyers in the United States were disbarred.[10] A study by the Center for Public Integrity published in 2003 reviewed 11,450 appellate court cases and found that more than 2,000 new trials were ordered because of serious misconduct by the prosecutors. However, only eleven prosecutors had their licenses temporarily suspended for their misconduct, and only one was disbarred.[11]

The ABA's Special Committee on Evaluation of Disciplinary Enforcement, chaired by former Supreme Court justice Tom Clark, called the failure of the legal profession's disciplinary mechanisms a "scandalous situation," and went on to note, "With few exceptions the prevailing attitude of lawyers toward disciplinary enforcement ranges from apathy to outright hostility. Disciplinary action is practically nonexistent in many jurisdictions; practices and procedures are antiquated; many disciplinary agencies have little power to take effective steps against malefactors."[12] A similar committee formed by the Bar of the City of New York found that well-placed, influential lawyers largely escaped disciplinary action for misconduct, and concluded that "the system catches only the small fish."[13] Ironically, the same professional organizations that claim to be watching out for the public's best interest have themselves been involved in repeated criminal activities. In the past, medical and bar associations commonly committed antitrust violations such as price-fixing and restraint of trade (see Chapter 2).

The failure of self-regulation in the accounting profession became a national scandal after Enron's outside auditor, Arthur Andersen, was caught in a massive scheme to hide evidence from the SEC of their complicity with Enron's illegal accounting schemes. As numerous other corporations were found to have used fraudulent bookkeeping schemes that never seemed to peak the interest of their auditors, public pressure forced Congress to act. The Sarbanes–Oxley Act of 2002 restricted outside auditors from providing the kind of lucrative consulting services Andersen did for Enron, and created a new board to oversee the accounting profession.[14]

A different approach to self-regulation occurs among corporations that utilize various techniques to root out illegal activities within their organizations. While these efforts are often reasonably successful, in most cases their focus is almost entirely on occupational crimes. Crimes by the corporation itself (especially when initiated by top management) are usually ignored. Many corporations in heavily regulated industries now have a compliance division or at least a compliance officer whose job is to ensure that the company's employees conform to the demands of the law. Not only does the operation of an effective compliance program reduce the risks of civil liability, but it serves to protect the company's public image and has often been used as an effective bargaining chip to head off more intrusive government regulation. John Braithwaite and Brent Fisse argue that such self-regulation could be more effective at preventing corporate crime than government enforcement actions if the corporations were legally required to maintain a vigorous compliance program.[15]

Government Regulation

The government bureaucracies set up to regulate various aspects of economic behavior have a far greater impact on the problem of white-collar crime than do the current attempts at self-regulation. Regulatory agencies have been established to do everything from maintaining free competition to protecting the health and safety of the public. Indeed, it is these agencies, not the traditional criminal justice system, that shoulder most of the burden of bringing organizational offenders to justice.

From the legislator's standpoint, regulatory agencies have two important advantages over the criminal justice system. First, they make the lawmaker's job easier by taking over the responsibility for the formulation of specific rules, standards, and guidelines. In the case of environmental pollution, for example, pollutants must be identified, their effects on the public's health must be determined, and safe exposure levels must be set. In addition, numerous other issues concerning the specific techniques to be used to achieve these goals must be decided. Although a legislative body could handle such questions, it would be an extremely time-consuming task involving matters well beyond the expertise of most legislators. But the availability of such expertise is not the only advantage legislators have seen in the creation of regulatory agencies. Second, such agencies provide a convenient place to pass the buck when politicians want to avoid making decisions that are likely to be unpopular with an important constituency.

Regulatory Agencies

Federal Agencies The primary responsibility for dealing with organizational crime, as well as many forms of collective embezzlement and market abuse, rests with a diverse group of federal regulatory agencies. Most of the older agencies, such as the Interstate Commerce Commission, the Federal Trade Commission, and the Securities and Exchange Commission, are organized as independent units under the direction of a group of commissioners appointed by the president. The original idea was to put the responsibility for regulatory problems in the hands of a group of experts and then to insulate them as much as possible from political interference. On the whole, however, this approach has failed to live up to its promise. The commissions were never really insulated from politics, and many of them became "captives" of the industries they were supposed to control—doing more to promote the interests of the regulated industry than of the public they were supposed to represent.

A new generation of reformers, concerned with such issues as environmental pollution and consumer protection, argued that a different organizational structure was needed. As a result, the newer regulatory agencies, such as the Environmental Protection Agency (EPA), are usually headed by a single administrator with a staff of assistants who are under much tighter legal restraints than they are in the older commissions.[16] For example, in order to give the Federal Trade Commission (FTC) maximum flexibility to do its job, Congress intentionally refrained from defining the "unfair methods of the competition" it was supposed to prevent. Yet the Clean Air Act of 1970 not only mandated that the EPA administrator set specific clean air targets to "protect public health," but also required that those targets be met no later than 1977.[17] Moreover, it gave "any citizen" the right to sue the EPA if it failed to carry out the act's requirements.[18] Another important difference between the commissions and the newer agencies is that the former have much greater freedom from presidential control. Commissioners are appointed for a fixed term and are subject to early removal only via congressional impeachment. Administrators, on the other hand, serve at the pleasure of the president and may be removed whenever the chief executive decides to do so.[19]

Space does not allow for a review of all the regulatory bodies that play a role in controlling white-collar crime, but we will examine the most important agencies, one of which is certainly the Federal Trade Commission. When it was created in 1915, the FTC was charged with preventing unfair competition and anticompetitive mergers, but over the years it took on responsibility for controlling a much wider variety of unfair trading practices, including false advertising, commercial bribery, and price discrimination. The FTC's responsibilities in the antitrust field are broadly defined. For example, the law calls on the agency to prevent "unfair methods of competition" and to stop mergers whose "effect may be to substantially lessen competition or tend to create a monopoly." Such general language is subject to many different interpretations, and FTC policy has tended to make wide swings back and forth as the political climate and the agency's commissioners have changed.

Because the Antitrust Division of the Justice Department handles many of the same kinds of antitrust cases as the FTC, there is considerable duplication of effort. The principal difference between the two organizations lies in their techniques of enforcement. The FTC is limited to civil and administrative action; if it decides to pursue a case after it conducts an investigation, it will either initiate a hearing before an administrative law judge or bring an action in civil court. The Antitrust Division of the Justice Department, in contrast, has jurisdiction over all criminal cases. Should the FTC decide that one of its cases warrants criminal action, it can recommend such action to the Justice Department. The final decision, however, rests with the attorney general, who is a political appointee, not a representative of an independent commission.[20]

The Securities and Exchange Commission (SEC) was created after the stock market crash of 1929 in an attempt to restore public confidence in the securities market. Although the SEC's responsibilities have expanded over the years, its overall objectives have remained much the same. It is the SEC's job to prevent misrepresentation in corporate financial statements and in the sale or exchange of securities. It also regulates procedures for the solicitation of proxies, enforces restrictions on insider trading, and supervises other aspects of securities transactions. The commission has the power to take a wide range of administrative actions. After an administrative hearing and a possible court appeal, the commissioners can expel members from stock exchanges, revoke the registration of brokers and dealers, or censure individuals for misconduct. If the facts warrant, they can also recommend criminal prosecution to the Justice Department. The SEC has usually enjoyed far more support from the industry it regulates than have other regulatory agencies. Despite frequent objections to specific SEC actions or policies, the most influential sectors of the financial community believe that the SEC plays an essential role in maintaining the trust on which the financial markets depend.

The Food and Drug Administration (FDA) operates under a very different kind of mandate. Rather than economic regulation, the health and safety of the public is its main concern. When it was created in 1906, the FDA made only spot checks on food and drugs to detect adulteration or mislabeling. But like other regulatory agencies, the FDA found its powers and responsibilities growing over the years, usually as a result of the public outcry about deaths from some dangerous new drug. After the sulfanilamide tragedy, the FDA was empowered to take steps to ensure that new drugs were safe before they were put out on the market. After the thalidomide case, the FDA was charged with ensuring that drugs were not only safe but also effective. The AIDS epidemic created new public pressures in the opposite direction. As the number of people found to be infected with the HIV virus exploded, the victims organized themselves and demanded speedier approval of new drugs—even if they have not yet been proven to be effective. Unfortunately, in the FDA's rush to create a "fast-track" approval system for such drugs, it has bowed to pressure from the pharmaceutical industry and included many drugs for diseases for which there are already safe and proven treatments.

In approving a new drug, the FDA has the difficult task of weighing its benefits against its possible dangers. The mere fact that a new drug has hazardous side effects is not sufficient to ban its use, because it may, for example, be the only effective treatment for a serious disease. Before permitting a drug to be put on the market, the FDA requires the manufacturer to conduct extensive tests first on laboratory animals and then on small groups of patients under carefully controlled conditions. Finally, the drug is released to a limited number of physicians to see how safe it is in ordinary medical use. Although these procedures appear to be careful and cautious, they are seriously weakened by the fact that the manufacturer, not the FDA, conducts the original tests. Because drug companies often have an enormous financial stake in the drugs they test, there is a strong motivation to bias the testing procedures or even falsify the data (see Chapter 2). Without undertaking its own tests, the FDA has no way of detecting such deception. Another serious weakness is the FDA's lack of authority over physicians. The misuse of prescription drugs accounts for numerous deaths and injuries that could well be prevented by more careful control of the way in which drugs are prescribed.

The Consumer Product Safety Commission (CPSC), a much newer agency than the FDA, was created to handle all consumer safety problems not already being dealt with by other government organizations. (Outside the CPSC's realm are food and drugs, which are the responsibilities of the FDA, and automobiles and tires, which are handled by the National Highway Traffic Safety Administration.) The CPSC has the responsibility to promulgate regulations protecting the public from unsafe products and to enforce both those standards and others created directly by legislative mandate. But unlike the FDA, the CPSC has no power to prevent dangerous new products from reaching the market. In most cases, it can act only after injuries and deaths have already occurred.

The Environmental Protection Agency's original mandate was to deal with air and water pollution, but over the years many other tasks have been added to its list of responsibilities, including the regulation of solid wastes, pesticides, noise pollution, and toxic substances. The EPA was given some very specific congressional mandates, but the effectiveness of this approach is a matter of debate. On the positive side, the mandates have forced the EPA to make controversial decisions it might otherwise have avoided and to act more expeditiously than many other regulatory agencies. The mandates have also proven to be an effective bargaining chip in the EPA's attempts to win industry cooperation. On the negative side, the deadlines set by Congress may occasionally have forced the EPA to act too hastily. Specific legislative mandates reduce the EPA's flexibility and, in some cases, have precluded the use of the most effective means of dealing with a particular environmental problem.[21] They have also made the EPA more vulnerable to time-consuming legal challenges from both environmentalists and polluters.[22]

Rosenbaum argues that the EPA's basic problem is simply that it has been given too much to do with too few resources. The environmental statutes "cover an enormous range of ecological problems, technical or scientific expertise, regulatory activity, and geographic space."[23] The EPA must regulate approximately 1,500 hazardous air pollutants under the Clean Air Act. It must evaluate more than 50,000 pesticides and test approximately 60,000 potentially hazardous chemicals. The 1990 amendments to the Clean Air Act alone fill 800 pages of small print. Rosenbaum also argues that the EPA suffers from excessive oversight from more than twenty often hostile congressional committees; deep internal divisions among the numerous managerial, professional, geographical, and political interests it encompasses; and fragmentation of its authority, which is shared with at least twenty-seven other federal agencies.[24]

One factor that sets the EPA apart from most other regulatory agencies is its political environment. In addition to a host of lavishly funded industry lobbies that attempt to obstruct its regulatory mission (a common problem for most such agencies), the EPA must reckon with powerful groups pushing the agency to carry out its statutory goals. This environmental lobby is both well organized and well financed—attributes of which few other citizen groups can boast.

The Occupational Safety and Health Administration (OSHA) was set up "to assure so far as possible every working man and woman in the nation safe and healthful working conditions." Its specific duties are to create safety regulations for the workplace and to carry out periodic inspections to make sure the regulations are being followed. Although a reading of the Occupational Safety and Health Act of 1970 (the legislation that created OSHA) would lead one to assume that the primary issue facing the agency concerns the technological feasibility of different safety and pollution control techniques, the real issue has turned out to be cost. The agency's principal objective has often seemed to be to balance the safety of workers against the cost of providing safe working conditions. Not surprisingly, its decisions have been highly controversial, and few other agencies have been subject to so great a barrage of criticism.

The Role of the States

Even though the lion's share of the responsibility rests with the federal government, the states play a significant role in the effort to control organizational crime. In some cases, the states conduct separate operations that run parallel to those of the federal agencies; in others, state and federal efforts are coordinated to achieve maximum efficiency. Some states are paid by the federal government to perform specific enforcement duties.[25]

States also have their own white-collar crime legislation. For example, most states have antitrust laws—fifteen of which actually preceded the Sherman Act.[26] Every state except Alabama has enacted what are known as "little FTC" laws, which cover unfair, deceptive, or anticompetitive business practices; and although federal preemption remains a problem, many states have enacted environmental or consumer protection laws that significantly strengthen national legislation. Organizationally, most states have followed the advice of the National Association of Attorneys General and have given their own attorney general the responsibility for enforcing those laws.

In comparison with the states, the federal government obviously has greater resources and broader jurisdiction, and often, tougher laws as well. Because the states lack both authority over interstate commerce and the financial means to handle large-scale complex cases, they have tended to concentrate on smaller violations. However, the states have on occasion combined forces against major offenders. In one case involving General Motors, for example, forty-six states undertook a joint effort to stop the automaker's practice of putting the engines built by one division in cars bearing the name of another.[27] Another problem for the states is that they are more vulnerable to threats by corporate criminals to move to another jurisdiction if the law is too vigorously enforced. The states do enjoy some advantages over the federal government, however. State enforcement agencies usually stay in better touch with local conditions, and they can often move much more rapidly than can the cumbersome federal bureaucracy.[28]

The Regulatory Process

Rule Making Unlike traditional law enforcement, many regulatory agencies not only enforce the rules but also create them. An appraisal of the effectiveness of such agencies thus becomes a far more difficult task. Even the strongest enforcement effort will have little impact if the regulations themselves are inadequate. Although the particulars vary from agency to agency, the process of formal rule making is a complex and time-consuming one that usually involves numerous staff and research reports, public hearings, and administrative procedures. The objective of such lengthy procedural requirements is to make sure that rule makers explore all sides of the issue at hand and arrive at a carefully considered judgment. However, when powerful interest groups utilize obstructionist tactics, the final result of this process is often a bureaucratic paralysis that frustrates the goals the agency presumably was established to achieve.

Some of the worst problems of this kind have cropped up at the Occupational Safety and Health Administration. Despite the rapidly growing list of potentially hazardous substances, since 1972 OSHA has enacted only seventeen final health standards—less than one per year.[29] This failure of the rule-making process has made it impossible for OSHA to ensure the level of occupational safety mandated by its enabling legislation. The FDA has had similar difficulties. The Food Additives Amendment requires that "potentially unsafe substances" be tested before being used as food additives, and the DeLaney Amendment forbids the marketing of any substance shown to cause cancer in laboratory animals. However, the FDA has repeatedly dodged these requirements by putting potentially hazardous substances on its list of additives that are "Generally Recognized As Safe" (GRAS). For example, the artificial sweeteners known collectively as cyclamates were not removed from the GRAS list until fifteen years after they were found to cause cancer in animals,[30] and the makers of another artificial sweetener, saccharin, won a special legislative exemption shielding their product from the requirements of the law. Numerous other additives have also been placed on the GRAS list even though serious safety questions have been raised about them.[31]

Intense political struggles often occur within a regulatory agency before strong new standards are proposed. But even if the proposals do ultimately call for tough standards, they are sometimes gutted or completely rejected by other agencies within the federal bureaucracy or by pressure from the president himself.[32] The Reagan administration, for example, was openly hostile to the regulatory process. But because the public support for environmental and safety regulation was far too strong for President Reagan to win outright repeal of this legislation, he proceeded largely through executive actions. Soon after taking office, Reagan ordered the Office of Management and Budget (OMB) to review all new regulatory actions, and specifically required a cost–benefit analysis for every new regulation. Critics charged that these actions transformed agency heads from "policy makers to policy pleaders in a tough unsympathetic court."[33] In addition, the Reagan administration used two other important antiregulatory strategies. The first, and perhaps most effective, was a concerted effort to make sharp cuts in the budgets and staff of regulatory agencies. The second involved the appointment of new administrators who were in tune with the administration's antiregulatory views, which in many cases meant that they were opposed to the objectives of the agencies for which they worked.[34]

The first Bush administration was less ideologically opposed to government regulation than its predecessor, and the executive review process was weakened by a 1990 Supreme Court decision holding that the OMB did not have the legal authority to block new regulations proposed by other agencies.[35] But like its predecessor, the Bush administration still allowed politically powerful corporate interests to stymie legally mandated regulations. The first President Bush created a new agency to review proposed regulations known as the Competitiveness Council, which functioned as a kind of court of last appeals, allowing powerful corporations to block many new regulations that they opposed.

The Clinton administration subsequently abolished the Competitiveness Council and was generally less inclined to interfere with the rule-making operations of the regulatory bureaucracy. Indeed, one of the first priorities of the second Bush administration was to suspend, modify, or repeal a host of new environmental standards promulgated in the last days of the Clinton administration.

Despite all these problems, the rule-making efforts of the federal regulatory agencies have not all been as dismal as might have been expected. The EPA, equipped with a strict legislative mandate and prodded by an active environmental lobby, has created some very significant regulations, and even OSHA and the FDA have promulgated standards restricting some of the most obvious threats to health and safety. But the fact remains that in most cases the rules made by regulatory agencies have fallen far short of the legislative standards they were required to meet.

Investigation and Case Selection

Once the rules and the standards are in place, the next step is to uncover the violations. Compared with traditional street crime, the task of unmasking white-collar criminals is far more difficult. For one thing, the wealth and influence of many offenders enable them to do a much more effective job of concealing their crimes, and the crimes themselves often involve a complex web of economic interactions that require a great deal of investigative work to reconstruct. A classic example of this problem can be found in the antitrust case the FTC brought against the oil industry in the early 1970s. The so-called Exxon case consumed 12 to 14 percent of the agency's entire antitrust budget.[36] However, after eight years of investigations and proceedings the case was simply dropped because of its "length and complexity."[37]

Another difficulty encountered by regulatory agencies is that the victims of organizational crimes often do not know they have been victimized or where to direct their complaints if they discover their problem. People who eat food with carcinogenic ingredients, buy short-weighted products, or breathe contaminated air seldom know with any degree of certainty that they have been the victims of a crime. Still, the regulatory agencies receive a large volume of complaints from businesses, special-interest groups, and the general public. The problem is that those complaints tend to be concentrated in a few narrow areas where the harm is most obvious, and many of the most serious types of white-collar crimes fail to spur public response.

To uncover these hidden offenses, regulatory agencies must conduct their own investigations—a costly and time-consuming chore for these chronically under-funded organizations. In a few industries—such as meatpacking, in which the law requires constant inspections—this problem has been resolved by requiring that each firm pay the cost of full-time inspectors. This system has obvious financial benefits for the government, but it is also conducive to corruption. A common problem is that inspectors come to see the firms they work with day in and day out as their real employer and neglect the public interest. Most often, however, inspectors are full-time employees of an enforcement division within a regulatory agency; accordingly, they examine many different firms and are less likely to identify with any single company. The problem here is that the enforcement agencies are grossly understaffed. As one commentator put it, "The typical establishment will see an OSHA inspector about as often as we see Halley's Comet."[38] The situation is, moreover, growing steadily worse. While the number of workers and the overall economy were undergoing enormous growth, a 1999 study by Public Citizen shows that the number of inspections OSHA carries out every year has declined steadily since 1975.[39]

Despite often meager investigatory resources, the regulatory agencies uncover or are made aware of many more violations than they can actually prosecute. Regulators are therefore faced with another dilemma: Do they go after the important, time-consuming cases and risk possible political reprisals from powerful corporate offenders, or do they pursue the less important cases that can be quickly resolved, thus producing the maximum number of convictions to impress congressional oversight committees? Even though the latter approach subverts the official goals of regulation, it has proven to have a powerful appeal to self-interested bureaucrats. The Federal Trade Commission provides a good example of this problem. Numerous reports in the late 1960s and early 1970s argued that the FTC was pursuing minor offenders and ignoring the major corporations that were doing most of the harm to the public.[40] Such attacks, combined with the reformist spirit stimulated by the Watergate scandals, led to a revitalization of the FTC, which was given new leadership, new programs, and new enforcement powers.[41] The commission then began to pursue more "structural" cases that directly attacked the oligopolistic control of major markets. In the 1980s, however, the Reagan administration and its supporters in Congress forced the FTC to back off from its aggressive enforcement policy, and none of the structural cases were resolved in a manner that provided any real benefits for the consumer.[42] Since then the federal government's antitrust efforts have reached near paralysis. Economists and corporate officials have argued that antitrust restrictions place an unfair burden on American corporations in an increasingly global economy, and no strong consumer lobby arose to challenge those contentions. Yet despite a major change in regulatory attitudes and the approval of numerous huge and probably very anticompetitive corporate mergers, no changes in the antitrust laws have been made—government enforcement agencies simply chose to ignore the law.

Regulatory Enforcement

Once a regulatory agency has decided to pursue a particular case, three courses of action are open to it. One is an administrative action, which usually involves an official agency hearing before an administrative judge. Representatives of the agency and the accused present their cases, and the judge makes a ruling that is subject to an appeal to a regular court. The second option is to take civil action by bringing suit against the offender in federal court. Finally, the agency can recommend that a criminal action be taken by the Justice Department or, in some cases, by a federal district prosecutor. Here, as noted earlier, the final decision rests with the Justice Department or the individual prosecutor.

Often an agency will initiate enforcement action by issuing a warning that further steps will be taken unless the illegal behavior stops. The agency may also enter into negotiations with the offenders, often in conjunction with other civil or administrative actions against them. Successful negotiations typically end with a corporate offender agreeing to administrative or court decrees banning future violations, but not admitting its guilt (an important factor in any future civil actions). Corporations that violate consent decrees are then subject to civil action by the agency or a contempt citation from the court. Unfortunately, regulatory agencies seldom devote sufficient resources to police the consent decrees, and most violations go undetected. The Federal Trade Commission resolves about 80 percent of its cases through negotiations with the offenders. Only about ten of SEC cases are referred for criminal prosecution.[43] In cases involving faulty products, regulatory agencies often seek a recall order under which the corporation will agree to repair the defective merchandise. Administrative agencies sometimes issue unilateral orders requiring either that remedial action be taken to correct past harm or that the offender cease and desist from further illegal actions. An agency may also seek a federal court injunction, which is backed by the power of contempt. Finally, many kinds of violations may result in fines handed down through administrative, civil, or criminal channels, and prison sentences may be given to individual offenders by the criminal court.

Given all these possible responses, the choice of sanctions obviously plays an important role in determining whether or not justice is ultimately done. Unlike the decision to pursue a case or not, the choice of sanction is a matter of public record that is easily available to criminologists. Far and away the most comprehensive study of this important issue was conducted by a research team headed by Marshall Clinard at the University of Wisconsin that resulted in the book *Corporate Crime*, published by Clinard and his associate Peter Yeager in 1980. Working with one of the few large government grants ever given for research into corporate crime, the Clinard study concluded that corporations were not subject to the "full force of the law."[44] The data amassed by the research team showed the legal response to be so feeble that in the vast majority of cases, the government was satisfied when the offending corporation merely agreed to stop breaking the law. Few actual punishments were handed out, even for serious corporate crimes. The study examined 1,529 sanctions given to 477 of the largest manufacturing firms in the United States in 1975 and 1976. Almost one-half (44.2 percent) of the "sanctions" involved only warnings, one-fourth (24.6 percent) were "future effect orders" usually requiring the corporation to stop its illegal activities, and 7 percent were retroactive orders requiring the offenders to take some action to rectify the harm their crimes had caused. Thus, more than three-fourths (75.8 percent) of the cases involved no actual penalties. Of the remainder, 21 percent were civil fines, and only 2.4 percent involved criminal fines.[45]

As low as they are, these figures still overestimated the percentage of firms that actually were punished. Although in theory fines do constitute a type of punitive action, corporate fines seldom equaled the amount of profit made from the illegal actions. Four-fifths of the fines in the Clinard study were for less than $5,000.[46] Moreover, the study found that the size of the fines did not increase with the size of the offender. The median fine against the smallest firms in the study was $750; for the medium-sized firms, $1,650; and for the largest firms, $1,000. A $1,000 fine against a multibillion-dollar corporation cannot be said to constitute a punishment in any realistic sense of the word. Some observers have argued that the stigma of a criminal conviction is in itself enough punishment, but this argument has rarely been applied to the lower-class offenders who commit most street crimes, and it holds even less weight when the offender is a large, impersonal organization.

Unfortunately, no comprehensive examination of this important issue has been done since the Clinard study, but the evidence we do have indicates that punishments meted out to white-collar offenders have increased considerably since then. One study from the late 1980s found that fines for average corporate offenders had increased to about $50,000, but they remained substantially less than the losses from the crimes themselves.[47] Today, penalties from the most publicized cases now sometimes run into the hundreds of millions of dollars. The largest criminal fines yet handed out occurred in May of 1999, when the Hoffmann–LaRoche Corporation agreed to pay $500 million as a penalty for its involvement in a price-fixing cartel in the vitamin industry (see Chapter 2).[45] Even the penalties in smaller-scale antitrust actions have gone up, as witnessed by the $100 million penalty for fixing the price of two agricultural products given the Archer Daniels Midland Company in 1996.[49] Another piece of evidence comes from Justice Department data on the prosecution of environmental crimes that shows a steady increase in the average fines for those offenses.[50] Legislative changes have also played a part. In 1990, for example, an amendment to the Clean Air Act increased criminal fines for violators to a maximum of $250,000 per day for individuals and twice that amount for corporations, and provided jail terms of up to five years for each offense.

But although the size of the fines may have increased, virtually everyone familiar with the enforcement efforts against corporate criminals agrees that only a tiny fraction of the offenses ever result in any kind of sanction. Moreover, even what seem to be huge fines are seldom really large enough to discourage potential criminals. For example, the $100 million penalty against Archer Daniels Midland Company just mentioned was the largest such fine ever levied by the Justice Department to that point, yet ADM's stock went up immediately after it was announced. Not only was the fine merely a fraction of the money ADM had made from its crimes, but the government also agreed to give ADM immunity from prosecution for price-fixing in the sale of high-fructose corn syrup, one of its leading products.[51] But while ADM emerged unscathed from the actions of the Justice Department, Dwayne Andreas, ADM's chief executive at the time the price-fixing took place, was not as lucky. In September of 1998, Andreas and two other ADM executives were convicted on price-fixing charges and sentenced to two years in prison and a fine of $350,000.[52]

Data concerning prosecutions from the savings and loan scandal also indicate that the government often fails to follow through and collect the fines that have been assessed. For example, a 1992 study by the General Accounting Office focused on the top 100 referrals for thrift fraud made to the Justice Department. Those cases involved total losses of almost $600 million and resulted in 219 indictments, 145 convictions, court-ordered restitution of $79 million, and $4.5 million in fines. But at the time of that study, only $349,810 in restitution and $15,200 in fines had actually been collected, which was less than one-half of 1 percent of the total amount.[53]

In addition to action against entire corporations, regulatory agencies can ask the Justice Department to prosecute individual executives. But such requests are relatively rare and seldom result in actual prison sentences. The Clinard study found only fifty-six cases during the two years from 1975 to 1976 in which executives had been convicted of criminal offenses because of their involvement in organizational crimes. Moreover, only sixteen of them served any time in jail.[54] A study of the antitrust cases brought from 1890 to 1969 reached similar conclusions. Despite explicit criminal sanctions in the Sherman Act, the study found that less than half (44.7 percent) of the 1,551 cases brought during that period involved criminal charges, and even after a criminal conviction, the chance of imprisonment was less than 1 in 20 (4.9 percent).[55] On the other hand, although the chances of an average white-collar criminal going to jail are slight, the odds that a "notorious" offender whose name is splashed across the headlines will go to prison appear to have greatly increased.

The Criminal Justice System

Although the regulatory bureaucracy shoulders most of the responsibility for dealing with organizational crimes, the traditional criminal justice system still plays an important role in the effort to control many types of white-collar crime. Police and prosecutors at the local, state, and national levels bear the primary responsibility for taking action against most individual white-collar criminals, and the criminal justice system takes over responsibility for corporate crimes when regulatory agencies come to the Justice Department to request criminal prosecution.

Law Enforcement Agencies

The local police, who are the front line in the struggle against street crime, have much less impact on the problem of white-collar crime. For one thing, most local police departments are too small and ill prepared to deal with the complexities of major white-collar crime, and even the large urban departments with the greatest resources devote surprisingly little effort to this sort of crime. Most urban police departments don't even have a fraud unit, and those that do exist tend to be underfunded and understaffed. Further, apart from small size and inadequate resources, local police are often excluded from white-collar cases for another reason as well: Because most major white-collar crimes transcend local and even state boundaries, the primary jurisdiction usually rests with the federal government.

More than two dozen federal law enforcement agencies exercise jurisdiction over some specific kinds of white-collar crime.[56] A number of federal departments, such as the Veterans Administration, Housing and Urban Development, and Defense have an inspector general with the authority to conduct audits and investigations. The U.S. Postal Inspection Service focuses on mail fraud, and the Criminal Investigation Division of the Internal Revenue Service deals with tax fraud. Although there is less than one criminal tax fraud conviction for every 9,000 civil tax penalties,[57] IRS investigators have proven to be important in bringing some major white-collar criminals to justice, since tax evasion can sometimes be the most easily proven offense in a complex web of illegal dealing.

However, the Federal Bureau of Investigation is the only national agency with broad police powers in this area. The FBI's primary focus in the field of white-collar crime has been on the individual occupational offenses, but its overall commitment to white-collar investigations has shifted back and forth with the political winds. For most of J. Edgar Hoover's long tenure as director, the FBI gave white-collar crime a low priority. After the Watergate scandals, however, the Bureau showed a new interest in the problem. In 1980, under Director William Webster, the Bureau claimed to have allocated 22 percent of its special agents and 15 percent of its budget to the investigation of white-collar crime,[58] but critics charged that most of that apparent increase was achieved by merely reclassifying already existing operations.[59] Whatever the case, this commitment lagged during the early years of the Reagan administration, only to be renewed in response to the public's outrage over the savings and loan scandal. The FBI is currently involved in the investigation of a wide range of white-collar offenses, including public corruption (especially by law enforcement), environmental crime, embezzlement, health care fraud, fraud in government procurement, securities and commodities fraud, and various kinds of "cyber crime."[60] Nonetheless, after the terrorist attacks of September 11, 2001, the investigation of white-collar crime has clearly been relegated to a position of secondary importance.

The Prosecutors

Unlike most street crimes, the bulk of the investigatory work for white-collar cases is often handled by the prosecutor's office, not the police. But the prosecutors, like most other parts of the justice system, are often ill prepared to meet the challenge posed by white-collar crime. A 1987 survey of California district attorneys found that although all the district attorneys' offices considered the prosecution of corporate crimes to be within their jurisdiction, they actually spent very little effort on that kind of work. Of the offices that responded, 62 percent prosecuted fewer than ten corporate financial offenses a year, and 81 percent prosecuted fewer than ten environmental offenses a year.[61]

There is, however, evidence that prosecutions have increased since then. In a later survey by the same team of researchers, one-quarter of the local prosecutors surveyed said that prosecutions of corporate crime had increased during their tenure of office, whereas only 1 percent said they had decreased.[62] A nationwide survey of 100 local prosecutors in larger American communities by the National Institute of Justice found that half have special environmental prosecution units and that two-thirds assign at least a part-time prosecutor to environmental offenses.[63] Overall federal prosecution for criminal environmental offenses has clearly been increasing year by year. In the entire decade of the 1970s only twenty-five cases were brought; in 1986 that number was ninety-four, and by 1993 it had increased to 186.[64]

On the other hand, another study found that only about 6 percent of the corporations prosecuted for federal environmental laws were among America's 500 largest companies, even though an estimated two-thirds of them were breaking those laws,[65] and there is no question that the overall level of prosecutions of white-collar offenses remains extremely low compared with the frequency and severity of the offenses themselves. In investigating the prosecutions involved in the savings and loan scandals, Tillman, Calavita, and Pontell found that only one in four of those referred to federal authorities for prosecution in California were ever actually indicted, and in Texas that figure was only one in seven.[66]

A growing body of research on the prosecution of white-collar crime is making the reasons for this neglect increasingly clear. One of the strongest limits on the prosecution of these cases is lack of sufficient staff and resources. White-collar crimes are far more difficult to investigate and prosecute than other offenses. A study by Donald Scott, for example, found that the average price-fixing case took twenty-one months to investigate and twenty-three more months to litigate.[67] As Michael Benson and his colleagues put it: "It is unlikely that district attorneys forgo prosecuting many serious street crimes because the effort is judged to be too costly or time-consuming. In corporate cases, administrative costs seem to take precedence over the traditional symbolic function of the law to maintain moral boundaries."[68] The problem many prosecutors face is that they are often evaluated by the kinds of statistics they produce—such as the number of cases prosecuted and the percentage of those cases that bring a conviction. As a result, the most attractive strategy is often to prosecute a lot of simple, easy-to-win cases and to avoid the big cases against powerful defendants. As Joan Neff Gurney concluded, a campaign against white-collar crime "can easily become a campaign against small-time con artists, embezzlers, and welfare cheaters unless more emphasis is placed on the quality of the cases as opposed to producing good stats."[69]

Another major factor is the political influence of the big corporations, which time and again have been able to divert prosecutorial attention to less controversial cases. On the local level, the fear of the economic damage a corporate offender could create by slashing payrolls or moving to another community places another powerful inhibition on prosecutorial zeal. In one survey, a surprising 25 percent of local prosecutors admitted that they allowed local economic considerations to affect their decisions, and many of the other respondents were undoubtedly less than honest in their response. Aside from local conditions, employees at all levels of government are often reluctant to antagonize powerful corporations because of the lure of a better-paying job they might someday win in the private sector. Finally, many prosecutors are simply not very concerned about white-collar crime. In one survey, only 4 percent of local prosecutors said that white-collar crime was a "very serious" problem.[70]

In examining the prosecutions brought as a result of the collapse of the savings and loan industry, Tillman, Calavita, and Pontell explored a variety of explanations of the reasons some suspected offenders were charged and others were not. They found that unlike most other types of offenses, "law enforcement may have been directed not at crime control but at damage control, the purpose of which was to restore confidence in a fraud-ridden industry close to the heart of the American economy."[71]

The Defense

Another factor that adds to prosecutors' reluctance to pursue major white-collar cases is the fact that the defendants tend to put up a far stronger legal defense than do common street criminals, because if nothing else they usually have far more financial resources on which to draw. Kenneth Mann's excellent study of attorneys who defend white-collar cases shows how differently the criminal justice system operates when dealing with white-collar and street criminals.[72] In theory, the law provides a strict system of procedural safeguards that protects all defendants from the vast power of the state. The defendant is supposed to be represented by an independent attorney who battles the prosecutor under the impartial eye of the presiding judge. But a large body of evidence shows that for most street criminals, the justice system actually functions more like an assembly line than a legal obstacle course. Since most of their clients have only limited means, defense attorneys have a strong interest in processing each case quickly and going on to the next client. The criminal attorney is also under intense pressure from the prosecutor and the court to move legal proceedings along as rapidly as the overburdened system will permit. The vast majority of cases against street criminals never come to trial but are settled by negotiated agreement in a process that has come to be known as "plea bargaining."

The operation of "white-collar justice" presents a startling contrast. As Mann shows, the white-collar criminal's attorney is intensely adversarial from the moment he or she first makes contact with the enforcement agency. Whereas the counsel for the average criminal is likely to be extremely limited in the amount of time and money that can be devoted to the client, attorneys for white-collar criminals prepare their cases with painstaking attention to detail, often employing the services of private investigators and other professionals. In fact, David Weisburd and his associates found that a sample of white-collar defendants from the Yale study were three and a half times more likely to have private counsel than was a comparable sample of conventional defendants.[73] The ratio would have been much higher if the study's definition of white-collar crime had not allowed inclusion of many low-income defendants who were not "persons of respectability and high social status," as Sutherland's original definition required (see Chapter 1).

One of the most important differences between these two types of cases is that the attorney of the white-collar criminal gets involved much earlier in the case's progress. While street criminals seldom get an attorney until they are arrested and charged with a crime, white-collar criminals usually learn about the allegations and hire an attorney at a much earlier stage in the legal process. Thus, attorneys for white-collar criminals spend most of their effort in preventing charges from being filed. Indeed, the white-collar attorneys Mann interviewed considered a case to be a failure if their client was charged with an offense, even if he or she was later acquitted. The key to this process is what Mann calls "information management"—the attempt to conceal incriminating evidence from the prosecutor. Not only do the attorneys try to place legal obstacles in the way of the government's efforts to gather evidence, but they also tell their clients exactly which kinds of evidence still in their control would be most damaging if revealed. Although it is illegal for attorneys to advise their clients to destroy such evidence, the intelligent and well-educated defendants typical of white-collar cases hardly need such explicit instructions.

As a result of all these efforts, suspected white-collar criminals are far less likely to actually face criminal charges than are conventional criminal suspects. When they are indicted, white-collar defendants and their attorneys are typically more adversarial. David Friedrichs estimates that white-collar offenders are about four times more likely to refuse a plea bargain and to take their case to trial than are other defendants.[74]

The Courts

The impact of the criminal courts on the problem of white-collar crime is limited by the action or inaction of the prosecutors and enforcement agencies. But the courts do play an important symbolic role in deciding what kind of punishment will be meted out in the relatively few cases that do end in convictions. One frequent criticism of the courts concerns the common use of the nolo contendere (no contest) plea. The legal consequences of this plea are similar to those of a guilty plea, except that the defendants do not officially admit their guilt, and their plea therefore cannot be used as evidence in subsequent civil cases. Although this may appear to be a minor difference, it is actually of great importance, because the criminal penalties handed down for white-collar crimes are often less severe than the civil liabilities such crimes create. The nolo plea deprives the victims of white-collar criminals of the benefit of using the government's investigatory efforts in their civil cases. Moreover, the fact that the defendants are never forced to admit their guilt tends to reduce the stigma otherwise attached to a criminal conviction. Some observers have also charged that judges often make a subtle distinction between a defendant who enters a plea of *nolo contendere* and one who pleads guilty, and that the former tend to receive a lighter sentence.[75] However, the U.S. Sentencing Guidelines now used in federal courts make no distinction between a nolo contendere and a guilty plea.[76]

Sentencing is an area in which a large body of research showing evidence of favoritism toward white-collar offenders has accumulated over the years. One of the best studies of sentencing was John Hagan and Patrice Parker's analysis of securities violations that occurred over a seventeen-year period in Ontario, Canada.[77] By measuring social class on the basis of structural position rather than occupational prestige, and by including data on the prosecutors' decision about which charges to bring, these researchers discovered significant differences in sentencing among different groups of high-status offenders. The employers (those who own a business and hold authority over others) at the top of the structural hierarchy received significantly more lenient sentences than did other white-collar offenders. This was primarily because employers were charged with less serious offenses than other criminals who had committed crimes of equal severity. In contrast, managers (those who hold authority over others but do not own the business) received more severe punishment than others. The researchers also found that the prosecution of securities offenders increased significantly in the post-Watergate era, and they concluded that managers had been the primary scapegoats for the public's demand to crack down on white-collar criminals.

Susan Shapiro's study of the Securities and Exchange Commission found that lower-status offenders were less likely to have legal action brought against them for minor offenses, but more likely to be criminally prosecuted for serious offenses. Although high-status defendants charged with criminal offenses had, on the average, committed more serious crimes, they were no more likely to receive a jail sentence than lower-status offenders.[78] In an analysis of 1,597 cases published in 1994, Albonetti also found that high-status, white-collar offenders were more likely to avoid punishment than were low-status offenders.[79] One contradictory conclusion was reached in a 1982 study by Wheeler, Weisburd, and Bode, which found that higher-status defendants charged with white-collar crimes were more likely to receive jail sentences than were lower-status defendants.[80] Although there is some disagreement about the reasons for this unexpected finding, there are two common explanations. First, the study was conducted just after the Watergate scandals at a time when concern about white-collar crime was unusually high. (John Hagan and Alberto Palloni's examination of the records of one federal district court, for example, showed that judges were tougher on white-collar offenders after the Watergate scandal than they were before it.[81]) Second, the study was conducted in urban federal districts with an especially high volume of white-collar-crime cases presided over by liberal judges.

Whatever the social status of the individual offenders, it is clear that those charged with white-collar crimes receive more lenient sentences than other offenders.[82] Although dated, the Clinard study of corporate crime is useful because it did not include defendants who would normally be considered street criminals as the Wheeler, Weisburd, and Bode study did. The study found that only 4 percent of the sanctions handed out for corporate crimes involved criminal cases against individual executives. Of the convicted executives, 62.5 percent received probation, 21.4 percent had their sentences suspended, and 28.6 percent received short jail sentences. The average sentence was 37.1 days. Excluding a single case in which two six-month sentences were handed out, the remaining fourteen defendants received sentences averaging only nine days.[83] McCormick's historical study found that fewer than one in twenty of those convicted on criminal antitrust charges went to jail.[84] Most ironic of all, however, was the fact that the first eleven men sent to prison under the Sherman Act were all labor, not business, leaders—even though the clear intent of Congress was to restrain big business, not the unions. The first business executive was not sent to prison under the Sherman Act until 1961—seventy-one years after its enactment.[85]

In an analysis of Medicaid provider fraud, researchers found that even if convicted, defendants in such cases were substantially more likely to escape punishment than were similarly charged non–white-collar offenders.[86] A 1994 study directed by Henry Pontell concluded that the median sentence for a defendant convicted of a serious criminal offense in the savings and loan scandal was one-third shorter than the sentence for the average burglar.[87] Finally, it is significant that no defendant in a white-collar case has ever received the death penalty, even though many white-collar crimes have resulted in the deaths of thousands of people.

There is, nonetheless, evidence that the punishment for white-collar offenses has been increasing in recent years. The biggest change has come from the U.S. Sentencing Guidelines for the federal courts, which went into effect in October of 1987 for individuals and November of 1991 for organizations. These guidelines were created in an attempt to restrict judicial discretion and standardize sentences for all types of federal crimes.[88] Although compliance with these guidelines is not mandatory, the Sentencing Commission keeps a record of each federal judge's "downward departures" (sentences that are less than the guidelines recommend), and many judges fear that those who are too lenient will have their future promotions blocked by Congress. Under these guidelines, the use of probation is sharply restricted and prison sentences are determined by a complex formula instead of the judge's individual discretion. The standards have also been tightened since their original inception. Most notably, the corporate scandals touched off by the collapse of Enron in the early years of the twenty-first century led to passages of the Sarbanes–Oxley Act, which mandated a significant increase in the recommended sentence for fraud that was put into effect in 2003.[89]

Although the effects of the federal sentencing guidelines on white-collar defendants have not yet been systematically studied, anecdotal evidence indicates that they have helped increase jail terms for many defendants, especially those charged with fraud. For example, in May 2004, not long after the new guidelines for fraud went into effect, Jamie Olis, a mid-level financial executive at a Texas energy firm, received a twenty-four-year sentence for a fraudulent scheme that inflated his company's cash flow by $300 million.[90] A decade before, he undoubtedly would have received a much lighter sentence. The effects of the sentencing guidelines are not, however, as straightforward as they might appear. Since well over 90 percent of all federal convictions result from plea bargaining, most defendants are probably not charged with the most serious offence they have committed. The prospect of long mandatory sentences may be a good tool to coerce a guilty plea from a defendant, but it may also discourage prosecutors from bringing criminal charges against many white-collar defendants and make it more difficult to obtain a conviction if the defendant refuses to cooperate. Moreover, another major goal of the guidelines—to create uniform punishments for all offenders—has clearly not been met. A 1999 study found enormous differences among the federal courts in different parts of the country. More than eight white-collar offenders were sent to prison for every ten who were convicted in the Western District of Wisconsin, whereas fewer than three of every ten were sentenced to prison in the District of New Jersey.[91] Those standards also have no effect on the fines assessed through civil actions, and as Kenneth Mann argues, the lower standard of proof required in civil cases and the declining difference between the access to information granted by the courts in civil and criminal trials have made civil proceedings against corporate criminals an increasingly attractive option.[92]

Another example of increasing punishments comes from the extension of manslaughter and homicide laws to cover corporations and their agents. As pointed out in Chapter 3, such prosecutions never occurred until the 1970s, and the first successful conviction did not come until the 1980s. Although this is obviously an indication of an increasing severity of punishment, such prosecutions remains extremely rare.[93] A good example of how difficult such cases are comes from the charges brought against a Chicago company known as Film Recovery Systems—a case that has often been cited as the first successful prosecution of corporate executives for criminal homicide. In June 1985, three officials of Film Recovery Systems, Inc. were found guilty of murder for the death of an employee. The victim was Stefan Golab, a Polish immigrant who worked around vats of sodium cyanide (used to remove silver from old film) in a poorly ventilated factory that was in violation of numerous health and safety codes. Golab repeatedly complained about headaches, nausea, and vomiting, and requested to be transferred to another part of the plant. While working near a chemical vat, Golab began shaking and foaming at the mouth; after being helped outside, he collapsed and died. The executives, who had heard numerous complaints from sick workers and knew of the safety violations, were found guilty of murder and sentenced to twenty-five years in prison and a $10,000 fine.[94] But in 1990, an appeals court threw out the convictions on what can only be described as a minor legal technicality.[95]

It is, moreover, important to recognize that despite the overall trend toward tougher sentences, those charged with white-collar offenses still get far less punishment than other offenders. As Table 4.1 shows, between 1997 and 2002 there was a slight increase in the length of the prison sentences handed out to defendants convicted of the offenses the U.S. Sentencing Commission classifies as white-collar crimes (fraud, embezzlement, forgery, counterfeiting, bribery, tax offenses, and money laundering). But on the average, those sentences were still only a third as long as those given for drug offenses, and the white-collar offenders were significantly more likely to receive probation.[96] In 2003, whereas 91 percent of those convicted of burglary went to prison, only 53 percent of the embezzlers and 20 percent of those charged with antitrust violations did. A similar disparity was evident in the length of the sentence among those who were incarcerated. The average burglar received thirty months; the embezzlers, seventeen months; and the antitrust offenders, only seven months.[97]

			TABLE **4.1**
Average Length of Prison Sentence (in months)			
	Violent Offenses	**Drug Offenses**	**White-collar Offenses***
1997	104.7	81	20.2
1998	105.7	78	19.2
1999	97.9	75	20.4
2000	102	74.3	20.5
2001	89.5	71.6	20.8
2002	NA	73.6	21.5

*Includes fraud, embezzlement, forgery, counterfeiting, bribery, tax offenses, and money laundering only.

Source: Bureau of Justice Statistics, *Sourcebook of Criminal Justice Statistics 2002* (Washington, D.C.: U.S. Government Printing Office, 2003), Table 5.30.

Civil Suits by Victims

Civil suits brought by the victims of street crimes are not usually considered to be part of the criminal justice process. But with the repeated failures of the government's enforcement efforts, such suits have become a significant factor in the control of white-collar crime. Indeed, the framers of some regulatory legislation (e.g., the Sherman Act) actually regarded private suits as an integral part of the enforcement process.

The lawsuits generated by white-collar crimes are usually aimed at one of two targets—the violators or the regulatory agencies. The specific legal mandates given the newer regulatory agencies have led to the numerous suits claiming that those agencies have not lived up to or have exceeded the requirements of the law. Business interests, for instance, have mounted a legal challenge to almost every OSHA health regulation,[98] and the EPA has repeatedly been sued by environmentalists seeking tougher action and by polluters seeking the opposite. The net effect of this litigation is difficult to gauge, for both the public and the corporations have won some important legal victories. However, to the extent that all the legal maneuvering tends to slow the enforcement process, it works to defeat the goals the regulatory agencies were originally intended to achieve.

The civil suits brought against corporate offenders have generally had far greater impact. We have already discussed the use of civil litigation by regulatory agencies; in addition, businesses bring suits against each other for a wide variety of reasons. Of course, most of these cases involve disputes over contracts and other everyday business relations, not white-collar crimes. But allegations of fraud, false representation, or antitrust violations are not uncommon. Of all types of suits, however, it is probably the fear of tort actions from the victims of white-collar crime that imposes the most significant restraints on illicit business activity. Indeed, the legislators of the 1890s apparently had such confidence that the treble-damage provision of the Sherman Act would stimulate effective civil actions that no funds were voted to enforce the act until well into the twentieth century. Even though the task of challenging the anticompetitive practices of the major corporations has in fact proven far too formidable for individual citizens, civil suits have come to play an extremely important role in restraining some other types of white-collar crime.

In the 1960s, the courts began to allow the victims of corporate crimes to band together in class-action suits. Such suits have proven to be a powerful weapon for the victims of some white-collar crimes. Although decisions by the more conservative courts that followed placed new procedural obstacles in the way of class-action suits, they still greatly increase the victims' chances of legal success. Indeed, several law firms now specialize in this difficult kind of litigation in the hopes of sharing in the multimillion-dollar judgments that are sometimes handed down.

Along with the development of the class-action suit, another important trend has been the growing popularity of product liability litigation. Current laws differ substantially from state to state, but individuals who have been injured by a defective product, or their survivors, now clearly have the right to sue its manufacturer for damages. A manufacturer's liability can run into hundreds of millions or even billions of dollars when a widely used product, such as the Ford Pinto or the Dalkon Shield, is involved. There has also been an increasing number of suits over injuries caused by unsafe working conditions. Although occupational injuries and some occupational diseases are covered by workers' compensation statutes that restrict private suits, the courts have held that a worker can still bring legal action if he or she can show that the company deliberately concealed information about occupational health hazards. These rulings have, for example, opened the door for suits from the tens of thousands of asbestos workers who are dying from previous on-the-job exposure.

Despite the huge size of some judgments, civil court actions seldom result in compensation for all the victims of a dangerous product. A study of civil suits in the nation's seventy-five largest counties found that in 1992 the defendants won only ninety-two professional malpractice suits, 142 product liability suits, and 202 suits involving toxic substances. The plaintiffs won about three-fourths of the toxic substances suits, but only 41 percent of the product liability suits and 30 percent of the malpractice suits. Moreover, despite the publicity surrounding a few multimillion-dollar judgments, the median award to the plaintiff in each type of suit was only $101,000, $260,000, and $156,000, respectively.[99]

In most cases, individual plaintiffs are outgunned by highly paid corporate lawyers whose legal maneuvers often succeed in obstructing entire groups of suits. For example, the makers of DES (diethylstilbestrol), a cancer-causing pregnancy drug, were able to win rulings that required the victims to prove which one of the 267 manufacturers of DES had made the particular drug they took—a decision that blocked most of the victims' suits. Years of legal battles were required before the courts finally formulated a new, and still not universally accepted, legal doctrine apportioning liability among all the manufacturers based on their share of the market.[100] But while the battle dragged on, needy victims were denied compensation or were forced to accept out-of-court settlements for only a fraction of the money they deserved.

A different sort of legal tactic was used by the Manville Corporation, the world's largest manufacturer of asbestos—a product that has caused hundreds of thousands of deaths and injuries to workers and the general public (see Chapter 2). Despite healthy profits and billions of dollars in assets, the company filed for Chapter 11 bankruptcy in August 1982, claiming that it could not pay all the potential judgments that might be made against it in the asbestos cases.[101] The battle between the company and its victims dragged on for six years before a settlement was finally reached and Manville emerged from bankruptcy. At the time, many hailed the agreement as a major victory for the victims, since Manville agreed to create an independently administered $2.5 billion fund to pay off the claims against it. It is now clear, however, that even such a huge sum was inadequate to pay for the damage Manville had wreaked, and the administrative structure of the fund itself was also deficient. By December 1992, more than a decade after the original bankruptcy filing and more than twenty years after the dangers of asbestos first won wide publicity, there were still more than 150,000 victims awaiting payment. Although there is no exact tally, there is little doubt that tens of thousands of victims died before the settlement money ever reached them.[102]

Even without such legal maneuvers and exemptions, civil action takes years, and many victims are forced to agree to quick settlements to meet their medical expenses. Victims are often unaware of their right to sue or cannot for one reason or another prove their case. Thus, it is common for a few victims to receive large settlements and for many others to get nothing.

Nevertheless, the threat of civil litigation is one of the strongest controls on corporate crime. The potential liability involved in the decision to market an unsafe product or expose the public to life-threatening pollutants is staggering, and corporations are responding in two different ways. Some corporations have come to realize that a better program of product testing, quicker recalls of faulty merchandise, and a more cautious approach to the disposal of toxic wastes are much cheaper in the long run than public denials and legal maneuvering. On the other hand, corporate interests have also attempted to change the law to make it more difficult for their victims to win big judgments in court. Such "tort reforms" are vigorously supported by a wide range of industries, and despite strong opposition from trial lawyers (which is often well funded) as well as consumer and environmental groups, at least eleven different bills have been enacted at the federal level since 1992 that limit victims' rights in cases involving such things as defective aircraft, faulty medical implants, Y2K computer glitches, securities fraud, and railroad accidents.[103] Ironically, long-established restrictions on the right to sue the government make it even easier for the government to avoid the responsibility for the victims of its mistakes than it is for the corporations.

The Effectiveness of Enforcement

Because government policies and priorities change from year to year and decade to decade, and because the dominant patterns of white-collar crime are subject to even more rapid change, it is difficult to make a flat statement about the effectiveness of the enforcement process. The elitist theorists who claim that the criminal activities of the elite receive only token punishment certainly overstate their case, but the pluralists' notion that pressure from other organized interests forces the justice system to treat the crimes of the privileged and the crimes of the powerless equally are even further from the mark. White-collar justice and the crimes it seeks to deter are far too complex a phenomenon to be appraised in a few simple generalizations, and a much more detailed analysis is necessary.

The principal goal of professional self-regulation is clearly to protect the interests of the professionals, not the public, and it need not concern us further. The operations of the various regulatory agencies are of much more importance. Some agencies appear to do a reasonably good job of meeting their statutory obligations, whereas others seem hopelessly inadequate. Much of this difference can be explained by the different configurations of pressure groups with which the agencies must contend. The relative success of the SEC can be attributed to the fact that, unlike most of the other agencies examined here, it enjoys strong business support. Of course, particular rulings and procedures are subject to attacks from business interests, but on the whole the business elite recognizes the need for the kind of control and regulation that the SEC provides.

The EPA has certainly not had such support. But in addition to the business lobby, which opposes its mission, it must confront a well-organized environmental lobby—a fact that goes a long way toward explaining why the EPA has been more successful than many other regulatory agencies. The EPA showed, for example, a remarkable resiliency in weathering what can only be described as an all-out attack from the Reagan administration and the corporate interests that supported it. Not only did Mr. Reagan appoint top administrators, such as agency head Anne Buford, who were openly hostile to environmental interests, but he slashed the agency's budget from $5.6 billion in 1980 to $4.1 billion in 1984 (a period of high inflation during which total federal expenditures increased more than 44 percent). But a scandal forced Buford's resignation, and the appointment of a director more friendly to environmental interests and pressure from

Congress and the general public forced the administration to ease up the pressure on the EPA's budget. By 1990, the EPA's budgetary outlays had once again reached their 1980 level,[104] and they have grown substantially since then. Nonetheless, the EPA is still highly vulnerable to political pressure. In 2001 and 2002 under the Bush administration, there were fewer than a quarter of the average number of annual citations issued for pollution during the last years of the Clinton administration.[105] Although the EPA has shown considerable resiliency in the face of determined and powerful opposition, it has still fallen far short of the urgent task it was created to accomplish. Every year more wilderness is destroyed, more animals are driven to extinction, more pollutants are dumped into the environment, and more people die from environmentally induced cancers.

Although its mission is much the same as that of the EPA, OSHA has been markedly less successful. OSHA has not promulgated an adequate number of regulations to control exposure to dangerous substances, and its enforcement efforts have been grossly inadequate.[106] OSHA has also been far less effective than the EPA in fending off attacks by its corporate opponents. A major factor in the failure of OSHA has been the lack of a grassroots movement for occupational safety comparable to the environmental movement. Although rank-and-file union members have often expressed concern about this issue, organized labor has never accorded top priority to health and safety issues. Conversely, business interests have mounted strong opposition to any effort to improve working conditions that involves significant financial costs.

The FDA presents a mixed picture, because it carries out two different tasks in regulating food and drugs. The FDA's reliance on safety tests conducted by the drug manufacturers clearly weakens its regulatory effectiveness, but on the whole, the FDA exercises tighter supervision of the U.S. drug market than many similar agencies do in other nations. In fact, the international community has grown so dependent on the FDA's supervision of the multinational pharmaceutical companies that an Australian expert on corporate crime, John Braithwaite, concluded that the "FDA is no longer only the guardian of the health of Americans; it is the guardian of the health of the world."[107]

This situation may, however, be changing. In response to pressure from AIDS patients, and, of course, the pharmaceutical industry, the FDA has been slackening its supervision of the drug market by instituting a "fast-track" approval system for promising new drugs. The results have been disastrous. The very first drug the FDA assigned for a fast-track six-month review process was Warner-Lambert's Rezulin—a drug combating a disease (diabetes) for which there were already many treatments. Rezulin was seen as a drug with a "blockbuster" sales potential, and after John L. Gueriguian, the FDA official originally charged with reviewing the drug, reached negative conclusions, Warner-Lambert pressured the FDA into removing him in November 1996. Once the drug was approved, its high-profile status as a fast-track drug made the FDA leadership especially reluctant to force its withdrawal from the market. A bitter internal battle raged on for months as the evidence built up of the drug's dangers to the liver. By the time it was finally withdrawn from the market in 1999, there were sixty-three confirmed fatalities, and an analysis by an FDA epidemiologist put the total figure at 400.[108]

The FDA's supervision of the quality and healthfulness of the food sold in U.S. supermarkets has fallen far, far short of its statutory mandates. The agency has failed to issue timely bans on carcinogenic substances, it does not adequately inspect the food supply, and it has promulgated lax labeling standards for potentially hazardous substances. One bright spot is that government regulators have made significant improvements in the labeling requirements for fat, calories, and other nutritional elements. But unlike the European countries, the FDA bowed to industry pressure and has refused to require the labeling of products that contain genetically engineered food.

Of all the regulatory agencies, those dealing with antitrust enforcement have one of the worst records of failure. Time after time, these agencies have won insignificant cases and ignored or lost the important ones. The crux of the problem lies in the lack of public involvement. Although many people recognize the problems created by the concentrated power of big business, there is little understanding of the complex legal technicalities involved in antitrust action. The antimonopoly movement of the late nineteenth and early twentieth centuries, which helped create the antitrust laws, has long since died away, and antitrust violations lack the drama that attracts media attention, as the more violent white-collar crimes sometimes do. The only antitrust violation that has received consistent government attention is price-fixing, and even then the enforcement effort has waxed and waned with the changes in the political climate.

A review of the enforcement efforts of the more traditional branches of the criminal justice system presents another complex picture. The available evidence on prosecution and sentencing shows that occupational criminals receive more lenient treatment than common street criminals. Enforcement agencies devote few resources to occupational crimes, and even after cases are filed and defendants convicted, white-collar offenders still receive lighter punishment. Convicted occupational offenders, however, do run a significant risk of imprisonment. In contrast, the individuals involved in organizational crimes run far less risk of significant punishment. The data examined in this chapter have shown that only a tiny fraction of the accusations brought against the individuals involved in corporate offenses end up in criminal court, and that even when convictions ensue, the "punishment" is often so insignificant as to be meaningless, at least as long as the corporations involved remain financially strong and influential. But the failure to prosecute is a far greater problem than judicial leniency. There are no statistics on how many serious organizational crimes are never prosecuted, but we do know that criminal prosecution is so rare that even the most notorious and most deadly cases, such as those involving the asbestos and cigarette manufacturers, seldom result in criminal charges (see Chapter 2).

The tort system was never intended to serve as a tool of criminal justice, but civil suits by victims have often proven to be a much more effective restraint on organizational crime than has the criminal justice system. To confirm this conclusion, one need only compare the minuscule criminal fines often given corporate offenders with the huge civil judgments sometimes passed against them. Although many factors contribute to this difference, one of the most important appears to be the nature of the plaintiffs involved. Even though private litigants lack the financial resources of the government enforcement agencies, they usually are firmly convinced of the justice of their claims and resolutely pursue the maximum possible recompense. In contrast, the government's enforcement efforts have repeatedly been compromised by political pressure. In the absence of unusually strong counterpressure to offset the political influence of the offenders, the government simply fails to do the job. It would, nonetheless, be a mistake to ignore the serious limitations that civil actions by victims have as a restraint on white-collar crime. As we have already noted, such tactics represent a viable alternative for only a small percentage of those harmed by white-collar offenses, and several important types of white-collar crime are seldom if ever subject to civil actions.

Two Case Studies

Despite some occasional successes, the broad strokes of our institutional analysis and the statistics generated by the justice system have painted a portrait of weak and ineffective enforcement. To flesh out this picture, we must explore the ways the justice system has dealt with specific cases and the political and economic pressures they generate. This section examines two cases of such enormous size and scope that they have taken on a historical significance all their own. In one of them the enforcement effort was largely successful, and in the other it was not. A comparison of the two cases speaks volumes about the true nature of white-collar justice.

Antitrust and the Petroleum Industry

Among the numerous antitrust cases brought against big oil, four stand out as serious efforts to break up the concentration of economic and political power in the petroleum industry: the early cases brought by the individual states under their own antitrust laws; the first federal case, instituted by President Theodore Roosevelt; the oil cartel case that began shortly after the end of World War II; and the Exxon case instituted by the FTC in the early 1970s.

The first legal challenge to the Standard Oil monopoly came in 1889, when Ohio attorney general David Watson happened across the text of the Standard Oil Trust Agreement in the appendix of a legal treatise. He was surprised to find that it violated the law in at least two important ways: First, it created a monopoly and was thus void and unenforceable at common law; and second, it forced Standard of Ohio to violate its state charter by operating under the direction of an out-of-state company. Watson took Standard to court, and after an extended legal battle, Standard of Ohio was ordered to withdraw from the trust. Although it appeared to commentators at the time that a death blow had been dealt to the oil trust's operations in Ohio, the use of delaying tactics combined with the court's failure to set a time limit for withdrawal from the trust allowed Standard to continue its operations without substantive change. In response to the original court order, Standard merely consolidated some of its companies and reshuffled its trust certificates. When Watson's trust-busting successor, Frank Monnett, discovered the deception, he launched a new case against Standard. The company's response was to reorganize itself as a holding company instead of a trust and to continue its delaying tactics. Finally, Monnett was replaced by an orthodox Republican who refused to continue the case, and the oil trust carried on with business as usual.[109]

Texas's assault on the Standard monopoly was carried out in a very different environment from the one in conservative, industrial Ohio. Not only was Texas a predominantly agricultural state, but its farmers were undergoing a long period of hard times that they blamed on the machinations of the eastern industrialists. Moreover, Texas had an exceptionally strong antitrust tradition bolstered by a constitution that contained explicit antitrust provisions.

The Texas representative of the Standard Trust, the Waters-Pierce Company, was renowned for the ruthless tactics it used against its competitors. The first moves against Waters-Pierce were made in 1894 by Governor Jim Hogg, who had already received wide acclaim for his contribution to the framing of a new state antitrust act. Although the early stages of the enforcement effort were marked by considerable ineptness on the part of the state prosecutors, they eventually won confirmation of the constitutionality of the Texas antitrust statutes in February 1897, a court ruling ordering the revocation of Waters-Pierce's Texas business license in the same year, and a final victory before the U.S. Supreme Court in March 1900.

After six years of legal battles, it appeared that the trustbusters had finally won. Henry Clay Pierce, however, continued to fight to retain control of the lucrative Texas market, and he began cultivating friends in high places. His most notable recruit was a rising young congressman, Joseph Bailey, who received more than $12,000 in interest-free loans from Pierce and his associates. Bailey was influential in persuading new Texas governor Tom Smith to grant Waters-Pierce a series of extensions. When the court order could no longer be evaded, Pierce reorganized his company, signed an affidavit certifying that Waters-Pierce (the company had not even changed its name) was no longer part of the Standard Trust, and won a new business license. The company continued to do business as usual in Texas until 1906, when Henry Pierce exploded a bombshell at a Missouri antitrust hearing by admitting that Standard Oil still controlled his company. The Texas attorney general filed suit ten days later and won a conviction in June 1907 that resulted in a $1.623 million fine and another revocation of Waters-Pierce's business permit. Although the attorney general later ran for governor on the strength of the successful antitrust case, his success was more appearance than reality. Standard continued to operate in Texas through its other subsidiaries until 1909, when a court ordered that its holdings in the state be placed in receivership and sold. However, it later was discovered that the purchaser, John Sealy, was himself a trustee of Standard Oil. The Waters-Pierce Company, meanwhile, was sold to a St. Louis businessman, Sam Fordyce, who turned out to be an old friend of Henry Pierce's, and together they promptly formed the Pierce-Fordyce Oil Association. Thus, although the Texas trustbusters had certainly made things difficult for the Standard Trust, they ultimately failed to expel the monopoly from their state.[110]

Altogether, ten states and the Oklahoma Territory filed antitrust suits against the Standard Oil combination between 1890 and 1911, but all the suits ultimately failed. In Tennessee, the combination dodged a 1909 court order banning Kentucky Standard from operating in that state simply by transferring its business to newly created Louisiana Standard. In 1910, Louisiana Standard sold 85.5 percent of the kerosene and 81.7 percent of the naphtha and gasoline sold in Tennessee. In Kansas, a petition charging Standard of New Jersey with antitrust violations led the state supreme court to appoint a commissioner to investigate the oil industry. The investigators took an incredible five years to come to the obvious conclusion that Standard did in fact monopolize the oil business in that state, and even after the report was completed, the attorney general took no action except to negotiate a meaningless consent decree. In 1908, the Missouri Supreme Court found three Standard companies guilty of antitrust violations. Each company was fined $150,000, the charter of one company based in that state (the infamous Waters-Pierce) was canceled, and the business licenses of the other two were revoked. But intense economic and political pressure from Standard, including suspension of the construction of a large Missouri oil refinery, forced the court to back down and reverse its decision.

On the federal level, the passage of the Sherman Act was met with administrative apathy. No federal charges were brought against Standard, the nation's most notorious monopoly, for 17 years. Although the act directed federal district attorneys "under the direction of the Attorney General" to institute antitrust proceedings against violators, in practice the decision to move against such politically powerful criminals was made by the president, not by the attorney general. Despite widespread public hostility toward the Standard combination and its obvious antitrust violations, Presidents Cleveland and McKinley took no action against the company. This was hardly surprising, for not only were both conservatives strongly allied with big business, but both had received substantial campaign contributions from Standard.[111]

The Justice Department finally brought suit against Standard for Sherman Act violations in May 1907. Although the case was marked by the same kind of legal maneuvering used in the state cases, the government won its final victory in May 1911, when the Supreme Court unanimously upheld a lower-court decision against Standard and ordered the combination dissolved into its constituent companies.

This decision was widely hailed as a devastating blow to the oil trust. Passing largely unnoticed was the fact that the technique of dissolution ordered by the Court, on the recommendation of the prosecutor, virtually ensured Standard's continued domination of the petroleum market. One problem with the dissolution order was structural. The different companies in the Standard combination had always specialized in the production, distribution, or marketing aspects of the business; and because the Court broke up Standard along the lines of existing companies, the newly created independent firms were virtually required to maintain close business relationships. A more serious problem resulted from the technique of stock distribution adopted by the Court. Instead of assigning stockholders blocks of stock in one of the new companies, the Court gave each stockholder a prorated share in each of the new companies. Because just eight stockholders held over 50 percent of the shares in Standard, this plan ensured that the same small group would own a controlling interest in each of the newly independent companies. Thus, even the dissolution of Standard Oil failed to break its hold on the domestic petroleum market. The question of why the prosecutors proposed such an obviously inadequate remedy cannot be answered with the available evidence, but one expert concluded that "they were more interested in winning a politically important case than restoring competition to the industry."[112]

Ironically, some measure of competition was soon to return to the petroleum industry—not as a result of the federal court's actions, but because of the discovery of large new oil fields in Texas and Oklahoma, which helped spawn the Texaco and Gulf petroleum companies. Moreover, Standard's foreign competitors, principally Shell and British Petroleum, were also growing stronger. In fact, the outbreak of competition eventually became so worrisome to the heads of the largest companies that they met in Achnacarry Castle in Scotland to hammer out the illegal cartel agreement discussed in Chapter 2.[113]

Details of the operation of the oil cartel were first uncovered by the Federal Trade Commission in the early 1950s. Although efforts were made to suppress the ensuing report on the grounds of "national security," the news leaked out and parts of the report were soon published. These disclosures came on the heels of evidence that some of the big oil companies had cooperated with the Germans during World War II. Together, these revelations generated a wave of public hostility that led President Harry Truman to order the Justice Department to begin a grand jury investigation of the oil cartel.[114] Shortly before leaving office, Truman decided to drop the criminal charges pending against the petroleum companies but ordered that the civil action be "vigorously prosecuted." When

President Eisenhower came to office, the oil cartel case, once seen as one of the most important cases ever brought by the Antitrust Division of the Justice Department, was slowly whittled away into insignificance. In the words of the director of the investigation, "The pressures were continuous from month to month, sometimes week to week, to downgrade the importance of the prosecution of the cartel case."[115] The final outcome of fifteen years of litigation was what John M. Blair, one of the foremost authorities on the petroleum industry, termed a "virtually meaningless consent decree."[116]

The last major challenge to the oligopolistic power of big oil was a suit launched by the FTC shortly after the first "oil crisis" in 1973—another time of strong public resentment against the petroleum industry. The suit charged Exxon and seven other major petroleum firms with collusive actions and sought to cut them up into separate production, pipeline, refining, and marketing companies in order to break their control of oil from wellhead to gasoline pump. Like all matters of this nature, the so-called Exxon case was massive and complex, consuming 12 to 14 percent of the FTC's entire antitrust budget for much of the 1970s.[117] Despite this effort, the FTC was hopelessly outmatched and little progress was made. The oil industry's legal team bogged down the government in endless maneuvers and finally swamped FTC investigators with massive requests for information and documents. With the coming of the Reagan administration, the political winds shifted against their effort, and in September 1981 the FTC finally gave up. The FTC's staff report recommended dropping the Exxon case because of the obstructionist tactics of the oil companies and the glacial slowness of the suit. One staff attorney was quoted as saying that the case "could continue without a final judgment on the merits or implementation of remedial provisions until 15 or 20 years after the filing of the complaint."[118]

The effort to prosecute antitrust violations in the petroleum industry has been a long and at times intense struggle, with key victories on both sides, but it is clear that the interests of the petroleum companies ultimately prevailed. Despite all the government's efforts, the petroleum companies succeeded in minimizing competition and maintaining the control of a small cartel. It was not a one-sided battle. The antitrust movement did succeed in limiting some of the worst abuses of the oil companies, both through direct court action and through the companies' fear of inciting more public demands for government action. But the fact remains that corporate interests ultimately defeated the antitrust laws.

The Rise and Fall of Michael Milken

From a sociological standpoint, the laws that regulate the securities markets have many similarities to the antitrust laws. They both seek to ensure fair competition and open markets. The offenses they define are usually well hidden behind corporate walls of secrecy, and the victims seldom complain to the authorities. Moreover, both sets of laws are complex and technical, and the public often has little understanding of the crimes they define. But as occurred after the revelation of the oil cartel agreements in the 1950s and the collapse of the savings and loan industry in the late 1980s, a wave of public indignation does occasionally demand strong enforcement action.

As we saw in Chapter 2, the fevered financial speculation of the 1980s was accompanied by a crime wave at the highest levels of the American financial community. Economists of this era dubbed it a "casino economy" in which the real money was not made through constructive investments but through various sorts of financial speculation that sought immediate gains regardless of the long-term consequences. Although many speculators, takeover artists, and savings and loan operations amassed enormous fortunes during this period, Michael Milken clearly stands out from the rest. Not only was he the dominant financial figure of this era, but he became a national symbol of its excesses.

The son of an accountant with an amazing memory and a head for figures, Milken grew up in a comfortable middle-class suburb of Los Angeles. While still an undergraduate at the University of California at Berkeley, he read a historical study showing that a portfolio of low-grade, high-interest bonds outperformed a comparable portfolio of blue-chip bonds. These so-called junk bonds not only became the focus of Milken's remarkable career, but they were to transform the financial landscape of the United States. After graduating from the prestigious Wharton School of Business at the University of Pennsylvania, Milken took a job with the Wall Street firm of Drexel Burnham Lambert, where he quickly became an outspoken advocate of the junk bond. Milken argued that the only problem with low-grade debt was its lack of liquidity, and he almost single-handedly created a lucrative market for high-yield (junk) bonds. When Milken first started trading in high-yield bonds in the 1970s, they were an obscure backwater of Wall Street's financial dealings. But at its peak in the late 1980s the market was more than $200 billion a year, and Michael Milken controlled 60 to 70 percent of the deals.[119]

In his early years, Milken saw himself as something of a crusader for economic growth as well as a financier. Milken's specialty was finding deserving companies that had been denied credit by the financial establishment and raising funds for them through the high-yield bond market; and he often pointed with pride to the jobs these companies helped create. But as Milken grew more and more successful, he turned what came to be known as his "money machine" to the biggest game around—financing corporate takeovers. By providing billions of dollars in junk-bond financing for such "corporate raiders," Milken fanned the flames of the takeover mania that gripped the United States in the 1980s. At the time, the corporate raiders claimed that they were performing a public service by dislodging overpaid and underperforming managers from their roosts at the top of the corporate pyramid, and wringing more profits out of their stodgy corporate targets. In reality, even unsuccessful raids usually left their corporate victims staggering under a huge burden of debt. As the takeover era of the 1980s came to a close, one corporate target after another collapsed into bankruptcy, throwing tens of thousands of workers from their jobs and contributing to the pervasive economic malaise of the early 1990s. Even the environment paid a price to make those corporate raiders into multimillionaires. One target of a Milken-financed raid, Pacific Lumber, reversed its environmentally enlightened policies and quickly set about clearcutting its old-growth redwoods in order to pay its junk-bond debt.[120]

Of course, the mere fact that these activities had devastating economic and social consequences does not make them illegal, and Milken probably could have built a considerable financial empire without ever breaking the law. But his near-total control of the multibillion-dollar junk-bond market and his insatiable desire to expand his power, wealth, and influence seemed to create irresistible temptations for a man who was to all outward appearances an exemplar of ethical behavior. Even though Milken often deceived (and in some cases cheated) his clients, his control of the junk-bond market gave them little choice but to continue to deal with him. The complexity of the laws and of the deals Milken put together makes it impossible to provide a full listing of his crimes, but in November 1990 he pleaded guilty to six felony counts that involved everything from security law violations (e.g., filing false disclosure statements) to mail fraud and tax violations.[121] Milken was given a stiff ten-year sentence (which was later reduced because of his good behavior in prison) and forced to pay $600 million for his crimes. Milken was also the target of numerous civil suits. In March 1992 he agreed to pay $500 million into a compensation fund, which, it is believed, still left him with at least $125 million in his own name and a family fortune estimated at half a billion dollars.[122] He was also given a lifetime ban on associating with any securities "broker or dealer." In 1998, several years after his release from prison, Milken was forced to pay $47 million to the SEC because a company he ran was involved in two banned transactions.[123]

How did the authorities succeed in bringing one of the richest and most powerful men in America to justice? As sometimes happens in investigations of syndicated crime, the case began with a small break that led to the arrest of one criminal, who was pressured to inform on bigger criminals, who in turn testified against still bigger criminals, until investigators worked their way up to the top of the chain. In this case it all began with an anonymous letter to the enforcement division of the Wall Street firm of Merrill Lynch, charging two of its brokers in Venezuela with insider trading. Merrill Lynch investigated and notified the SEC, which then carried on the case. It turned out that the two traders were "piggybacking" (copying the buy and sell orders) on the trades carried out for a client of a Swiss bank in the Bahamas. Further investigation revealed that this client, known as Mr. Diamond, was actually Dennis Levine, an investment banker with Shearson Lehman Hutton and later with Drexel Burnham Lambert. Levine eventually pleaded guilty to four felony counts and agreed to cooperate with the authorities and implicate others involved in his insider-trading schemes. Chief among them was Ivan Boesky, the financial world's most celebrated speculator in takeover stocks. Like Levine, Boesky was eventually sent to prison, and he also agreed to inform on others to win a lighter sentence for himself. Prosecutors generally demand that informers turn in someone of greater importance than themselves to get such deals, and among others Boesky implicated Michael Milken. In fact, Boesky went so far as to wear a concealed microphone to record one conversation with Milken.[124]

Milken put on a tenuous defense against the accusations of the investigators. His lawyers argued that any criminal charges would come down to a case of Milken's word against that of a convicted felon, and Milken even hired a public relations firm to help wage a battle in the media. (The government is, of course, legally prohibited from publicly discussing most aspects of a pending legal case and was therefore unable to answer many of his charges.) But despite all these efforts, the investigators were eventually able to get supporting evidence from several of Milken's former employees, and he agreed to plead guilty to the felony charges mentioned earlier.[125]

Why was the government able to bring Milken to justice when it was so notably unsuccessful in its actions against the oil companies? Many of Milken's supporters charged that the government's actions were part of an effort by the corporate establishment to stop the upstart Milken and his corporate raiders. It is true that Milken, Boesky, Levine, and most of the other key figures in the scandal were Jews, and most of them no doubt were seen as outsiders by the Waspish corporate establishment. There is, however, no evidence to suggest that Milken's downfall was part of a conspiracy or that the investigators had any idea where the trail would ultimately lead. If Milken suffered from being an "outsider," it was not that the enforcement agencies were out to get him, but that he lacked the political power to force them to back down. Milken and the others involved in the scandal were so consumed with their financial concerns that they paid little or no attention to cultivating political influence until it was too late to do them much good. Big oil, on the other hand, has long maintained one of Washington's most powerful lobbies. While those involved in the prosecution of the oil cartel case reported constant political pressure to back down, those involved in the Milken case experienced few such problems aside from the negative media attention generated by Milken's last-minute public relations campaign. In fact, the political pressure probably ran in the other direction. The chief prosecutor involved in the case, Rudolph Giuliani, was politically ambitious, and Milken's conviction was clearly a feather in his cap during a period when the savings and loan scandal was a hot topic of public concern (several insolvent savings and loans were heavy purchasers of Milken's junk bonds). Thus, while Milken's "outsider" status was not the cause of his legal problems, his lack of political influence commensurate with his financial strength left him more vulnerable to the law than better-connected corporate offenders.

Why Justice Fails

The evidence leaves little doubt about the failure of the current system to mete out equal justice to all offenders. It now remains only to explain why white-collar offenders receive the favored treatment outlined in these pages. At a general level, it is clear that the enforcement effort against white-collar crime so often fails both because such crimes are hard to detect and because the wealth and influence of the criminals enable them to avoid the full weight of the law. A growing body of research, however, allows us to go beyond such generalities and to specify some of the particular techniques that have been used to stymie the enforcement process.

Two Red Herrings

Our first order of business is to dispose of two widely held misconceptions that simply do not fit the facts. One is the belief that white-collar crimes are non-violent offenses that cause little real harm to the public. If one accepts that assumption, it follows that fewer enforcement resources should be spent on white-collar crimes than on street crimes, which pose a real public danger. But the data reviewed in the first chapter of this book clearly show the fallacy of this argument. Not only do white-collar crimes cost the public considerably more money than do all other types of crime combined, but many white-collar crimes are very violent indeed. In fact, the evidence indicates that white-collar offenses kill and cripple far more people than all the street crimes put together.

A more widely accepted derivative of the first argument holds that whatever the actual harm caused by white-collar crime, the public is less concerned about it than street crime and consequently puts less pressure on the enforcement agencies to do a thorough job.[126] But once again the evidence fails to support this contention. Although the public is unlikely to show interest in any individual crime unless the media publicizes it, decades of opinion polls have shown intense resentment about the crimes of those in positions of trust and responsibility. In a 1969 Harris poll, 68 percent of the people questioned felt that a businessman who illegally fixes prices was worse than a burglar, as opposed to only 28 percent who thought the burglar was worse.[127] Another survey from the late 1960s found that the public considers an embezzler to be a more serious offender than a burglar, prostitute, or looter, but not an armed robber or murderer.[128] In a 1972 sample, 120 Baltimore residents were asked to rate the seriousness of several different criminal acts. "Manufacturing and selling drugs known to be harmful to users" and "knowingly selling contaminated food which results in a death" were held to be more serious than such crimes as armed robbery or assault with a gun.[129] When that study was replicated a decade later in a rural area of Illinois, researchers found even stronger resentment against white-collar criminals. To the Illinois residents, the intentional sale of a contaminated drug that results in the death of a user was more serious than forcible rape or selling secrets to a foreign nation.[130] A study that was published by the U.S. Department of Justice in 1984 and involved more than 60,000 respondents showed the same intense concern about white-collar crime among the general public. For example, a factory that polluted a city's water supply and killed twenty people was ranked seventh out of the 204 offenses studied. This piece of research, like virtually all the others, also made it clear that the more physical harm an offense causes, the more serious it is considered to be. A factory that killed one person with its waste was ranked thirteenth of the 204 offenses and a factory that made twenty people sick was ranked thirty-first, whereas a factory that was said only to pollute a city's water without mention of any injuries was ranked sixty-fourth.[131] Forty-five percent of respondents in a survey published by the National White Collar Crime Center in 2000 said that selling tainted meat that caused one person to become ill was worse than an armed robbery that caused a serious injury. In contrast, only 36 percent held the robbery to be more serious. Similarly, most respondents held a contract "fraudster" to be a more serious offender than a "street" thief (44 percent to 38 percent).[132]

Evidence also shows that the public favors tougher penalties for white-collar offenders than are given out by the justice system. A study by Donald Newman asked 178 people to recommend the penalties for a number of actual cases involving violation of the Food, Drug, and Cosmetic Act. Four out of the five respondents recommended harsher penalties than were handed down by the courts.[133] Don Gibbons's sample of residents of the San Francisco area showed that 70 percent favored prison sentences for antitrust violators and 43 percent agreed that incarceration was the appropriate penalty for advertisers who misrepresent their products.[134] In the Gibbons survey, 85 percent of the respondents favored prison sentences for embezzlers, as did 88 percent of the subjects in a national sample taken by other researchers at about the same time. In a survey taken in Illinois, almost 90 percent of the respondents agreed with the statement, "White-collar criminals have gotten off too easily for too many years; they deserve to be sent to jail for their crimes just like everyone else." On the other hand, less than 15 percent agreed with the statement, "Since white-collar criminals usually don't harm anyone, they shouldn't be punished as much as regular criminals."[135] Interestingly, surveys indicate that the people who are least concerned about white-collar crime may be those who work in criminal justice agencies. When the same questions asked in the Baltimore study mentioned earlier were put to a sample of police chiefs[136] and to probation officers and attorneys working for criminal justice agencies,[137] both groups indicated less concern about white-collar crime than the general public did. The survey by the National White Collar Crime Center found that while the public felt that a "fraudster" and a robber deserved equal punishment, they believed that the robber was likely to be more severely punished.[138]

Hollow Laws

A cursory examination of the laws designed to control white-collar crime reveals an imposing structure of rules and regulations. But a closer look uncovers numerous flaws, loopholes, and omissions that benefit elite interests, whereas the penalties provided by laws are often inadequate to the tasks they are supposed to achieve.

The courts have occasionally also helped to thwart the enforcement process. The Supreme Court's original ruling that the Sherman Act applied only to "unreasonable" restraints of trade, even though the legislation contained no such language, certainly made the federal regulators' job more difficult, as did the more recent decision requiring OSHA investigators to obtain a warrant before inspecting a workplace that an employer wished to conceal. A long series of court rulings favorable to advertisers have allowed them to make false statements without legal penalty, as long as those statements remain sufficiently general. But by no means have the rulings all been one-sided, and court-imposed restrictions do not seem to have been as critical to the failure of justice as the inherent shortcomings in the laws themselves.

Complaints have often been voiced about the vague, general language in the enabling legislation for many regulatory agencies, but a case can be made both for and against this practice. On the one hand, the battle over the interpretation of ambiguously worded legislation inevitably ends up in court, where elite interests enjoy the advantages of vast financial resources and the best legal talent. On the other hand, it can also be argued that more specifically worded legislation cannot deal effectively with the subterfuges white-collar criminals so often use to get around the letter of the law. As a congressional report on the original proposals to create the FTC put it, there is "no limit to human inventiveness in this field. If Congress were to adopt the method of definition, it would undertake an endless task."[139] But whatever the problems inherent in more specific legislative mandates, the evidence we have examined shows that the process of regulatory rule-making has been thoroughly corrupted by the political influence of powerful corporate offenders—both inside the regulatory agencies and in the "economic impact" reviews made by other government agencies.

The penalties available to enforcement agencies vary enormously from crime to crime and agency to agency. In many cases even the maximum penalties are hopelessly inadequate, and powerful offenders seldom receive the maximum possible punishment. As we have seen, however, there is a trend toward much larger fines and stiffer penalties to be handed down by criminal courts. Although the federal sentencing guidelines have contributed to the increase in penalties for convicted white-collar offenders, these offenders still typically receive only a fraction of penalties given street criminals who have committed comparable offenses.[140] Similarly, while the criminal statutes covering such things as manslaughter and murder are slowly being extended to cover corporations as well as individuals, actual prosecutions remain extremely rare.

The Paucity of Resources

One of the most fundamental reasons for the failure of the enforcement effort is a chronic shortage of personnel and resources. Of the more than one-half million police officers and tens of thousands of government prosecutors and enforcement officials in the United States, only a handful are assigned to deal with the nation's most serious crime problem. The combined manpower of the fraud sections of all the federal prosecutors' offices around the country is only a few hundred, yet they must handle the bulk of all federal prosecutions for occupational crimes. In the words of August Bequai, "They are asked to do a Herculean task, which is far beyond the resources and the power at their disposal."[141]

If anything, the situation is worse at the regulatory agencies that carry the major burden for controlling corporate crime.[142] The Consumer Product Safety Commission has the staggering responsibility of not only creating regulatory standards to ensure the safety of the millions of products sold in the American marketplace, but also enforcing those standards. Yet its total staff in 2003, including administrators, rule makers, and enforcement agents, was 480 persons.[143] The Federal Trade Commission, which is given the similarly gargantuan task of "ensuring that competition in the market place is vigorous, free and fair . . . by eliminating threats to fair and honest competition from all sources," had barely more than a thousand full-time positions that year.[144] Moreover, these acute shortages of resources show no signs of easing. The federal agencies with responsibility for controlling corporate crime had around 26,000 budgeted staff positions in 1980, but by 1983 their staff had declined by almost a fifth; and it did not return to its 1980 level until the end of the Reagan administration. In 2003, the total was still only around 31,500 budgeted positions.[145] That was only a 22 percent increase during a period when gross domestic product almost doubled.[146]

The situation is bad enough in normal times, but when a particularly large scandal engulfs the system it can be completely swamped. Such was the case with the savings and loan fiasco. One frustrated official told a team of criminologists investigating the problems that, "I feel like it's the Alaskan oil spill. I feel like I'm out there with a roll of paper towels . . . the task is so huge, and what I'm worrying about is where I can get some more paper towels. I stand out there with my roll and I look at this sea of oil coming at me, and it's so colossal and at the same time people are yelling at me, 'The birds and fish are dying! Do it faster!' I'm going as fast as I can."[147]

In addition to the severe shortage of personnel, the fact that government employees receive much lower pay than they would in the corporate sector poses another serious problem. In the mid-1990's, for example, a staff lawyer with the SEC with ten years' experience earned only about $70,000 a year, whereas a partner in a top law firm (the kind that have the corporations the SEC regulates as clients) made between $370,000 and $1.4 million.[148] The lure of a higher-paying job in private industry has led many government staffers to cultivate the favor of private interests at the expense of their legal duty. The salary gap also makes it difficult for regulatory agencies to hire top-quality professionals, especially lawyers and scientists. For example, Paul Quirk reports that the FDA has had "trouble recruiting high-caliber scientific and medical personnel" and has been forced to hire many physicians with no expertise in drug research because the agency could not match the salaries specialists are paid in private industry.[149] Similar problems at the FTC and the Antitrust Division of the Justice Department have led to rapid turnover in their legal staffs and the loss of much of their best legal talent.[150] Thus, these agencies are forced to fight long legal battles against some of the nation's best attorneys with a constantly changing team of young, inexperienced lawyers.

The Personal Advantages of Privilege

The wealth and influence of white-collar criminals give them a significant advantage over the lower-class offenders typically involved in street crime. As we have seen, it has often been claimed that the common cultural background shared by regulators, prosecutors, judges, and white-collar defendants leads to greater leniency than is shown to street criminals. But whether or not high socioeconomic status produces more lenient treatment in and of itself, the evidence clearly indicates that the legal system shows greater leniency toward defendants who commit crimes as part of white-collar occupations than toward those who commit similar nonviolent street crimes. It appears that those who make the laws and work in the criminal justice system understand the pressures that lead white-collar workers to abuse their positions but have less sympathy for those living in the alien world of the street criminal.

The white-collar defendant's ability to pay for a first-rate defense—the best lawyers, numerous appeals, and if necessary, private investigators and expert witnesses—is another factor of critical importance. Many former defendants have openly admitted that their ability to "hire the best" was the decisive factor in their case. Conklin cites the example of a Texas oil millionaire who admitted that he was acquitted on wire-tapping charges because he spent more than $1 million on his defense. A different businessman put it this way: "Law is like a cobweb; it's made for flies and smaller kinds of insects, so to speak, but lets the big bumblebees break through. When technicalities of the law stood in my way, I have always been able to brush them aside as easy as anything."[151]

The Advantages of Corporate Organization

In addition to the benefits of wealth and status, those involved in organizational crimes enjoy another special advantage: The law is written with a strong individualistic bias that makes it difficult to deal with such crimes. To convict someone of a criminal offense, the law normally requires not only that he or she be shown to have committed the criminal actions, but also that the person acted with criminal intent. For example, a corporate spokesperson who falsely claims that a deadly product is safe has committed a criminal act only if he or she knows the statement to be false. But someone in public relations would be unlikely to be given such information, even if the dangers of the product were common knowledge in other parts of the organization. Somewhere in the corporate organization there would undoubtedly be an individual who both knew about the dangers of the product and ordered or permitted the release of the false statement—but that is extremely difficult to prove. If corporations as a collectivity were put on trial, criminal intent (i.e., knowledge that the statement was fraudulent) would be much easier to establish. Although there are clear legal precedents for this kind of criminal case (see Chapter 2), such charges are seldom filed.

The evolution of the laws regulating corporate behavior shows that the rights and duties assigned to individuals have slowly been extended to corporations but that they have been given more of the former than the latter. It is widely held that even though corporations can be fined for their crimes, they cannot be imprisoned or executed like individual criminals. But, in fact, corporations can be imprisoned in everything but the most literal sense of the word by being placed on probation with conditions that tightly restrict their freedom of action, and it seems that the court-ordered dissolution of corporations that have repeatedly been convicted of serious crimes would be not only feasible but highly appropriate in many circumstances.

Another important advantage enjoyed by corporate offenders is the potential confusion caused by their great size and complexity. Even when a lower-level employee is caught red-handed in some illegal activity, it is extremely difficult to trace criminal responsibility back to the higher-ups who are ultimately responsible. Because of this diffusion of responsibility, it is often difficult to identify who actually ordered a particular illegal action. Many top corporate managers intentionally avoid any direct knowledge of their subordinates' criminal activities, even while indirectly encouraging them. Such was the case in the price-fixing conspiracy in the heavy electrical equipment industry. The conspirators testified that although their bosses did not order them to fix prices, the company demanded a level of profitability that both parties knew could be achieved only by illegal means. A special committee of outside experts created by Merck & Company reached the same conclusion about middle-level management's involvement in international bribery. The committee found that middle managers did not usually report their bribery operations to top management "on the assumption that, despite the atmosphere of acceptance, top management did not want to be involved."[152]

Hidden Crimes

Secrecy is the white-collar criminal's first line of defense. Of course, street criminals also do their best to conceal their crimes, but white-collar criminals enjoy some very significant advantages in this endeavor. Unlike the victims of most street crimes, the victims of white-collar criminals are often unaware of the causes of their problems. Because the costs of such offenses as price-fixing or environmental pollution are spread over a very large number of people, individual victims often suffer so small a loss that they have little to gain in pressing for legal action—if they even know they have been victimized. Organizational criminals enjoy the added protection of working behind the walls of secrecy that the government and the corporations erect around themselves. Moreover, the extreme complexity of corporate financial transactions makes it relatively easy to conceal illegal dealings from overworked government regulators.

The corporations' influence on the media also enables them to minimize public awareness of their crimes. Not only are most newspapers and radio and television stations owned by big corporations, but the media's dependence on advertising revenue for financial survival gives corporations with big advertising budgets added leverage. Moreover, most white-collar crimes lack the sensationalistic appeal that sells newspapers and boosts television ratings. Relatively "dull" crimes that involve powerful corporate interests, such as antitrust violations, usually receive minimal media attention despite the huge losses that may be involved. For example, the 1961 heavy electrical equipment price-fixing case was the most highly publicized antitrust case of its time, yet a study of major American newspapers found that only 16 percent featured the story on page1, and about a third made no reference to it at all.[153] When Sandra Evans and Richard Lundman selected a very similar antitrust case—the folding-carton price-fixing scandal of 1976—and replicated the earlier study, they found that although the 1976 case involved about the same amount of damages over a similar period of time, it received even less coverage than its predecessor. They concluded that "newspapers protect corporate reputations by failing to provide frequent, prominent, and criminally oriented coverage of common corporate crimes such as price-fixing."[154] The media reacted in a similar fashion to the collapse of the savings and loan industry. The media was generally very late in beginning its coverage of the scandal and never gave it the attention its staggering financial costs would seem to have warranted.[155] When the California energy crisis first hit in 2000 and the state underwent rolling blackouts and staggering increases in the cost of electricity, the media downplayed the claims by state officials that the big energy corporations were manipulating the prices and laid the blamed on California's failure to build new power plants. It was not until May of 2002, when the public's attention had long since turned to other problems, that Enron memos leaked out detailing their illegal schemes and the media finally admitted the true source of the problem.[156]

Violent white-collar crimes that leave a dramatic toll of deaths and injuries often get more attention, but the press still tends to construct those crimes in ways that minimize corporate responsibility. The release of a huge cloud of toxic gas by a Union Carbide plant in Bhopal, India, that killed more than 2,000 people was consistently characterized by the American press as a disaster, not a crime, and Union Carbide was usually described as the victim, not the criminal. In contrast, the Indian press was far more likely to call Union Carbide negligent and irresponsible, and to refer to the incident as criminal activity.[157] Wright, Cullen, and Blankenship found a similar pattern of media coverage of the 1991 fire in a North Carolina chicken processing plant that killed twenty-five workers and injured fifty-six others. The media originally attributed the "disaster" to lax enforcement of health and safety standards, not illegal corporate behavior, and there was little publicity when criminal indictments were handed for three company officials or when the owner of the plant pleaded guilty to manslaughter.[158]

The Techniques of Obstruction

If their crimes are detected, white-collar criminals use a variety of techniques to obstruct the process of justice. One of the most effective is the delaying game. A corporation will often refuse to voluntarily turn over data and documents requested by government regulatory agencies, thus forcing a time-consuming legal battle to obtain the information. If a court orders that the information actually be divulged, the alternative tactic of "overcompliance" is commonly used. In one case, IBM responded to a private suit seeking information for an antitrust case with more than 75 million pages of material.[159] Many government enforcement agencies have also been swamped in a similar sea of paper. Our review of the antitrust actions against the petroleum industry showed how that industry used an almost endless chain of legal appeals and maneuvers to bog down understaffed government agencies. The effectiveness of this tactic can be seen in the FTC's capitulation in the Exxon case, when the government openly admitted that it gave up because the case would take too long to pursue. The delaying game has often been used against other regulatory actions as well. Investigative reporter Mark Dowie gave the following description of the techniques commonly used to combat new government safety standards: "(a) Make arguments in succession, so the feds can be working on disproving only one at a time; (b) claim that the real problem is not X but Y; (c) no matter how ridiculous each argument is, accompany it with thousands of pages of highly technical assertions that will take the government months or, preferably, years to test."[160]

Some techniques of obstruction are far less subtle. Outright threats and coercion are often used to prevent the law from being enforced. This is a particularly effective tactic against state or local cases. Just as Standard Oil threatened economic reprisals against the state of Missouri if it continued its antitrust action, so numerous other businesses have threatened to leave states that pursue tough enforcement and regulatory actions. Even the federal government is subject to this kind of blackmail, when multinationals threaten to move their operations to Third World countries that have no effective environmental or safety legislation. Another kind of intimidation is brought to bear when corporations make dire predictions about the economic damage that regulation would cause. But as Mark Green and Norman Waitzman have pointed out, when new regulations have actually been put into effect, they seldom have produced the economic horrors predicted by the corporations.[161]

The Corruption of Enforcement

On top of chronic shortages of resources and all the difficulties inherent in proving charges against powerful white-collar defendants, the enforcement process is further weakened by its own corruption. A host of political and economic rewards may await employees who are willing to neglect their legal responsibilities, whereas those who show too much zeal may risk arousing the displeasure of their superiors. To complicate matters further, bonds of friendship, sympathy, and common background may give the agents of enforcement reason to pause before demanding that the full weight of the law be brought to bear against white-collar defendants.

Political pressure is the elite's most powerful weapon in its effort to corrupt the enforcement process. The history of enforcement in the petroleum industry, for example, shows that major antitrust cases are seldom initiated without prior political approval. The impetus for the major cases against big oil came from periodic waves of public indignation, not from routine administrative actions on the part of the enforcement agencies. When public concern died down, the same cases that were launched with so much fanfare were either settled quietly through meaningless consent decrees or simply dropped.[162]

Even the regulatory agencies charged with protecting the health and safety of the public operate in the same highly politicized environment. When Assistant Secretary of Labor George Guenter wrote a memo to his Nixon administration superiors promising to promulgate "no highly controversial standards (cotton dust, etc.)" so as to use "the great potential of OSHA as a sales point for fund raising and general support by employers,"[163] he was unusual only in his willingness to put in writing the kinds of political considerations that often guide regulatory agencies. Moreover, Guenter's tactics were apparently highly effective: After his nonenforcement pledge, textile interests contributed $1 million to Nixon's reelection effort.[164] Of course, other political forces may push for tougher enforcement—particularly after a highly publicized disaster or scandal—but the constant, day-to-day pressure usually runs in the other direction.

Another major source of corruption is the control that corporations often exert over the selection of candidates to run the agencies regulating their industry. To cite one notorious example, the members of the Federal Home Loan Bank Board (FHLBB) that supervised the savings and loan industry at the time of its collapse were drawn almost entirely from that industry. Until the scandal earned almost daily media attention, the U.S. League of Savings Associations (a lobbying group for the industry) held a virtual veto power over the nominees to head the FHLBB.[165] But the political pressure on regulatory agencies is not always transmitted via politicians and their appointees. Business interests also operate effective lobbies aimed directly at the enforcement agencies. These lobbyists attempt to curry favor with regulators and enforcement officials, often offering free seminars, dinners, and travel.

Corporations also hold out the alluring possibility of high-paying jobs in private industry for those who "understand" business interests. Take, for example, the study of the EPA's pesticide program by the Environmental Working Group. The report found that two-thirds of the highest EPA officials who worked in the programs since its inception in 1977 received at least part of their paychecks from pesticide interests in 1999. Four of the six former assistant administrators for Pesticides and Toxic Substances and two of four former directors of the Office of Pesticide Programs worked for the pesticide industry, as did a large group of former staffers involved in the evaluation of pesticide safety.[166] This so-called revolving door between regulatory agencies and the industries they regulate obviously fosters a pro-business attitude that makes it difficult to pursue tough enforcement actions. Moreover, corporations often go far beyond the use of ingratiating lobbyists and the lure of future employment. As the cases described in earlier chapters have shown, outright bribery is commonly directed at enforcement agents—especially field inspectors. Similarly, campaign contributions and direct payoffs are used to gain allies among influential politicians outside the executive branch who are in a position to obstruct the process of justice.

Review Questions

- How have the professions attempted to regulate themselves? How successful have those efforts been at stopping white-collar crime?

- What federal and state agencies are charged with regulating corporate and business abuses? Discuss the strengths and weaknesses of the current efforts to create and enforce those regulations.

- What role does the criminal justice system play in the control of white-collar crime? How effective has it been?

- What impact do civil lawsuits have on the problem of white-collar crime?

- Compare and contrast the case of the antitrust violations in the petroleum industry with the case of Michael Milken.

- What are the reasons that the promise of equal justice for street offenders and white-collar offenders so often fails to come true?

Notes

1. Robert Derbyshire, quoted in Boyce Rensberger, "Few Doctors Ever Report Colleagues' Incompetence," *New York Times*, January 29, 1976, p. 1 passim.
2. Martin Garbus and Joel Seligman, "Sanctions and Disbarment: They Sit in Judgment," in Ralph Nader and Mark Green, eds *Verdicts on Lawyers* (New York: Thomas Y. Crowell, 1976), p. 50.
3. Eliot Freidson, *The Profession of Medicine* (New York: Dodd Mead, 1970), pp. 71–72.
4. Public Citizen, "20,125 Questionable Doctors." http://www.citizen.org, August 21, 2001.
5. "Doctors Sanctioned for Sex Offenses Still Practicing, Report Finds," *Corporate Crime Reporter*, June 22, 1998, p. 1.
6. Stephen M. Rosoff, Henry N. Pontell, and Robert Tillman, *Profit Without Honor: White Collar Crime and the Looting of America* (Upper Saddle River, N.J.: Prentice Hall, 1998), p. 344.
7. Ibid., p. 434.
8. Garbus and Seligman, "Sanctions and Disbarment."
9. Philip Hager, "Lawyer Discipline Systems Held Inadequate to Protect Public," *Los Angeles Times*, May 21, 1991, pp. A1, A22; S. G. Bene, "Why Not Fine Lawyers? An Economic Approach to Lawyer Disciplinary Sanctions," *Stanford Law Review* 43 (1991): 864–941.
10. Erin Condon, "HALT Survey Finds Toothless Lawyer Discipline." http://www.halt.org/news/00-summer/page.cfm?page5tlrpg7, July 26, 2001.

11. Henry Weinstein, "Prosecutor Misconduct Probed in National Study," *Los Angeles Times,* June 26, 2003, P. A24.

12. Quoted in Garbus and Seligman, "Sanctions and Disbarment."

13. Quoted in Jethro K. Lieberman, *Crisis at the Bar: Lawyers' Unethical Ethics and What to Do About It* (New York: W. W. Norton, 1978), p. 206.

14. AICPA, "Summary of the Sarbanes–Oxley Act of 2002," November 9, 2004, http://www.aicpa.org; Caroly Said, "Bush Can't Sign Fraud Bill Fast Enough," *San Francisco Chronicle,* July 31, 2002, pp. A1 and A13; CBS News "Corporate Fraud Bill Sent to President," July 25, 2002, http://www.cbsnews.com.

15. John Braithwaite and Brent Fisse, "Self-regulation and the Control of Corporate Crime," in C. Shearing and P. C. Stenning, eds., *Private Policing* (Newbury Park, Calif.: Sage, 1987), pp. 221–46.

16. Marshall B. Clinard and Peter C. Yeager, *Corporate Crime* (New York: Free Press, 1980), p. 76; James Q. Wilson, *The Politics of Regulation* (New York: Basic Books, 1980), pp. 357–94; Bruce Ackerman and William T. Hassler, *Clean Coal—Dirty Air* (New Haven: Yale University Press, 1981), pp. 1–12.

17. See Clinard and Yeager, *Corporate Crime,* p. 76, n. 3.

18. Clean Air Amendments of 1970, 304, 42 USC (Supp II 1978).

19. See Arthur Belonzi, Arthur D'Antonio, and Gary Helfand, *The Weary Watchdogs: Governmental Regulations in the Political Process* (Garden City, N.Y.: Avery Publishing Group, 1977), pp. 31–32.

20. See Mark J. Green, Beverly C. Moore, and Bruce Wasserstein, *The Closed Enterprise System: Ralph Nader's Study Group Report on Antitrust Enforcement* (New York: Grossman, 1972); Suzanne Weaver, "Antitrust Division of the Justice Department," in Wilson, *Politics of Regulation,* pp. 123–51; Robert A. Katzman, "Federal Trade Commission," in Wilson, *Politics of Regulation,* pp. 152–87.

21. Ackerman and Hassler, in Clean Coal–Dirty Air, provide an insightful examination of the effects of the specific legislative mandates on the effort to minimize the air pollution from coal-generated electric power.

22. For example, see Alfred Marcus, "Environmental Protection Agency," in Wilson, *Politics of Regulation,* pp. 267–305.

23. W. A. Rosenbaum, "The Clenched Fist and the Open Hand: Into the 1990s at EPA," in N. J. Vig and M. E. Kraft, eds., *Environmental Policy in the 1990s: Toward a New Agenda,* 2nd ed. (Washington, D.C.: Congressional Quarterly Press, 1994), p. 126.

24. Ibid., pp. 121–43.

25. Marshall B. Clinard, Peter C. Yeager, Jeanne Brissetts, David Petrashek, and Elizabeth Harries, *Illegal Corporate Behavior* (Washington, D.C.: U.S. Government Printing Office, 1979), p. 41.

26. Ibid., p. 45.

27. For a more detailed description of this case and its outcome, see ibid., p. 45.

28. For a good discussion of the role of the states in the enforcement efforts against corporate crime, see ibid., pp. 41–53.

29. Peter Lurie, Marti Long, and Sidney M. Wolfe, "Reinventing OSHA: Dangerous Reductions in Enforcement During the Clinton Administration," September 6, 1999, Public Citizen, http://www.citizen.org/hrg/PUBLICATIONS/1494.htm.

30. James S. Turner, *Chemical Feast* (New York: Grossman, 1970), pp. 5–29.

31. Ibid., pp. 138–68.

32. George C. Eads and Michael Fix, *Relief or Reform? Reagan's Regulatory Dilemma* (Washington, D.C.: Urban Institute Press, 1984), pp. 45–50; Larry N. Gerston, Cyn-

thia Fraleigh, and Robert Schwab, *The Deregulated Society* (Pacific Grove, Calif.: Brooks/ Cole, 1988), pp. 42–43.

33. Howard Ball, *Controlling Regulatory Sprawl: Presidential Strategies from Nixon to Reagan* (Westport, Conn.: Greenwood Press, 1984), p. 71.

34. Gerston, Fraleigh, and Schwab, *The Deregulated Society*, pp. 53–55.

35. David G. Savage, "OMB Can't Block Safety Regulations, Court Says," *Los Angeles Times*, February 22, 1990, p. A16.

36. Katzmann, "Federal Trade Commission," p. 157.

37. Robert L. Jackson, "FTC Drops Huge Antitrust Suit against Eight Oil Firms," *Los Angeles Times*, September 17, 1981, pp. 1, 13.

38. Robert S. Smith, *The Occupational Safety and Health Act* (Washington, D.C.: American Enterprise Institute, 1976), p. 62.

39. Lurie, Long, and Wolfe, "Reinventing OSHA."

40. For example, Edward F. Cox, Robert C. Fellmeth, and John E. Schultz, *The Nader Report on the Federal Trade Commission* (New York: Baron, 1969); Green, Moore, and Wasserstein, Closed Enterprise System; American Bar Association, *Report of the Commission to Study the Federal Trade Commission* (Chicago: American Bar Association, 1969).

41. See Clinard and Yeager, *Corporate Crime*, p. 77.

42. See, for example, Mark Green and Norman Waitzman, *Business War on the Law: An Analysis of the Benefits of Federal Health/Safety Enforcement*, rev. 2nd ed. (Washington, D.C.: Corporate Accountability Research Group, 1981).

43. Hongming Chen, "Securities and Exchange Commission," pp. 722–25 in Lawrence M. Salinger, ed., *Encyclopedia of White-Collar and Corporate Crime* (Thousand Oaks, Calif.: Sage, 2005).

44. Clinard and Yeager, *Corporate Crime*, p. 122.

45. Clinard et al., *Illegal Corporate Behavior*, p. 291.

46. Clinard and Yeager, *Corporate Crime*, p. 125.

47. M. A. Cohen, "Corporate Crime and Punishment: A Study of Social Harm and Sentencing Practices in the Federal Courts, 1984–1987," *American Criminal Law Review* 26 (1989): 605–62.

48. "Hoffmann–LaRoche and BASF to Pay Record Criminal Fines for Participating in International Vitamin Cartel, LaRoche to Pay $500 Million, Highest Criminal Fine Ever," *Corporate Crime Reporter*, May 24, 1999, p. 3.

49. Kurt Eichenwald, "Archer Daniels Agrees to Big Fine for Price Fixing," *New York Times*, October 15, 1996, pp. A1, C3.

50. Michael A. Verespej, "The Newest Environmental Risk: Jail," *Industry Week*, January 22, 1990, pp. 47–49; Patrick Lee, "Exxon Indictment Unusual in Many Ways, Experts Say," *Los Angeles Times*, March 2, 1990, p. D2.

51. Robert Sherrill, "A Year in Corporate Crime," in *Criminology 99/00* (Guilford, Conn.: Duskin 1999), pp. 108–13.

52. Rebecca S. Katz, "Archer Daniels Midland," in Lawrence M. Salinger, ed., *Encyclopedia of White-Collar and Corporate Crime* (Thousand Oaks, Calif.: Sage, 2005), pp. 51–52.

53. Robert A. Rosenblatt, "U.S. Recoups Only Fraction of Funds from S&L Frauds," *Los Angeles Times*, February 7, 1992, pp. A1, A23.

54. Clinard and Yeager, *Corporate Crime*, p. 291.

55. Albert E. McCormick, "Rule Enforcement and Moral Indignation: Some Observations on the Effects of Criminal Antitrust Convictions upon Societal Reaction Processes," *Social Problems* 25 (October 1977): 30–39.

56. David O. Friedrichs, *Trusted Criminals: White Collar Crime in Contemporary Society* (Belmont, Calif.: Wadsworth, 1996), pp. 272–73.

57. D. Burnam, *A Law unto Itself: The IRS and the Abuse of Power* (New York: Random House, 1989), p. 79.

58. William H. Webster, "An Examination of FBI Theory and Methodology Regarding White Collar Crime Investigation and Prevention," *American Criminal Law Review* 17 (Winter 1980): 275–86.

59. D. R. Simon and S. L. Stewart, "The Justice Department Focuses on White Collar Crime: Promises and Pitfalls," *Crime and Delinquency* 30 (1984): 91–106.

60. http://www.fbi.gov

61. Michael L. Benson, William K. Maakestad, Francis T. Cullen, and Gilbert Geis, "District Attorneys and Corporate Crime: Surveying the Prosecutorial Gatekeepers," paper presented at the meetings of the American Society of Criminology, Montreal, November 1987.

62. Michael L. Benson, William K. Maakestad, Francis T. Cullen, *Local Prosecutors and Corporate Crime* (Washington, D.C.: National Institute of Justice, January 1993).

63. *Environmental Crime Prosecution: Results of a National Survey* (Washington, D.C.: National Institute of Justice, December 1994).

64. Yingyi Situ and David Emmons, *Environmental Crime: The Criminal Justice System's Role in Protecting the Environment* (Thousands Oaks, Calif.: Sage, 2000), pp. 147–48.

65. R. W. Adler and C. Lord, "Environmental Crimes: Raising the Stakes," *George Washington Law Review* 59 (1991): 781–891.

66. Robert Tillman, Kitty Calavita, and Henry Pontell, "Criminalizing White Collar Crime Misconduct: Determinants of Prosecution in Savings and Loan Fraud Cases," *Crime, Law and Social Change* 26 (1997), pp. 53–76.

67. Donald W. Scott, "Policing Corporate Collusion," *Criminology* 27 (1989): 559–87.

68. Benson et al., "District Attorneys and Corporate Crime: Surveying the Prosecutorial Gatekeepers."

69. Joan Neff Gurney, "Factors Influencing the Decision to Prosecute Economic Crime," *Criminology* 23 (November 1985): 623.

70. Benson et al., "District Attorneys and Corporate Crime: Surveying the Prosecutorial Gatekeepers"; Michael L. Benson, Francis T. Cullen, and William K. Maakestad, "Local Prosecutors and Corporate Crime," *Crime and Delinquency* 36 (1990): 356–72.

71. Robert Tillman, Kitty Calavita, and Henry Pontell, "Criminalizing White Collar Misconduct: Determinants of Prosecution in Savings and Loan Fraud Cases," *Crime, Law and Social Change* 26 (1997): 53–76.

72. Kenneth Mann, *Defending White Collar Crime: A Portrait of Attorneys at Work* (New Haven: Yale University Press, 1985).

73. David Weisburd, Stanton Wheeler, E. J. Waring, and Nancy Bode, *Crimes of the Middle Class* (New Haven: Yale University Press, 1991), p. 100.

74. Friedrichs, *Trusted Criminals*, p. 315.

75. See Clinard and Yeager, *Corporate Crime*, pp. 285–86; Bureau of National Affairs, "White Collar Justice: A BNA Special Report on White Collar Crime," *United States Law Week* 44 (April 13, 1976): 12.

76. Gary S. Green, "Sentencing Guidelines," in Lawrence M. Salinger, ed., *Encyclopedia of White-Collar and Corporate Crime* (Thousand Oaks, Calif.: Sage, 2005), pp. 732–37.

77. John Hagan and Patrice Parker, "White Collar Crime and Punishment: The Class Structure and the Legal Sanctioning of Securities Violations," *American Sociological Review* 50 (June 1985): 302–16.

78. Susan P. Shapiro, "The Road Not Taken: The Criminal Prosecution for White Collar Offenders," *Law and Society Review* 19 (1985): 179–217.

79. C. A. Albonetti, "The Symbolic Punishment of White Collar Offenders," in G. S. Bridges and M. A. Myers, eds. *Inequality, Crime and Social Control* (Boulder: Westview Press, 1994), pp. 269–82.

80. Stanton Wheeler, David Weisburd, and Nancy Bode, "Sentencing the White Collar Offender," *American Sociological Review* 47 (October 1982): 641–59.

81. John Hagan and Alberto Palloni, "'Club Fed' and the Sentencing of White Collar Offenders," *Criminology* 24 (1986): 603–22.

82. Bureau of Justice Statistics, *Compendium of Federal Justice Statistics, 1999* (Washington, D.C.: U.S. Department of Justice, 2001), Table 5.25.

83. Clinard and Yeager, *Corporate Crime,* p. 291.

84. McCormick, "Rule Enforcement and Moral Indignation."

85. See Hans B. Thorelli, *The Federal Antitrust Policy: Origination of an American Tradition* (Baltimore: Johns Hopkins University Press, 1955).

86. Robert Tillman and Henry N. Pontell, "Is Justice 'Collar-Blind'? Medicaid Provider Fraud," *Criminology* 30 (1992): 547–74.

87. Henry N. Pontell, *Fraud in the Savings and Loan Industry: White Collar Crime and Government Response* (Washington, D.C.: National Institute of Justice, 1994).

88. See Gary S. Green, "Sentencing Guidelines," in Lawrence M. Salinger, ed., *Encyclopedia of White-Collar and Corporate Crime* (Thousand Oaks, Calif.: Sage, 2005), pp. 732–37.

89. "Corporate Crime: Bosses Behind Bars," *The Economist,* June 12, 2004, pp. 59–60.

90. "Sentencing of White Collar Criminals Varies Widely Throughout the Federal System, Report Finds," *Corporate Crime Reporter,* November 8, 1999, p. 3.

91. Kenneth Mann, "Procedure Rules and Information Control: Gaining Leverage over White Collar Crime," in Kip Schlegel and David Weisburd, eds., *White Collar Crime Reconsidered* (Boston : Northeastern University Press, 1992), pp. 332–51.

92. Ibid.

93. Leo G. Barrile, "Determining Criminal Responsibility of Corporations," paper presented at the American Society of Criminology, San Francisco, November 1991.

94. Barbara J. Hayler, "Criminal Prosecution of Corporate Crime: The Illinois Corporate Murder Case," paper presented at the meetings of the Western Political Science Association, Eugene, Oregon, March 20–22, 1986; Larry Green, "3 Officials Guilty of Murder in Cyanide Death at Plant," *Los Angeles Times,* June 15, 1985, pp. 1, 5; Ray Gibson and Charles Mount, "3 Former Executives Guilty in Cyanide Death," *Chicago Tribune,* June 15, 1985, pt. I, pp. 1, 5.

95. Barrile, "Determining Criminal Responsibility of Corporations."

96. Bureau of Justice Statistics, *Sourcebook of Criminal Justice Statistics 2002* (Washington, D.C.: U.S. Government Printing Office, 2003), Table 5.30.

97. Ibid., Table 5.25.

98. Steven Kelman, "Occupational Safety and Health Administration," in Wilson, *Politics of Regulation,* p. 259.

99. Carol J. DeFrances et al., *Civil Jury Cases and Verdicts in Large Counties* (Washington, D.C.: Bureau of Justice Statistics, July 1995).

100. See Cynthia Laitman Orenberg, DES: *The Complete Story* (New York: St. Martin's Press, 1982), pp. 137–57; Edwin Chen, "Liability Suits: Few Guidelines," *Los Angeles Times,* October 6, 1982, p. 1 passim.

101. Henry Weinstein, "Manville Move Brings Asbestos Battle to Head in Courts and Congress," *Los Angeles Times,* August 27, 1992, pt. IV, p. 1 passim; Martin Boron, "Asbestos Maker Files for Bankruptcy, Cites Lawsuits," *Los Angeles Times,* October 6, 1992, pt. I, pp. 1, 13.

102. Reuters, "Court Rejects Settlement for Manville Trust," *Los Angeles Times,* December 5, 1992, p. D2.

103. "Tort Reform, In Great Detail," Nader 2000, http://www.votenader.org/issues/tort_full.html, July 26, 2001.

104. U.S. Bureau of the Census, *Statistical Abstract of the United States, 1991* (Washington, D.C.: U.S. Government Printing Office, 1991), p. 321.

105. Seth Borenstein, "How Has America's Environment Fared under Bush?" *San Luis Obispo Tribune,* October 18, 2004, p. A7.

106. "Number of OSHA Inspections Under Clinton Less than During Any Prior Administration, Report Finds," *Corporate Crime Reporter,* September 13, 1999, p. 3.

107. John Braithwaite, *Corporate Crime in the Pharmaceutical Industry* (London: Routledge and Kegan Paul, 1984), p. 277.

108. David Willman, "The Rise and Fall of the Killer Drug Rezulin," *Los Angeles Times,* June 4, 2000, p. 1A passim; "Public Citizen Calls for Criminal Investigation of Warner-Lambert Over Rezulin Diabetes Drug. FDA Doctor's Job on the Line," *Corporate Crime Reporter,* March 20, 2000, p. 1; David Willman, "FDA's Approval and Delay in Withdrawing Rezulin Probed," *Los Angeles Times,* August 16, 2000, p. 1A passim.

109. Bruce Bringhurst, *Antitrust and the Oil Monopoly: The Standard Oil Cases, 1890–1911* (Westport, Conn.: Greenwood Press, 1979), pp. 10–39.

110. Ibid., pp. 40–68; Carl Solberg, *Oil Power* (New York: Mason/Charter, 1976), pp. 52–54.

111. Solberg, *Oil Power,* p. 49.

112. Bringhurst, *Antitrust and the Oil Monopoly,* p. 147.

113. For details, see John M. Blair, *The Control of Oil* (New York: Vintage Books, 1976), pp. 54–71.

114. Burton I. Kaufman, *The Oil Cartel Case: A Documentary Study of Antitrust Activity in the Cold War Era* (Westport, Conn.: Greenwood Press, 1978), pp. 19–37.

115. Quoted in Blair, *Control of Oil,* p. 75.

116. Ibid.

117. Katzmann, "Federal Trade Commission," p. 157.

118. Robert L. Jackson, "FTC Drops Huge Antitrust Suit against Eight Oil Firms," *Los Angeles Times,* September 17, 1981, pt. I, pp. 1, 13.

119. James B. Stewart, *Den of Thieves* (New York: Simon & Schuster, 1991), pp. 43–47; Connie Bruck, *The Predators Ball* (New York: Penguin Books, 1988), pp. 286–87, 356.

120. Stewart, *Den of Thieves,* pp. 185–86.

121. James Bates and Paul Richter, "Stiff Prison Term Surprises Foes, Friends Alike," *Los Angeles Times,* November 22, 1990, pp. D1, D3; Stewart, *Den of Thieves,* p. 437.

122. Scot J. Paltrow, "Judge Stuns Milken with 10-Year Sentence," *Los Angeles Times,* November 22, 1990, pp. A1, A27; Victor F. Zonana, "Judge Approves Milken–Drexel Settlement Plan," *Los Angeles Times,* March 10, 1992, pp. D1, D4.

123. "U.S. Attorney White Finds that Milken Did Not Violate Probation, But He Will Pay $47 Million to Settle SEC Charges," *Corporate Crime Reporter,* March 2, 1998, p. 3.

124. Paul Richter, "Wall St. Scandal Leaves Many to Cope with Shame," *Los Angeles Times*, December 25, 1988, p. IV, pp. 1, 5; Stewart, *Den of Thieves*, pp. 231–98.

125. Stewart, *Den of Thieves*, pp. 299–443; Platrow, "Judge Stuns Milken with 10-Year Sentence."

126. Various versions of this argument can be found in George B. Vold, *Theoretical Criminology* (New York: Oxford University Press, 1958), p. 259; Ernest W. Burgess, "Comment," *American Journal of Sociology* 46 (July 1940): 38; Vilhelm Aubert, "White Collar Crime and Social Structure," *American Journal of Sociology* 58 (November 1952): 265; and Marshall B. Clinard and Richard Quinney, *Criminal Behavior System: A Typology* (New York: Holt, Rinehart and Winston, 1967), p. 137.

127. "Changing Morality: The Two Americas: A Louis Harris Poll," *Time* 93 (June 6, 1969): 26.

128. Joint Commission on Correctional Manpower and Training, *The Public Looks at Crime and Corrections* (Washington, D.C.: Joint Commission on Correctional Manpower and Training, 1968).

129. Peter Rossi, Emily Waite, Christine Berk, and Richard Berk, "The Seriousness of Crimes: Normative Structure and Individual Differences," *American Sociological Review* 39 (1974): 224–37.

130. Francis Cullen, Gregory Clark, Bruce Link, Michael Mathers, Jennifer Niedospial, and Michael Sheahan, "Dissecting White Collar Crime: Offense Type and Punitiveness," *International Journal of Comparative and Applied Criminal Justice* 9 (Spring 1982): 16–27.

131. Bureau of Justice Statistics, *Bulletin: The Severity of Crime* (Washington, D.C.: U.S. Government Printing Office, January 1984).

132. National White Collar Crime Center, *The National Public Survey on White Collar Crime* (Morgantown, W.V.: National White-Collar Crime Center, 2000), pp. 12–13.

133. "Changing Morality."

134. Don C. Gibbons, "Crime and Punishment: A Study of Social Attitudes," *Social Forces* 47 (June 1969): 395.

135. Francis I. Cullen, Richard A. Mathers, Gregory A. Clark, and John B. Cullen, "Public Support for White Collar Offenders: Blaming the Victim Revisited?" *Journal of Criminal Justice* 11 (1983): 481–93.

136. Henry Pontell, Daniel Granite, Constance Keenan, and Gilbert Geis, "Seriousness of Crimes: A Survey of the Nation's Chiefs of Police," *Journal of Criminal Justice* 13 (1985): 1–13.

137. Richard McCleary, Michael J. O'Neil, Thomas F. Epperlein, Constance Jones, and Ronald H. Gray, "Effects of Legal Education and Work Experience on Perceptions of Crime Seriousness," *Social Problems* 28 (February 1981): 276–89.

138. National White Collar Crime Center, *The National Public Survey on White Collar Crime* (Morgantown, W.V.: National White-Collar Crime Center, 2000), pp. 18–19.

139. U.S. House of Representatives, Report 1142, 63rd Cong., 2nd sess. 19, 1914, as quoted in Clinard and Yeager, *Corporate Crime*, p. 76.

140. Bureau of Justice Statistics, *Sourcebook of Criminal Justice Statistics 2002* (Washington D.C.: U.S. Government Printing Office, 2003), Table 5.30.

141. August Bequai, *White Collar Crime: A 20th Century Crisis* (Lexington, Mass.: Lexington Books, 1978), p. 150.

142. For data on the EPA see, Situ and Emmons, *Environmental Crime*, p. 149.

143. *Appendix: Budget of the United States Government, Fiscal Year 2003* (Washington, D.C.: U.S. Government Printing Office, 2002).

144. Ibid.

145. Calculated from data given in the federal budgets. These figures are for the FDA, OSHA, CPSC, EPA, NHTSC, FTC, and the Antitrust Division of the Justice Department. The exact totals for allocated full-time positions are 25,818 for 1980; 20,864 for 1983; 29,041 for 1992; 25,358 for 1996; 30,611 for 1999; and 31,505 for 2003.

146. Data for GDP from U.S. Department of the Census, *Statistical Abstract of the United States, 2003* (Washington, D.C.: GPO, 2004), p. 438.

147. Tillman, Calavita, and Pontell, "Criminalizing White Collar Misconduct," p. 71.

148. Scot J. Platrow, "The Revolving Door," *Los Angeles Times,* March 13, 1994, pp. D1, D4, D6.

149. Quirk, "Food and Drug Administration," p. 207.

150. See Katzmann, "Federal Trade Commission," p. 175.

151. Quoted in Frank Pearce, "Crime, Corporations, and the American Social Order," in Ian Taylor and Laurie Taylor, eds. *Politics and Deviance: Papers from the National Deviancy Conference* (Baltimore: Penguin Books, 1973), p. 22.

152. Quoted in John Braithwaite, *Corporate Crime in the Pharmaceutical Industry* (London: Routledge and Kegan Paul, 1984), p. 9; Clinard and Yeager, *Corporate Crime,* pp. 279–80.

153. "Notes and Comment: Corporate Crime," *Yale Law Journal* 71 (December 1961): 288–89.

154. Sandra S. Evans and Richard J. Lundman, "Newspaper Coverage of Corporate Price-Fixing: A Replication," *Criminology* 21 (November 1983): 529–41.

155. E. Hume, "Why the Press Blew the S&L Scandal," *New York Times,* May 24, 1990, p. A25; L. Martz, "S & Ls: Blaming the Media," *Newsweek,* June 25, 1990, p. 42.

156. Nancy Rivera Brooks, Thomas S. Muligan, and Tim Reiterman, "Memo Shows Enron Role in Power Crisis," *Los Angeles Times,* May 7, 2002; Richard Simon, Ricardo Alonso-Zaldivar, and Tim Reiterman, "Enron Memos Stir Calls for Wider Investigation," *Los Angeles Times,* May 8, 2002.

157. Michael J. Lynch, Mahesh K. Nalla, and Keith W. Miller, "Cross-Cultural Perceptions of Deviance: The Case of Bhopal," *Journal of Research in Crime and Delinquency* 26 (1989): 7–35.

158. John P. Wright, Francis T. Cullen, and Michael B. Blankenship, "The Social Construction of Corporate Violence: Media Coverage of the Imperial Food Products Fire," *Crime and Delinquency* 41 (1995): 20–36.

159. Lewis Beman, "IBM's Travails in Lilliput," *Fortune* (November 1973): 158.

160. Mark Dowie, "Pinto Madness," in Jerome Skolnick and Elliot Currie, eds. *Crisis in American Institutions,* 4th ed. (Boston: Little, Brown, 1979), pp. 33–34.

161. Green and Waitzman, *Business War on the Law.*

162. On this point, see Bringhurst, *Antitrust and the Oil Monopoly.*

163. Green and Waitzman, *Business War on the Law,* p. 99.

164. Ibid., p. 108.

165. Kitty Calavita and Henry N. Pontell, "'Heads I Win, Tails You Lose': Deregulation, Crime and Crisis in the Savings and Loan Industry," *Crime and Delinquency* 36(3) (July 1990): 309–41.

166. "EPA Pesticide Program Is a Farm Team for Pesticide Lobby, Report Finds," *Corporate Crime Reporter,* August 2, 1999, p. 3.

The Causes

*I*n all the social sciences, no notion is more elusive than the concept of causality. Although its meaning seems clear enough in everyday conversation, the task of constructing a precise, scientific explanation of the cause of even the simplest human behavior is maddeningly complex. As the researcher painstakingly isolates and quantifies the factors that are presumed to have caused the behavior, new theories continually pop up to offer rival explanations. The interaction between the numerous variables and the procedures of measurement and investigation render the interpretation of even the most straightforward data ambiguous and uncertain. Thus, more than a little hubris is involved in any attempt to lay out a unified theory of the causes of as diverse a group of phenomena as those housed under the rubric of white-collar crime. It is not a hopeless endeavor, however, as long as one is willing to accept the inherently probabilistic and tentative nature of any conclusions. Although the white-collar crimes are diverse, there are, as we have seen, many underlying commonalities. There is also a growing body of research and analysis on the causes of these crimes that can guide our efforts.

The aim of this chapter is to bring this research together into a unified theoretical structure that can make sense out of the complex phenomenon of white-collar crime. Our final product will, however, bear little resemblance to the conclusive and unambiguous explanations for which many scientists long. The theory of white-collar crime more closely resembles a tapestry in which numerous causal strands are woven together into an integrated, if as yet incomplete, whole.

The basis of this analysis is the simple notion that all criminal behavior requires two elements—motivation and opportunity—that must coincide before a crime can occur. At first it may appear that this reflects a strict division between the social psychological causes (motivation) and the structural causes (opportunity) of white-collar crime, but that is not so. An opportunity must ultimately become psychologically available to individual actors, or it will remain merely a theoretical possibility; and conversely, the roots of individual motivation can be found in the culture and structure of industrial society.

Because of the complexity of the problem of motivation, we will break down our analysis of this topic into two parts. The first explores the formulation of the original motivation for white-collar crime. But a mere attraction to the rewards of criminal behavior is not enough, for society erects strong ethical barriers to restrain such behavior. The second part, therefore, deals with the ways in which white-collar criminals, or the organizations in which they work, neutralize those controls. Finally, we will conclude this chapter with an analysis of the creation and distribution of the opportunities for white-collar crime.

Formulating the Motivation

Understanding human motivation is no easy task, and we will begin with one of the most often discussed, but most poorly researched, issues in the study of white-collar crime—the role of individual personality. From there we will move on to a discussion of the ways in which individuals construct the personal realities that guide their behavior and explore the structural roots of those systems of meaning.

The Personality Factor

The public tends to see criminals as a breed apart from "normal" women and men. The deviants among us are branded as insane, inadequate, immoral, impulsive, egocentric, or any of a hundred other epithets. In seeing the deviant as a wholly different kind of person from ourselves, we bolster our self-esteem and repress the fear that under the right circumstances we too might violate the same taboos. But this system of facile psychological determinism collapses when applied to white-collar criminals. The embezzling accountant or the corporate manager serving in her firm's illegal schemes conforms too closely to the middle-class ideals of American culture to be so easily dismissed.

Edwin Sutherland repeatedly used the belief in the psychological normality of the white-collar criminal as an argument against the psychological explanation of any crime:

> The criminal behavior of businessmen cannot be explained by . . . feeble-mindedness or emotional instability. We have no reason to think that General Motors has an inferiority complex or that Aluminum Company of America has a frustration–aggression complex or that U.S. Steel has an Oedipus complex. . . . The assumption that an offender must have some such pathological distortion of the intellect or the emotions seems to be absurd, and if it is absurd regarding the crimes of businessmen, it is equally absurd regarding the crimes of persons in the lower classes.[1]

Whether or not Sutherland's conclusions concerning the causes of "lower-class" crimes are accurate, it is generally agreed that personal pathology plays no significant role in the genesis of white-collar crime. In fact, this conclusion has been so widely accepted that only a few empirical studies of the issue have actually been done. But the available data do support the notion that white-collar criminals are indeed psychologically normal.[2]

The fact that most white-collar offenders are free from major psychiatric disorders does not prove, however, that their personality structures played no part in the genesis of their crimes. Recognizing this problem, Sutherland tried to show that the rates of corporate crime were unrelated to the personalities of corporate employees, and he argued that individual personality was therefore not an important etiologic factor in white-collar crime. To support his case, Sutherland pointed out that a corporation may violate the law in some parts of its operations but not in others, even though the entire operation is under the direction of the same individuals. He also emphasized the fact that many corporations continue long-term patterns of criminal activities despite undergoing complete changes in personnel.[3] The problem with this line of argument is that even if it can be shown that variations in the personalities of corporate employees have little effect on the rates of corporate crime, it does not prove that personality is not an important factor in an individual's decision about whether to become involved in illegal corporate activities, or that personality has no influence on the rates of other types of white-collar crime, such as embezzlement. Sutherland did not even prove his claim that personality variations play no part in the genesis of corporate crime, for it is possible that corporate managers are more likely to promote individuals with a particular type of personality. In other words, the mere fact that top management has changed does not prove that the personality characteristics of top management have also changed.

While Sutherland's arguments are too weak to justify rejecting the psychology approach out of hand, the evidence in its support remains ambiguous at best. Moreover, white-collar crime remains a thorn in the side of those who use some kind of psychological variable as a general explanation for all types of crime. Gottfredson and Hirschi's "general theory of crime," which is often known as self-control theory, is the most noteworthy recent example.[4] The core of their argument is that crime is caused by the weak self-control of the offenders and that, given the opportunity, those with weak self-control will get involved in crime when others will not. The problem that arises with white-collar offenders is obvious, since most people would agree that corporate executives and most other higher-level offenders actually have high levels of self-control.

Herbert, Green, and Larragoite attempt to save Gottfredson and Hirschi's theory by arguing that all corporate crimes are individual crimes committed by individual employees and that their behavior can indeed best be explained by their lack of self-control. Herbert, Green, and Larrogoite do not dispute the fact that most corporate executives are self-controlled, but in an unusual twist they claim that, compared with the huge number of business transactions that occur every day, the rate of white-collar crime is actually very low.[5] As Yeager and Reed point out, however, that argument makes no more sense than claiming that the rate of rape is extremely low because there are so many interactions between men and women that do not result in a rape.[6] Moreover, the idea that corporate crimes are nothing more than crimes by individual executives flies in the face of generations of sociological work from Durkheim onward that has explored the autonomous influence exerted by social organizations over their members.

The few studies that have carried out empirical research on the personality or personal history of white-collar offenders have reached divergent conclusions, but some traits do recur in sufficient numbers to be worthy of mention. Almost all the studies have agreed on one point: Most white-collar offenders are psychologically "normal," if by that term we mean that they have no symptoms of major psychiatric disorder (hallucinations, delusions, neurotic compulsions, etc.). In addition, two studies agree that white-collar criminals are "egocentric," and two others characterize white-collar offenders as "reckless." In his study of war crimes such as spying and sabotage, Lonell Selling concluded that such offenders were egocentric and antisocial. However, in many places Selling's conclusions, formed from interviews with convicted offenders he encountered in the course of his psychiatric practice, are so obviously prejudiced and ill conceived as to cast grave doubt on the validity of his entire study.[7] Walter Bromberg's methodology was similar to Selling's in that he examined criminals he happened to encounter in his work (at Bellevue Psychiatric Hospital); but despite the obvious flaws in his sampling technique, the moderate tone of his writings gives us hope of greater objectivity. Bromberg cites the case of a successful banker, convicted of various illegal financial manipulations, as typical of many white-collar criminals. Bromberg wrote, "[he] impressed the examiners as a realistic, though relatively uncompromising, individual, independent rather than stubborn, yet unaware of his rather strong tendency toward recklessness. On a deeper level, one could sense in him a certain rigidity of character expressed openly in stubbornness, independence, and lack of compromise. Egocentricity and an unconscious feeling of omnipotence shone through [his] character structure."[8]

In an interview with a sample of thirty white-collar offenders from Leyhill Prison in Great Britain, John Spencer also found a high degree of recklessness among his subjects. He described the outstanding features of these offenders' personalities as "their ambition, their drive, their desire to mix with people of higher social position than their own, and to give their children an expensive private education, and their willingness to take financial risks in the process." Spencer went on to characterize their behavior as "reckless and ambitious."[9] However, he was more careful to qualify his conclusions than was Bromberg, noting that "it would be a mistake to see the adventurous and ruthless gambler as typical of the white-collar criminal. Such men did not account for more than one-third of the sample."[10] Spencer found that just as many of his subjects were "muddlers and incompetent men" without firm principles who had simply drifted into criminal behavior.

Richard Blum's study of industrial spies was one of only two studies to use a control group of nondeviant subjects, but the methodological advantages of this procedure were outweighed by the extremely small sample used—only three industrial spies and six controls. Like other psychologically oriented researchers, Blum found the white-collar offenders (and, for that matter, the control group as well) to be "remarkably free from instability or disabling psychopathology."[11] He focused his investigation on the life histories of his subjects. The main difference Blum discovered between the two groups was that the offenders reported a far greater number of troubling "life experiences," especially during childhood. The average was only three such experiences for the controls and eleven for the offenders.[12] In a much better designed study that compared 350 incarcerated white-collar offenders with a control group of nondeviant executives, J. M. Collins and F. L. Schmidt found a significantly higher degree of irresponsibility, lack of dependability, and "disregard for the rules" among the convicted offenders.[13] However, whether such characteristics are personality traits, or simply attitudes the offenders have learned, is open to question.

Taken as a group, the conflicting conclusions of these studies provide scant evidence for the proposition that white-collar criminals have significant psychological differences from other white-collar workers. However, it would be unwise to disregard the personality factor completely, pending the arrival of more conclusive data. It is easy to imagine how personality differences could lead one executive to embrace criminal activities and another similarly placed executive to reject them. It seems likely, however, that a particular personality orientation will facilitate criminal activities in one occupational situation and discourage them in another, so that no single set of characteristics is conducive to crime in all situations. For example, nonconformists might well be more likely to become involved in an occupational crime directed against an employer but less likely to go along with organizational crimes demanded by their employer. A strict conformist could be expected to show the opposite tendencies.

Stanton Wheeler's work on the motivation of white-collar criminals illustrates the way in which psychological variables can operate in conjunction with situational factors.[14] The beginning of Wheeler's investigation is a question that has long puzzled both the general public and many criminologists as well: "Why do people who are already extremely wealthy individuals risk involvement in white collar crimes, when the money they make can add little or nothing to their already lavish standard of living?" Certainly, such behavior runs counter to the expectations of classical economic theory. Wheeler answers this question in terms of personality. Such individuals are, he claims, "risk seekers" who derive a high degree of satisfaction from increasing their wealth regardless of the actual utility of those gains. These people are characterized by "greed as a personality trait: people who want even more, the more they already have."[15] In contrast, Wheeler argues that other white-collar criminals are motivated by a very different drive— the "fear of falling" and losing some of the wealth and status they have already achieved.

However, the overall impact of personality on the problem of white-collar crime is still open to question for at least two important reasons. First, because the culture of industrial capitalism tends to encourage values, attitudes, and personality structures conducive to white-collar crime, there are always a large number of people with the needed characteristics. Moreover, the operation of the corporate system and the competitive struggles of small business give such individuals a far greater chance of reaching key decision-making positions. As Willem Bonger put it way back in 1905, "As always it is the environment that is the cause of the crimes taking place; it is the individual differences which explain in part who is the one to commit them."[16] Another limitation on the value of personality variables in explaining white-collar crime is the fact that the structural demands in many occupational positions virtually force their occupants to violate the law, regardless of their personal desires or characteristics. For example, when J. Scott Armstrong asked business students to play the role of board members of a pharmaceutical company and presented them with a problem faced by an actual company—a very profitable drug was found to be dangerous to the public—79 percent of the students made the same decision as the real company's management did. They not only refused to withdraw the drug from the market, but they undertook legal and political maneuvers to prevent the government from banning it.[17] Weisburd and Waring's analysis of data from a broad sample of convicted white-collar offenders points to the same conclusion: "there was little in their (the convicted white-collar offenders) records that indicated a predisposition to criminality. Indeed, there was frequently evidence to the contrary. A specific crisis or special opportunity appears to have drawn otherwise conventional people across the line to crime."[18]

The Culture of Competition

Whether or not the personality of the offender is considered important, conventional wisdom offers an even more popular explanation of the motivation for white-collar crime. White-collar criminals break the law, according to this view, because it is the easiest way for them to make a lot of money. Robert Lane found that the business and government officials he studied saw the desire for financial gain as the principal cause of white-collar crime: "Most businessmen and most responsible government officers, at least from the sample interviewed, believe that businessmen run afoul of the law for economic reasons—they may want to 'make a fast buck.'"[19] Those who are familiar with criminological theory will recognize these views as an unknowing restatement of the principles of the classical criminology created in the late eighteenth and early nineteenth centuries by Cesare Beccaria and Jeremy Bentham[20] and carried on by its more modern descendants, such as those promoting rational choice theory. According to this perspective, people violate the law because, after evaluating their situation, they believe some criminal activity will bring them more pleasure and less pain than the other courses of action available to them.

The longevity of this kind of explanation is not hard to understand. Although it may not provide a very convincing account of the reasons a woman would murder her husband in a fit of rage, it is highly persuasive when applied to rational, calculating crimes. But Lane's formulation is too narrow, for although the desire to get rich quick is certainly a motivating factor in many white-collar crimes, other kinds of financial motivations are often equally important. Many white-collar offenders are driven by the fear that they will lose what they already have rather than by the desire for more. For example, when David Weisburd and his colleagues examined the statements of a sample of convicted white-collar criminals made in their presentence information reports, they found that this "fear of falling" was a central motivating force for a large group of offenders. Such offenders would have been "reasonably happy with the place they have achieved through conventional means if only they could keep that place. But the fate of organizational success and failure, or the changing nature of the economy in their line of work, may put them at least temporarily under great financial pressure, where they risk losing the lifestyle that they have achieved. . . . The motivation for their crime is not selfish ego gratification, but rather the fear of falling—of losing what they have worked so hard to gain."[21] Of course, the desire to make more money and the desire to protect what one already has are two closely related aspects of the same phenomenon, which may be termed financial self-interest.

But the numerous case studies we have examined make it clear that financial self-interest, even in its most general sense, is only part of a larger motivational complex that is deeply ingrained in white-collar workers. Along with the desire for great wealth goes the desire to prove oneself by "winning" the competitive struggles that play such a prominent role in our economic system, and this desire to be "a winner" provides another powerful motivation for white-collar crime. One illustration of the need to win without a concomitant financial motivation can be found in the Soap Box Derby. Although no great financial rewards are involved, the Derby creates fierce competition among the entrants. The rules of the Derby require that the young contestants build their own cars, but the desire to win is so strong that many use illegal outside help (in fact, some racers have been built by professionals at a cost of as much as $20,000). The conventional wisdom among contestants has been that forbidden modifications to the cars are necessary to win in the final heats. In addition to prohibited modifications to chassis and wheels, one winner was found to have installed a magnet in the nose of his racer so that its attraction to the swinging starting gate would give him a quicker start.[22] Clearly, these contestants and their supporters were driven by a consuming desire to be winners in the competitive struggles of American life, not just the quest to advance their financial self-interest. Interestingly, Bromberg found virtually identical motivations among the adult white-collar criminals he and his associates examined. He concluded that those offenders had "become identified with the common business ideal of success at any price."[23]

The definition of wealth and success as the central goals of human activity is part of what may be termed the culture of competition, which is particularly characteristic of social systems based on industrial capitalism. This culture of competition defines the competitive struggle for personal gain as a positive, rather than a negative or selfish, activity. Competition is seen not only to build the character and endurance of the competitors (one of the theoretical benefits of the Soap Box Derby) but also to produce the maximum economic value for society as a whole. Not surprisingly, the competitive economic struggles typical of industrial capitalism are seen by and large as a fair battle in which the most capable and the hardest-working individuals emerge victorious. This belief in turn becomes an important legitimation for social inequality, as it implies that the poor deserve their inferior position because they are lazy or incompetent.[24] The winners, on the other hand, are admired for the ability and drive that made them successful.

This adoration of the rich and successful and the stigmatization of the poor not only provide strong reinforcement for the drive for personal success but also contribute to the pervasive sense of insecurity and the fear of failure that are such a powerful undercurrent in the culture of competition. Malcolm X expressed these feelings well in his autobiography: "Full-time hustlers never can relax to appraise what they are doing and where they are bound. As is the case in any jungle, the hustler's every waking hour is lived with both the practical and subconscious knowledge that if he ever relaxes, if he ever slows down, the other hungry, restless foxes, ferrets, wolves, and vultures out there with him won't hesitate to make him their prey."[25] Although Malcolm X was describing a subculture of the lower classes in a capitalist society, the same insecurities are equally common among respectable businesspeople and politicians.

But neither the desire for wealth and success nor the fear of failure can account for all the motivations behind white-collar crimes. Some of these crimes are clearly rooted in the offenders' efforts to live up to the expectations of the significant others in their occupational world. This is particularly true of the various functionaries who, out of an unreflective sense of obedience, carry out their superiors' orders to commit some illegal act, as well as the members of occupational subcultures who go along with illegal activities in order to win the acceptance and support of their peers. In such cases, the offenders often ignore the larger society's condemnation of their crimes and accept their occupational associates' definition of such actions as acceptable and even necessary behavior.

Yet, when one extends this analysis beyond single individuals to encompass the entire group that sustains such criminogenic attitudes, the influence of the culture of competition usually reappears. Whereas the lower-level functionaries involved in organizational crimes may act out of conformity and obedience, the executives giving the orders are usually pursuing those elusive goals of wealth and success. Similarly, while individual members of a deviant occupational subculture (e.g., that found among corrupt police officers) may merely be conforming to the expectations of their peers, the collective desire for financial gain is the primary force that creates and sustains those expectations.

Of course, the culture of competition is only one of the many diverse strains of contemporary culture, and there are other constellations of values that reject or mitigate this kind of orientation. How, then, do we explain why one individual comes to see the world in a way that is highly conducive to criminal behavior and another does not? Sutherland answered this question with his famous theory of differential association: "The hypothesis of differential association is that criminal behavior is learned in association with those who define such behavior favorably and in isolation from those who define it unfavorably, and that a person in an appropriate situation engages in such criminal behavior if, and only if, the weight of the favorable definitions exceeds the weight of the unfavorable definitions."[26] Sutherland argued that criminal behavior is learned like any other behavior, and that the criminal must learn both the techniques of crime and motivations favorable to criminal behavior. He further held that the "specific direction of motives and drives is learned from definitions of the legal codes as favorable or unfavorable."[27]

Sutherland's contention that criminal behavior is learned can hardly be challenged, and his forceful insistence on this point has been of lasting benefit to modern criminology. In other respects, however, his theory is too narrow. Positive or negative definitions of the law constitute only one small component of the attitudes that influence criminal behavior. Many people with positive attitudes toward the law break it anyway, and many with negative attitudes do not. In other cases, criminals may be ignorant of the law, or the law itself may change.

Another, more fundamental problem with Sutherland's theory is his insistence that the construction of personal reality is entirely a product of one's associations with others. Sutherland felt that individuals automatically adopt the definitions of those with whom they have the greatest frequency, duration, and intensity of association. But if that were true, how could those definitions ever change? For that matter, how could they have originated in the first place?

In fact, individuals constantly create new ideas and definitions. Most are quickly discarded because they do not conform to the accepted structure of social reality, but a few have what Max Weber called an "elective affinity" for the social conditions of a particular group and thus are integrated into its cultural system.[28] Some individuals also persist in maintaining idiosyncratic conceptions of reality with little social support, despite the stigma that it may involve. Sutherland's view was that all criminals are ultimately conformists, but true deviance does in fact exist. Contemporary society would hardly have been possible without it.

Despite these objections, it seems fair to say that most of our attitudes, values, and definitions are learned from others. But that does not explain the origins of those ideas. To do so, we must look for their structural causes.

Anthropological studies of the few remaining foraging societies where people live primarily from hunting and collecting edible plants indicate that their people are generally not acquisitive or competitive. Most of those societies are, moreover, strongly egalitarian, with no social classes or even much in the way of permanent political leadership. The enormous differences between foraging societies and the industrial societies with which we are familiar can be traced to their relationship to the environment and the economic system it creates. The cooperative, egalitarian ethos of most foraging societies can be attributed, at least in part, to the fact that such societies produce little surplus wealth. Thus, the economic base cannot support the system of status competition based on the accumulation of wealth that is found in the industrial societies. Significantly, the Indians living along what is now the northwestern coast of the United States and Canada, whose fishing activities generated a more substantial surplus, were in some important respects less egalitarian and more competitive than other foraging peoples.[29]

Willem Bonger, one of the first criminologists to systematically examine the relationship between crime and economic conditions, realized the important role that surplus wealth plays in the displacement of egalitarian social relations. He argued that the growth of commercial exchange made possible by an increasing surplus had a profound sociological impact:

> As soon as productivity has increased to such an extent that the producer can regularly produce more than he needs, and the division of labor puts him in a position to exchange the surplus for things that he could not produce himself, at this moment there arises in man the notion of no longer giving to his comrades what they need, but of keeping for himself the surplus of what his labor produces, and exchanging it. Then it is that the mode of production begins to run counter to the social instincts of man instead of favoring it as heretofore.[30]

Whether or not social evolution proceeded in the order that Bonger postulates, his work points out the important role of market exchange in the development of the culture of competition.

Ethnographic studies of foraging societies have shown that their system of exchange is generally based on sharing and reciprocity. For example, Richard Lee found that the bands of !Kung bushmen in the Kalahari Desert share all the available food equally.[31] Each day a group of adults leaves camp and forages for food. When they return, all the food is divided among the members of the band. Everyone receives an equal share whether they have been foraging, hunting, or sleeping. Robert Dentan found similar patterns of distribution among the Semai of Central Malaya.[32] Even a hunter who succeeds in killing a large animal and dragging it back to camp through the dense jungle has no more claim on its meat than any other member of the band. The meat is cut up into equal portions and distributed to all who are hungry. The hunter is not given a special status because of his accomplishments—indeed, he is not even thanked by the other members of the group, for, as Dentan put it, "Saying thank you is very rude, for it suggests first that one has calculated the amount of a gift, and second that one did not expect the donor to be so generous."[33]

The culture of competition that plays such an important role in white-collar crime is rooted in the structure of the industrial economy. Most obviously, the enormous surplus wealth generated through industrial production provides a vast store of material goods to be competed for—a condition largely absent from foraging societies. A second key factor is the displacement of the open sharing of reciprocal exchange with the calculated self-interest of market exchange. Of course, reciprocal exchange still persists in industrial capitalism, particularly among relatives and close friends, but market exchange is the dominant mode, and that mode of exchange fosters a very different kind of personal outlook from that found among foragers.[34] Market exchange is inevitably tied to the notion of profit and loss: The gain of one trading partner often comes at the expense of the other. Thus, as production for market replaces production for immediate consumption, competition and the quest for personal gain replace the more cooperative sentiments fostered in reciprocal exchange. In addition, the use of money provides an objective, impersonal standard by which to measure profit and loss in industrial society, thus further reinforcing the spirit of competition and the goal of the personal acquisition of wealth.[35]

While it may appear to some that those criminogenic conditions prevail only in the capitalist nations, the same conditions that create a culture of competition could also be found in the communist nations as well—at least to the extent that they underwent a process of industrialization. For one thing, all industrial economies produce a substantial amount of surplus wealth, even if the amount of those surpluses was somewhat smaller in the communist than in the capitalist countries. Although markets in the communist nations did not operate as freely as do those in the West, goods and services were still allocated largely on the basis of monetary exchange. Ideological claims notwithstanding, the systems of stratification in communist nations were always characterized by sharp class divisions. Moreover, there is a considerable amount of social mobility in all industrialized nations, whether communist or capitalist, and that inevitably entails the competition for advancement and a fear of downward mobility.

This does not mean, however, that we should assume that all the industrialized nations are essentially similar. The culture of competition may vary significantly even among the rich, industrialized nations, just as their economic systems show considerable variance. Edwin Schur has argued that the United States puts a greater emphasis on competitive individualism than can be accounted for solely on the basis of its capitalist economic system: "It is difficult not to conclude that American society has what might be termed capitalism with a vengeance—a reverence for the values of individualism, competition, and profit of such intensity as to provide incentives to crime that go well beyond a level that must be considered inevitable in a modern complex society, even a basically capitalist one."[36] Although there is little hard empirical work on this point, Schur is certainly not alone in this belief. Many observers have argued that the nexus of values we have called the culture of competition is stronger in the United States than in any capitalist nation of Western Europe, Oceania, or Asia. Even if this contention is accurate, however, it does not necessarily follow that the rates of white-collar crime must be higher in the United States. Given the persuasiveness of the culture of competition in all industrialized societies, it appears that the crime rates for white-collar offenses are more likely to be determined by the availability of attractive opportunities than by differences in motivational patterns.

Neutralizing Social Controls

The culture of competition receives strong social support in the industrialized nations, but so do the ethical standards that attempt to restrain it. Schools teach general moral principles at all grade levels, and religious institutions place even greater emphasis on such values. Newscasts, popular television programs, and the pronouncements of corporate and government leaders frequently proclaim the importance of maintaining high ethical standards, and even the shadiest operators claim to share them. The network of laws based on those values provides another powerful support. In addition to the threat of punishment, the law has enormous symbolic importance. It provides official reinforcement for the principles it embodies, and it creates a stigmatizing label for those who violate its standards—a label that is, moreover, especially repugnant to the respectable businesspeople, politicians, and professionals who constitute the majority of white-collar criminals.

Techniques of Neutralization

The conflict between the culture of competition and other ethical standards is carefully papered over in public. An elaborate pretense is maintained that there is no contradiction and that unethical behavior is ultimately rewarded with failure and disgrace. In private, of course, the fact that "bending" the rules of the game provides an important competitive advantage is much too obvious to ignore, and other ways must be found to resolve this contradiction. Some people openly reject the ethical standards of their culture, whereas others find nothing appealing in the values of materialism and competition, but most people are attracted by both ideals. One way to construct a personal reality that accommodates both is through the use of what Gresham Sykes and David Matza have called "techniques of neutralization."[37] A technique of neutralization is essentially a device that enables individuals to violate important normative standards but to neutralize the definition of themselves as deviant or criminal. Such techniques take many forms, but in essence they are rationalizations that deviants use to justify their actions. For example, a physician may justify claiming Medicaid reimbursements for services that were never performed by telling himself that his actions didn't really harm anyone, while salespeople pass off their deceptive statements on the grounds that "everyone does it."

But techniques of neutralization are not just ex post facto rationalizations—they are available to the potential deviant before the offense actually occurs and thus form part of the motivation for the original act.[38] A physician does not file fraudulent Medicaid claims and then suddenly make up a rationalization to justify her actions. Rather, she is aware from the beginning that her schemes will not cause any direct harm to her patients and that rationalization makes it psychologically feasible for her to carry out her plans.

Of all types of white-collar criminals, embezzlers have been the subject of the most scientific study, perhaps because so many people have difficulty understanding why trusted, well-paid employees would jeopardize their position by stealing from their employers. Most of the research on embezzlement has attributed the offenders' crimes to their need for money. More specifically, these studies found the major causes of embezzlement to be gambling, extravagant living, and costly personal problems.[39] But the fact that embezzlers feel they need more money than they can legitimately earn is hardly a sufficient explanation in itself, for the culture of competition and the advertising that supports it have planted the desire for more money and more possessions in the minds of most people. So the question remains: Why do some individuals with the opportunity to embezzle actually do it, whereas others do not?

Donald R. Cressey's detailed study of the motivations for embezzlement was the first to provide an answer to this question.[40] Based on intensive interviews with a sample of incarcerated embezzlers, Cressey concluded that three distinct elements are necessary for embezzlement to occur: The perpetrators must have a nonshareable financial problem, they must have the opportunity and the knowledge necessary to commit an embezzlement, and they must apply a suitable rationalization to "adjust" the contradiction between their actions and society's normative standards. Of these three propositions, the first is the most questionable, for there appears to be no necessary reason why an embezzlement must result from a nonshareable problem instead of a simple desire for more money. Indeed, Gwynn Nettler interviewed several embezzlers who did not have such nonshareable problems (at least not until after they committed their crimes), and Dorothy Zietz's study of female embezzlers reached a similar conclusion.[41] Cressey's second proposition, in contrast, is almost self-evident: To be an embezzler, an individual must have the opportunity and knowledge necessary to commit the crime. Of greatest relevance to our discussion is Cressey's third proposition and his investigation of the specific types of rationalizations that embezzlers use to justify their actions.

Most embezzlers, according to Cressey, rationalize their crimes by telling themselves they are just borrowing the money and will soon return it. As one subject put it, "I figured that if you could use something and help yourself and replace it and not hurt anybody, it was all right."[42] Cressey found that his respondents continued to use this rationalization to justify their embezzlement while they became more and more deeply involved in crime. Eventually they were either caught or realized they would never be able to pay back all the money they had taken, and they were finally forced to accept the criminal nature of their behavior. Cressey's respondents reported using several other rationalizations as well, but the borrowing rationalization was by far the most common, probably because it is so well suited to neutralize the ethical standards condemning embezzlement.

The borrowing rationalization does not work as well for other white-collar crimes. Fortunately, there are numerous studies that examine the rationalizations criminals use to justify other kinds of white-collar crimes. One of the most common is the claim that the crimes do not harm anyone. If one's actions do not hurt other people, the argument goes, then there is nothing unethical about them. When a Westinghouse executive on trial for price-fixing was asked if he thought his behavior had been illegal, he responded, "Illegal? Yes, but not criminal. . . . I assumed that a criminal action meant damaging someone, and we did not do that."[43] Lawrence Zeitlin found similar justifications in his study of workers discharged for stealing from their employers. As one of his subjects put it, "It's not really hurting anybody—the store can afford it."[44] Survey data have shown that the public is more tolerant of theft from large businesses and the government than it is of theft from smaller, more vulnerable organizations—probably because theft from a larger organization is perceived as less harmful to the victim.[45]

Those involved in business crimes frequently justify their behavior by claiming that the law itself is unnecessary or unjust. Businesspeople complain loudly about "government interference" in their affairs, often using the ideology of laissez-faire capitalism to point out what they consider to be inappropriate statutes and regulations. According to such beliefs, it is the law that causes harm to the public and not the illegal activities of business. Given this system of beliefs, a host of business crimes can easily be justified. Marshall Clinard, for example, concluded that gasoline dealers' belief that wartime rationing of gasoline was unnecessary was a "rationalization for the violations which were occurring."[46] Among small businesses, ideological considerations are probably less important than the owners' perception of whether the regulations are fair to them. In a study of rent control in Honolulu, Harry Ball found no significant difference in violation rates among landlords who felt that rent control was necessary and those who did not. But he found significantly higher rates among landlords who felt that the rent ceilings applied to their property were less than the "fair" rental value.[47]

Another common technique of neutralization is the claim that one's criminal behavior was necessary in order to survive or to achieve vital economic goals. Many employees use this appeal to necessity to explain why they went along with illegal activities expected by their employers. Sutherland cited the case of an idealistic young college graduate who had lost two previous jobs because he refused to become involved in unethical activities. After taking his third job, this time at a used car dealership, he found out that they too expected him to become involved in shady business practices. "When I learned these things I did not quit as I had previously. I sometimes felt disgusted and wanted to quit, but I argued that I did not have much chance to find a legitimate firm. I knew the game was rotten, but it has to be played—the law of the jungle and that sort of thing."[48] Ian Smith, a former city councilman in Britain, used a similar argument to justify his part in a corruption scandal: "I am by nature a wheeler-dealer. How else can you be a successful politician?"[49]

Even representatives of giant corporations use this justification, although such firms are unlikely candidates for economic extinction. The Westinghouse executive quoted earlier went on to justify his involvement in the price-fixing conspiracy by saying, "I thought we were more or less working on a survival basis in order to try to make enough to keep our plant and our employees." The former sales manager of a "competing" company made the same point: "The spirit of the [price-fixing] meetings only appeared to be correcting a horrible price level situation . . . [there was no] attempt to actually damage customers, [or] charge excessive prices. There was not personal gain in it for me [sic]. The company did not seem actually to be defrauding [anyone]. Corporate statements [show] that there have been poor profits during all these years."[50] It is also worthy of note that this executive, like most other white-collar criminals, freely combined different justifications of his behavior. In addition to claiming that his activities were necessary to his employer, he denied that his illegal activities harmed others.

A case reported by Gary Reed and Peter Yeager of a middle manager who helped cook his company's books to inflate its profits shows a watered-down version of this argument of necessity in which criminal behavior was not necessary for corporate survival but was simply the least unpalatable course of action available. When describing the actions of his boss, who had pressured him into his illegal activities, this manager said: "What he did was not unethical. . . . What he did was he made the best of a bad situation without having to sacrifice the company's progress. If we wouldn't have gotten the [profits increased this way] we might have had to cut back on some things we didn't want to sacrifice, like our marketing budget, or on people. You know, I mean the alternatives . . . were probably a lot uglier."[51]

Another version of this argument of necessity often used to justify occupational offenses is that the crime was necessary to help one's family. Kathleen Daly's research found evidence of significant gender differences in the use of this rationalization. In her study of the presentence reports of convicted white-collar offenders, the female embezzlers were about twice as likely to cite the needs of their family members as a justification than were male embezzlers, whereas males were much more likely to cite business needs.[52] However, every one of the males incarcerated for economic crimes who were interviewed by Willott, Griffin, and Torrance's mentioned the need to provide support for their families as a justification for their crimes. As one of their respondents put it: "You see, none of us was taking this money to live a raucous life-style. . . . A sort of selfish, you know, quixotic sort of life-style. . . . it was as a genuine need to look after others, our families, our children, our borrowings."[53]

The argument of necessity can be even more persuasive in government than in private settings. The participants in many political crimes and violations of civil liberties rationalize their illegal activities in terms of "national security." Indeed, some criminals even claim that it is their patriotic duty to break the law in order to promote the long-term interests of the nation.[54]

A justification that is often combined with the argument of necessity is the claim that "everybody else is doing it." As one of Cressey's subjects put it, "In the real estate business you have to paint a pretty picture in order to sell the property. We did a little juggling and moving around, but everyone in the real estate business has to do that. We didn't do anything that they all don't do."[55] This kind of rationalization is frequently used to justify "fudging" on income tax returns, and Michael Benson found it to be just as popular among those convicted of criminal tax fraud. According to one respondent, "Everybody cheats on their income taxes, 95 percent of the people. Even if it's ten dollars, it's the same principle."[56]

Another version of the "everybody's doing it" justification holds that it is unfair to condemn one violator unless all the other violators are condemned. A defendant in a British corruption case said, "I will never believe I have done anything criminally wrong. I did what is business. If I bent any rules, who doesn't? If you are going to punish me, sweep away the system. If I am guilty, there are many others who should be by my side in the dock."[57] Yet another version of this justification is that criminal behavior must be some sort of individual choice, and that people are not responsible for their actions when they are merely conforming to the expectations of others. Corrupt employees often claim that they haven't done anything wrong, because they were merely going along with a pattern of behavior accepted among their peers.[58]

Finally, many occupational crimes are justified on the grounds that the offender deserves the money. This rationalization is particularly common in cases of employee theft. In his study of dock workers, Gerald Mars found that pilferage was defined as a "morally justified addition to wages" or an "entitlement due from exploiting employers."[59] Lawrence Zeitlin discovered similar attitudes among employees who stole from retail stores. One of his subjects felt that the "store owed it to me," and another said, "I felt I deserved to get something additional for my work since I wasn't getting paid enough."[60] The same rationalizations have been used to justify corruption among government employees, who often see themselves as underpaid in comparison with their counterparts in private industry. One former city councilman gave the following account of his reasons for becoming involved in corruption: "People like me are expected to work full time without salaries, without staff, or even postage stamps. I for one couldn't afford such a situation. And that is where Poulson [a businessman seeking special favors] filled the gap. . . . I came to the conclusion that I was missing out, that I could combine my real desire to give public service with what they call a piece of the action."[61]

Of course, many other justifications are used to neutralize normative controls, but the six rationalizations just discussed seem to be the most common. Before moving on, however, we must explore an important question concerning their origins. Cressey argued that individual offenders do not invent their own rationalizations but simply apply existing definitions to their own behavior: "Each trusted person does not invent a new rationalization for his violation of trust, but instead applies to his own situation a verbalization which has been made available to him by virtue of his having come into contact with a culture in which such verbalizations are present."[62] While this is probably true much more often than not, individuals do construct their own justifications based on individual circumstances and rework previously learned rationalizations to better fit their own experience. For example, employees who justify their thefts by holding that the company will not be harmed generally pick up this rationalization directly from other employees or from widely held cultural beliefs. But employees who find themselves confronted with a special problem not shared by their coworkers may develop unique rationalizations. For example, a woman singled out as a target for her boss's sexual advances and the jealousy of her male coworkers might use those facts to construct a particularistic justification for her criminal behavior.

With all this said, it is clear that most of the techniques of neutralization are still culturally learned. Of particular importance in this regard are the various occupational subcultures that not only supply their members with a set of appropriate rationalizations but also help to isolate them from contact with those who would pass harsher judgment on their criminal activities. Many of the ways occupational subcultures encourage criminal behavior were examined in Chapter 2. Police subcultures, for example, often distinguish between "clean" payoff money and "dirty" payoff money, holding that there is nothing unethical about accepting the former. Moreover, the workers in many factories make clear distinctions between which property it is permissible to steal and which property it is not, and many politicians learn to see the exchange of political favors for campaign contributions or personal rewards as a normal part of their job.

Such deviant subcultures need not be confined to a single employer or even to a single profession. The business culture that is shared to one degree or another by most businesspeople not only provides incentives for illicit activities but also contains justifications that can be used to neutralize ethical restraints. The common expression that "business is business" reflects the subculture's belief that harsh necessity justifies both the unethical and the illegal activities of the business world. Polls indicate that the "everybody else is doing it" rationalization also has a strong affinity to the attitudes and opinions of the business subculture. Most businesspeople apparently believe not only that their peers and competitors are willing to commit unethical acts, but that they are actually doing it. Four out of five executives surveyed by the *Harvard Business Review* felt that some of the generally accepted practices in their industry were unethical, and four out of seven believed that other executives would violate a code of ethics if they felt they would not be caught.[63] A 1975 study of top officials in the fifty-seven largest U.S. corporations found that the officials believed unethical behavior to be so widespread that it had to be accepted as part of everyday business activities.[64] A study of business attitudes undertaken by the Uniroyal Corporation found that "most managers believed that their peers would not refuse an order to market off-standard and possibly dangerous products (although a majority insisted they would personally reject such orders), and a majority thought young managers automatically go along with superiors to show loyalty."[65]

Organizational Conformity

Up to this point we have been discussing the causes of white-collar crime in general, but now some special attention must be devoted to organizational crime. Although the same process of motivation and rationalization occurs in both individual and organizational crime, the structural demands of formal organizations create unique pressures that require careful analysis. Modern organizations are, in a sense, machines for controlling human behavior. To survive, a large corporation must directly control the behavior of thousands of employees and indirectly influence the activities of much larger groups on the outside. Although organizations may well encounter special problems in persuading employees to engage in illegal activities, the mechanisms for achieving conformity to organizational expectations are much the same whatever the legal standing of the organization's demands.

One of the most powerful techniques to win conformity with organizational demands is the threat of dismissal. John Z. DeLorean, a former top executive of General Motors and founder of his own unsuccessful automobile firm, gave the following description of the pressure applied to an engineer who objected to dangerous design elements in the notorious Chevrolet Corvair: "Charlie Chayne, vice-president of engineering, along with his staff, took a very strong stand against the Corvair as an unsafe car long before it went on sale. . . . He was not listened to but told in effect, 'You're not a member of the team. Shut up or go looking for another job.'"[66] Of course, such threats are seldom made so blatantly, but even so, employees understand what is involved in going against the company's demands.

The fear of losing an important assignment or being passed up for the next promotion is just as much a threat for the achievement-oriented executive as the possibility of dismissal. In the social world of the modern corporation, dedication to the company and conformity to the wishes of one's superiors are seen as essential to success. Regular promotions are an expected part of the climb up the corporate ladder, and overly scrupulous managers are likely to find the promotions they expected going to those who have been more cooperative. For example, court testimony from General Electric executives involved in the heavy electrical equipment price-fixing cases indicates that they were under intense pressure from their superiors to participate in the price-fixing conspiracy. Their primary fear was not so much the loss of their jobs (although, ironically, many of them were fired after the scandal broke) as the loss of the particular assignments they had been given, and the negative effects that event might have had on their careers.[67] As one executive put it, "If I didn't do it, I felt someone else would. I would be removed, and somebody else would do it."[68] The consuming desire for success and the notion that conformity and obedience to superiors are essential to achieve that goal make executives fearful of questioning their orders, even if they involve illegal activities. A report to the Securities and Exchange Commission concerning Lockheed's involvement in overseas bribery noted, "Employees learned not to question deviations from standard operational procedure and practices. Moreover, the Committee was told by several witnesses that employees who questioned foreign marketing practices damaged their claims for career advancement."[69] Thus, top corporate leaders are able to persuade their subordinates to engage in illegal activities, often without specifically ordering them to do so, because their position in the organization gives them control of rewards and punishments that are enormously important to those below them.

Organizational control nonetheless involves much more than simply handing out sufficient rewards and punishments to ensure employee obedience. A large organization harbors a unique social world all its own, and the subculture embodied in the organization shapes its members' behavior in countless ways—many times without conscious awareness on the part of the employees. At the most fundamental level, the way an organizational subculture defines the work situation and the role of various employees creates the context for all organizational behavior. The ethos of a corporation also helps shape the moral sensibilities and perspectives of its employees—especially those in managerial positions. Certainly, any decision to engage in illegal activity is profoundly affected by the social world sheltered within the organization.

One important element of this social world is its "moral tone"—that is, its ethical system and its attitudes toward illegal behavior. As one student of the Equity Funding fraud wrote, "Corporations can and do create a moral tone that powerfully influences the thinking, conduct, values, and even the personalities of the people who work for them. The tone is set by the men who run the company, and their corruption can quickly corrupt all else. A startling thing about Equity Funding is how rarely one finds, in a cast of characters big enough to make a war movie, a man who said, 'No, I won't do that. It's wrong.'"[70]

In describing his research sponsored by the accounting firm of Peat, Marwick, and Mitchell, Donald R. Cressey writes: "I interviewed about two dozen internal and external auditors. Every one of these financial executives said that the ethical behavior of a company's personnel is determined by the example set by top management."[71] Clinard and Yeager found much the same attitudes in a series of interviews they conducted among top corporate managers.[72]

But although such beliefs are accurate, they are also misleading, because they hinge on a single fact taken out of the social and economic context in which it is embedded. Of course top management influences the ethical tone of the organization—but top managers' ethical standards are not simply their own personal beliefs. The ethics and outlook of those who come to hold the most powerful positions in an organization are molded and shaped by the same process of socialization that influences other, less successful managers. Indeed, promotion to the highest ranks generally requires a much higher degree of ethical conformity than is expected of lower-level employees.[73] Those who refuse to change personal standards that are incompatible with the demands of their corporate employer seldom reach the top.

Much has been written about the numbing effects modern bureaucracies have on the moral sensibilities of their employees. Numerous writers have chronicled the growth of what William H. Whyte called the "organization man," who is under such overwhelming pressure to conform that individuality and personal ethical standards must be sacrificed for the sake of a career.[74] According to Diane Margolis, the "new men" who took over American business as it became more routine and more bureaucratic "had to be less autonomous and more passive, less ambitious and more malleable; team players, not loners—in short, other-directed, not inner-directed."[75] Frank Howton used similar terms in describing the modern-day corporate functionary as a "new kind of man who in his role of servicing the organization is morally unbound. . . . His ethic is the ethic of the good soldier: take the order, do the job."[76]

Howton argues convincingly that these amoral functionaries have become so common because they are necessary to bureaucratic organization. A bureaucracy, as Max Weber pointed out, is an impersonal system of interrelated roles whose rights and duties are spelled out in formal rules.[77] One of the principal strengths of bureaucratic organization is that individual employees are dispensable—one employee can be replaced by another with a minimum of disruption. But this interchangeability requires that individual employees think and act in a similar fashion, and the existence of widely divergent ethical standards and attitudes among members of the workforce might interfere with the smooth operation of the organization. Thus, the efficient bureaucracy breeds moral conformity—or perhaps more often, a kind of amoral pragmatism.

The process of socialization into the corporate ethic occurs at all levels of the organization, but a particular effort is made to shape aspiring managers accord-ing to the corporate image. The transfer is one of the devices commonly used to achieve this goal. By continually moving young executives from one area to an-other, the firm weakens outside ties that might interfere with their socialization. These transfers make managers more dependent on the corporation to satisfy their social needs and bring them ever more deeply into its social world. The long hours of work required of up-and-coming executives have a similar effect. The burden of overwork disrupts commitments to family, friends, community, and other interests that might place conflicting pressures on the manager. As Margolis put it, "What is to be accomplished is not a total change in the young man's values or attitudes but merely their reorder. The priority of the corpora-tion must be established. For that to happen, exhausting workloads are less strate-gic than work situations that put the corporation into competition with other institutions or persons who might lay claim on the man. These competitions, which always have the appearance of accidents, are in fact intentional enforcers or tests of the man's loyalty to the corporation."[78]

This rigorous process of socialization can produce a kind of "moral numb-ness" in corporate managers.[79] The well-socialized executive tends to display a narrow, pragmatic approach to his or her work, acting in the best interests of the corporation with little thought of its moral implications. C. Wright Mills held such attitudes to be part of the "structural immorality" of American society,[80] but perhaps the phenomenon can more appropriately be termed "structural amorality," for the well-trained bureaucrat does not oppose or reject popular morality, but is often indifferent to it.

Socialization into a bureaucratic organization does much more than merely dull the initiate's ethical sensibilities, however. As James March and Herbert Simon, Charles Perrow, and other sociologically oriented organizational theorists have pointed out,[81] an organization also controls its members through its in-fluence on the definition of the situations they face on the job. The organization provides definitions about what needs to be done, the importance of various tasks, and the effects of those tasks on the company and the community. The organization defines the goals it is pursuing and the ways those goals are to be achieved. It provides repertoires of actions to be used in response to given situations, and it teaches employees to direct their attention to certain aspects of their environment and to ignore others.

This network of definitions often makes unethical or illegal activities appear to be a normal part of the daily routine. Time after time, individuals unlucky enough to have been caught committing corporate crimes have expressed surprise and even shock that their actions were really considered criminal by the world outside their organizations. One General Electric executive involved in the heavy electrical equipment scandals said that price-fixing "had become so common and gone on for so many years that we lost sight of the fact that it was illegal."[82] James Carey's description of the attitudes of those involved in the marketing of MER/29 applies equally well to many other organizational criminals: "No one involved expressed any strong repugnance or even opposition to selling the unsafe drug. Rather, they all seemed to drift into the activity without thinking a great deal about it."[83]

The organizational structure of modern bureaucracy greatly facilitates its ability to manipulate employees' definition of their occupational world. The mammoth size of many of these organizations, their labyrinth of organizational units, and the ever-increasing trend toward specialization fragment the responsibility of individual employees. Most employees work on only a small part of a much larger overall operation, and many never see—or choose to ignore—the potential impact of the project as a whole. Employees who question the ethical or legal implications of their work are told to carry out their duties and not to worry about things that are the responsibility of top management.

At the same time, top managers often make an intentional effort to avoid legal responsibility for the illegal activities they encourage. In the heavy electrical equipment price-fixing cases, for example, top management first set quotas and goals that virtually required price-fixing to achieve, and then they made it clear that they did not want to hear anything about the criminal activities of their subordinates.[84] Surveys indicate that many middle-level managers are afraid to be honest with their bosses, and that the number of managers reporting this problem has steadily increased.[85] This same process goes on in government as well. The scandal that developed over the sale of arms to America's adversaries in Iran and the use of some of the profits to illegally support the rebels seeking to overthrow the government of Nicaragua provides a classic example. It is clear that President Reagan ordered his subordinates to find some way to aid the Nicaraguan rebels, even though a specific prohibition on the use of government funds for such a purpose had already been enacted into law. Former national security adviser John M. Poindexter, who directed the Iran-Contra scheme, testified before Congress in July 1987 that although he was confident that the president would have approved the plan, he did not ask his permission in order to protect him from the political damage that would occur if the plan became public.[86]

Another factor that facilitates corporate control of managers is their relative isolation from the outside world. In one of his most-well-known works on business administration, Peter Drucker compared the isolation of the executive with that of monks in a monastery. He went on to note that the executive's "contacts outside of business tend to be limited to . . . people of the same set, if not to people working for the same organization. The demand that there be no competing outside interests and loyalty applies to the corporate executive as it does to the army officer. Hence executive life not only breeds a parochialism of the imagination comparable to the 'military mind,' but places a considerable premium on it."[87] This isolation is important, because it insulates the white-collar criminals from the condemnation they would otherwise receive from those outside the social world of their organization, and also because it discourages normal skepticism about attitudes and goals that executives learn on the job.

The Distribution of Opportunity

No matter how strong an individual's motivation, by itself it can never provide a complete explanation of criminal behavior. If there is no opportunity, there is no crime. In this short discussion, we cannot hope to list all the opportunities associated with the myriad occupational positions created by modern industrial economies. We can only provide a general description of the overall distribution of the opportunities for white-collar crime and examine some of the reasons those opportunities are distributed the way they are. But before we proceed, we have to clarify exactly what we mean by an opportunity. In everyday speech, "opportunity" has a positive connotation—an opportunity is a favorable set of circumstances that allows us to do something we desire. Thus, we speak of an opportunity to double an investment, not an opportunity to have cancer surgery. Here, however, the term will be used in a more neutral way. For our purposes, an opportunity is merely a possible course of action, and different opportunities can be evaluated on the basis of their attractiveness to different individuals or groups.

Rational choice theory holds that we do this evaluation on the basis of reason and logic. But although this is often the case, the choices made by even the most rational corporate executives are influenced by a host of other factors. Critics of this approach, such as Diane Vaughn, have pointed out that there clearly are social and cultural restraints on the exercise of rational choice.[88] The attitudes of our friends and associates, the subculture within an organization, or the cultural perspective of an entire society can, for example, blind an individual decision maker to many options that would appear to be highly attractive rational choices or make a highly irrational decision look extremely attractive.

There has, unfortunately, been little effort to measure criminal opportunities directly. But because the culture of competition has diffused the motivation for white-collar crime so widely, it seems justified to use an indirect measure and assume that high crime rates reflect the presence of attractive criminal opportunities. The only other important factor affecting the crime rates would appear to be the distribution of rationalizations—for some types of crime are more easily justified than others. But in light of the ingenuity people have shown at creating flattering definitions of their own behavior, there is little doubt that crime rates and the distribution of criminal opportunity are strongly correlated. Nonetheless, there is still a serious problem with using available data on crime rates as an indicator of the distribution of opportunities for white-collar crime, because virtually all the quantitative measures of white-collar crime used in criminological research are based on reports by regulatory and criminal justice agencies. Although those statistics are certainly influenced by the underlying crime rate, they also reflect a number of extraneous variables, such as the likelihood of detecting a particular crime, and the priorities and procedures of the agencies themselves. Despite these difficulties, some preliminary conclusions are necessary, both as a summary of the current state of our knowledge and as a basis for further research.[89]

Industries

Both the distribution of opportunities and their relative attractiveness vary significantly from one industry to another. One question that has created a great deal of interest among scholars is the role of the market structure of an industry in corporate crime. However, many contradictory claims have been made about which type of market structure is the most conducive to criminal activity. On the one hand, it can be argued that competitive markets in which many different firms struggle to keep afloat are the most likely to have high crime rates, because the combatants will use every possible means to survive and prosper. On the other hand, it appears that price-fixing and other antitrust conspiracies are far easier in markets dominated by a few large firms. Thus, it would seem that industries with many small, highly competitive firms would be characterized by a high rate of crimes that are intended to improve competitive performance, such as fraud, false advertising, and espionage, and that collusion and antitrust activities are most common in more concentrated industries.

Most of the empirical research on this issue has focused on the antitrust laws. Although it would seem to be impossible for hundreds of small firms to join together in an illegal conspiracy without being detected, many researchers have compared the rate of antitrust violations in moderately concentrated and highly concentrated industries. Jeffrey Pfeffer and Gerald Salancik, J. F. Burton, and Marc Riedel[90] found the greatest number of antitrust violations in industries with intermediate levels of concentration, whereas George Hay and Daniel Kelley[91] found more violations among highly concentrated firms. Peter Asch and J. J. Seneca[92] concluded that high concentration is associated with higher rates of crime in consumer goods industries and with lower rates of crime in producer goods industries.

Finally, Richard Posner[93] and the Clinard study[94] found little relationship of any kind between these two variables. As Clinard and Yeager suggested, quantitative research on this topic is extremely difficult, and more sophisticated methodology is needed before these contradictory findings can be resolved.[95]

The much slimmer body of research on bribery also concentrates on the issue of market structure. Pointing out the numerous bribery scandals involving the sale of everything from aircraft to beer, Clinard and Yeager argued that bribery is most likely to occur in highly competitive industries.[96] This position has obvious appeal, because it pictures bribery as simply one more type of competition between firms seeking to sell their products—the more competition, the greater the need to resort to bribery. Yerachmiel Kugel and Gladys Gruenberg, however, argued that oligopolistic markets are most conducive to bribery: "Since oligopoly markets are characterized by lack of price competition, international payoffs become a kind of nonprice competition."[97] Data from the international payoff scandals in the 1970s appear to support Kugel and Gruenberg's thesis. Of the thirty-two companies that were found to have spent more than $1 million in "questionable payments" abroad, half were in just four industries. The heaviest concentration of offenders was in the drug industry, where seven different firms admitted making more than $1 million in foreign payments. The second greatest concentration of offenders was in the aircraft industry, where four firms surpassed the $1 million mark, followed by the oil industry, with three million-dollar offenders and the food industry, with two.[98] All these industries are oligopolistic ones in which a few giant firms dominate the American market.

The matter is, however, more complicated than it may appear, for a high concentration ratio in the United States does not necessarily mean that there is no international competition. Despite a high degree of domestic concentration in the aircraft industry, the international aircraft market is often fiercely competitive, and most of the reported bribery in this industry was indeed intended to promote aircraft sales. In contrast, the petroleum industry has long been characterized by cartels and collusion, and there generally is less competition in either domestic or international markets. Significantly, most of the bribery reported in the petroleum industry was intended not to directly promote the sales of a particular company's products, but to preserve and enhance a political climate favorable to the operations of all international oil companies. Thus, intense competition appears more likely to be associated with commercial bribery intended to promote the sale of a firm's products, whereas firms in noncompetitive industries may have more of a tendency to be involved in political bribery aimed at influencing government policies and programs.

Because all the quantitative studies just discussed rely on official records and reports as their only measure of white-collar crime, it is difficult to know how much confidence we should place in their conclusions. The case study method, which analyzes the conditions that contribute to particular white-collar offenses in particular industries, has so far produced better results. Harvey Farberman[99] and William Leonard and Marvin Weber,[100] for example, all concluded that the economic organization of the automobile industry virtually forced individual dealers to engage in shady business practices. They argued that the oligopolistic firms that control the supply of new automobiles pressure their franchises to sell cars at an extremely low price in order to increase their sales volume, and dealers are therefore forced to make up their losses through repair and service rackets and other fraudulent activities. Norman Denzin found similar conditions in the liquor industry.[101] Distillers impose rigid sales quotas on their distributors that force them to give untaxed, under-the-table incentives to retailers to keep up their volume.

Martin Needleman and Carolyn Needleman have, however, criticized the assumption in such studies that the participants are coerced into criminal activity.[102] They argue that in most cases, it is more accurate to talk about "crime facilitative" rather than "crime coercive" systems. Their study of the securities industry, for example, found many conditions that made criminal activities easier but did not actually force individuals to participate. More specifically, the Needlemans found that the legal doctrines limiting the financial risk in handling stolen securities, the strong financial incentives to keep up market flow, and the traditions of trust and professional solidarity in the industry all combined to facilitate securities theft. Moreover, the repeated waves of financial scandals and the numerous statements from insiders familiar with the operations of the stock market and commodity exchanges suggest an extremely high rate of other criminal activities among those involved in the financial markets as well (see Chapter 2). Not surprisingly, David Weisburd and colleagues' analysis of convicted white-collar offenders found a higher crime rate in the securities industry than in any of the six other industries they analyzed.[103]

Another variable influencing the opportunity structure within an industry is what Edward Gross called "organizational sets"—groups of similar organizations whose actions are visible to each other.[104] The key point is that these sets tend to have an internal system of stratification with dominant organizations, middle-level organizations, and marginal organizations. The relatively small number of firms at the top of these stratified organizational sets greatly increases the attractiveness of antitrust conspiracies, because it reduces the number of firms that must become involved and thus reduces their chances of being uncovered. Citing the Equity Funding case, Gross also argued that both the tendency for organizations to focus their attention almost exclusively on the activities of other members of their set and the great complexity of relations among participants in different sets make it easier for outsiders to conceal fraudulent schemes that cut across set boundaries. Some researchers feel also that the fact that some corporations are structurally bedded in an organizational network may help insulate them from mechanisms of social control that would otherwise restrain their criminal behavior.[105]

Variations in the regulatory environment also play a major role in determining the opportunity structure in different industries. The more tightly an industry is regulated, the more likely it is that attractive opportunities will be illegal, and the more white-collar crime we can expect. One of the most important influences shaping an industry's regulatory environment is the products it makes. Industries whose products cause serious and clearly identifiable harm to the public or the environment tend to be subject to more stringent regulation than those that do not. Examples include the pharmaceuticals industry, whose products may mean life or death for their users; the automobile industry, which has been subject to an increasing number of safety and environmental regulations; and the chemical and petroleum industries, which produce a wide variety of hazardous substances, often using industrial processes that pose great environmental risks as well. It is not surprising, then, that the Clinard study of corporate crime found all these industries have unusually high crime rates.[106]

Banking is another industry that has traditionally been subject to strict regulation, not because its products are particularly dangerous but because numerous frauds and failures over the years have forced the government to play a strong supervisory role. Banks and savings and loans had not been considered particularly high-crime industries until the 1980s, when there was a virtual explosion of crime and corruption among the nation's thrift institutions. Although many factors were involved, a principal cause was the deregulation of the industry, which stripped away most of the restrictions that had been imposed on the way these institutions could use funds from publicly insured deposits, and helped to create a kind of "casino mentality" among savings and loan operators. Even more important was the fact that the antiregulatory fervor of the Reagan administration prevented it from adequately funding federal inspectors and auditors, thus leading many savings and loan operators to believe that they could get away with almost any kind of fraudulent activities without fear of detection (see Chapter 2 for more details).

Finally, there is considerable evidence that illegal practices spread from one organization in an industry to another.[107] Some of this tendency can be attributed to the diffusion of motivations and rationalizations discussed earlier in this chapter, but other processes appear to be involved as well. For one thing, knowledge about the availability of criminal opportunities and the specific techniques necessary to carry them out diffuse within an industry, just as the rationalizations do.[108] Moreover, the illegal activities of a firm have a direct impact on its competitors. Seeing a competitor increase its profits by illegal means is likely to enhance the attractiveness of such behavior, whereas the failure of a competitor's illegal enterprise is likely to have the opposite effect. Profits generated by illegal means may also allow a firm to lower its prices or take other advantages over its competition, thus reducing the attractiveness of the competition's legitimate opportunities and encouraging all the firms in the industry to become involved in similar illegal schemes.

Organizations

The goals an organization pursues are certain to have a major impact on both the type and the amount of its criminal activities, but there is considerable disagreement about what those goals actually are. According to the theory of laissez-faire capitalism advanced by Adam Smith and his followers, the principal goal of all private enterprise is profit. Corporations are money-making machines; if they fail to make money, the logic of capitalism says they should go bankrupt. However, some defenders of contemporary business downplay the importance of profit as a business goal, pointing out that business firms pursue many other objectives as well. J. K. Galbraith has held that the giant multinational firms typical of the corporate sector have become increasingly conservative, and that their sights have turned from achieving the maximum possible profits to a quest for security and self-protection.[109]

In this view, managers aim for a "satisfactory" level of profitability that offers stability and security, rather than taking greater risks to achieve higher profits. The size and influence of the firm, Galbraith has argued, are often more important to today's professional managers than are exorbitant profits. Because managers are no longer the major stockholders in their firms, high profits and dividends are supposedly less attractive than the status derived from being at the helm of a huge firm with vast power and influence. Even among the owner-operated firms of the small business sector, the argument goes, there are constraints on the pursuit of profit, such as limitations on how much time and effort the owner is willing to devote to the business.

Although there is some truth in these arguments, the central importance of profit to contemporary business should not be underestimated. Modern-day managers may not struggle for every last dime in profits, but they know that a decline in profitability poses a direct threat to their careers. Once "satisfactory" levels of profitability have been achieved, firms may pursue other goals, but the primacy of the profit motive quickly reemerges if profits decline. After a careful statistical analysis of the reasons for the dismissal of top corporate executives, David James and Michael Soref concluded that "profit criteria appear to be the most important standard by which corporate chiefs are judged, and dismissal is the ultimate sanction that conditions their behavior."[110] Thus, the corporate executive who lets the profitability of his or her firm decline runs a very real risk of being fired.[111]

Modern corporations are, however, far too complex to operate with only a single goal. A corporation can hardly tell its manufacturing division or sales division that its goal is simply to make profits. Each organizational unit must be given specific subgoals that ultimately contribute to the overall organizational goals. The sales division, for example, might be given a particular quota to reach, while the manufacturing division is told to produce a certain number of items at a particular cost.

Corporate managers have little discretion in selecting the primary corporate objective (profitability), but they are responsible for the subgoals. Moreover, the specific targets selected by top management may have an important influence on middle-level employees' decisions about whether to stay within the confines of the law. For example, Ronald Kramer argues that the goals set for the Ford Pinto—that it weigh less than 2,000 pounds and cost less than $2,000—ultimately caused the safety problems for which it became notorious, because such goals led to the rejection of safety modifications that would have increased the weight and cost of the car.[112]

The retired middle managers studied by Marshall Clinard expressed the belief that top management is responsible for setting the overall ethical standards of the corporation. Many of them drew a distinction between "financially oriented" managers and "technical and professional types." The interviewees believed that financially oriented managers were primarily interested in quick profits and personal prestige, and were therefore more inclined to engage in criminal activities. Professionally oriented managers were held to be less willing to risk criminal activities and more concerned with the long-term well-being of the corporation.[113]

It would be a mistake, however, to attribute too much independence to those at the top. Even the highest-ranking managers are often as constrained by the structural realities of the organization and its external environment as are its lower-level employees. For one thing, top management faces a complex balance of political forces within the organization that places clear limits on its discretion. Individuals and groups who occupy strategic lower positions within the organization may have great power over certain types of corporate operations. One study of the Australian Trade Practices Act, for example, concluded that most violations did not originate at the top, but with other factions within the corporations involved.[114] Those at the top often find that they have great power only as long as they utilize it in the ways that are expected of them. The culture and traditions of an organization have a resilient strength that is difficult for even the most capable leader to overcome. Moreover, most upper-level executives have been socialized into the same organizational culture as other employees, and that culture plays an important part in determining their decisions.[115]

In addition to those powerful internal forces, top management is restrained by the external environment of the organization. Many critical definitions, ideas, and beliefs come from the industry in which a firm operates and from the general ethos of corporate culture. Government controls and the climate of public opinion place another set of restraints on contemporary corporations, as do the economic realities of the marketplace. Under many circumstances, top management may have little choice but to engage in illicit activities, if it is to meet the overriding demand for profits. If, for instance, a competitor is cutting costs by violating pollution and safety standards, it may be impossible to maintain competitive prices without engaging in similar activities.

Given the primacy of the profit motive, it is not surprising that the research shows that firms with declining profitability are more likely than others to break the law. In a study of wartime price control legislation, George Katona found that compliance in the meat and laundry industries "seemed to be more satisfactory among firms with rising profits than among those with declining profits."[116] Robert Lane's study of New England shoe manufacturers also found fair trade violations to be more common when profits were declining,[117] and Geis concluded that there was more price-fixing in the heavy electrical equipment industry when market conditions were poor.[118] In a study of 500 major corporations, Barry Staw and Eugene Szwajkowski found that firms cited for antitrust violations had been making lower profits than had other firms in their industry.[119] The Clinard study of corporate crime reached similar conclusions. In the words of Clinard and Yeager, "Firms in depressed industries as well as relatively poorly performing firms in all industries tend to violate the law to a greater degree."[120] Sally Simpson's study of antitrust violations found that firms in a difficult economic environment committed more serious violations, whereas in good economic times, firms committed more minor violations.[121] Finally, A. Jenkins and John Braithwaite found lower rates of fraud in nonprofit nursing homes than in those operating as profit-making organizations.[122]

Many observers have claimed that there is a relationship between the size of a firm and its involvement in illegal activities, but they do not agree on whether large or small firms are most likely to break the law. John Conklin, for example, suggested that the anonymity and impersonality of the large corporations and the way responsibility for important tasks is fragmented among many different employees actually encourage white-collar crimes.[123] Others, especially those working for large corporations, have claimed that small firms are more likely to violate the law, because they lack the professional expertise to decipher the maze of government regulations that control business activities.[124]

The research on this point is as contradictory as the claims. Neither Katona nor Clinard was able to arrive at definitive conclusions about the relationship between the violation of wartime price regulations and firm size. Lane found that larger firms were much more likely to violate labor regulations and trade-practices legislation than were smaller firms, but he found the opposite to be the case for violations of the Fair Labor Standards and the Public Contracts Acts in the metal and metal products industry.[125] In two other industries, Lane found no relationship at all between size and legal offenses. His overall conclusion was that there is "no clear relationship between size and violation; each industry and each regulatory measure has a pattern of its own."[126] The Clinard study of corporate crime reached similar conclusions. Although larger firms were found to have more total violations, the relationship disappeared when controls were introduced to compensate for the greater volume of business carried on by the big firms.[127] Roger Riis and John Patric found some evidence that dishonest practices were more common among large than among small car and radio repair shops,[128] and a study of income tax compliance found that erroneous returns were more commonly filed by large firms than by small ones.[129] Thus, despite the efforts of these researchers, no clear relationship between firm size and criminal conduct has been established.

Occupations

All occupations offer some illicit opportunities, even if it is only to evade the taxes on the money we earn. These opportunities are, however, unevenly distributed, and some occupations clearly hold far greater possibilities for illicit gain than others. Unfortunately, the great diversity of occupational categories and the paucity of sociological research on this subject make it possible to present only a few basic generalizations and hypotheses. The attractiveness of the opportunities for bribery, for instance, appears to depend on the economic value of the services the holder of a particular job can offer in exchange for corrupt payments. One of the reasons police corruption is most common among officers involved in the enforcement of narcotics and vice laws is that organized criminals are willing to pay those officers large sums of money to look the other way.[130] Other occupations with rich opportunities for corruption include purchasing agents, government inspectors, and politicians.

The government's increasing role in regulating private business has created burgeoning opportunities for corruption over the last fifty years as the number of rule makers and inspectors has increased.[131] Another structural condition that encourages government corruption is the increasing cost of running for public office. Because of the widely held belief that an expensive advertising campaign is necessary to win high office, even the most scrupulous politicians are tempted to trade political favors for the campaign contributions necessary for such efforts. The simultaneous expansion of the politicians' need for money, and private industry's desire to purchase special favors from them, has produced a situation uniquely suited to foster corruption.

Opportunities for embezzlement seem to vary with the degree of financial trust placed in the holders of different occupational positions. Accountants, book-keepers, and clerks have many opportunities for embezzlement, whereas other employees in the same organizations may have none. Opportunities for fraud and other illegal financial manipulations appear to be greatest in occupations with direct involvement in financial dealings, such as salespeople and upper-level executives. A study of presentence reports in federal court by David Weisburd and his colleagues found that managers were convicted of the most serious crimes, the crimes of owners were second, and lower-level employees committed the least serious offenses.[132]

In general, it appears that the opportunities for employee pilferage are more widely dispersed than the opportunities for fraud or embezzlement. Most employees have the opportunity to steal from their employer at one time or another, and a great many actually do. Such opportunities are not, however, evenly distributed throughout the occupational structure. John Clark and Richard Hollinger's comprehensive survey found that employees with access to and knowledge about vulnerable targets for theft (e.g., sales clerks in stores, engineers in factories, and nurses and technicians in hospitals) were the most likely to report having actually committed a theft.[133] Occupations also differ in terms of the size of the reward they offer to the potential thief. Whereas the television assemblers in Donald Horning's study usually took small objects of little value,[134] stockbrokers and securities dealers have the opportunity to steal far more valuable items.

One of the most important determinants of the illicit opportunities available to professionals is the financial arrangements that determine their remuneration. Professionals working on a fee-for-service basis have numerous opportunities to persuade their clients to consent to profitable but unnecessary procedures, whereas those working on salary have little to gain from such activities. Another important factor is the ignorance of clients about what kind of services they really need, and the strong emphasis on mutual trust in the professional–client relationship that leads many clients to an unquestioning acceptance of the professional's judgment. The fact that a substantial portion of medical and dental bills are paid by insurance further decreases the clients' concern about unnecessary services and overcharging.

Occupational subcultures play an important role in facilitating many types of white-collar crimes by promoting the spread of the knowledge and techniques necessary to transform a potential course of criminal action into a psychologically available opportunity. Because these subcultures typically have members from many different industries, they provide a source of communication independent of the industry or organization in which an individual works. For example, accountants, physicians, and lawyers learn about opportunities for white-collar crime as they learn their profession and are socialized into its subculture. Similarly, the striking parallels in the patterns of corruption found in many different police departments strongly suggest the transmission of criminal techniques through an occupational subculture shared by officers. Although subcultures in law, medicine, and the other professions do not directly condone criminal behavior, the sense of mutual solidarity and self-protection does make criminal opportunities more attractive by reducing the chances of receiving severe punishment. Occupational subcultures thus serve as part of a network of communication that transmits information about opportunities, techniques, and motivations, as well as a protective shield that reduces the visibility of professional misconduct.

Gender

Gender is one of the strongest predictors of criminality, and in general, men commit far more crimes than women. A quick examination of the statistics on criminal arrests, however, might lead one to believe that this generalization is far less applicable to white-collar crimes. Although only 23 percent of the persons arrested in the United States in 2002 were female, women made up half (49.8 percent) of those arrested for embezzlement and 45.1 percent of those arrested for fraud—a higher percentage than for any other crimes except prostitution and vice.[135] Moreover, the percentage of those arrested for white-collar crimes who are women has been increasing rapidly in recent years. In the last decade alone, the percentage of women arrested for embezzlement increased 28 percent and the percentage of women arrested for fraud increased 7 percent.[136]

However, any appearance of gender equality is largely a statistical artifact. For one thing, many people arrested for embezzlement or fraud do not hold a job at the white-collar level. Moreover, the arrest statistics provide virtually no useful data on the highest-status white-collar criminals, for their numbers are small and their chances of being arrested are far lower than those for other white-collar offenders (see Chapter 4). Yet it is precisely in the upper-level corporate and organizational crimes that women are most underrepresented. Since patriarchal society denies women equal access to the upper levels of the economic world, it also denies them opportunities for the white-collar crimes those positions offer.[137]

Kathleen Daly's analysis of a sample of presentence reports from seven federal court districts shows very significant differences between the male and female offenders who are arrested for white-collar offenses.[138] The women in Daly's sample were younger, were less educated, and had lower-status positions and lower incomes than the men. She also found that the women made less money from their crimes and were less likely to commit their offenses as part of a group. Although this study included many offenses that do not fall within the definition of white-collar crime used in this book (e.g., welfare fraud), a comparison of the gender differences among specific white-collar offenses produces some interesting results. Women were extremely underrepresented among those charged with the two offenses that are most likely to be corporate crimes. An overwhelming 98 percent of those charged with antitrust and SEC violations were male. In contrast, 45 percent of those charged with bank embezzlement were female. However, the women charged with bank embezzlement were more likely to be tellers, whereas the men were more likely to be bank officers or financial managers. The crimes of the women were also "generally less sophisticated than men's, of shorter duration, and less likely to be carried out with others."[139]

One possible explanation of these findings is that differences in social expectations and socialization create different motivational patterns for women and men. For example, some studies of moral reasoning indicate that women are more likely to see moral issues in terms of a network of interconnecting responsibilities, whereas men are more prone to see such issues in terms of individual rights based on formal rules.[140] Such differences might contribute to the lower overall crime rate among women and their relatively greater involvement in white-collar than street crimes. Other social–psychological research indicates that men are more task oriented in their group behavior,[141] which might help explain why men's white-collar crimes have generally involved a larger group of conspirators. At this point, however, such contentions are mere speculation. Little empirical research has yet been done on gender differences in the motivation of white-collar criminals, and none of it specifically addresses these points.

What the available research does show is that men and women tend to use different rationalizations to justify their white-collar crimes. The most comprehensive study of this issue was conducted by Dorothy Zietz, who found that many of the generalizations Cressey had made about male embezzlers did not apply to the embezzlers she interviewed at the California Institution for Women.[142] Cressey's subjects needed money because of nonshareable problems they had brought upon themselves, and they rationalized their crimes by telling themselves that they were only borrowing the money. Zietz's subjects, on the other hand, cited problems for which they were not responsible and seldom used the borrowing rationalization. Zietz's embezzlers were far more likely to justify their offenses in terms of the needs of their spouse or children.

Zietz's findings have, however, received mixed support from other researchers. In a small case study of convicted embezzlers, Sue Mahan concluded that Cressey's theory was in fact applicable to some female embezzlers.[143] On the other hand, Zietz's conclusion about the use of family-based rationalizations by female offenders finds support in Daly's research. Although Zietz found that all of her subjects used the family rationalization and only 29 percent of Daly's sample of embezzlers used that rationalization, Daly still found that the family rationalization was used about twice as often by women as by men. However, the impact of the differences in the distribution of rationalizations among females and males remains unclear. For one thing, both genders appear to share many rationalizations. Moreover, the different rationalizations preferred by males and females all appear to provide effective justifications for white-collar crime, and it is difficult to determine whether this difference has any impact on the actual incidence of embezzlement or other crimes.

Although the issue of motivational differences remains unresolved, differences in the opportunity structure for women and men clearly have a powerful effect on white-collar criminality. Daly's finding that very few women are involved in corporate crimes obviously reflects the gross underrepresentation of women in the highest circles of corporate decision making. Of course, this same pattern of discrimination continues down through the middle and lower levels of the corporate hierarchy and has a similar effect in patterning the distribution of white-collar offenses. The fact that female bank embezzlers are more likely to be tellers, whereas males have a greater likelihood of holding managerial positions, seems to be an obvious reason for women's crimes having been less sophisticated, having netted lower returns, and being less likely to be committed by a group of offenders. Yet we cannot assume that men and women in the same occupational position are necessarily presented with the same opportunities for white-collar crime. Steven Box argues that female workers are more closely supervised than their male counterparts in the same job and therefore have fewer criminal opportunities.[144] Research on women managers also indicates that they are often excluded from the social networks of their male colleagues[145]—another condition that might reduce the availability of criminal opportunity.

The Whole Picture

As we have seen, the pattern of etiologic factors that generate white-collar crime is a complex one indeed. Although social scientists have tended to focus on either the social psychological or the structural level, a complete understanding of the causes of white-collar crime requires us to recognize the interdependence of those two approaches. Social psychological analysis alone leaves us ignorant of the structural and historical forces that shape all human behavior, but an analysis focused exclusively on structural variables neglects the personal dimension of human behavior and cannot ultimately account for any individual offenses.

Our analysis has shown that white-collar crime is caused by the coincidence of three necessary conditions, the first of which is motivation. There must be some reason for an individual to turn to white-collar crime. In most cases, the motivation is the desire for financial gain, the wish to be seen as a success in the eyes of others, or the fear of losing what one already has. Although many people believe such motivations to be a part of human nature, that is clearly not the case. Rather, the political economy of industrial society, with its enormous economic surplus and reliance on a system of market exchange, has given rise to a culture of competition that fosters these motivations.

The second requirement is the neutralization of the ethical restraints that inhibit criminal behavior. On the individual level, this is achieved through the use of various rationalizations that justify the offender's behavior. Often these rationalizations are learned on the job, but there are many other sources as well. In the case of organizational crime, the process of neutralization is greatly facilitated by the power of large organizations to shape the definitions that guide the behavior of their employees. Thus, criminal activities may be defined in such a way as to make them appear to be routine, unproblematic behavior, or at least a necessary part of the job.

Finally, along with the desire, there must be an opportunity. The fact that popular mass movements have been able to force the adoption of legal restrictions on many abuses of those in privileged positions but have often been unable to win effective enforcement of those standards creates a rich profusion of attractive opportunities for white-collar criminality. But it is clear that some people have greater and more attractive opportunities than others. The distribution of those opportunities was found to be influenced by many different variables among the various occupations, organizations, and industries in which people are employed.

Review Questions

- What role does personality play in the motivation of white-collar crime?
- What is the culture of competition and how does it encourage white-collar crime?
- What are techniques of neutralization, and what role do they play in the formulation of the motivation for white-collar crime?
- How do complex organizations encourage their members to engage in illegal acts?

- How does the structure of opportunities for white-collar offenses differ among different industries, organizations, and occupations, and between the genders?
- Summarize the theory of the causes of white-collar crime presented in these pages.

Notes

1. Albert Cohen, Alfred Lindesmith, and Karl Schuessler, eds., *The Sutherland Papers* (Bloomington: Indiana University Press, 1956), p. 96.
2. Richard H. Blum, *Deceivers and Deceived* (Springfield, Ill.: Charles C Thomas, 1972), pp. 145–57; Walter Bromberg, *Crime and the Mind: A Psychiatric Analysis of Crime and Punishment* (New York: Macmillan, 1965), pp. 377–400; Lonell S. Selling, "Specific War Crimes," *Journal of Criminal Law, Criminology, and Police Science* 34 (January–February 1944): 303–10; John C. Spencer, "White Collar Crime," in Edward Glover, Hermann Mannheim, and Emanuel Miller, eds., *Criminology in Transition* (London: Tavistock, 1965), pp. 233–66.
3. Edwin H. Sutherland, *White Collar Crime* (New York: Dryden Press, 1949), pp. 257–66.
4. Michael Gottfredson and Travis Hirschi, *A General Theory of Crime* (Stanford: Stanford University Press, 1990).
5. Carey Herbert, Gary S. Green, and Victor Larragoite, "Clarifying the Reach of a General Theory of Crime for Organizational Offending: A Comment on Reed and Yeager," *Criminology* 36 (1998): 867–83.
6. Peter Cleary Yeager and Gary E. Reed, "Of Corporate Persons and Straw Men: A Reply to Herbert, Green, and Larragoite," *Criminology* 36 (1998): 885–97.
7. Selling, "Specific War Crimes."
8. Bromberg, *Crime and the Mind*, p. 388.
9. Spencer, "White Collar Crime," p. 259.
10. Ibid., p. 261.
11. Blum, *Deceivers and Deceived*, p. 154.
12. Ibid., pp. 145–57.
13. J. M. Collins and F. L. Schmidt, "Personality, Integrity and White Collar Crime: A Construct Validity Study," *Personnel Psychology* 46 (1993): 295–311.
14. Stanton Wheeler, "The Problem of White Collar Crime Motivation," in Kip Schlegel and David Weisburd, eds. *White Collar Crime Reconsidered* (Boston: Northeastern University Press, 1992), pp. 108–23.
15. Ibid., p. 112.
16. Willem Bonger, *Criminality and Economic Conditions*, abridged by Austin T. Turk (Bloomington: Indiana University Press, 1969; originally published in 1905 as *Criminalité et Conditions Économiques*), p. 137.
17. J. Scott Armstrong, "Social Irresponsibility in Management," *Journal of Business Research* 5 (1977): 185–213.
18. David Weisburd and Elin Waring, *White-Collar Crime and Criminal Careers* (Cambridge: Cambridge University Press, 2001), p. 146.
19. Robert E. Lane, *The Regulation of Businessmen: Social Conditions of Government Economic Control* (New Haven: Yale University Press, 1954), p. 90.

20. Cesare Beccaria, *An Essay on Crimes and Punishments* (London: Almon, 1767); Jeremy Bentham, *An Introduction to the Principles of Morals and Legislation* (London: Pickering, 1823).

21. David Weisburd, Stanton Wheeler, E. Waring, and Nancy Bode, *Crimes of the Middle Classes: White Collar Offenders in the Federal Courts* (New Haven: Yale University Press, 1991), p. 224. Italics in original.

22. Richard Woodley, "The Importance of Being Number One," in Leonard D. Savitz and Norman Johnston, eds. *Contemporary Criminology* (New York: Wiley, 1982), pp. 117–25.

23. Bromberg, *Crime and the Mind,* p. 389.

24. Joe R. Feagin, *Subordinating the Poor: Welfare and American Beliefs* (Englewood Cliffs, N.J.: Prentice-Hall, 1975), does an excellent job of showing how the "ideology of individualism" serves to legitimate the American system of stratification and to subordinate the poor.

25. Malcolm X, *The Autobiography of Malcolm X* (New York: Grove, 1965), p. 109.

26. Sutherland, *White Collar Crime,* p. 234.

27. Edwin Sutherland, *Principles of Criminology* (Philadelphia: J. B. Lippincott, 1947), p. 6.

28. See Max Weber, *Ancient Judaism,* trans. Hans Gerth and Don Martindale (New York: Free Press, 1932), esp. p. 80; Hans Gerth and C. Wright Mills, trans., *From Max Weber: Essays in Sociology* (New York: Oxford, 1946), esp. p. 280.

29. See Ruth Benedict, *Patterns of Culture* (Boston: Houghton Mifflin, 1934). Also see Marvin Harris, *Culture, People, Nature,* 3rd ed. (New York: Harper & Row, 1980), pp. 233–37.

30. Bonger, *Criminality and Economic Conditions,* p. 7. On this point, also see Eleanor Leacock, "Women's Status in Egalitarian Societies: Implications for Social Evolution," *Current Anthropology* 19 (June 1978): 247–55.

31. Richard Borshay Lee, The !Kung San: *Men, Women, and Work in a Foraging Society* (Cambridge: Cambridge University Press, 1979).

32. Robert Knox Dentan, *The Semai: A Nonviolent People of Malaya* (New York: Holt, Rinehart and Winston, 1968).

33. Ibid., p. 49.

34. Numerous scholars in the Marxist tradition have commented on this point, including Friedrich Engels, *The Origin of the Family, Private Property, and the State* (New York: International, 1972); Leacock, "Women's Status in Egalitarian Societies"; Bonger, *Criminality and Economic Conditions,* esp. pp. 37–38.

35. See James William Coleman, "Crime and Money: Motivation and Opportunity in a Monetarized Economy," *American Behavioral Scientist* 35 (July 1991): 827–36.

36. Edwin M. Schur, *Our Criminal Society: The Social and Legal Sources of Crime in America* (Englewood Cliffs, N.J.: Prentice-Hall, 1969), p. 187.

37. Gresham M. Sykes and David Matza, "Techniques of Neutralization: A Theory of Delinquency," *American Sociological Review* 22 (December 1957): 667–70.

38. See Donald R. Cressey, *Other People's Money: A Study in the Social Psychology of Embezzlement* (Belmont, Calif.: Wadsworth, 1971; originally published in 1953).

39. G. E. Levens, "101 British White Collar Criminals," *New Society,* March 26, 1964, pp. 6–8; Virgil W. Peterson, "Why Honest People Steal," *Journal of Criminal Law and Criminology* 38 (July–August 1947): 94–103; "Postwar Embezzler Is Younger, Lives Faster, Is Less Inclined to Suicide," *Journal of Accountancy* 90 (October 1950): 344;

Svend H. Riemer, "Embezzlement: Pathological Basis," *Journal of Criminal Law and Criminology* 32 (November–December 1941): 411–23; Cressey, *Other People's Money.*

40. Cressey, *Other People's Money.*

41. Gwynn Nettler, "Embezzlement without Problems," *British Journal of Criminology* 14 (January 1974): 70–77; Dorothy Zietz, *Women Who Embezzle or Defraud: A Study of Convicted Felons* (New York: Praeger, 1981).

42. Cressey, *Other People's Money,* p. 101.

43. Quoted in Gilbert Geis, "The Heavy Electrical Equipment Cases of 1961," in Gilbert Geis and Robert F. Meier, eds. *White Collar Crime* (New York: Free Press, 1977), p. 122.

44. Lawrence R. Zeitlin, "A Little Larceny Can Do a Lot for Company Morale," *Psychology Today* 14 (June 1971): 22 passim.

45. Erwin O. Smigel, "Public Attitudes toward Stealing as Related to the Size of the Victim Organization," *American Sociological Review* 21 (June 1956): 320–26.

46. Marshall B. Clinard, *The Black Market: A Study of White Collar Crime* (New York: Rinehart and Co., 1952), p. 169.

47. Harry V. Ball, "Social Structure and Rent-Control Violations," *American Journal of Sociology* 65 (May 1960): 598–604.

48. Sutherland, *White Collar Crime,* p. 236.

49. Steven Chibnall and Peter Saunders, "Worlds Apart: Notes on the Social Relativity of Corruption," *British Journal of Sociology* 28 (June 1977): 138–54.

50. Geis, "Heavy Electrical Equipment Cases," pp. 122, 123.

51. Gary E. Reed and Peter C. Yeager, "Organizational Offending and Neoclassical Criminology: Challenging the Reach of A General Theory of Crime," *Criminology* 34 (1966): 357–82. Also see Kathy E. Kram, Peter C. Yeager, and Gary Reed, "Decisions and Dilemmas: The Ethical Dimension in the Corporate Context," in James E. Post, ed., *Research in Corporate Social Performance and Policy* (Greenwich, Conn.: JAI Press, 1989).

52. Kathleen Daly, "Gender and Varieties of White Collar Crime," *Criminology* 27 (1989): 769–94.

53. Sara Willott, Christine Griffin, and Mark Torrance, "Snakes and Ladders: Upper-Middle-Class Male Offenders Talk About Economic Crime," *Criminology* 39 (May 2001): 441–66.

54. See Gary Cavender, Nancy C. Jurik, and Albert K. Cohen, "The Baffling Case of the Smoking Gun: The Social Ecology of Political Accounts in the Iran-Contra Affair," *Social Problems* 40 (1993): 152–66.

55. Cressey, *Other People's Money,* p. 35.

56. Michael L. Benson, "Denying the Guilty Mind: Accounting for Involvement in White Collar Crime," *Criminology* 23 (1985): 585–607.

57. Chibnall and Saunders, "Worlds Apart," p. 142.

58. See Geis, "Heavy Electrical Equipment Cases," p. 123.

59. Gerald Mars, "Dock Pilferage: A Case Study in Occupational Theft," in Paul Rock and Mary McIntosh, eds. *Deviance and Social Control* (London: Tavistock, 1974), p. 224.

60. Zeitlin, "A Little Larceny Can Do a Lot," p. 22.

61. Chibnall and Saunders, "Worlds Apart," p. 143.

62. Cressey, *Other People's Money,* p. 137.

63. Raymond C. Baumhart, "How Ethical Are Businessmen?" *Harvard Business Review* 39 (July–August 1961): 5–179.

64. L. Howard Silk and David Vogel, *Ethics and Profits: The Crisis of Confidence in American Business* (New York: Simon & Schuster, 1976).

65. Carl Madden, "Forces Which Influence Ethical Behavior," in *The Ethics of Corporate Conduct* (Englewood Cliffs, N.J.: Prentice-Hall, 1977). Also see Marshall B. Clinard and Peter C. Yeager, *Corporate Crime* (New York: Macmillan, 1980), pp. 67–68.

66. *Time,* November 19, 1979, p. 85.

67. See Geis, "Heavy Electrical Equipment Cases," p. 124.

68. Ibid.

69. Quoted in Clinard and Yeager, *Corporate Crime,* p. 65.

70. William E. Blundell, "Equity Funding: I Did It for the Jollies," in Donald Moffitt, ed. *Swindled! Classic Business Frauds of the Seventies* (Princeton, N.J.: Dow Jones Books, 1976), p. 46.

71. Donald R. Cressey, "Employee Theft: The Reasons Why," *Security World* (October 1980): 31–36.

72. Clinard and Yeager, *Corporate Crime,* p. 60.

73. See Diane Rothbard Margolis, *The Managers: Corporate Life in America* (New York: William Morrow, 1979).

74. William H. Whyte Jr., *The Organization Man* (Garden City, N.Y.: Anchor Books, 1957).

75. Margolis, *The Managers,* p. 118.

76. Frank W. Howton, *Functionaries* (Chicago: Quadrangle, 1969), pp. 5–6.

77. Max Weber, *The Theory of Social and Economic Organization,* A. M. Henderson and Talcott Parsons, trans. (New York: Free Press, 1964), pp. 329–41.

78. Margolis, *The Managers,* p. 63.

79. See ibid., pp. 41–66, for an excellent description of this process.

80. C. Wright Mills, *The Power Elite* (New York: Oxford University Press, 1959), p. 343.

81. James G. March and Herbert A. Simon, *Organizations* (New York: John Wiley and Sons, 1958); Charles Perrow, *Complex Organizations: A Critical Essay* (Glenview, Ill.: Scott Foresman, 1972), esp. pp. 145–76.

82. Quoted in Geis, "Heavy Electrical Equipment Cases," p. 123.

83. James T. Carey, *Introduction to Criminology* (Englewood Cliffs, N.J.: Prentice-Hall, 1978), p. 384.

84. See Geis, "Heavy Electrical Equipment Cases."

85. Baumhart, "How Ethical Are Businessmen?"; S. N. Brenner and E. A. Molander, "Is the Ethics of Business Changing?" *Harvard Business Review* 55 (January–February 1977): 59–70.

86. Sara Fritz and Karen Tumulty, "Did Not Tell Reagan of Funds Diversion, Poindexter Testifies," *Los Angeles Times,* July 16, 1987, pt. I, p. 1 passim.

87. Peter F. Drucker, *Concept of the Corporation,* rev. ed. (New York: John Day, 1972), p. 88. Sutherland also examined the issue of the isolation of corporate executives; see *White Collar Crime,* pp. 247–53.

88. Diane Vaughan, "Rational Choice, Situated Action, and the Social Control of Organizations," *Law & Society Review* 32(1) (1998): 23–61.

89. For a more detailed analysis, see James William Coleman, "Toward an Integrated Theory of White Collar Crime," *American Journal of Sociology* (September, 1987): 406–39. A similar analysis of the opportunity structure can be found in Neal Shover and Kevin M. Bryant, "Theoretical Explanations of Corporate Crime," in Michael B. Blankenship, ed., *Understanding Corporate Criminality* (New York: Garland, 1993), pp. 141–76.

90. J. F. Burton Jr., "An Economic Analysis of Sherman Act Criminal Cases," in J. M. Clabault and J. F. Burton Jr., eds., *Sherman Act Indictments, 1955–1965: A Legal and Economic Analysis* (New York: Federal Legal Publications, 1966); Jeffrey Pfeffer and Gerald R. Salancik, *The External Control of Organizations: A Resource Dependence Perspective* (New York: Harper & Row, 1978), esp. pp. 124–25, 183; Marc Riedel, "Corporate Crime and Interfirm Organization: A Study of Penalized Sherman Act Violations," *Graduate Sociology Club Journal* 8 (1968): 74–97. Also see Clinard and Yeager, *Corporate Crime,* pp. 50–51.

91. George Hay and Daniel Kelley, "An Empirical Survey of Price-Fixing Conspiracies," *Journal of Law and Economics* 17 (April 1974): 13–39.

92. Peter Asch and J. J. Seneca, "Is Collusion Profitable?" *Review of Economics and Statistics* 58 (February 1969): 1–12.

93. Richard Posner, "A Statistical Study of Antitrust Enforcement," *Journal of Law and Economics* 13 (October 1970): 365–420.

94. Marshall Clinard, Peter Yeager, J. M. Brissette, D. Petrashek, and E. Harries, *Illegal Corporate Behavior* (Washington, D.C.: U.S. Government Printing Office, 1979).

95. Clinard and Yeager, *Corporate Crime,* p. 51.

96. Ibid., pp. 165–66.

97. Yerachmiel Kugel and Gladys W. Gruenberg, *International Payoffs* (Lexington, Mass.: Lexington Books, 1977), p. 36.

98. Ibid., p. 47.

99. Harvey A. Farberman, "A Criminogenic Market Structure: The Automobile Industry," *Sociological Quarterly* 16 (Autumn 1975): 438–57.

100. William N. Leonard and Marvin Glenn Weber, "Automakers and Dealers: A Study of Criminogenic Market Forces," *Law and Society Review* 4 (February 1970): 407–24.

101. Norman Denzin, "Notes on the Criminogenic Hypothesis: A Case Study of the American Liquor Industry," *American Sociological Review* 42 (December 1977): 905–20.

102. Martin L. Needleman and Carolyn Needleman, "Organizational Crime: Two Models of Criminogenesis," *Sociology Quarterly* 20 (Autumn 1979): 517–28.

103. David Weisburd, Elin Waring, and Stanton Wheeler, "Examining Opportunity Structures in White Collar Crime: The Roles of Social Status and Structural Position," paper presented at the meetings of the American Society of Criminology, Montreal, November 1987.

104. Edward Gross, "Organizational Structure and Organizational Crime," in Gilbert Geis and Ezra Stotland, eds. *White Collar Crime: Theory and Research* (Beverly Hills, Calif.: Sage, 1980), pp. 52–77.

105. See Nancy Reichman, "Regulating Risky Business: Dilemmas in Security Regulation," *Law and Policy* 13 (1991): 263–95; Mary Zey, *Banking on Fraud: Drexel, Junk Bonds and Buyouts* (New York: Aldine de Gruyter, 1993).

106. Clinard et al., *Illegal Corporate Behavior,* pp. 102–107.

107. Edwin H. Sutherland, *White Collar Crime: The Uncut Version* (New Haven: Yale University Press, 1983, originally published in 1949), pp. 246–50; Clinard and Yeager, *Corporate Crime,* pp. 60–63; Donald R. Cressey, "Restraints of Trade, Recidivism and Delinquent Neighborhoods," in James Short Jr. ed. *Delinquency, Crime and Society* (Chicago: University of Chicago Press, 1976).

108. See Harold C. Barnett, "Branch Culture and Economic Structure: Correlates of Tax Noncompliance in Sweden," revised version of a paper presented to the American Society of Criminology, Cincinnati, Ohio, November 9, 1984.

109. John Kenneth Galbraith, *The New Industrial State* (New York: Signet Books, 1967).

110. David R. James and Michael Soref, "Profit Constraints on Managerial Autonomy: Managerial Theory and the Unmaking of the Corporation President," *American Sociological Review* 46 (February 1981): 1–18.

111. In further contradiction of Galbraith's thesis, Larner found no significant differences in the profit orientation of manager-controlled and owner-controlled firms. See Robert Larner, *Management Control and the Large Corporation* (New York: Dunellen, 1970).

112. Ronald C. Kramer, "Corporate Crime: An Organizational Perspective," in Peter Wickman and Timothy Dailey, eds. *White Collar and Economic Crime* (Lexington, Mass.: Lexington Books, 1982), pp. 75–94.

113. Marshall B. Clinard, "Corporate Ethics, Illegal Behavior, and Government Regulation: Views of Middle Management," report to the National Institute of Justice (Washington, D.C., 1982).

114. Andrew Hopkins, "The Anatomy of Corporate Crime," in Paul R. Wilson and John Braithwaite, eds. *Two Faces of Deviance: Crimes of the Powerless and the Powerful* (St. Lucia, Queensland: University of Queensland Press, 1978), pp. 214–31.

115. On the limitations on the power of those at the top of the corporate hierarchy, see Rosabeth Moss Kanter and Barry Stein, eds., *Life in Organizations: Workplaces as People Experience Them* (New York: Basic Books, 1979), pp. 3–21.

116. George Katona, *Price Control and Business* (Bloomington: Indiana University Press, 1946), p. 241.

117. Robert E. Lane, *The Regulation of Businessmen: Social Conditions of Government Control* (New Haven: Yale University Press, 1954), p. 94.

118. Geis, "Heavy Electrical Equipment Cases."

119. Barry M. Staw and Eugene Szwajkowski, "The Scarcity-Munificence Component of Organizational Environments and the Commission of Illegal Acts," *Administrative Science Quarterly* 20 (September 1975): 345–54.

120. Clinard and Yeager, *Corporate Crime*, p. 129.

121. Sally S. Simpson, "The Decomposition of Antitrust: Testing a Multi-Level Longitudinal Model of Profit-Squeeze," *American Sociological Review* 51 (December 1986): 859–75; also see Sally S. Simpson, "Cycles of Illegality: Antitrust Violations in Corporate America," *Social Forces* 65 (June 1987): 943–63.

122. A. Jenkins and John Braithwaite, "Profits, Pressure and Corporate Law-Breaking," *Crime, Law and Social Change* 20 (1993): 221–32.

123. John E. Conklin, *Illegal but Not Criminal: Business Crime in America* (Englewood Cliffs, N.J.: Prentice-Hall, 1977), pp. 64–65.

124. See Lane, *Regulation of Businessmen*, pp. 96–97; Clinard, *The Black Market*, p. 325; Katona, *Price Control and Business*, pp. 128–29.

125. Lane, *Regulation of Businessmen*, pp. 97–98.

126. Ibid., p. 98.

127. Clinard and Yeager, *Corporate Crime*, p. 130.

128. Roger William Riis and John Patric, *Repairmen Will Get You If You Don't Watch Out* (New York: Doubleday, Doran & Co., 1942).

129. Eileen Shanahan, "Tax Errors Seen among Concerns," *New York Times*, July 21, 1975, pp. 31–32.

130. Knapp Commission, *The Knapp Commission Report on Police Corruption* (New York: George Brazillier, 1972); Pennsylvania Crime Commission, *Report on Police Corruption and the Quality of Law Enforcement in Philadelphia* (1974).

131. For an analysis of some of the factors contributing to corruption in local land use regulation, see John A. Gardiner and Theodore R. Lyman, *Decisions for Sale: Corruption and Reform in Land-Use and Building Regulation* (New York: Praeger, 1978), pp. 138–80.

132. Weisburd, Waring, and Wheeler, "Examining Opportunity Structures in White Collar Crime."

133. John P. Clark and Richard C. Hollinger, *Theft by Employees in Work Organizations* (Washington, D.C.: National Institute of Justice, September 1983).

134. Donald N. M. Horning, "Blue Collar Theft: Conceptions of Property Attitudes Toward Pilfering and Work Group Norms in a Modern Industrial Plant," in Erwin O. Smigel and H. Lawrence Ross, eds., *Crime Against the Bureaucracy* (New York: Van Nostrand Reinhold, 1970).

135. Bureau of Justice Statistics, *Sourcebook of Criminal Justice Statistics, 2003* (Washington, D.C.: U.S. Government Printing Office, 2004), Table 4.8.

136. Ibid.; *Sourcebook of Criminal Justice Statistics*, 1993, Table 4.9.

137. See James Messerschmidt, *Masculinities and Crime: Reconceptualization of Theory* (Lanham, Md.: Rowman & Littlefield, 1993).

138. Kathleen Daly, "Gender and White Collar Crime," paper presented at the meetings of the American Society of Criminology, Atlanta, October 1986, p. 18.

139. Ibid.

140. Carol Gilligan, *In a Different Voice: Psychological Theory and Women's Development* (Cambridge, Mass.: Harvard University Press, 1982); Josephine Donovan, *Feminist Theory* (New York: Frederick Ungar, 1985).

141. See Alice H. Eagly, *Sex Differences in Social Behavior: A Social-Role Interpretation* (Hillsdale, N.J.: Lawrence Erlbaum, 1987), pp. 108–10.

142. Dorothy Zietz, *Women Who Embezzle or Defraud: A Study of Convicted Felons* (New York: Praeger, 1981).

143. Sue Mahan, "Opportunities for Women in White Collar Crime," paper presented at the meeting of the American Society of Criminology, Montreal, 1987.

144. Steven Box, *Power, Crime and Mystification* (New York: Tavistock, 1983).

145. See, for example, Barbara Reskin and Irene Padavic, "Sex Differences in Moving Up and Taking Charge," in Estelle Disch, ed., *Reconstructing Gender* (Mountain View, Calif.: Mayfield, 1997), pp. 364–78.

six

The Criminal Elite

*T*hrough the pages of this book we have seen that white-collar criminals are indeed members of a criminal elite. In comparison with other criminals, they make more money from their crimes, they run fewer physical risks, their chances of arrest or conviction are lower, and if convicted they receive lighter penalties. Although precise quantitative data are lacking, we have also seen that criminal activities are surprisingly common among elite groups that might be thought to have little to gain from such behavior. Thus, we have a criminal elite in another sense as well—an elite frequently involved in crime but one that often seems able to ignore the laws that constrain the other strata of society.

White-collar crime is an enormously complex phenomenon. To handle so cumbersome a topic, it was necessary to break it down into many smaller units. But all the issues we have examined—the legal definition of white-collar crime, its causes, the enforcement effort, and the characteristics of the crimes themselves—are facets of a single problem. This topical approach tends to isolate the issues from one another. As a result, we risk losing sight of their subtle interconnections. Our next task is therefore to present an integrated restatement of the main points of this study that makes these interconnections explicit.

The Problem of White-Collar Crime: A Summary

The problem of white-collar crime is rooted in the social contradictions of industrial society. One of the most important of these is class conflict, especially the struggle for power and profits waged between the dominant elite and the less privileged strata of society. Most of the laws creating organizational crimes resulted from the interaction between (1) the efforts of farmers, consumers, workers, or the general public to limit abuses of the elite, and (2) the response of the elite to those social movements. On the other hand, the origins of laws prohibiting such individual crimes as embezzlement and employee pilferage can be traced to the efforts to protect the interests of more privileged groups by regulating the behavior of the lower classes. The same class conflicts can be seen in the enforcement process—for example, in the success the elite has had in weakening the enforcement of legislation that threatens its interests or its use of law enforcement as a tool to suppress the political activities of its leftist critics.

The battle lines do not always coincide so neatly with the divisions of the class system, however. The efforts of women and minorities to win equal treatment from our economic institutions are a major example. Indeed, elite groups are themselves divided by conflicting economic interests. The conflicts between the major stockholders in savings and loan institutions and their high-rolling executives are an obvious example, as is the medical profession's struggle to minimize the legal profession's ability to hold physicians civilly accountable for their errors and misdeeds.

Another fundamental contradiction exists between our relentlessly materialistic culture's demand for ever-greater affluence and the environmental and human carnage often produced by the effort to achieve it. As is often the case, the defenders of the status quo have enormous political and economic advantages over those who advocate fundamental reforms. But periodic environmental crises have repeatedly galvanized the forces of reform, not only winning popular support but even lending strength to those voices calling for a different kind of cultural orientation.

The laws defining white-collar crime have diverse historical origins, but most of them can be traced back to the dislocations and conflicts caused by the growth of industrial capitalism. Antitrust legislation was a response to the economic squeeze put on small farmers and businesspeople by the growth of the giant corporations. Consumer protection laws can be seen as substitutes for the informal controls that regulated commerce in more traditional societies. Legislation regulating political campaigns formed part of an effort to maintain and improve democratic institutions in the face of the growing centralization of economic power. Worker and environmental protection legislation can be traced to the recognition of the dangerous side effects of industrial technology. But such problems do not automatically generate new laws. Rather, legislative change comes about as a result of the conflict between organized groups reflecting many divergent interests.

Most legislation concerning white-collar crime has been the product of the struggle between popular mass movements (with occasional support from some segments of the upper class) and well-entrenched elites. The efforts of the antimonopoly, populist, consumer, and environmental movements all fit a similar pattern. At first, the reformers encounter a stone wall of elite opposition that frustrates their efforts. But if the movement is able to take advantage of such factors as well-publicized disasters and scandals, widespread popular support, and effective organization and leadership, it may ultimately win passage of new legislation. Yet even when elite interests fail to defeat reform legislation, they still exert great influence in shaping its final form.

The prohibition of such activities as embezzlement and industrial espionage followed a different pattern, which might be called "reform from the top." Because the changes were initiated by elite interests, they did not require popular pressure for enactment. Indeed, many reforms arose from new judicial interpretations that involved no changes in statutory law at all. When new legislation was enacted, the legislative process generally occurred with a minimum of public involvement and without great media attention.

The enactment of laws is not, as it is so often pictured, the end of the struggle for reform; it is the beginning. The same interests continue their conflict, this time over control of the enforcement process; and in this second struggle, elite interests are in an even stronger position than they are in the legislative arena. Despite the elite's power to manipulate the media, the political process is far more open to public view than the enforcement bureaucracy, and the voting power of the masses may help counter the political influence that inevitably flows from vast concentrations of wealth and power. However, the popular appeal of reformist movements is of considerably less strategic significance in influencing the enforcement process.

A comparison of the treatment of white-collar criminals and street criminals demonstrates the justice system's double standard. For one thing, white-collar criminals are much less likely to be arrested. And even if they are arrested and convicted, they typically receive lighter punishment than those who have committed street crimes of equal severity. Despite this overall pattern of leniency, many individual white-collar criminals do receive jail sentences or other meaningful punishment; but that is less often true of those involved in organizational crimes. Those who work to illegally promote the interests of their powerful corporate employers are commonly given nothing more than a warning or an order to stop. Many times, when punishments are meted out they involve only fines that do not even equal the profit the offenders made from their crimes. But with all this said, it is true that punishment handed out to white-collar offenders has slowly been growing more severe over the years.

The reasons for the double standard of justice can be traced to the great structural advantages enjoyed by white-collar criminals. For one thing, the organization of the justice system favors the white-collar criminal. The investigation of occupational crimes is usually left in the hands of small, understaffed fraud units in the offices of state or local prosecutors, whereas local police departments with much greater investigative resources largely ignore the problem. Influential professions such as law and medicine have won broad powers of self-regulation that often serve as a shield against outside "interference" from the criminal justice system. Finally, most white-collar defendants in criminal or civil court enjoy the advantages of wealth, prestige, and the best legal representation.

The responsibility for dealing with most corporate crimes has been shifted away from the criminal justice system to specially created regulatory agencies that are more inclined to negotiate cooperative settlements than to pursue tough criminal sanctions. Moreover, elite interests have generally been successful in preventing the allocation of sufficient resources to those agencies to enable them to carry out their legislative mandates effectively. Regulatory agencies are almost always underfunded and understaffed, especially in comparison with the vast resources at the disposal of the corporate offenders they must police. In criminal cases, organizational offenders also benefit from the individualistic bias of our legal system, which often makes it necessary to sift through complex networks of organizational interactions to prove the criminal intent of each individual defendant.

Compared with other offenders, the social and political power of corporate criminals puts them in an entirely different position vis-à-vis the justice system. Corporate criminals often have the strength to fend off, wear down, or even overpower the enforcement effort. Delaying tactics have proven to be one of the corporate criminal's most effective strategies. Whereas the strength of the enforcement effort waxes and wanes with changes in the political climate, the profit-seeking private corporation never wavers in the pursuit of its own interests. Thus, corporate criminals seek to delay legal proceedings as long as possible, while waiting for a change in the political climate that will let them off the hook. In some cases powerful corporate criminals use direct intimidation, threatening to close a large plant or to move overseas if enforcement agencies do not adopt a more "reasonable" attitude. In other cases, they attempt to corrupt individual officials with the lure of high-paying jobs in private industry, big campaign contributions, or sometimes outright bribes.

Secrecy is one tool used by white-collar and street criminals alike, but white-collar criminals (and especially organizational criminals) enjoy some important advantages in its use. For one thing, the victims of white-collar crime are often unaware of the causes of their problems and thus cannot complain to enforcement agencies. Another major advantage enjoyed by organizational criminals is the wall of secrecy that corporations and government agencies build to protect themselves from outside scrutiny. In many cases there is a legitimate need to protect sensitive information, but the same security measures can also serve to conceal illegal activities.

It would be easy to conclude that the principal cause of white-collar crime is the offenders' belief that they run little risk of significant punishment, but the matter is a good deal more complex than that. It is as necessary to explain the offenders' motivations and the structure of illicit opportunities as it is to account for the failure of the mechanisms of social control. Certainly, no single factor can account for the complex interrelationships between the social–psychological and structural variables that lie at the root of the problem of white-collar crime.

On the social-psychological level, individuals are pushed toward white-collar crime by the same craving for money and success that motivates so many other crimes. Such motivations are often combined with the pressures exerted by occupational subcultures or superiors that encourage or even demand illegal activities. The occupational subculture in many urban police departments, for example, requires officers to participate in some degree of petty corruption if they want to be considered "one of the gang." Similar pressures are often brought to bear on government or corporate employees to carry on criminal activities for the sake of their organizations.

The combination of such motivations can create strong psychological pressure to become involved in white-collar crime; however, a belief in moral or ethical principles often generates a powerful contravening force of its own. Thus, the way an individual resolves this conflict will obviously have a great influence on his or her potential for criminal behavior. White-collar offenders use a variety of common rationalizations to neutralize those ethical standards and maintain a positive self-image despite their deviant behavior. Typically, they justify their behavior by telling themselves that no one is really being harmed by their activities, that the laws are unjust, that some criminal activities are necessary for economic survival, that everybody else is doing it, or that they deserve the extra money their crimes produce.

Although many criminologists are content with such personal explanations, the origins of these psychological processes lie in the structure of contemporary industrial society. The desire for wealth and success, more than merely an individual personality trait, is part of the culture of competition found to one degree or another in all industrial societies. These societies generate large economic surpluses and are characterized by high degrees of inequality; yet, unlike agricultural societies, they have considerable social mobility. Great importance is given to material well-being in these societies, and personal wealth is a key determinant of social status. This combination inevitably encourages the desire to outdo one's fellows in the accumulation of material goods and the symbols of success that lie at the root of so many white-collar crimes.

The political economy of industrial capitalism and the diverse interest groups it creates also structure the definitions of criminal behavior. Once the laws and the enforcement priorities have been set, structural variables determine the distribution of the most attractive opportunities for white-collar crime. Thus, crime rates in the pharmaceutical and automotive industries are high because the dangers associated with their products create strong public pressure for government regulation and, thereby, the temptation to violate those regulations. In a more general way, the demand for profitability, which the economic system places on all private businesses, is a primary motivation for organizational crime. A business must make profits to survive and prosper, and criminal activities often provide an effective way of making those profits. Criminal opportunities also vary greatly from one occupation or structural position to another, as they do between the genders.

What Can Be Done?

Crime, as Emile Durkheim pointed out long ago, is inevitable in modern societies. The function of criminal law is to create crime by branding certain people and certain behaviors as deviant. A law that no one broke would be an unnecessary law. Thus, a certain amount of white-collar crime is inevitable in any society that bases its legal system on universal standards that apply to all social strata. But as we have seen, the incidence of white-collar crime goes far beyond this inevitable minimum. No other kind of crime—indeed, few problems of any sort—can even approach the hundreds of thousands of lives and billions of dollars lost every year through white-collar crime.

The aim of this final section is to explore some of the ways of dealing with this pressing problem. Although its conclusions are based on the preceding analysis, a crystal ball is not part of the standard inventory of sociological tools. The sociology of deviance has shown the unexpected damage done by past efforts to deal with such problems as drug use and prostitution through criminal law,[1] and there are no guarantees that any of the following proposals would have the desired effects. Yet there is good reason to believe that the growing body of research into the problem of white-collar crime can help us avoid the mistakes made by the moral crusaders of the past.

Ethical Reforms

When we hear news reports about some heinous new crime, the easiest response is to blame it on the moral failings of the criminal. By branding the offender as one kind of deviant or another, we avoid recognizing our own antisocial impulses or the ways we participate in the social arrangements that produce such acts. Sociologists have long opposed such one-sidedly individualistic explanations, which are especially suspect when applied to white-collar crime. There is no denying that an individual's moral and ethical standards are society's first line of defense against all sorts of criminal behavior. The problem is the failure to recognize that those standards not only are the result of the personal decisions of countless autonomous individuals, but also are the product of the cultural and social organization of our society. Thus, any successful effort to strengthen our ethical standards must focus on cultural and structural changes as much as on individual actors. As long as the values of competitive individualism dominate our cultural horizons, there is little likelihood that ethical reforms can be a very effective tool in the battle against white-collar crime. This does not mean that the numerous proposals aiming to promote more ethical behavior are without merit. However, their greatest chance for success is within the context of a direct challenge to the legitimacy of the values of competitive individualism.

One proposal comes from Melvin DeFleur, who argues that "because it is impossible to police everyone . . . a reduction in illegal corporate behavior depends on the development of stronger codes of ethics in business."[2] But how can that be done? He makes three recommendations: (1) Courses in ethics should be made mandatory in business schools, (2) trade associations should establish uniform ethical codes for each industry, and (3) individual corporations should make systematic efforts to develop ethical codes and instill them in their employees. To more structurally oriented sociologists these recommendations appear rather naive, for it is hard to imagine that a single college class, or even a series of them, would be likely to stimulate achievement-oriented young managers to defy the expectations of the organizations on whose approval their futures depend. It is equally difficult to imagine that an industry trade association would promulgate any standards of behavior that run counter to the financial interests of its members, or that the members would follow the standards if they did. High-sounding codes of ethics may make for good public relations, but by themselves they are unlikely to have any effect on the "ethical climate" of the government or the business world. After making a careful statistical comparison of corporations with codes of ethics with explicit penalties, corporations with codes but without penalties, and corporations with no codes at all, M. Cash Mathews concluded that "it just didn't make a difference."[3]

More structurally oriented criminologists argue that ethical standards will change only when the structural rewards for unethical behavior change, and that what is necessary is some way to make ethical behavior more rewarding than criminal behavior. The most obvious course of action would be to increase the civil and criminal penalties for such offenses, and we will examine those alternatives in the following section. Christopher Stone and Donald R. Cressey, among several others, have proposed another approach—the creation of a public award to be given to corporations that maintain high ethical standards.[4] Such awards would be highly publicized, and corporations would be encouraged to use them in advertising campaigns. Corporations that fail to meet ethical standards would then face negative publicity, especially since their competitors would be free to advertise their ethical superiority. This proposal still leaves many unanswered questions concerning the nature of those ethical standards and the best ways to evaluate corporate performance, but it does merit further study. A similar proposal made by W. Brent Fisse would use publicity as a sanction against corporate offenses. However, instead of a public award, Fisse calls for new legislation requiring convicted corporate offenders to pay for advertising that would inform the public of their offenses.[5]

Because occupational criminals are not supported by large impersonal organizations, individual ethical standards are probably more important in controlling their behavior. Tougher punishments would once again be helpful, but there are limits to the effectiveness of even a well-organized and well-financed criminal justice system. As long as the culture of competition remains a central part of our society, the level of occupational crime is likely to remain high. There are, however, some ways that the criminogenic elements in occupational subcultures might be more directly attacked. Our analysis suggests, for example, that the attempts at police reform that usually occur after each corruption scandal ought to give central importance to changing the occupational subculture of the department. Although providing better training programs for new officers and hiring top managers with a fervent opposition to even the most minor corruption could certainly help, it is likely that long-term cultural changes can be achieved only by encouraging large numbers of officers who have accepted the old subcultural norms to resign or retire, and by dissolving or reforming organizational units with a particularly strong reputation for corruption. Professional subcultures are generally less amenable to such changes, and they are probably best reformed from within by focusing more public attention on the examples of unethical professional conduct and challenging more reputable practitioners to do something about it.

Enforcement Reforms

Of all the reforms discussed here, the idea that white-collar criminals must be more severely punished is probably the most widely accepted. Of course, one of the reasons for this belief—that all criminals should be given their "just deserts" and that white-collar offenders have been getting off too lightly—has little to do with preventing crime.[6] Although most criminologists advocate strong enforcement as a means of deterrence, there has been very little research about how effective a deterrent our current enforcement efforts against white-collar crime actually are. What little research there is does not indicate that deterrence has been very effective.[7] There are, however, many different proposals for improving the situation. Foremost among these suggestions are the calls for greater resources and new priorities for enforcement agencies, a greater effort to isolate those agencies from outside political pressures, and legislation that is less ambiguous and easier to enforce.

The data given in Chapter 4 clearly show the need for more resources. Regulatory agencies and prosecutors are often hopelessly outmatched by their corporate opponents, who command larger and more skilled legal staffs and much greater financial support. There are too few government inspectors to detect more than a small fraction of the pollutants illegally released into the environment, and the same is true of occupational health and safety hazards and dangerous consumer products. Regulatory agencies even lack the resources to test all the potentially dangerous substances so that appropriate regulations can be promulgated. To remedy this situation, regulatory and enforcement agencies must be given substantial increases in their budgets. Certainly, funding at twice or three times the current levels would not be out of line with the importance of the problem. The most pressing needs are for larger research budgets to permit regulatory agencies to actively search out threats to public health and safety before disaster strikes; for substantial increases in the ranks of investigators and prosecutors; and for higher pay for the legal, medical, and scientific personnel who now are often lured away to better-paying jobs in private industry. Greater support is also needed for the local agencies that bear the primary responsibility for dealing with occupational crimes.

An increase in resources must be accompanied by a greater effort to insulate enforcement agencies from undue political pressure. Although there appears to be no certain way to achieve that end, several possibilities have been suggested.

First of all, along with an increase in pay, the employees of regulatory agencies could be required to sign an agreement, backed up by explicit legal penalties, promising never to work for any of the firms that fall under their regulatory jurisdiction. Currently there is a two-year moratorium on such employment changes, but many believe that a longer time period is necessary and that regulatory agencies would be better off without an employee who would refuse to sign such an agreement. Second, to defuse the threat of punitive budgetary cutbacks for agencies that offend powerful special interests, as well as to lighten the financial burden on the public, enforcement and regulatory agencies could be made more self-supporting. This could be accomplished by legislation requiring that convicted offenders pay the full cost of the government's investigation and prosecution. This money, along with any punitive fines, would then be turned over to the agencies involved in the case. An alternative approach would be to assess special fees on the firms in industries that require a high level of supervision, such as chemical manufacturing or banking.

The system of fines and penalties for the individuals involved in white-collar crime has been significantly revamped in recent years. The general guidelines created by the U.S. Sentencing Commission have resulted in an increase in fines and jail sentences for many types of white-collar offences, even though the typical offender is still only receiving a fraction of the sentence given for comparable street crimes.[8] Other legislative changes have also been made in recent years. The penalties for corporate fraud, for example, were increased as a result of the wave of public indignation following the financial scandals at such corporations as Enron and WorldCom. The Sarbanes Oxley Act of 2002 doubled the maximum jail time for executives who commit mail or wire fraud to ten years, created a new crime of securities fraud, and provided prison terms up to five years for chief executives and financial officers who certify false financial reports.[9] Such penalties are certainly severe enough to deter potential white-collar offenders, if they actually believe they are likely to receive them, but that unfortunately is seldom the case. As we have seen, no action is taken against the vast majority of offenders, and those who are the object of prosecution are often able to negotiate some kind deal with the enforcement bureaucracy that results in a lighter punishment.

The treatment of organizational offenders is far more lenient. Time and again, the penalties given corporations have not even equaled the profits made from their crimes, much less posed a credible deterrent. Some have argued against the imposition of large fines and financial penalties because they may force some offenders into bankruptcy, thus punishing the innocent along with the guilty. In fact, there seems little doubt that financial penalties based on a realistic estimate of the damage done by organizational crime would indeed cause some firms to go bankrupt, as occurred to the A. H. Robbins and Manville Corporations as a result of the civil actions by their victims. But there are good grounds for believing that such an event would ultimately work to the public good. Although some workers might lose their jobs, the assets of bankrupt firms do not vanish; they are purchased by other businesses. Most of the workers probably would be quickly rehired—hopefully, by a more reputable employer. If necessary, new legislation could be enacted mandating the bankruptcy courts to take special action to protect the interests of the workers in such cases. Stockholders would suffer a more permanent loss, but that is part of the risk investors take when they buy stocks rather than invest in more secure investments such as insured bank accounts. The example of a major corporation being forced into bankruptcy because of the legal penalties for its criminal behavior could pose a powerful deterrent to other offenders, and it might also spur stockholders to monitor the activities of management more closely.

One way to minimize the problem of a legal action that inadvertently harms innocent people is to focus more heavily on the prosecution and imprisonment of the executives responsible for corporate offenses. The weakness in this approach lies in the great difficulty prosecutors have in proving that a specific individual was responsible for a particular corporate crime. But there is little doubt that a credible threat of prosecution and imprisonment would be an extremely powerful deterrent to most high-status offenders, who seldom see themselves as criminals and often place great importance on the public esteem they enjoy.

According to the polls discussed in Chapter 4, the public is most concerned about white-collar crimes that cause direct physical harm to people. It therefore makes sense to give such crimes as environmental pollution, occupational safety violations, and the manufacture of unsafe products a high priority in the enforcement effort. According to those same polls, the public believes that such violent white-collar crimes deserve punishments at least as severe as those given for violent street crimes. A much more vigorous effort is therefore needed to investigate, prosecute, and imprison violent white-collar offenders. For example, a greater volume of cases is necessary to establish clear legal precedents for the prosecution of negligent corporate executives for manslaughter and murder and to make such legal actions a routine and expected response to violent organizational crime.

Another promising approach to corporate crime focuses on incapacitation rather than punishment. The idea here is that after a corporation is convicted of a criminal offense, the judge would place it on probation and restrict its freedom of action so that it can no longer carry on its criminal activities. For example, the judge might seek to penetrate the organizational shell of the corporate offender by placing enforcement agents in a position to prevent it from repeating its crimes. Under such a strategy, a firm that has committed repeated environmental violations would be required to pay the cost of hiring enough government inspectors to continually monitor the firm's compliance with the law. For such a system to function effectively, it would probably be necessary to rotate the inspectors periodically to prevent them from becoming too closely identified with a single firm. Other possible forms of corporate incapacitation include requiring a firm to divest itself of particularly crime-prone divisions or lines of work, or in the most extreme cases, imposing corporate capital punishment (i.e., a judicial order dissolving the corporation). As in the case of the fines discussed earlier, some of these actions carry the potential to harm innocent people along with the guilty, and care must be taken in crafting a response that is appropriate to each individual case. However, the argument that a corporation should not be punished for its crimes because it would cause financial harm to others makes no more sense than the argument that a convicted murderer should go free because his incarceration would cause his wife and children to suffer.[10]

A different approach to prevention is to enact legislation creating a system of licensing for executives of the major corporations, as there is in the other professions. Such a license need not be difficult to obtain. A simple test on the legal and ethical requirements of corporate management would be sufficient. The main value of this licensing system would be to create a mechanism for disbarring corporate officers who violate their ethical obligations to the public or to the corporation itself (as in the case of embezzlement). A special regulatory agency might be established to hear the cases against individual executives. If the evidence warranted, the hearing officer would be empowered to prohibit an offender from working for any major corporation for a fixed number of years. Although many disbarment cases would undoubtedly be appealed to the federal courts, such a procedure would provide a means of sanctioning executive misconduct without having to prove criminal intent.

As we have seen, the system of self-regulation that already exists for the professions such as law and medicine has proven woefully inadequate to the job. The fundamental problem is that the organizations created to regulate professional conduct are dominated by the members of the same profession they are supposed to be regulating. The best way to deal with this problem is to restructure the entire system of professional licensing so that its primary responsibility is to the public, not the professionals. States might, for example, be encouraged to create a consolidated Bureau of Professional Licensing, staffed by full-time examiners and investigators and headed by an elected administrator.

One largely untapped resource in the battle against organizational crime can be found in the outside auditors that publicly traded firms must hire to examine their financial reports. These auditors are in an excellent position to uncover many types of corporate illegalities. However, the American Institute of Certified Public Accountants, along with most individual practitioners, has traditionally held that "the normal audit arrangement is not designed to detect fraud and cannot be relied upon to do so."[11] The attitude of most accounting firms is reflected in the following statement by one member of a major firm concerning its responsibility to report bribery payments: "We are not required to audit below the normal levels of materiality in search for illegal payments. Our responsibility in this connection is to our clients. It does not extend to informing the SEC about immaterial payments if we find them. We are not police for the commission."[12]

Auditors may not be policemen, but increasing pressure is being brought to bear on them to guarantee the honesty of their audit reports. The bankruptcy of Arthur Andersen because of its complicity in Enron's accounting schemes sent a clear message to the accounting profession, as did the Sarbanes–Oxley Act of

2002. This bill restricted the kinds of lucrative consulting services that firms like Arthur Andersen provided for the companies they audited, and it set up a five-member board to oversee the accounting industry. Although these reforms and the attention brought by the wave of financial scandals in early part of the twenty-first century will undoubtedly have some important short-term impact, the same old problems are likely to resurface in the years ahead. The fact is that outside auditors still face a built-in conflict of interest. Although an individual auditor's employer may be an independent accounting firm, that firm is still paid by the corporation whose books he or she is examining. A firm that gains a reputation for "overzealousness" in checking for corporate illegalities runs the risk of losing many important clients.

As a result, although outside auditors are in a unique position to assist law enforcement, they have seldom seen that to be their role. A few basic reforms could greatly enhance their role in protecting the public from corporate fraud. For one thing, auditors could be legally required to actively search out fraud, deception, and indications of other illegalities in corporate financial statements and to report all suspected problems to enforcement agencies. But in order to carry out this new role, the accounting firms will have to be insulated from their clients' financial pressures. To achieve this goal, major corporations could be required to pay an audit fee to a government clearinghouse, which would then select the firm to do the actual audit so that the auditors would feel no undue pressure to compromise the integrity of their reports.

Structural Reforms

Criminologists have long held that the best way to deal with crime is to attack it at the source rather than to depend on the criminal justice system to punish the offenders after the fact—and that is exactly what proposals for structural reforms try to do. Yet these proposals are highly controversial, both because they arouse strong ideological disputes and, more important, because they threaten powerful vested interests. Nevertheless, this approach offers some of the most promising avenues for achieving long-range solutions to the problem of white-collar crime.

Many proposals for dealing with organizational crime involve basic changes in corporate organization to reduce the incentives for illegal activities or at least to make such activities more difficult. Christopher Stone, among others, has proposed that public representatives be added to the boards of directors of all major corporations.[13] These directors would have their own staffs and be charged not only with representing the public interest in the boardroom but also with supervising corporate behavior, hearing complaints, and uncovering corporate illegalities. In a variation on this idea, several European nations, including Sweden and Germany, now require worker representation on corporate boards. Such workers' representatives might well be combined with Stone's public representatives to further broaden the spectrum of interests participating in corporate decision making.

How effective would these new board members be at making corporations more responsible? Studies of the European experience have shown that worker representation on corporate boards has not brought radical changes in corporate policies, for the new board members' main concerns have been in the areas of job security and working conditions.[14] Thus, there is reason to doubt that, in itself, worker representation in corporate decision making would do much to improve the integrity of the business, discourage environmental pollution, or encourage safer products. Impetus for such reforms must come from public representatives. As long as stockholders continue to dominate corporate boards, the likelihood of major internal reforms will be limited. However, if the worker representatives and the public representatives worked together, and if their combined votes exceeded those of the stockholders, fundamental changes would be far more likely to occur.

Ralph Nader's Corporate Accountability Research Group has argued that stricter standards of corporate accountability can be imposed by means of the chartering process.[15] If an individual state tried to impose tough new standards under the current chartering system, major corporations could simply move their headquarters to another state that gave them a better deal. The Nader group therefore proposed a system of federal chartering that would prevent corporations from playing off one state against another. Under this proposal the federal chartering agency would require corporate boards to take a much more active role in guiding these firms. The boards also would be expanded to include worker representatives, and the corporations would be required to give the public much greater access to their records on such things as product safety research, plant emissions, and plans for factory closings.

However it is achieved, a freer flow of information among top management, corporate directors, regulatory agencies, and the general public would help discourage corporate crime and make the enforcement agencies' job an easier one. Too often, top managers and directors are able to cultivate selective ignorance about the criminal activities of their subordinates, the dangerous emissions of their plants, or the hazards of their products. Today corporate spokesmen who make false public statements that cause serious harm to others can avoid criminal liability for fraud simply by claiming that they honestly believed their statements to be true.

One way to deal with this problem would be to require corporate decision makers to review explicit reports on such things as product safety research, environmental pollution, and unethical practices. As those reports moved up the chain of command, officials at each level would be required to describe their effort to conform to legal regulations and to report any knowledge they have of possible illegalities. After the reports had been signed by the corporate board, they would be given to an appropriate federal agency for legal review. In addition to alerting enforcement agencies to possible problems, such a reporting system would make it impossible for top managers to claim that they were unaware that, for example, the statements made by the sales division were contrary to the findings of the research department.

John Braithwaite has made another kind of proposal to provide a structural barrier to corporate crime. Whether by new legislation, by court order, or by voluntary corporate reform, Braithwaite argues that those assigned the responsibility for keeping a corporation in compliance with the law must be given greater strength within the corporation. Among other things, he suggests that compliance personnel be given a more professional status, a high-level ombudsman be established to hear complaints, reports be made directly to the chief executive officer in writing (thus "tainting" him or her with the knowledge of potential criminal activities), and corporate decisions about ethical and legal matters be written down to create a kind of "corporate case law," which would then provide a guide for employees who must make a difficult decision.[16]

A different approach to the control of corporate crime would be the selective nationalization of firms that have long records of criminal violations. Nationalization may sound like an extreme measure, but all the government would have to do is buy up enough stock to gain a controlling interest in the firm. The old management would then be replaced by a new group of managers, who would be instructed to reform and restructure the corporation. After the reforms had been effected and the corporation was operating in a responsible manner, the government could sell its stock and return the firm to private ownership. A program of nationalization might also focus on industries rather than on individual firms. The rationale behind this approach is that some industries (e.g., petroleum) have such a long history of antitrust violations that they clearly are no longer regulated by the free market, and the government therefore needs to step in to protect the public interest. This could be done in several ways. All the firms in the industry could be nationalized—but that, of course, would produce even less competition, albeit with public instead of private control. A more attractive alternative would be to nationalize a single large firm and to use it to reintroduce competition into the oligopolistic industry. A third alternative would be to start an entirely new, government-owned firm to compete with the existing oligopoly.

On the whole, occupational crimes are not as amenable to structural solutions as are organizational crimes. But there are two important exceptions—occupational crimes among government employees (discussed in the next section), and occupational crimes in the health-care professions. Our previous analysis has shown that the fee-for-service approach to payment lies at the root of a wide variety of crimes in the health-care industry. The motivation for performing unnecessary tests and treatments, for example, comes from the fact that physicians and laboratories are paid for each service they perform; thus, they are rewarded for "overdoctoring." If the health-care system were to pay professionals on a salary basis rather than on the volume of services performed, the motivation for many offenses would be eliminated.

Political Reforms

White-collar crime differs from most other types of crime in that there are so many promising proposals for dealing with it. There is little doubt that if some reasonable combination of the proposals discussed earlier were vigorously applied to the problem, the incidence of white-collar crime would decline. The difficulty in dealing with white-collar crime lies not so much in discovering viable responses but in winning their implementation. In other words, this is primarily a political problem that can be solved only by reforming the political process.

The most urgent need is for radical changes in the present system of campaign financing. The fact that most politicians have to rely on campaign contributions from well-endowed special interests has clearly had a paralyzing effect on the battle against white-collar crime. As the aide to one presidential candidate put it when asked about his candidate's position on corporate crime: "No Democratic presidential candidate has ever made corporate crime an issue," because "the money will dry up."[17]

The simplest way to resolve this problem would be to create a system of federal and state financing for election campaigns. The current provision for matching funds in presidential elections is certainly an improvement over the old system, but it is only a halfway measure for a single office. It would be far better to provide complete government funding for all major elections. Each candidate would be given the same amount of money to spend, and large blocks of free television and radio time could be set aside for the candidates to discuss the issues. The main difficulty in formulating such a system is to create a fair way to determine who is to receive government funds. On the one hand, a large number of frivolous candidates might run for office if no cost were involved. But on the other hand, the large, established parties currently in power might well write the campaign financing legislation in such a way as to exclude small-party candidates. Nonetheless, some fair system could certainly be worked out. One promising approach would be to require petitions with a minimum number of signatures to qualify for funding in the primary, and then to use the primary returns as the basis for funding eligibility in the general election.

Another essential step toward reform is the provision of stronger protections for individual civil rights and the freedom of political expression. As we have seen, the government not only has established systematic programs for the surveillance of those who voice unpopular opinions or challenge the political interests of the elite, but has actually taken direct covert action to repress their political activities. It would be helpful to have a new federal law explicitly criminalizing any activities on the part of government agents that interfere with the freedom of expression. Although most such activities are already illegal, such a law would still have an important symbolic value.

But because there is some question about how effectively the government can ever police itself, it is crucial that the public be given access to the broadest possible range of information about the government's activities. When a government agency begins an investigation of a political group, it should be required to notify the group of that fact. The activities of all government agents, operatives, and informants involved in such political cases should be periodically reviewed by a panel of federal judges to make sure that the government is staying within the bounds of the law and the standards of ethical conduct. Individuals should be given speedy access to all files kept on them by public or private organizations, without having to take costly legal action. All citizens should also be able to have inaccurate information removed from their files and be guaranteed the right to sue for any damages caused by the dissemination of false information. Perhaps most important, much stronger laws should be enacted to give the public and the media the greatest possible access to information about the activities of the government. The federal government creates millions of "secrets" every year that are exempt from the disclosure provisions of the Freedom of Information Act.[18] The government's ability to cloak its activities behind a veil of secrecy needs to be greatly reduced.

A Concluding Note

This book must convey a rather dismal picture of the world to most of its readers. The repeated examples of respected men and women using the most unscrupulous means to enlarge already ample fortunes, of major corporations' indifference to the injuries and deaths they cause innocent people, of the government's violations of human rights, and of the weakness and corruption of the enforcement effort certainly cast our society in a dark light.

It is the responsibility of the sociological enterprise to probe the depths of society's problems, and such an endeavor is unlikely to produce comforting results. Good sociology often contains a disquieting glimpse behind the social illusions we erect to conceal unpleasant realities. It is nonetheless true that there are countless honest corporate executives, diligent government servants, and dedicated professionals who have been ignored in these pages. Social problems are not, however, created or resolved on the basis of the personal moral characteristics of individual decisions, but by the social conditions that underlie them.

In the last analysis, the problem of white-collar crime is one strand in a seamless web of social relations that transcend the neat categories sociologists create to contain them. The kinds of changes necessary to provide a permanent solution will require a major restructuring of our social and economic relationships. If such changes are made, they will not come about because of the problem of white-collar crime alone, but because of a confluence of many social forces pushing in the same direction. The one thing that is certain is that our social relations will indeed change—but only time will tell if those changes will leave us with a more humane society.

Review Questions

- Briefly summarize the problem of white-collar crime and its causes.
- Describe some of the proposals for dealing with the problem of white-collar crime and evaluate their possible effectiveness.

Notes

1. See, for example, James William Coleman, "The Myth of Addiction," *Journal of Drug Issues* 6 (Spring 1976): 135–41; Troy Duster, *The Legislation of Morality* (New York: Free Press, 1970); Edwin M. Schur, *Crimes Without Victims* (Englewood Cliffs, N.J.: Prentice-Hall, 1965).
2. Melvin L. DeFleur, *Social Problems in American Society* (Boston: Houghton Mifflin, 1983), p. 352.
3. Quoted in Paul Richter, "Big Business Puts Ethics in Spotlight," *Los Angeles Times,* June 19, 1986, pt. I, p. 28; also see Marilynn Cash Mathews, "Codes of Ethics: Organizational Behavior and Misbehavior," in William C. Frederick, ed. *Research in Corporate Social Performance and Policy* (Greenwich, Conn.: JAI, 1987). For a discussion of corporate codes of ethics, see Donald R. Cressey and Charles A. Moore, *Corporation Codes of Ethical Conduct* (New York: Report to the Peat, Marwick, and Mitchell Foundation, 1980).
4. Christopher D. Stone, *Where the Law Ends: The Social Control of Corporate Behavior* (New York: Harper & Row, 1975), p. 243.
5. W. Brent Fisse, "The Use of Publicity as a Criminal Sanction against Business Corporations," *Melbourne University Law Review* 8 (June 1971): 113–30.
6. For arguments along these lines, see Kip Schlegel, *Just Deserts for Corporate Criminals* (Boston: Northeastern University Press, 1990).
7. Sally S. Simpson, "Corporate-Crime Deterrence and Corporate-Control Policies," in Kip Schlegel and David Weisburd, eds. *White Collar Crime Reconsidered* (Boston: Northeastern University Press, 1992), pp. 289–308; John Braithwaite and Toni Makkai, "Testing an Expected Utility Model of Corporate Deterrence," *Law and Society Review* 25 (1991): 7–39.
8. Bureau of Justice Statistics, *Sourcebook of Criminal Justice Statistics 2002* (Washington D.C.: U.S. Government Printing Office, 2003), Table 5.30; Also see, R. W. Adler and C. Lord, "Environmental Crimes: Raising the Stakes," *George Washington Law Review* 59 (1991): 781–861.
9. AICPA, "Summary of the Sarbanes-Oxley Act of 2002," November 9, 2004, http://www.aicpa.org; Caroly Said, "Bush Can't Sign Fraud Bill Fast Enough," *San Francisco Chronicle,* July 31, 2002, pp. A1 and A13; CBS News "Corporate Fraud Bill Sent to President," July 25, 2002, http://www.cbsnews.com.
10. See John Braithwaite and Gilbert Geis, "Theory and Actions for Corporate Crime Control," *Crime and Delinquency* 28 (1982): 304–14; Steven Walt and William S. Laufer,

"Corporate Criminal Liability and the Comparative Mix of Sanctions," in Schlegel and Weisburd, eds., *White Collar Crime Reconsidered,* pp. 309–31.

11. C. David Baron, Douglas A. Johnson, D. Gerald Searfoss, and Charles H. Smith, "Uncovering Corporate Irregularities: Are We Closing the Expectation Gap?" *Journal of Accountancy* (October 1977): 56.

12. Walter Guzzardi Jr., "An Unscandalized View of Those 'Bribes' Abroad," *Fortune* (July 1978): 178.

13. Stone, *Where the Law Ends.*

14. See Martin Carnoy and Derek Shearer, *Economic Democracy: The Challenge of the 1980s* (White Plains, N.Y.: M. E. Sharpe, 1980), pp. 249–57.

15. Ralph Nader, Mark J. Green, and Joel Seligman, *Taming the Giant Corporation* (New York: Norton, 1976).

16. John Braithwaite, *Corporate Crime in the Pharmaceutical Industry* (London: Routledge and Kegan Paul, 1984), pp. 290–388.

17. *Corporate Crime Reporter* 1 (April 13, 1987): 50.

18. Associated Press, "Government Created 6.8 Million Secrets in 1990, Not Counting War," *San Luis Obispo Telegram-Tribune,* April 3, 1991, p. A7.

Index